NATURAL RIGHTS ON THE THRESHOLD OF THE SCOTTISH ENLIGHTENMENT

NATURAL LAW AND
ENLIGHTENMENT CLASSICS

Knud Haakonssen
General Editor

NATURAL LAW AND
ENLIGHTENMENT CLASSICS

Natural Rights on the Threshold of the Scottish Enlightenment

The Writings of Gershom Carmichael

Edited by James Moore
and Michael Silverthorne

Texts translated from the Latin
by Michael Silverthorne

Foreword by James Moore

LIBERTY FUND

Indianapolis

This book is published by Liberty Fund, Inc., a foundation established to encourage study of the ideal of a society of free and responsible individuals.

⬠ 𐎀𐎅

The cuneiform inscription that serves as our logo and as the design motif for our endpapers is the earliest-known written appearance of the word "freedom" (*amagi*), or "liberty." It is taken from a clay document written about 2300 B.C. in the Sumerian city-state of Lagash.

Cover art: Glasgow College as it appeared in 1693, taken from John Slezer, *Theatrum Scotiae* (1693), reproduced courtesy of the Department of Special Collections, Glasgow University Library

06 05 04 03 02   C   5 4 3 2 1
06 05 04 03 02   P   5 4 3 2 1

Library of Congress Cataloging-in-Publication Data
Carmichael, Gershom, 1672–1729.
[Works. English. 2002]
Natural rights on the threshold of the Scottish enlightenment : the writings of Gershom Carmichael / edited by James Moore and Michael Silverthorne ; texts translated from Latin by Michael Silverthorne ; foreword by James Moore.
p.   cm. — (Natural law and enlightenment classics)
Includes bibliographical references and index.
ISBN 0-86597-319-9 (alk. paper)—ISBN 0-86597-320-2 (pbk. : alk. paper)
1. Natural law.   2. Law—Philosophy.   3. Law—Scotland.
I. Moore, James, 1934–   II. Silverthorne, Michael.
III. Title.   IV. Series.
K457.C37 A2 2002
340'.112—dc21   2002029377

LIBERTY FUND, INC.
8335 Allison Pointe Trail, Suite 300
Indianapolis, Indiana 46250-1684

CONTENTS

Foreword   ix

Acknowledgments   xvii

I. *Natural Rights*

From *Supplements and Observations upon Samuel Pufendorf's On the Duty of Man and Citizen according to the Law of Nature, composed for the Use of Students in the Universities*

Editorial Note   7

1. On Moral Philosophy, or the Science of Natural
   Jurisprudence   9

2. On Lasting Happiness and the Divine Law   21

3. On Human Action in the Divine Court   30

4. Law, Rights, and Justice   39

5. On Natural Law   46

6. On Duty to God   54

7. On Duty to Oneself   59

8. On Duty to Others, or Sociability   73

9. Natural Rights and Agreements   77

10. On the Right of Property   91

11. Contracts and Quasi Contracts   106

12. Dissolution of Obligations ... 118

13. The State of Nature ... 124

14. On the Rights of Husbands and Wives ... 128

15. On the Rights of Parents and Children ... 134

16. On the Rights of Masters and Servants ... 138

17. On the Origin of Civil Society, or the Original
    Contract ... 146

18. On the Constitution of Civil Government ... 157

19. On the Limits of Sovereign Power and the Right of
    Resistance ... 162

20. On Conquest and Patrimonial Kingdoms ... 175

21. On the Rights of Citizens ... 188

22. On the Rights of War and Peace ... 199

23. Appendix: The Rights and Duties of Men and
    Citizens ... 211

II. *Natural Theology*

Synopsis of Natural Theology
(Edinburgh, 1729)

Contents ... 223

Preface: Natural Theology and the Foundations
of Morals ... 227

On the Scope of Natural Theology ... 233

1. On the Existence of God ... 234

2. On the Attributes of God and First, on the
   Incommunicable Attributes ... 248

3. On the Communicable Attributes of God ... 257

4. On the Divine Operations, or Actions
   Involving External Objects ... 270

III. *Logic*

A Short Introduction to Logic

Editorial Note 287

Preface 289

A Short Introduction to Logic 292

1. On Apprehension 293

2. On Judgment in General, and on Immediate
   Judgment in Particular 298

3. On Mediate Judgment or Discourse 304

4. On Method, and Logical Practice 309

IV. *Early Writings: Philosophical Theses*

1. *Philosophical Theses*, 1699 325

2. *Philosophical Theses*, 1707 357

V. *Gershom Carmichael's Account of His Teaching Method*

379

Bibliography 389

Index 397

FOREWORD

It is a remarkable feature of the enlightenment in eighteenth-century Scotland that many of the most distinguished moral philosophers of that era assigned to their students texts based upon the writings of the early modern natural jurists. The works of Grotius, Pufendorf, and Locke were commented upon, supplemented, annotated, and adapted for the use of students at the universities of Glasgow, Edinburgh, and Aberdeen—only St. Andrews seems to have been the exception—from the end of the seventeenth century to the late eighteenth century. The professors who lectured on natural rights theories included Francis Hutcheson, Adam Smith, and Thomas Reid at the University of Glasgow; William Law, William Scott, John Pringle, and James Balfour at the University of Edinburgh; and George Turnbull and David Verner at the University of Aberdeen. What prompted these professors, civic authorities, and noble patrons of universities to insist upon instruction of pupils in the language and literature of natural rights?

The attractions of the natural rights tradition for the political and academic leadership of post-revolutionary Scotland were many. It was a body of writing consistent with the principles of the Revolution of 1688. In the writings of Grotius, Pufendorf, and, especially, Locke, students would find exposed the errors of the political thinking of the pre-revolutionary era: of patriarchalism, the divine right of kings, and indefeasible hereditary right. They would learn instead that men have a natural right to life, liberty, and property; that they have a natural right to defend themselves and others; that there is a natural obligation to keep promises; that governments have their origin in the consent, express or tacit, of the people. The derivation of rights and obligations from the law or laws of nature appealed to Scottish legislators and professors for another reason. Scottish civil law, particularly in the seventeenth and eighteenth centuries, was much indebted to Roman law. Grotius, Pufendorf, and the many commentators on their writings who taught in universities in Europe illustrated their moral and political principles by rules and cases drawn from Roman civil jurisprudence. Scottish students of law frequently completed or supplemented their legal studies abroad; study of the writings of the natural jurists prepared them for those studies and for the practice of law in Scotland. Further, the moral philosophy courses offered in Scottish universities in the seventeenth century had been systems of scholastic ethics which exhorted students to cultivate a way of life which would lead to beatitude, or lasting happiness. The difficulty with these systems, as identified by representatives of the Scottish universities in the 1690s, was not the end or objective of these studies; longing for beatitude was acknowledged to be the law of nature; the weakness of those systems was the method proposed for the attainment of this end, the method of scholastic Aristotelianism. Natural jurisprudence set before the student a different method and agenda for the attainment of happiness; the systems of Grotius, Pufendorf, and Locke were all of them explicitly opposed to scholastic Aristotelianism. Their systems offered instead an understanding of the law or laws of nature attended by rights and obligations which comprised a new ordering of the duties of men and citizens.

It was Gershom Carmichael (1672–1729), the first Professor of Moral Philosophy at the University of Glasgow, where he taught from 1694 until his death, who introduced the natural rights tradition to the universities of Scotland. He did so in a manner which reconciled the natural rights theories of Grotius, Pufendorf, and Locke with Roman law and with the law of nature understood in the scholastic manner as longing for beatitude or lasting happiness.

Gershom Carmichael was born in London. He was the son of Alexander Carmichael, a Scottish Presbyterian clergyman, who died in 1677. His mother, Christian Inglis, later married the Scottish theologian and mystic James Fraser of Brae. Gershom Carmichael was educated at the University of Edinburgh, 1687–91. He taught briefly at the University of St. Andrews, 1693–94. In 1694 he was appointed at the University of Glasgow through the good offices of the family of the Duke and Duchess of

Hamilton and their son, to whom he dedicated the first of his *Philosophical Theses* (printed below), and his relative, John Carmichael, Earl of Hynd-ford, to whom he dedicated a second set of *Philosophical Theses*, 1707 (also printed below). In 1727, when the regenting system at the University of Glasgow was terminated, he was appointed Professor of Moral Philosophy.

He was reputed to be a demanding teacher. Robert Wodrow, one of his students in the 1690s, described him as "a hard student, a thinking, poring man . . . singularly religious. . . . A little warm in his temper, but a most affectionate, friendly man."[1] Some years later he was considered by an-other of his students to be the "best Philosopher here."[2] As a regent he was responsible for teaching all parts of the philosophy curriculum: logic, metaphysics (ontology and pneumatology, or science of the mind or soul, which was taken to include natural theology), moral philosophy, and nat-ural philosophy. He composed his own introduction to logic (printed be-low) which was designed as a commentary on the Port Royal logic, or *The Art of Thinking*. He also composed a short system of natural theology (also printed below) which provides a succinct exposition of Reformed scholas-tic, or dogmatic, theology. It was written originally to supplement, and in part replace, the texts he assigned his students in metaphysics, the *Pneu-matological and Ontological Determinations* of the Dutch metaphysician Gerard de Vries. His particular specialty was moral philosophy. The ex-tended exposition of natural rights (printed below) derives from a com-mentary on Samuel Pufendorf's shorter work *On the Duty of Man and Citizen*. The main outlines are present in lectures delivered at the Univer-sity of Glasgow in 1702–3; the details, as they appear below, were worked out over many years of reflection and debated with the outstanding moral philosophers and natural jurists of Europe. In the fourth and final year, he taught physics; his texts were the *Physica* of Jean Le Clerc and the physics of Newton adumbrated by David Gregory and later by Willem Jacob 'sGravesande.

1. Wodrow, *Analecta*, IV, p. 96.
2. Letter of 21 August 1715 from Jonathan Woodworth to the Rev. Peter Walkden, in Bromley, "Correspondence of the Rev. Peter Walkden," p. 27.

In his selection of texts for students and in his manner of commenting upon them, Carmichael was careful to exclude from consideration the canonical texts of Aristotle. He described "the forms of speaking of the Aristotelian School" as "obscure, ambiguous and, as it were, deliberately fashioned for deception."[3] He maintained, however, that the scholastic ethics taught in Reformed or Presbyterian universities in the seventeenth century had propounded a truth of fundamental importance. It was that all human beings long for lasting happiness, or beatitude. We can never achieve lasting happiness in this life, given the fallen, imperfect condition of mankind. But longing for happiness is an inescapable condition of life. And this longing is most appropriately expressed in veneration of God.

This was the first law of nature in Carmichael's natural jurisprudence, that every man signify his longing for lasting happiness in reverence for God. One may signify such reverence directly, in worship of God, or indirectly, in respect for God's creation: in self-respect and in respect for others. These were the second and third laws of nature, that one respect oneself and that one be sociable, or have respect for others. And there was no more appropriate way of signifying respect for persons, in Carmichael's view, than to acknowledge that every individual should be considered to enjoy certain natural rights. And it was the proper vocation of the moral philosopher to specify those rights and indicate how they apply to oneself and to others in various conditions of life.

Carmichael's understanding of the laws of nature permitted him an appreciably different perspective on social life from that of Pufendorf. Pufendorf had argued that the cultivation and preservation of sociable living obliged all members of society to obey superior powers: husbands, fathers, masters, rulers. Carmichael thought otherwise. He maintained (with Grotius and Locke and against Pufendorf) that every individual has a natural right of self-defense. He concurred with Locke's reasoning that in the state of nature (in a world not yet occupied or appropriated, a negative community, as Pufendorf had conceived it) every man may have a right to property in things on which he has labored (without waiting upon the agreement of others, as Pufendorf had maintained). He argued further,

3. See below, p. 229.

again on the authority of Locke, but putting the matter more unequiv-
ocally than Locke had ever done, that no man has the right to enslave
another, "for men are not among the objects which God has allowed the
human race to enjoy dominion over."[4] He defended the theory, common
to all the early modern natural jurists, that civil or political societies have
their origin in an original contract, a theory which appealed to post-
revolutionary Scottish thinkers, inasmuch as it excluded (particularly in
Locke's formulation) any claim to political power on the grounds of hereditary right.

One of the persistent themes in Carmichael's commentary was his insistence, against Pufendorf, that individuals and peoples have a right to
resist governments which invade their rights and liberties. Carmichael
considered such a right of resistance to be a corollary of the respect for
oneself and for others required by the law of nature. The same concern for
the rights of individuals and of peoples led him to challenge Pufendorf's
theory that subjects may be forced to consent to a government imposed
by a conqueror for the sake of peace and sociable living. Carmichael's concern was again the loss of liberty and self-respect of individuals and peoples. He insisted, against Pufendorf, on the continuity of the Scottish
people and, against George Mackenzie, on the limited government of
Scotland in ancient times. He believed that the liberty and dignity of the
Scottish people had been well secured by the limitations insisted upon in
the Act of Union of 1707 and by the accession of the House of Hanover,
"a family which has given us the most Serene King George, today happily
ruling over us, and which will continue to afford a line of pious Kings,
who will endure, if Britain's prayers prevail, as long as the sun and the
moon."[5]

The academic world which Carmichael inhabited included moral philosophers and natural jurists beyond the boundaries of Scotland and Great
Britain. Pufendorf's texts on moral philosophy and the law of nature were
required reading for university students across Protestant Europe. The
common language of academic life, Latin, facilitated direct exchange, mu-

4. See below, p. 140.
5. See below, p. 187.

tual assistance in the clarification of ideas, and debate. Carmichael referred frequently in his observations on the law of nature to Gottlieb Gerhard Titius (1661–1714), author of a commentary on Pufendorf, and a distinguished professor of Roman law at the University of Leipzig. Titius was particularly critical of Pufendorf's depiction of the state of nature as a condition of indigence, weakness, and malice. Titius described the state of nature as a condition of natural sociability and moderate self-love. He was also critical of Pufendorf's account of the pretended advantages of civil society. Titius reminded readers that in society subjects often suffer from persecution and cruelly conducted wars. He described slavery, in language noted by Carmichael, as "a sure sign of the death of sociability."[6]

The outstanding authority on natural jurisprudence in the early eighteenth century was Jean Barbeyrac (1672–1744). His translations and voluminous commentaries on the writings of Grotius, Pufendorf, and Cumberland were remarkable for their erudition. He considered the early modern natural law tradition the most effective antidote to skepticism in morals and politics. But he also acknowledged the validity of many of the insights of Pierre Bayle and others. He corresponded with Locke and shared many of Locke's theological convictions. He quarreled with orthodox members of the Reformed Church in the cities where he taught: in Berlin, Lausanne, and Groningen, where he spent the latter part of his life (1717–44).

Carmichael wrote to Barbeyrac and sent him a copy of the first edition of his *Supplements and Observations* on Pufendorf's work *On the Duty of Man and Citizen.* Barbeyrac responded in kind,[7] sending Carmichael the fourth edition of the same work, which contained Barbeyrac's long rejoinder to criticisms of Pufendorf that had been made by Leibniz. He subsequently acknowledged assistance he had received from Carmichael in interpreting Pufendorf and on points of translation.[8] The two men agreed that Pufendorf had made insufficient provision for the natural right of self-defense. They agreed that Locke's explanation of the right of property as

6. See below, p. 145.

7. Letter of 3 February 1720 from Jean Barbeyrac to Patrick Simson, in Glasgow University Archives MSS Murray 660, fol. 1.

8. Pufendorf, *Of the Law of Nature and Nations,* p. 437.

the product of labor was more satisfactory than Pufendorf's account, which made proprietorship dependent on consent. They further agreed that a people must be allowed a right of resistance to a government that attempts to deprive its subjects of their rights. But they frequently differed: on the interpretation of contracts; on quasi contracts, or obligations arising from the circumstances of life; on the rights of slaves; on whether societies, as distinct from governments, had their beginnings in a contract; and on the rights of conquerors. Their differences turned ultimately on whether considerations of humanity, of a disposition of reverence for the deity, of the relevance of the divine court or forum should have a place in natural jurisprudence. Barbeyrac was skeptical of the appropriateness of such considerations in natural law. In Carmichael's understanding of the law of nature, reverence for God and for God's creation were matters of fundamental importance.

Carmichael was succeeded as Professor of Moral Philosophy at the University of Glasgow by Francis Hutcheson, who generously acknowledged his debt to Carmichael in his own work prepared for the instruction of students, *A Short Introduction to Moral Philosophy:*

> The learned will at once discern how much of this compend is taken from the writings of others, . . . to name no other moderns, from Pufendorf's smaller work, *de officio hominis et civis,* which that worthy and ingenious man the late Professor Gershom Carmichael of Glasgow, by far the best commentator on that work, has so supplied and corrected that the notes are of much more value than the text.[9]

Hutcheson's relationship with Carmichael is complicated by the fact that the distinctive feature of Hutcheson's moral philosophy, as expressed in his English language writings directed to adult readers—his theory of a moral sense which brings ideas of virtue and vice before the mind—has no parallel in Carmichael's work. Hutcheson was also concerned to emphasize that moral distinctions did not depend upon whether or not one might be judged to have acted in a spirit of reverence for the deity. Insofar as the enlightenment in Scotland may be considered to have been a repu-

---

9. Hutcheson, *A Short Introduction to Moral Philsopohy,* p. i.

diation of Reformed or Presbyterian scholasticism, Carmichael must be perceived to have been a figure of a pre-enlightened era. But in his closely argued, often inspired celebration of the natural rights of individuals and of peoples, Carmichael's work may be seen to have marked an enduring moment in moral and political speculation. It contributed, very funda-mentally, to shape the agenda of instruction in moral philosophy in eighteenth-century Scotland. It may also be found to be relevant today.

ACKNOWLEDGMENTS

Our work on the writings of Gershom Carmichael began many years ago. In the course of our studies we have incurred many obligations.

The Social Sciences and Humanities Research Council of Canada provided generous support in the early stages of research. We are also grateful for hospitality extended to us by the Institute for Advanced Studies in the Humanities of the University of Edinburgh on different occasions.

Our appreciation of the contexts and significance of Carmichael's thinking has been enhanced by discussions at many seminars and colloquia where we have presented our interpretations of the texts. The scholars who have assisted us in our understanding of his writings are too numerous to be mentioned here. We are grateful for the encouragement and support we have received from colleagues and friends.

We have depended heavily on the collaboration of librarians and archivists. The assistance of David Weston, of the Department of Special Collections of the University of Glasgow, and of Arnott Wilson, formerly of Glasgow University Archives, has been indispensable. The resourcefulness of the inter-library loan staffs at McGill University and Concordia University has been much appreciated.

We must also record our indebtedness to Leszek Wysocki, who transcribed some of Carmichael's dictates and reviewed an early draft of the translation.

Our wives, finally, have been tolerant of our enthusiasm and of the time we have spent on this project. We are gratified by the opportunity this series of books affords to make Carmichael's writings available to a wider public.

xvii

ഇൠ PART I ഇൠ

Natural Rights

From *Supplements and Observations upon Samuel Pufendorf's On the Duty of Man and Citizen according to the Law of Nature, composed for the use of students in the Universities,* by Gershom Carmichael, Professor of Philosophy in the University of Glasgow: the second edition with additions and amendments (Edinburgh, 1724)

Supplements and Observations
upon The Two Books of Samuel Pufendorf's
On the Duty of Man and Citizen
according to the Law of Nature
composed for the use of students in the Universities

by Gershom Carmichael

Professor of Philosophy in the University of Glasgow

the second edition with additions and amendments

What is true and fitting is the aim of my careful inquiry
—Horace

Edinburgh

Printed by John Mosman and Partners, at the expense
of John Paton, Bookseller and are for sale at his Premises
in Parliament Square

1724

To the Most Noble and Illustrious Lord
Whose ample Merits have Deserved So Well of his Country

JAMES

Earl of Hyndford, Viscount Nemphlear,
Lord Carmichael of the same,
Head of the Name and family of Carmichael, &c. &c.
Together with
his First-Born Son and Heir, the Noble Youth,

JOHN

Lord Carmichael
Who gloriously emulates the Virtues
of his Father and Grandfather:

I, Gershom Carmichael,

in gratitude and ready obedience,
Give and dedicate
This my humble service of adding supplements and
observations to
an outstanding work of a most noble author

Editorial Note

In the last paragraph of his preface (pp. 19–20), Carmichael refers his readers to an appendix located at the end of his commentary (pp. 211–17) in which he sets out the propositions of moral science in what he takes to be their proper order. The chapter headings and the sequence in which the chapters are arranged in this edition for the most part follow the order which Carmichael proposes in his appendix. The organization of this edition therefore attempts to reflect the distinctive character and argument of Carmichael's natural jurisprudence.

Readers interested in consulting Carmichael's Latin text may be guided by the note numbers. Carmichael himself numbered each of his annotations after the book, chapter, and section of Pufendorf's *On the Duty of Man and Citizen.* We have followed this practice and appended Carmichael's number to each of the annotations. Thus II.4.5.i appended to the note on pp. 141–42 refers to Carmichael's first note to *On the Duty of Man and Citizen,* book II, chapter 4, section 5.

The editors have included all the significant annotations that Carmichael published. Some smaller notes, which consist largely of cross-references and elementary explanations, have been omitted.

On Moral Philosophy, or the Science of Natural Jurisprudence

Greetings to the generous reader[1]

No one with the least tincture of learning can be ignorant of the fact that philosophy has been brought to a much happier condition in our own lifetime and in that of our parents than it had previously enjoyed. This has happened in two ways: philosophy has been purged of the absurdities of previous ages, and it has been enriched by outstanding improvements. And it has occurred not only in natural philosophy, where it has not escaped the attention of the general public that advances have been made by distinguished scientists which have contributed also to the refinement of the arts, but the other parts of philosophy have been no less happily cultivated. And of these none owes more to the achievements of the hundred years just past than *Moral Science.*

This science had been most highly esteemed by the wisest of the ancients, who devoted themselves to its study with great care. It then lay buried under debris, together with almost all the other noble arts, until a little after the beginning of the last century, when it was restored to more than its pristine splendor (at least in that part of moral science which concerns the mutual duties of men and which is much the greater part because of the variety of cases that occur here) by the incomparable Hugo Grotius in

---

1. Carmichael's "Preface" to his 1724 edition of *Supplements and Observations.*

9

his outstanding work *The Rights of War and Peace*.[2] And from that time the most erudite and celebrated scholars in Europe, as if aroused by the sound of a trumpet, have vied with one another in the study of this noblest and most useful branch of learning.

For more than fifty years, scholars more or less confined their studies within the limits set by Grotius; inasmuch as some reduced his work to epitomes, others illustrated it with notes and commentaries, and others made various criticisms of it. I do not include in this company those famous Englishmen, Selden and Hobbes, since the one restricted himself to the so-called books of Noah and the teaching of the Hebrew doctors built upon them,[3] while the other set out, not to illustrate the study of the law of nature, but to corrupt it.[4] But then that most-distinguished man, Samuel Pufendorf, decided that something more should be attempted. By arranging the material in the work of Grotius in a more convenient order and by adding what seemed to be missing from it to make the discipline of morals complete, he produced a more perfect system of morals in those books that bear the title *Of the Law of Nature and Nations*.[5] Subsequently, he reduced this system to a compendium in this elegant treatise to which we have devoted some little care of our own.[6]

When this treatise was published, it began to be used for teaching purposes in the universities. And it was recognized by reasonable judges of these things that there is no other genuine *philosophy of morals* than the philosophy that elicits and demonstrates *from evident principles founded in the nature of things* those *duties* of *men* and *citizens* which are required in the individual circumstances of human life. And so the science of *the law of nature,* however different in appearance it might seem from the ethics which had long prevailed in the schools, was no different in aim and sub-

---

2. Grotius, *De Jure Belli ac Pacis* (1625); all references to this work are to *The Rights of War and Peace* (1738).

3. Selden, *De Jure naturali.*

4. Hobbes, *Elementa Philosophica De Cive;* references are to *On the Citizen* (1998); and Hobbes, *Leviathan* (1946).

5. Pufendorf, *De Jure Naturae et Gentium;* references are to *Of the Law of Nature and Nations* (1749).

6. Pufendorf, *De Officio Hominis et Civis* (1673); references are to *On the Duty of Man and Citizen* (1991).

ject matter; it was the same subject, more correctly taught, and therefore better able to reach the goal which the other had sought with uncertain direction.

For all writers on *ethics* had always professed that it was the *science which would direct human actions to goodness,* that is, to *conformity with the law of nature* or, as they commonly say in the schools, with the *right dictates of reason.*[7] But by what means can any science direct human actions to conform with the law of nature unless it is by *showing* what that law prescribes, what it forbids, and what sanctions it employs to enforce its precepts, that is, what good awaits those who observe its precepts and what evil will ensue for those who neglect them? Whatever distinctions one may make between scholastic ethics[8] and natural jurisprudence, one must not attribute them to the nature of moral science itself but to the spurious or genuine manner of teaching it. The same observation is made by the distinguished Titius in the prolegomena, section 48, to his own *Observations* on this treatise of Pufendorf's.[9]

Nor should it be objected that the subjects which form a great part of the scholastic ethics are not to be found in recent writings on the doctrine of natural law. For if one cuts out some of the things which appear too frequently in every part of scholastic philosophy, empty quibblings and arguments about words which ought to be excluded from the whole range of the sciences, if one also excises those things which can be defined only on the basis of supernatural revelation and must be left therefore to theology, if, finally, one sets aside those purely theoretical questions which are more appropriately treated today in pneumatology, what remains can easily find its place in the study of natural law, although it has been too much neglected until now by recent writers; and so it will be included in what follows.

---

7. *Recto rationis dictamine:* possibly a misprint for *rectae rationis dictamine* ("the dictates of right reason").

8. Three treatises of "scholastic ethics" were widely used in universities in Great Britain in the seventeenth century: Eustache, *Ethica* (references are to the 1693 edition); Burgersdyck, *Idea Philosophiae* (references are to the 1654 edition); and Heereboord, *Collegium Ethicum* (references are to the 1658 edition).

9. Titius, *Observationes,* p. 21.

No one who cares sincerely about duty, and recognizes that a common rule of duty is given to all men, can doubt that every individual is obliged to seek some knowledge of this rule, and a more accurate knowledge must be sought by some in proportion to the talents they have been given and have a duty to employ in this life. But if there are any who do not think that the *discipline of philosophy* is necessary for this pursuit, even though it offers more complete and more accurate knowledge of this kind drawn from nature itself, it is because some have persuaded themselves that *moral theology,* or as it is more popularly called, *casuistry,* can take the place of philosophy, others think this knowledge may be found in study of the civil law, while still others suppose that they can solve the moral problems considered here without any particular training or reflection, by the sole resource of common sense. Pufendorf himself found it necessary to confront these errors in his own preface,[10] and anyone will be capable of defending himself against them after a little attention to this science, so that it will not be necessary to dwell unduly on them here.

But the need for a thorough grounding and training in moral science should be sufficiently evident when one considers the innumerable delusions which tend to creep into questions of this kind and divide men every day into parties, not without great disturbance of the public peace. Nay, one may affirm that the perverse and malignant spirit which inspires evil citizens among us to unsettle the public happiness enjoyed by these nations under the just and flourishing reign of our most Serene King, and agitates the same individuals to initiate endless rebellions in favor of the papal *Pretender* to the throne, has no other source (so far as this source can be imputed to opinions rather than to evil passions) than ignorance of the true principles of *natural right.*

The importance of keeping moral philosophy distinct from *revealed theology* is acknowledged by the most acute among the theologians themselves,[11] who do not claim that scripture fixes or removes the boundaries of civil rights as they call them: they assume that these rights are just the

10. Pufendorf, *On the Duty of Man and Citizen,* pp. 6–13.

11. Carmichael appears to have in mind, among others, the work of the moderate Reformed Dutch theologian Hermann Witsius, *Miscellaneorum.* Gerard de Vries, *De Natura Dei,* also stressed the separation of moral philosophy from revealed theology.

same as nature or the consent of men has made them. I would add that it is not a useless exercise to derive the more general moral precepts contained in the Holy Book from the nature of things, not only for the sake of those who do not know or do not acknowledge the Divine Word but also for our own sake who embrace it. For our human frailty needs all the assistance that God has given us to discover and adhere to the truth. And finally it is an important consideration in support of the divine origin and authority of the Sacred Books that they conform with the understanding of *the nature of God* and *the duties of men* which one may gather from the nature of things by the right use of reason. This conformity can never be appreciated by those who neglect the study of moral science or confuse it with revealed theology. For these reasons I have never been able to approve of the practice of those who have insisted that what they call *Christian ethics,* or morals deduced from the testimony of the holy scriptures, should be taught in the schools for the moral part of philosophy. An occasion for this delusion may have been afforded by the even more serious error of those for whom ethics was nothing more than a confused assortment of doctrines, pillaged from the bookshelves of pagan philosophers, on the assumption *that one should determine what can or cannot be known by the light of nature from what was or was not known to the pagan philosophers,* an assumption that has been the cause of many aberrations and which is worthy only of those strangers in their own home who have never known enough to consult nature herself concerning the demands of nature.

Nor can the place of moral philosophy be taken by the *Roman* or any other particular system of jurisprudence. For we are seeking a common norm for all men which will mediate the mutual duties of men who are not obliged to each other by their common subscription to any particular civil law. The same norm must also provide the source of those mutual obligations which exist between rulers and subjects in civil societies; it must supply the grounds for the obligation of the civil law and indicate how those laws are best interpreted; and it must direct us finally, to the most beautiful aspects of virtue which are not comprehended within codes of public law. From all of this it is clear that no merely human law can suffice. One does find in the books of Roman law innumerable declarations of the law of nature, in light of which Ulpian says that he and his friends aspire to true *philosophy*.[12] But we should not credit any man or any nation with authorship of the laws of nature; this belongs to nature alone. (Compare what is said by Titius, the distinguished scholar mentioned above, in the preface to his *Observations on Lauterbach*.)[13] And just as the authority of the Roman government adds nothing to the sanctity of the laws of nature; so the mixture of natural laws with merely civil laws and things of that order prevents one from deducing the natural and genuine precepts contained in the books of Roman law from their own principles and from seeing that those precepts are connected with each other by the native genius of the Roman jurists. Those jurists, to say nothing of their interpreters, may have expounded philosophies which acquired the force of laws, but when they found some rule established by positive law or uniformly accepted customs, they did not normally trouble themselves to deduce that law from some higher source nor was it pertinent to their task to do so.

They are therefore merely dabblers in one or in both kinds of law who persuade themselves that an accurate knowledge of natural law can be derived from the study of Roman law or of any civil law whatsoever. This is not to denigrate the study of civil jurisprudence, however; for besides the value of studying the law that is used in the courts for the authority of such law in addition to its manifest equity, I also readily acknowledge that the civil law of the Romans often illustrates the natural law, reflecting the light which it receives from it. So just as it is reasonable to teach moral science to those students of the civil law who want it, a knowledge of civil law is virtually necessary in the present state of our moral studies. Indeed the need is so great that the science of natural law will never reach perfection or be cultivated with felicity, until the philosophers know more about the civil law and the jurists know more about philosophy; until, that is, the philosophers recover, or the jurists restore, the garments borrowed from philosophy which at one time added luster to the attire of Roman jurisprudence.

Some understanding of the nature and utility of the science expounded

---

12. Justinian, *Digest*, I.1.1.i (an excerpt from Ulpian).
13. Titius, Preface, *Observationum ratiocinantium*.

in this volume can be gained from the foregoing. It remains for us, Reader, to give you some account of the labors that have gone into the volume itself.

It has been for a long time a concern of the *Scottish* universities to allow their students to drink from the pure and abundant springs of every discipline, whatever may be said by some who pronounce on matters they have little investigated. I note[14] in particular a most ingenious man, who has deserved excellently of his country on many accounts, Sir Richard Steele, who declares, in the Epistle Dedicatory to Pope Clement XI, prefaced to *An Account of the State of the Roman Catholic Religion,* edited by himself,[15] that in the Scottish academies they scrupulously abstain from every attempt to investigate the truth deeply, or make further advances in the sciences. He relies on a single argument: that there are certain dogmas concerning the weightier articles of religion, to which assent is demanded of those who are admitted to the task of teaching in our churches or academies. But it is certain that we have not for this reason ever encountered any barrier to the progress of learning, nor will we ever suspect that there can be such a barrier until perhaps someone proves that what is most conducive to making successful advances in the knowledge of truth is that we have nothing ever certain, nothing undoubted, not even in matters of the greatest importance; that the truth of what we have understood most evidently from the sacred oracles or from the actual nature of things, we ourselves call into doubt; or that we should be afraid to enable our descendants to see the truth as little obscured by the clouds of error as it is within our power to permit. We are indeed able to make mistakes, and not infre-

14. The remainder of this paragraph appears as a long footnote in Carmichael's text, pp. xiv–xv.

15. *An Account of the State of the Roman-Catholick Religion* was a collaborative production to which Sir Richard Steele, Benjamin Hoadly (Bishop of Bangor), and Michel de la Roche (later the first editor of the *Bibliothèque Angloise,* 1717–19) all made contributions. The Epistle Dedicatory (pp. i–lxx), though signed by Sir Richard Steele, appears to have been the work of Benjamin Hoadly. The Epistle was reprinted in *The Works of B[enjamin] Hoadly,* vol. I, pp. 534–53, by his son, John Hoadly, who attributes it to his father (pp. xix and 534). G. A. Aitken, *The Life of Richard Steele,* vol. II, p.546. The criticism of Scottish universities appears at pp. xliii–xliv of the 1716 edition, as printed at *Works,* vol. I, p. 546.

quently we do: but we know also that there can be certain truth in a judgment, by which one gives assent to things evidently perceived, even though in making a judgment one is not exempt from all risk of error in other respects. Nor do we suspect that because things seen in dreams very occasionally deceive us, therefore what we see in front of us when we are awake and which we touch with our fingers should be considered dubious or fanciful; this is because of that quality of self-evidence which easily distinguishes things received by the external senses from the fantasies of dreamers. Those who contend that certain knowledge of truth and the law of acting in conformity with it, cannot be obtained without an infallible judge, let them see what cause they serve.[16]

So, in my endeavor to adorn the *Sparta* where I was born, so far as my feeble abilities permitted, I decided not to burden my students any longer with dictates of systems of philosophical science in the received manner. It seemed to me that nothing could be more suitable for prelections in moral philosophy than this treatise of the famous Pufendorf. But as I lectured, I came across many things which needed comment or supplementation. So I imparted to my students brief notes for them to write in the margins of their books beside certain passages. At the same time I included in these annotations passages from Grotius where the arguments were treated, along with references to my Ethical Theses which I had also circulated among them;[17] although these were composed principally as material for public disputation, they still served the purpose of a supplement to those parts of moral science which are touched on lightly or not at all by Pufendorf. The university printer asked me to include my comments in a new edition of Pufendorf's treatise which he was preparing. And as most of those parts of my Ethical Theses which differed from the teachings of Pufendorf had been included in the book, together with a good deal more, it gradually developed into that lengthy commentary which issued from our academic press a few years ago as supplements to Pufendorf's work.[18]

16. Carmichael's response recalls a similar argument for the self-evidence of perceptions and judgments based upon them used in his *Philosophical Theses* of 1699, sec. 11. See below, p. 332.

17. The *Philosophical Theses* of 1707. See below, pp. 353–76.

18. Carmichael, *Supplementa et Observationes.*

These have been at length revised and here and there augmented. I am permitting them to be published once more with the same intention as before of promoting the moral studies of young people in our universities.

I have attempted to take particular care in this commentary to deduce the obligations of the law of nature and its fundamental precepts from *the existence, perfection, and providence of the supreme being*;[19] so that the manifest connection between *moral science* and *natural theology* would be evident to the reader; for moral doctrine is in truth the practical part of natural theology. In this way I have sought to elevate moral science from the human forum to which it has been too much reduced by Pufendorf to the loftier forum of God. I have done this particularly in Supplement I[20] and in the first part of Supplement II.[21] And by these means I hope that I have answered the particular or at least the juster part of the criticisms made of Pufendorf's system by the celebrated Gottfried Wilhelm Leibniz in a letter that has been several times reprinted.

This letter appears among the appendices to an edition of this work [the *De Officio* of Pufendorf] by the distinguished Alexander Arnold Pagenstrecher, published in Groningen in 1712.[22] The letter also appears in a French version, translated by the famous Barbeyrac, with his animadversions upon this letter, in an entirely new edition of his French translation of this text.[23] Whether I have contributed anything toward the formulation of that more perfect system of moral doctrine whose absence the same excellent philosopher lamented in his letter I do not know; the reader must

19. See the parts of Carmichael, *A Synopsis of Natural Theology*, printed below; hereafter, *Synopsis*.

20. Pp. 21–29, below.

21. Pp. 46–53, below.

22. This sentence and the following were printed as a footnote in the original (p. xvii). The edition to which Carmichael refers is Pufendorf, *De Officio Hominis et Civis* (1712). Leibniz's letter has been translated into English by Patrick Riley, "Opinion on the Principles of Pufendorf," in *The Political Writings of Leibniz*, pp. 64–75.

23. Barbeyrac's translation and commentary on Leibniz's letter, "Jugement d'un Anonyme sur l'original de cet Abrégé, avec des réflexions du traducteur," was included in the fourth edition of his translation of Pufendorf's *De Officio Hominis et Civis*, published as *Les devoirs de l'homme et du citoyen traduits du Latin du Baron de Pufendorf*. The edition of Barbeyrac's translation and commentary referred to in these notes is the sixth edition, published in 1741.

form his own judgment on the basis of those principles I have laid down at the end of Supplement II and from the method I have sketched in the appendix.[24]

I have tried not to overlook altogether the subjects which are normally taught in the usual course on ethics and which are lacking in the system of Pufendorf. And so I have included everything from them that seemed most useful and suitable for treatment here. I will not delay to speak now of what can be read in Supplements I[25] and III[26] of supreme beatitude, of the morality of human actions, and the moderation of appetite and all those feelings which the author has described in his larger work. As for the virtues and vices, Aristotle's *Ethics* contains almost all that needs to be said on the subject and comprehends virtually everything of practical import in the moral doctrines of the scholastics, although it was transmitted by them in a confused and often feeble manner. We have confined our exposition on this subject to a very brief account of the ideas of *virtue* and *vice* in an observation at pp. 42–43, below, merely to dispel the inaccurate notions which are commonly bandied about on this subject and to indicate how one may recapture the basic distinctions. I thought it plainly superfluous to enter into a more particular discourse on them, as if the doctrine of virtue were entirely distinct from the doctrine of duties. For anyone who understands what he should do in life, and what he should not do, cannot be ignorant of what should be classified as virtue and vice. And if I had thought it relevant to expand upon the names of virtue and vice, I would not have devoted a separate discussion to the matter: I would have indicated instead the tendency of individual virtues and vices to obedience to or violation of the precepts.

I am not ignorant of the fact that several scholars before me have devoted their labors to illustrating and enriching this treatise of Pufendorf's. But I had the opportunity to make use of very few of those writings in preparing this edition. I gladly acknowledge that these comments owe

24. Pp. 46–53, 211–17, below.
25. Pp. 21–29, below.
26. Pp. 59–67, below.

much to two distinguished men who preceded me in this undertaking, Titius and Barbeyrac. But I had already communicated to my pupils my opinions about the most important articles, most of it in writings much as I have presented them here,[27] before I saw the *Observations* of Titius (and, before they were seen by anyone in these regions, if I am not mistaken), if not before they were published, and before Barbeyrac's *Annotations* on either of Pufendorf's works were published.[28] When I subsequently consulted them, I was delighted that my thoughts on *the legitimate reasons for requiring obedience, on the fundamental precepts of natural law, on obtaining compensation for damages,* and on several other questions of importance were confirmed by the authority of such great men. I mention this here so that no one will be surprised that I do not refer to their writings when I amend Pufendorf's text in almost the same manner as these distinguished men in works published before mine. The perceptive reader will quickly recognize that their observations have prompted not a few of mine when he remarks not only how much my work is indebted to them but how often I have defended Pufendorf's system from their criticisms when these seemed to me to be unjustified.

Further, concerning the order of investigating the social duties, outlined in the appendix according to the various classifications of rights which belong to men in opposition to each other, I must advise you, Reader, that after I had time and again dictated my Ethical Theses in almost the same order as here and presented them for consideration by public disputation, I discovered not without particular pleasure, obvious traces of the same method in the work of the famous Ulrich Huber, in his noble treatise *On the Rights of Civil Society,* book II, sections IV and VI (a work I had had no opportunity to see before).[29] There is this difference in our

27. Surviving manuscript notes from Carmichael's lectures on ethics from as early as 1702/3 to some extent substantiate this claim.

28. Titius, *Observationes,* was published in 1703. Barbeyrac's translations and commentaries on *De Jure Naturae et Gentium* (1672) and *De Officio Hominis et Civis* (1673) were published in 1706 and 1707, respectively.

29. Huber, *De Jure Civitatis,* pp. 384–416, on the right of property; and pp. 431–72, on personal rights or rights which have their origin in agreements.

approaches, however: that erudite scholar refers all the rights which he discusses to civil society and so he does not consider rights in the full scope in which they may be seen in the more comprehensive view of moral science presented here.

[The preface concludes with three short paragraphs which pertain exclusively to technical points in the original edition: whether or not to include material from other works of Pufendorf, on the numbering of the paragraphs, on the preparation of the index, etc. These paragraphs have no relevance for the present edition and for this reason they are not included here.

The preface is subscribed. . . .]

From my house in the college of Glasgow, December 27, 1723.

CHAPTER 2

On Lasting Happiness
and the Divine Law[1]

*Which treats some of the more general and
fundamental points of moral doctrine which Pufendorf
omitted or did not explain with sufficient clarity*[2]

1. It is natural for man to strive to be as happy as he can and to avoid
misery so far as possible. It follows that he will use the faculties in which
man excels so that his will may be determined to choose and perform those
actions which he thinks will lead to his greatest happiness, and which will
permit him most effectively to escape misery. And he will consider not
only the good which he pursues and the evil he would avoid, but the reasonable expectation attending any action that it will lead to the one and
not to the other.[3]

---

1. Supplement I of the 1724 edition of *Supplements and Observations.*

2. The argument of this chapter had been used by Carmichael to expound the first
principles of his moral philosophy from a very early stage in his teaching career. The
same line of reasoning appears in "Dictates" of his ethics recorded in 1702–3 in the
first chapter of his "Ethics, part one" (Glasgow University Archives MS. Gen. 168, fols.
12–20). This discussion became the first supplement in his *Supplements and Observations* (Supplementa et observationes). The presentation in the second edition (1724),
translated here, follows the 1718 edition, with four minor verbal changes.

3. The assumption that it is natural for a man to seek the most lasting happiness
available to him was a common premise of treatises in scholastic ethics (see below,
p. 23, n. 7).

2. But man is also endowed with a faculty of reasoning which, when he employs it correctly, allows him to understand that he was created not by himself or for himself alone: that he and all he has derives from God, who is alone all that is both great and good. And since God has created all things and disposes them with supreme justice and wisdom for the manifestation of his glory, he must govern the human race to the same end, in a manner suitable to its nature.[4]

3. Man is able to recognize God as the source of all good things, and in light of his knowledge of the good to direct his actions by the power of his will. He is also able either so to arrange his actions as to testify to his love and veneration for his creator and Lord, and so in an active way to serve his glory; or on the other hand in such a way, that in betraying neglect or hatred of him, he obscures that glory, so far as he is capable of doing so.

4. That an agent of this kind may be directed to the glory of God agreeably with his nature, he must be so placed that his happiness is connected with the preservation of due subordination to God, and his misery with the violation of that subordination. Consequently, he can only acquire or preserve that happiness to which he constantly aspires by the original law of his nature, avoiding the misery which he no less shuns by the same law, when he signifies by his actions the highest esteem for the Deity, the most intense love, and the most devoted veneration.[5] And so far as he turns aside from this norm (i.e., by actions or omissions which betray contempt, neglect, or hatred of God), so far he may wander from the path of his own happiness, and veer toward the corresponding misery. Man easily understands, therefore, that this condition has been given him by God. And if

4. Eustache, *Ethica*, p. 18; Burgersdyck, *Idea Philosophiae*, p. 37; Heereboord, *Collegium Ethicum*, p. 5.

5. Carmichael understood the relation between God and man as a relation of *signification* by word and deed. His insistence on signification is consistent with the emphasis in his natural theology on the incommunicable attributes of the deity (see *Synopsis*, ch. 2): certain properties or attributes of the deity cannot be shared; they can, however, be signified. In this respect Carmichael's understanding of the relation between God and man differed from that of his scholastic predecessors insofar as they held (with Aquinas and other Aristotelian scholastics) that the relation between God and man was a relation of participation.

happiness and misery are not always dispensed in this life on these terms, he can quite clearly infer from this very fact that some future state of the soul is to be expected.[6]

5. Moreover, there is strong confirmation that each man has more regard for his own happiness, the more he gives evidence in his individual actions of a soul devoted to God. For the great and good God, as he is the supreme *dispenser* of every kind of happiness or misery for men, so is he also the unique *object* of the most consummate beatitude which can come to man. Man cannot achieve beatitude either in the consciousness of his own finite perfections, or in the possession of things of less value than himself, or in the contemplation of abstract truths. He can enjoy it only in an immediate vision of God himself which will last forever, a vision of God reconciled with him, and preserving him with fatherly care; and this is necessarily accompanied by the most ardent love and unspeakable joy.[7]

6. The desire which God has given man for the most consummate happiness is strong evidence that such beatitude is available to him if he perseveres in due subordination to God. But if he defects from that straight path (and each man finds within himself innumerable symptoms of such defection) and loses the right to obtain this beatitude, offered by divine grace, one must not conclude that the glory of the divine perfection in the determination of man's eternal state will be diminished. Rather grace should be illustrated still more clearly, whether in mercifully restoring that lost beatitude or in inflicting a punishment, whose severity and duration

6. Carmichael disagreed fundamentally with Pufendorf's opinion that natural law must abstract from belief in the immortality of the soul and an afterlife. See ch. 3, p. 30.

7. In treatises of scholastics ethics, the distinction between God as "the unique object of the most consummate beatitude" and "the immediate vision of God which will last forever" was expressed in the distinction between *objective beatitude* and *formal beatitude*. The scholastic moralists were also unanimous in thinking that the proper object of beatitude cannot be discovered in external goods or in the goods of the body or in the goods of the mind; but only in a vision of God (beatific vision) and in actions consistent with that vision: Eustache, *Ethica*, pp. 20–23 and 24–27; Burgersdyck, *Idea Philosophiae*, pp. 20–21 and 28–38; Heereboord, *Collegium Ethicum*, pp. 13–17 and 17–22. Carmichael had already made explicit use of this distinction between objective and formal beatitude in his "Dictates" on moral philosophy: in 1702–3, sec. 21 (Glasgow University Library MS. Gen. 168, fol. 17).

may attest how great was the beatitude lost, and how great the offense of *lèse-majesté* against God.

7. It is not easy to determine from nature how far in this degenerate condition of the human race, any ordering of our actions can contribute to obtaining that beatitude or avoiding an equal misery. But it is clear enough that if any way is left to man to secure the one and avoid the other (and on this matter the kindly dispensation of divine providence toward the human race bids one not simply to despair altogether), each man is able to hope with some prospect of justice that he will obtain it the more he gives evidence of devoted affection toward the Deity in his individual actions. And even the least likelihood of obtaining infinite good or escaping infinite evil ought to have more influence with us than all the considerations opposed to it.

8. We are also led to the same conclusion by the fact that the human mind is fitted to feel the greatest pleasure and delight in actions which are most comformable to reason. Such actions are, above all, those which show love, esteem, and veneration for a most perfect object. By contrast we feel the greatest repining and remorse in their opposites. Hence it is rightly said from of old: *virtue is its own reward, vice its own punishment.*[8]

9. All the considerations we adduce seem to conspire to suggest that the key to the significance of actions within a man's power to bring happiness and avoid misery lies in the evidence they give in individual actions of the most intense love and reverence for the great and good God, and scrupulous avoidance of anything that suggests the contrary sentiment.

10. In every duty which has reference to God and in which his approval is expected, the intention of the divine will is of the first importance; and *the will of God demands certain actions of men as a sign of love and veneration*

8. The ancient Stoic idea that virtue alone is conducive to happiness, and vice is itself the greatest misery, may be found in various classical sources: Zeno, in Diogenes Laertius, *Lives of Eminent Philosophers,* VII.94; Cicero, *Tusculan Disputations,* V.5; Epictetus, *The Discourses,* as reported by Arrian, III.7; Marcus Aurelius, *Meditations,* IX.42. For commentary, see Davidson, *The Stoic Creed,* p. 159. The scholastic moralists thought that happiness cannot consist in moral virtue alone; virtue must also be directed to knowledge and love of God (Burgersdyck, *Idea Philosophiae,* p. 37).

of himself and interprets contrary actions as indications of contempt or hatred, connecting the offering of the one or the absence of the other with the happiness of man, and the commission of the one or the neglect of the other with his misery; and therefore that will, declared by suitable signs, is called *the divine law.*[9] And from what has been said it is clear that this law must be recognized as the highest norm of human actions. The actions which the law requires as a sign of love and devoted affection toward God are said to be *prescribed* by law. Actions, on the other hand, which the law requires us to interpret as indications of contempt, neglect, or hatred toward God are said to be *forbidden* by law. He who performs prescribed actions because they are prescribed (and as so performed they are called *morally good*), or omits forbidden actions, because they are forbidden, is said to *obey* the law; but he who commits forbidden actions (which are usually called *morally bad*), or omits prescribed actions, is said to *transgress* or violate the law. If an action prescribed by law is done, by someone either in ignorance that it is prescribed, or without regard to the prescription, that action is said to be not *formally* but *materially* good.

11. From this, we may determine those actions or omissions of men which are liable to the direction of law, and thus capable of moral good or evil. It is those actions and omissions *which are done by men knowingly and voluntarily and not involuntarily or,* which comes to the same thing, *which are in the power of the agent to do or not to do, or depend on the determination of his will.* Those sorts of actions and omissions, popularly called *free,* where there is a law laid down by which they are prescribed or forbidden,

---

9. The notion that actions are morally right or good only when they signify love and veneration of God, i.e., only when they are in conformity with the divine will or the divine law, would have appeared perfectly correct to any student or reader reared upon the teachings of Calvin and the Reformed or Presbyterian Churches. John Calvin, *Institutes of the Christian Religion,* ch. 1: "Seeing our condition, the Lord has provided us with a written law to teach us what perfect righteousness is and how it is to be kept: that is, firmly fixed in God, we turn our gaze to him alone, and to him aim our every thought, yearning, act, or word" (p. 17). The same primacy of the divine or moral law was impressed upon Presbyterians in the *Confession of Faith;* see esp. pp. 110–13, 246–48, 414–15.

are imputable to man, for praise or for censure, reward or punishment; seeing that there may be in each and every one of them an appropriate or inappropriate sentiment toward God the author of the law.

12. Therefore no one can be held responsible for *necessary* things because they happen, or *impossible* things, because they do not. Only those things should be regarded as necessary which happen whether anyone wishes them to or not; not all these things are effectively determined by the mind willing them. Equally, those things alone should be said to be impossible which do not occur, whether anyone wishes them or not; not by any means all the things which the mind lacks the requisite disposition to will seriously.

13. But for any human action, or omission of it, to become a *moral act,* and thus imputable to man as *good* or *evil* according to what was said above, a law must exist which prescribes or forbids that action. This law is the will of God, as we described it in section 10, declared by suitable signs: that is, signs by which a man would be able to know the will of God and the duty which is incumbent on him in this respect according to the law, if he employed his reason rightly upon them and with due attention, as well as on the existence of the conditions which perhaps that law presupposes. That is, when these conditions are present, a man is not to be considered blameless if he is ignorant of the morality of his action, and, if he does that action, he is also to be regarded as consenting in some way to the morality involved in it.

14. We infer that where there is a law, the morality of every one of our free actions or omissions is to be judged on three heads: *first, from the value of what is done or omitted,* both considered in itself and clothed in all the circumstances which may urge that it be done or omitted here and now; *second,* from the *manner* and *measure of knowledge* which one may have about the action or its omission morally considered; i.e., about the law and the circumstances just mentioned; *third,* from the *greater or lesser inclination* of the will to what is done or *aversion* from what is omitted; including the motives by which the will is directed to the one or to the other.

15. As regards the *first,* it is certain that no circumstances of an action or omission, no effects or consequences, have any power to constitute, intensify, or reduce its morality, before God and conscience, further than these

things could be known or foreseen by the agent, if he brought due attention to bear. Nor is it less certain that all circumstances (at least those of any importance) are relevant to the morality of any human action, insofar as they can be known or guessed; and therefore all consequent goods and evils, however remote, even those caused more directly by other men, so far as they could be foreseen with appropriate diligence by the man on the point of action, as in all probability more likely to follow that action than its omission. Likewise consequences are also relevant to the morality of an omission, so far as they could be foreseen as more likely to happen in all probability, if the proposed action were omitted, than if it were performed.

16. However, this should not be taken to mean that all the effects which it was given to us to foresee as more likely to follow an action or omission of ours than its contrary, should be imputed to us, to the same degree (as often happens) or even in the same way, as if they had been produced directly by us; we mean only that all consequences of this kind ought to be included in the more general calculation, if not in the particular calculation. Hence it would not be a right action if it were likely that some evil would be caused or some good prevented; nor would it be right to forgo an action by which evil could possibly be avoided or good procured; the greater prospect of obtaining some good or avoiding some evil must determine our choice of action.

17. Both knowledge and *intention* are relevant, as we indicated in the *second* and *third* points above [sec. 14] to estimate the morality of an action or its omission. In order that an action or omission be good in these respects in the eyes of God (that is, in order that it be accepted by him as a sign of love and veneration toward him), it is required both that what is done be prescribed by law in the given circumstances, and what is omitted forbidden; and that this can be known by the man who acts or refrains from acting. It is also required that he actually know, or at least judge with probability, that the thing is so, and he must not only agree to conform to the law but also must be primarily concerned, in his action or omission, to show regard for the law. For no one can be said to be obeying the law, or showing devout affection toward God, who is doing what is prescribed by the law in ignorance or without contemplation of God and his law.

18. The evil of an action or of an omission admits various degrees based

on these factors. On the basis of knowledge, it varies according to the different degrees of knowledge or suspicion that what is done is forbidden by law, or what is omitted is prescribed; or, if this is not known, in accordance with various reasons for that ignorance. On the basis of intention, it varies in accordance with the different degrees of inclination or aversion of the will; in accordance with the more estimable or more odious nature of the reasons by which one is induced to sin; and by the various degrees of weight which the consideration of moral evil has in checking the impulse to sin.

19. I have everywhere related the morality of actions to the divine law alone, since by itself it obliges and every obligation of human laws is ultimately to be resolved into it. Divine law is declared by two means. It may be declared by express signs, for example by voices and writing, and when declared by this means it is called the *positive law of God.* It may also be declared by the very constitution of human nature and of the other things which are open to men's observation by these things and by the transcendent perfections of the Deity which shine forth from them, certain actions of men, in certain circumstances, necessarily signify in the one case love and veneration toward the Deity and in the other case contempt and hatred; and thus they must be regarded by God Himself as signs of moral sentiment: and when the will of God is signified in this latter mode, it is called the *natural law.*

20. Since therefore the will of God himself is made known to us by these natural means of producing obligation; since God himself has placed the same means within the sphere of our observation (means, that is, by which are declared to us both the distinction between actions prescribed by law and actions forbidden by law, and also the importance which the former have for bringing happiness and the latter for misery); since finally the same God has allowed us a rational faculty, by whose right use we may have the power to reflect on the things presented to us and from observation of them and continual comparison of one with another to deduce true and certain conclusions about the morality of our actions and thus of their moral effects; it is clear that the natural law is the true and *divine law* in the proper sense, seeing that it is ordered, sanctioned, and promulgated by God himself.

21. The *discipline* which *teaches the prescriptions of the natural law in themselves,* i.e., which elicits them from nature herself and demonstrates them, or, and this comes to the same thing, *which directs human actions in conformity with that law* is that very discipline which is called *ethics or moral philosophy;* and therefore we find no reason to distinguish it from *natural jurisprudence.*

∞ CHAPTER 3 ∞

On Human Action in the Divine Court[1]

[Carmichael disagreed fundamentally with Pufendorf's opinion that natural law must abstract from belief in the immortality of the soul and an afterlife. Pufendorf had said in his preface: "The greatest difference [between natural law and theology] is that the scope of the discipline of natural law is confined within the orbit of this life" (Pufendorf, *On the Duty of Man and Citizen*, p. 8). In a note to this preface Carmichael offered the opposite point of view.]

We are taught by the light of nature as the fruit of acting well, to hope, and indeed to expect, not only felicity in this life in particular (although this is most closely attached to duties enjoined by natural law) but also, in general, some greater happiness or greater alleviation of misery, if not in this, at least in a future life, than evildoers will be able to attain. Furthermore, if any way of obtaining the greatest happiness after this life is left to man, [we are] to conceive of the hope of it as the more probable, the more, in the individual actions of life, we render ourselves obedient to the divine law. It is not correct, therefore, to say that the end of the discipline of natural law is confined to the scope merely of this life. ["Author's Preface," 6.1]

[Carmichael also disagreed with Pufendorf's position ("Author's Preface," secs. 6 and 7) that natural law, like human jurisdiction, "is concerned only with a man's external actions and does not penetrate to what is hidden in the heart . . ." (Pufendorf, *On the Duty of Man and Citizen*, p. 9). Carmichael comments:]

1. From Carmichael's notes in *Supplements and Observations*, 1724, to the "Author's Preface"; and bk. I, ch. 1, "On Human Action."

Since the law of nature has been ordered and sanctioned by God himself, we are warranted in saying that its edicts are particularly applicable in the court of God and of conscience and, just as evidently, direct the internal motions of the mind as well as external modes of behavior. But the contrary follows from the premises established by Pufendorf; although he attempts to soften the actual conclusion and seems to hint elsewhere at something else.[2] See the criticism of Pufendorf by the distinguished Leibniz (the so-called Anonymous) in Barbeyrac's examination of this subject.[3] ["Author's Preface," 6.3]

The *internal* acts of the mind are themselves *human,* and so far as *external* acts depend for their direction on internal acts, they derive their qualification [as human] from that source. It is not necessary [for acts of the mind] that there be a previous dictate of the intellect and command of the will: this would involve an infinite regress. It is enough that internal conscience and self-approval be intimately and essentially involved in all those [mental actions]. *Human* actions therefore are those actions which above we called *free* and taught that they are in every case and peculiarly subject to moral rule (pp. 25–26). This is not the place to discuss whether the schools are right to call other motions that proceed from our faculties *human actions.*[4] [I.1.2.i]

It is a dispute about a word whether judgments, together with the operations which the mind performs upon ideas previously impressed upon it by objects, should be counted as acts of *intellect* or *will.* It makes no difference how we settle it, provided that we always recognize that the mind behaves actively in them, and hence freely, and that those acts therefore (contrary to what some think) are not devoid of morality. It is therefore perhaps a scholastic prejudice that all our modes of thought must be reduced to two or, as it is commonly expressed, must be attributed to one

2. Pufendorf thought that while natural jurisprudence must be abstracted from Christian theology, the "Christian virtues too do as much as anything to dispose men's minds to sociability" (Pufendorf, *On the Duty of Man and Citizen,* p. 9). See also Moore and Silverthorne, "Protestant Theologies," pp. 173 ff.

3. See ch. 1, nn. 22, 23.

4. Burgersdyck and Heereboord included under the rubric of human actions not only *free* actions, but also *involuntary* actions (*actiones invitae*) or *passions: Idea Philosophiae,* ch. V; *Collegium Ethicum,* ch. VI; see ch. 1, n. 8, above.

or other of two faculties; a discussion of this is more appropriate in a different forum.[5] [I.1.4.i]

There are two senses in which a man is said to *be able to understand* the natural law or certain of its precepts. In the *first* sense this phrase is taken in a wide sense to mean only that a faculty of reason has been implanted in man by God, and signs of the true and the good have been manifested in nature, by means of which a man might get to know the difference between what should be done and what omitted, if he used that faculty rightly. In the *second* sense, the phrase, taken more narrowly, means that there is such a vigor of intellect in a man and such clear signs in nature of a law which prescribes some things and forbids others, that he could understand the duty laid upon him by law, using the ordinary diligence which one who is not plainly negligent of duty is rightly expected to use. These two senses must be carefully distinguished. For in the former sense, what is asserted here is true of all men; but in the latter sense (which Pufendorf seems to have had particularly in mind),[6] it is true only of men of mature years and sound mind. In the former sense, it should be extended to all the precepts of natural law, as each man has opportunity to observe them; in the latter sense, only to the more general and more obvious precepts. Finally, in the former sense, the law must be supposed to be *knowable* so that one may be condemned for violation of it even in the court of God, since not even in the court of God is one thought to be personally responsible for violating a law which was not properly declared to him, that is, a law which he was capable of understanding by his own nature but which was not clearly signified to him; but in the latter sense, the necessity of supposing the law to be knowable is restricted to the human court. [I.1.4.ii]

[Pufendorf had defined right conscience (*conscientia recta*) as a well-informed understanding of "what is to be done or not done," which is supported by "certain and incontrovertible reasons." He acknowledged that most persons do not act upon such an understanding; they are guided rather by "probable conscience."[7] Carmichael observed:]

5. See below, p. 339.
6. Pufendorf, *On the Duty of Man and Citizen,* I.4, pp. 17–18.
7. Ibid., I.5, p. 18.

The distinguished Gerhard Titius, *Observations,* no. 17, seems to criticize this term ["right conscience"] unnecessarily, contending that conscience as here defined ought to be called *certain conscience,* inasmuch as probable conscience is also *right.* But against this one must say that merely *probable* conscience, even though it is sometimes *true* (which is all that the author admits) yet falls short of rectitude precisely insofar as it fails to achieve certainty. For inasmuch as there are sure indications of promulgated law exhibited to men, one should permit as little latitude as possible in the court of God to a kind of culpable weakness when men claim that they do not know with certainty the provisions of the law. Besides, the distinguished commentator admits at *Observations,* no. 19.4, that probable conscience is not sound, but requires a remedy. [I.1.5.iii]

If it is a question of what is required in the divine court, without a doubt conscience must be rightly instructed, and one must embrace what is supported by sound reasons. But secondly, if it is a question of choosing the [course of action] which is merely less dangerous, then one must adopt the rule proposed by Pufendorf,[8] provided that it is only a question of whether to undertake or omit some action. Sometimes, however, it is clear that one or the other of two things must be done; that in fact it is less harmful that one of them be done than that both be omitted. Then, and even though it is doubtful whether either course of action is right, we must still exempt such cases from the rule proposed by Pufendorf, as Grotius correctly taught,[9] and which Pufendorf and Barbeyrac improperly reject.[10] [I.1.6.i]

8. Ibid., I.6, p. 18: his rule is that "one should suspend action as long as the judgment as to good and bad is uncertain."

9. Grotius said: "This Rule, of abstaining from a doubtful Action does not hold when we are oblig'd to do either this or that, and yet are unsatisfied in either, whether it be just or not; for then we are allow'd to choose that Side which appears less evil or unjust. For whensoever we are under the Necessity of making a Choice, the lesser Evil assumes the Character of Good" (Grotius, *Rights of War and Peace,* II.23.2, cited in Pufendorf, *Of the Law of Nature and Nations,* I.3.8, pp. 29–30).

10. It is characteristic of Carmichael as a moral philosopher that he supported the more affirmative and active orientation of Grotius's and Locke's natural jurisprudence against the more cautious and obedience-oriented approach to natural and civic duty of Pufendorf and (on certain matters) Barbeyrac. In *Les Devoirs* (1741), pp. 12–13, Barbeyrac complained that Carmichael had failed to provide an illustration of an action which must be done even though the outcome might be of doubtful merit. The only

It is not without justification that the distinguished Titius here reproaches the author for treating *spontaneity* and *liberty* as different conditions of the will or of its acts, despite the fact that by the definitions of both given here, he makes the former a part of the latter. For he places spontaneity in an indifference to act or not to act; but he places liberty both in that indifference to act or not to act which is called *contradiction,* and in the indifference to doing this [particular] thing or its contrary, which is called *contrariety.*[11] But it is of greater importance to observe that neither the indifference of contradiction nor that of contrariety belongs to the genuine spontaneity or liberty of the will or of its acts. Man does indeed experience that he is an agent who is not only *spontaneous* but *free,* i.e., that he acts from a principle which is not only internal but rational, by means of a determination of the will, and the fact itself proclaims that this condition is requisite to the morality and imputability of human actions. But neither reason nor experience suggests that absolute indifference opposed to all previous determination is necessary for this effect, or that it is actually found in our freest actions.[12] On the contrary, that hypothesis not only derogates from the absolute power of the Supreme Deity over created things, but also is opposed to the very nature of causality. For just as no effect exists without some adequate cause, so neither is it possible to acknowledge that any cause is adequate which does not determine the

---

illustration which occurred to Barbeyrac of the kind of case Carmichael could have had in mind was the case of a subject who has been ordered by a legitimate ruler to perform one or more dubious actions. Like Pufendorf, Barbeyrac thought that the circumstance that an act had been commanded by a superior imparted moral merit to the act. For Carmichael, on the other hand, the moral merit of an action was always signified by the disposition or sentiment in which it was performed. Accordingly, we find Carmichael inclined to support actions which manifest or exhibit the appropriate disposition (reverence or veneration of the deity), even when no rule or law made by a (human) superior demands it.

11. Pufendorf, *On the Duty of Man and Citizen,* I.9–10, pp. 19–20, and *Of the Law of Nature and Nations,* I.IV.1–2; Titius, *Observationes,* no. 29.

12. The idea that liberty of the will depended upon indifference had been argued by the Jesuits (Molina, Suarez, and others). Among the scholastic moralists whose texts were regularly assigned in moral philosophy courses in British universities in the seventeenth century, only Eustache offered a qualified defense of the liberty of indifference: *Ethica* (1693), pp. 12–13 and 64–65.

existence of the effect. Nor can any effect be determined to exist by a cause containing nothing that requires its existence rather than its nonexistence. Compare the *Demonstration of God* of the distinguished [Joseph] Raphson, part II, proposition 11.[13] And of course it is far from being the case that man is made the master of his own action by absolute indifference in acting; on the contrary, the action itself is conceived, on that hypothesis, as some sort of entity which is independent or born as of its own accord from nothing. But these points belong elsewhere.[14] [I.1.9.i]

I have sufficiently indicated in the preceding paragraph what sort of spontaneity and liberty we should affirm. It is the conception which is briefly explained at pp. 25–26 and at much greater length and with much greater power by the famous John Locke, *Essay Concerning Human Understanding,* book II, chapter 21, where it is centered on this point: *that one acts or does not act as one wishes to act or not to act.*[15] In whatever created thing therefore this condition of action is found, it is precisely there that there is room for reasons drawn from the representation of good or evil. And in a mind capable of knowing spiritual things, the strongest of these ought to be those which are drawn from the prescriptions of the divine law, so that as one is prompted by these reasons to perform at the command of God's will the actions He prescribes, and to omit those He forbids, so one is to be considered as giving evidence of, on the one hand, love and veneration of God himself, and on the other hand, of neglect and contempt. One must therefore expect the consequences of the two actions which it is worthy of the majesty, wisdom, and sanctity of the supreme deity to dispense on the one hand to his worshippers and on the other to those who despise him. The prejudice that absolute indifference is required for this effect is puerile, and is perhaps the "archetypal lie" of all the errors in this doctrine.[16] It is indeed true that duty, even when it is left

13. Raphson, *Demonstratio de Deo.*
14. See below, *Philosophical Theses* (1699), pp. 339–41.
15. Locke, *Essay,* bk. I, ch. 21, sec. 21, pp. 244 ff.
16. On the "archetypal lie," or *proton pseudos,* see Aristotle, *Analytica Priora,* 56a15. The circumstance that liberty of indifference was conceived by Jesuit writers to

undone, may be said to be capable of being chosen, so far as it is capable of being known (see above, p. 32). Thus it may be said, *first,* in the wider sense, that a faculty of reason is implanted in the mind, and signs of good and evil are manifested, such that if a man used his reason with the greatest care, he would be determined to embrace the good. Or it may be said, in a narrower sense, that there is in the mind a vigor of reason and that the signs of good and evil are so clearly represented to it that a man would be determined to embrace the good, provided ordinary constancy of will accompanied ordinary attention of intellect. Of these the former is the standard for imputation in the court of God and of conscience: but we do not deny that the latter is rightly the most that is required in the human court. [I.1.10.i]

The author does not seem to have intended here to teach a complete distribution of goods, but only of terrestrial goods, the same distinction of goods as is suggested by the Apostle (1 John, II.16).[17] Therefore, since that *good* toward which the will is perpetually set serves toward attaining or preserving happiness, that is, pleasure or immunity from pain, an aim to which it contributes either *directly* or *indirectly,* it is clear that all that is good is *pleasant* or *useful* (taking these terms in a rather wide sense). [I.1.11.i]

Actions which are *involuntary because of force,* or *compelled,* should rather be called *passions* (*passiones*) as the distinguished Gerard de Vries noted, *Pneumatological Determinations,* section II, chapter VII.6.[18] Also when it is a question of actions which are *involuntary by reason or ignorance,* or *mixed,* the same author gives an equally correct account: in the former, the so-called involuntary element is something which is merely incidental to the action, apart from the intention; the latter are actually free

---

counter the determinism of Protestant moralists may account in part for the ferocity of Carmichael's repudiation of this doctrine ("the archetypal lie," etc.).

17. Pufendorf, *On the Duty of Man and Citizen,* I.1.11, p. 20. The First Letter of John, 2.16: "For all that is in the world, the lust of the flesh, and the lust of the eyes, and the pride of life, is not of the Father, but is of the world." The biblical saying cited by Carmichael is significant in its underlining of the ascetic dimension of Carmichael's moral philosophy, as contrasted with the Epicurean orientation of much of Pufendorf's moral thought.

18. De Vries, *De Natura Dei,* p. 32.

actions, since they have been undertaken as a result of a previous choice, though joined with a tendency in the opposite direction. [I.1.16.i]

It is his own *free* actions and omissions, as we have defined them at pp. 25–26 and above at 35–36, which are in a man's power to do or not to do. If anyone insists that some notion of *indifference* is relevant here, it is obvious that this indifference is contained in the notion of *freedom* given in the aforesaid passages, in that an agent is *determined to act or not to act precisely in the same way that he is determined to will or not to will.* We do not deny that the one is connected with the other in a man (and perhaps in any free created agent), *because if we look at its mere essence, he may be determined to either of the two.* But if anything beyond the indifference explained here is required for the effect of imputation in the *human court,* it includes only this, that a *man being placed in such circumstances* (so far as these can be known by men before the actual event) without the supernatural intervention of the Deity, *can be determined to choose either direction.* But this is not required in the *divine court* either. Further, actual imputation also requires a law by a man who pays due attention and when known may move him to obedience, provided only he rightly trains his reason. We have indicated above, p. 32, and pp. 35–36, in what sense both points ought to be understood with regard to both the divine and the human court. [I.1.17.i]

[Pufendorf held that a man is not responsible for actions taken under duress: when one is forced to do or suffer something, or secondly, when one is threatened with some serious harm unless one acts or abstains from acting. Carmichael comments:]

This second mode of compulsion, as it does not prevent the action from being truly free (that is, undertaken here and now by command of the will), cannot diminish responsibility for it either. (Whether it excuses an action which would otherwise have been bad, and makes it good, is another question.) But it cannot be admitted in the court of God with respect to actions by which reverence for the Deity is directly violated, a perfect right of another man is injured, or harm inflicted in other ways on us or on other innocent persons, especially a greater or an equal harm to those things which a man has no right to freely dispose of, such as life and limbs.

Otherwise, the infliction of a serious injury may necessitate many actions which it would not be right to do apart from that. And it often extenuates those actions which it does not excuse in the divine court, and usually removes responsibility in the human court, if the evil represented would cause terror to a grave and constant man. [I.1.24.i]

This [absence of responsibility of an agent who acts simply as the instrument of another] is never to be admitted in actions in which a man interposes the command of his will, whatever necessity he may be under. But it is true that these actions are not always imputed to the immediate agent, nor are they of the same type of morality (far less of the same degree) as if he had done them of his own accord. This is all that the author seems to mean here, as in every passage where he denies responsibility for such actions. But this should not be extended to those actions which we have said in the previous note cannot be excused by the second kind of compulsion. [I.1.27.i]

Laws, Rights, and Justice[1]

The author is right to point out here that it contributes to the security of the human race that men's actions be restrained by a certain rule; he illustrates the same point more fully at *Of the Law of Nature and Nations,* II.I. But the assertion that man actually is subject to such a rule needs to be proved from the supreme perfections of God himself, from the rational nature of Man, and from the total dependence of man on God. Cf. the early part of Supplement I, pp. 21 ff. [I.2.1.i]

[Pufendorf defines Law as "a decree by which a superior obliges one who is subject to him to conform his actions to the superior's prescript." Carmichael comments:]

The distinguished [commentators] Titius and Barbeyrac[2] object that this definition is insufficiently general, arguing that there are laws which are purely *permissive* as well as laws *which give rise to obligation.* In any case they are wrong to add in confirmation of this that all rights emerge from purely permissive laws. On the contrary, since, by the distinguished writers' own admission, rights and obligations go hand in hand and are correlative, since it is their special property to be imposed and cancelled together, the same law which gives someone a right which is valid against others, also by that very fact imposes on those others the corresponding obligation; cf. Grotius, I.I.9. Nor should a right to mere *license* which does

---

1. From the notes to bk. I, ch. 2, "On the Rule of Human Actions, or on Law in General."

2. Titius, *Observationes,* no. 50. Barbeyrac, *Discours sur la permission des loix,* which is bound with Pufendorf, *Les devoirs de l'homme et du citoyen.*

not involve such an obligation, such as the Hobbesian *natural right of all men to all things,* be taken as a law at all, but rather as the negation of all laws. However I do not deny that an explicit act on the part of the maker of a law often intervenes to dissolve an obligation previously imposed by law; such an act simply repeals a previous law, and is also often called a *law,* whether rightly or wrongly is not worth arguing. [I.2.2.i]

We cannot have a properly clear and distinct idea of *moral rightness* unless we refer it ultimately to the *divine law.* This is why we determined to establish the notion of divine law (as the sufficient norm and measure of all morality) at the very beginning. This is not the point to discuss *law* in general; for human laws can be conveniently discussed among the innumerable other circumstances, in the face of whose diversity the divine law itself requires many different duties from us. As for the obligatory force of human laws, the plan of the course requires us to delay this until much later. [I.2.3.i]

A *superior* is one who has *good reasons* why he may require, under threat of penalty, that another man submit his freedom of will to his discretion. Such a one is either God, whose strength can never fail, or someone to whom God has, directly or indirectly, granted this authority. The divine power is understood to be ready to support such a one, by exacting a penalty from those who resist him, if he happens on occasion not to have sufficient strength in his own hands for this purpose. [I.2.5.i]

[On the grounds which Pufendorf gives for obligation to a superior, Carmichael comments:]

With the exception of the final argument (which is the foundation not of original but only of derived power),[3] the reasons which the author gives here, whether taken separately or together, are not sufficiently powerful. (Cf. *Of the Law of Nature and Nations,* I.VI.12.) We will be more correct in saying that the reason for the *original* power which belongs to God alone is to be sought in the *infinite perfection of God and in the total dependence of ourselves and of all things upon him as the first and independent*

---

3. The "final argument" is this: "If [he] has voluntarily submitted to him and accepted his direction."

cause; and that the primary root of derived power is the *Law of God,* by which He gives one man the right or capacity to rule another, though often certain human acts also are a part of the process, and notably the act mentioned in the final clause of this section, that *a man voluntarily submits himself to another and accepts his direction.* [I.2.5.ii]

It is a celebrated question, whether *dispensation* has a place in the natural laws. It cannot be doubted that God has sometimes, by a positive declaration of his will, made that just which otherwise would have been unjust by natural law, and vice versa. But many reasonably deny that in these cases God has made a dispensation from any precept of natural law. They contend that the condition of the object has been so altered by God, not as Legislator but as supreme Lord or supreme Judge of all created things, that what would have been forbidden apart from that individual case, is now enjoined by natural law, or *vice versa.* See Suarez, *On Laws,* book I.⁴ Civil rulers set the limits of right and wrong by positive laws rather differently than the law of nature does. They make use of the right which individual citizens have given them against themselves, of accommodating their own rights to the safety and security of the state. Yet they are no more to be said to be granting dispensation from the laws of nature, than a creditor in remitting a debt is said to detract in any way from the law on paying debts. [I.2.9.i]

[Pufendorf says: "Those actions for which the law makes no provision in either way are said to be licit or permitted." Carmichael comments:]

In ethics these actions are commonly called *indifferent.* Not without reason most of the scholastics deny that any human action, *taken as a whole,* i.e., with all its circumstances, is indifferent. We however recognize that innumerable actions are indifferent, not only *in kind,* that is, in abstraction from all circumstances, but also taken in conjunction with all those circumstances which can be known and weighed by other men; and therefore no man may be convicted of wrong by another man for doing or omitting them. [I.2.11.i]

Justice, and moral *goodness (bonitas)* and *badness (malitia)* in general, is

---

4. Suarez, *Tractatus de Legibus;* see also bk. II, ch. 15, pp. 93–99: "Whether the absolute power of God is able to dispense from the natural law."

attributed primarily to actions (on the goodness and badness of which, see Pufendorf, *On the Duty of Man and Citizen,* I.2.11, and our Supplement I.10, pp. 24–25) and secondarily to persons insofar as they are endowed with the *habit* of performing such actions. The moral goodness of a person is called *virtue,* and can be aptly defined as *a habit tending toward obedience to the Divine Law,* that is, to doing actions prescribed by the law with the intention of doing so, and to omitting forbidden actions with that intention. Likewise the moral badness of a person is called *vice,* which is defined as *a habit tending toward transgression of the Divine Law,* that is, to committing forbidden actions with whatever intention or to omitting prescribed actions.

But *justice* as attributed to actions, as the author explains in the following paragraph, is simply their goodness considered with reference to a person to whom a particular act is due; and therefore *justice* attributed to persons, if taken in an equally broad sense, as a constant and perpetual will to perform the duties which are owed to each and every one (that is, to God, to ourselves, and to other men), covers the whole range of moral virtue.

Yet the usual enumeration of the *Cardinal Virtues* as four is not completely without foundation. For the other three (so far as they are moral) are contained within the scope of *justice* as just defined; yet each one of them by itself is in some way a general virtue and relates to all kinds of duties. *Prudence,* for instance, leads to full investigation and careful judgment as to what we owe, in particular circumstances, to God, ourselves, or other men. And *temperance* and *fortitude,* if taken in a sufficiently broad sense, remove two particular obstacles to right action, i.e., an excessive grasping after the goods, and excessive fear of the ills of this life. Thus the former teaches *self-restraint,* the latter *endurance,*[5] which, as Epictetus cleverly remarked, contain between them the sum of all moral philosophy. Cicero too put it very well at *On Duties* I.ii: *no one can be just, who fears death, pain, exile or poverty, or who prefers their opposites to equity.*[6]

---

5. *apexesthai* and *anechesthai:* Neatly expressed at fragment 10.6: " 'And so,' he says, 'if a man should take to heart these two words and observe them in controlling and keeping watch over himself, he will, for the most part, be free from wrongdoing, and will live a highly peaceful life.' These two words, he used to say, were *anechou* and *apechou*" (Oldfather, ed. *Epictetus,* vol. II, p. 455).

6. The quotation is to be found at Cicero, *De Officiis* [On Duties], II.[xi].38.

Because of that one principle from which flows all genuine obedience to law (i.e., love of God tempered with reverence, and a habitual will to show it in all one's actions), we have defined virtue, or justice, taken broadly, in a collective rather than an indefinite sense; and so we should inquire not into the various *kinds of virtue* but into the various *relations or parts of virtue.* The best way of analyzing these is by the variety of duties which they lead one to do, or if you prefer, to the variety of precepts which they incline one to obey. The broadest division is into *piety,* which has regard to the duties to be offered directly to God, and *probity,* which has regard to the duties owed to ourselves or to other men. Goodness toward ourselves, taken in its full range, is not distinguished, so far as I know, by a single name; for *temperance,* even if taken in a wide sense, is only a certain part of it, and does not cover the whole range. However, probity toward other men is *justice* itself in the narrower sense, as our author defines it at section 14. [I.2.12.i]

The unjust man does the just things which he does, either because of the penalty attached to the law, or for some other similar reason different from sincere respect for the divine law. By a sincere respect for that Law, we mean a respect which is founded in a habitual will to obey God in all things, or keeping conformity with the divine law always before our eyes, above all other considerations which can be opposed to it. This is the regard for law which should be understood at pp. 24–25 and in other passages where we speak of obedience to law and actions truly good. [I.2.12.ii]

Justice, in the broad sense here explained, as it is nothing other than *goodness* in relation to the person in whom the action terminates, can have regard to the agent himself as well as to any other man. [I.2.13.i]

The *justice* which is here analyzed as above is justice toward other men. *Universal* justice, however unsuitable that name may be, should be confined to duties which another person could not require in his own right. Otherwise one member of the division would exhaust the whole which was being divided.

But to penetrate this distinction more deeply, notice that *justice toward other men,* i.e., the habitual will to perform the duties which are due to them and to abstain from the contrary actions, assumes in the person for whom justice is to be done, some *right* or *facility afforded by law, of doing, having, or obtaining something from someone else,* and in the party which is doing justice, it assumes the corresponding *obligation* of permitting him so to do or to have, or of providing that which the other has the right of obtaining from him. Furthermore, just as right on the one hand and obligation on the other are founded (as will be said below)[7] in the importance of the duty in question to the preservation and advancement of social life among men, so both the right and the corresponding obligation vary according to the varying degrees of importance. There are some duties which are so absolutely necessary to social life that human society itself would be unsociable in their absence, and therefore they are rightly enforced even on those who do not want to do them. But there are other duties, which pertain to the comfort or ornament of social life more than to its essence, and are therefore left to the discretion and honor of each individual. One is said to have a *perfect right* to the former, a right which is often distinguished by the term *suo jure*. To the latter one has only an imperfect right. Likewise, the obligation of performing the former is called *perfect,* of the latter, *imperfect*. Finally, the *justice* which disposes one to the performance of perfect duties is called *particular* justice; Grotius calls it *expletive (expletrix);* it is what we have called justice in the strictest sense, which is defined by the jurists as *the constant and perpetual will to give each man his due*.[8] The justice which inclines men to imperfect duties is called *universal;* Grotius calls it *attributive (attributrix);* it embraces all the other virtues which pertain to other men.[9]

Note in passing that in civil society the distinction between *perfect* and *imperfect* right, and so between *expletive* and *attributive* justice, is normally to be found in the civil laws, which grant or deny an action in the courts. [I.2.14.i]

A *wrong (injuria)* is a *violation of another's perfect right,* whether it comes about by unjust action or by omission of a due action, whether by deliberate intention or by culpable negligence or recklessness. Hence Justinian teaches that the *lex Aquilia,* which was directed against those who wrongfully inflict loss, applies to those who harm others not only by *fraud* but also by *fault* (*Institutes,* IV.3.3). [I.2.15.i]

---

7. Ch. 2 and ch. 23.
8. Cf. Justinian, *Institutes,* I.1.
9. Grotius, *Rights of War and Peace,* I.I.8.

A right may relate simply to doing or to having something; corresponding to this right is an indefinite obligation on others to permit one so to do or to have. Or a right may relate to requiring something from another person; to this corresponds a more specific obligation upon the other to do that particular thing. A wrong is committed by the violation of either of these rights. The author seems to imply this distinction in the immediately preceding words. Two of the three precepts of law given at *Institutes,* I.1.3, seem to make the same point: namely, the two which relate to others, *not to harm another* and *to give each man his due.* Further, the former right is violated by harming, without just cause, either the man himself or his possessions, or by taking them away without such a cause. The latter right is violated by refusing either a thing or a service which is due by perfect obligation. [I.2.15.ii]

Among these many philosophical comments, may I also be permitted here to suggest one philological observation, with due deference to others' judgment. This is that a law is not properly spoken of as introduced (*latam*) by the person who *commands (iubet)* a law, and in whose command the force of the law lies. For *the introduction of a law or legislation (legislatio),* so far as I have had occasion to observe, was not, among the Romans, attributed either to the free People or in later times to the Emperors, but only to the magistrate who was the author of the law which was to be commanded by the people.[10] And this is the only sense in which the *Legislators* of the Greek states, *Solon, Lycurgus, Zaleucus,* etc., are so called by Roman writers.[11] [I.2.16.i]

---

10. Thus the "lex Porcia" is named for M. Porcius Cato, who as praetor introduced or proposed it before an assembly of the Roman people in 198 B.C. See also p. 157 and n. 3, below.

11. Solon, reformer and lawgiver of Athens, early sixth century B.C.; Lycurgus, the legendary legislator of the Spartan way of life, perhaps of the late seventh century B.C.; Zaleucus of Locri, reputed to be the earliest composer of a written legal code in any Greek city, perhaps about 650 B.C.

On Natural Law[1]

The basic precepts of natural law[2]

Pufendorf's doctrine of the fundamental precept of natural law, which he lays out in chapter 3 [Pufendorf, *On the Duty of Man and Citizen*, I.3], has long been criticized by many grave and learned men as unsatisfactory and inadequate to the end it seeks to achieve. So instead of making individual notes on this chapter we will attempt to give some idea, in the most summary form possible, of a doctrine of the precepts of Natural Law which may be seen to be less open to those criticisms.

1. In the first place, we must keep before our eyes the notion of the *Divine Law* and of the duty it *prescribes* which we established at pp. 24–25. That notion is that when God prescribes something to us, He is simply signifying that he requires us to do such and such an action, and regards it, when offered with that intention, as a sign of love and veneration toward him, while failure to perform such actions, and, still worse, commission of the contrary acts, he interprets as an indication of contempt or hatred. Since a man can give evidence in his actions of both of these sentiments toward God, either immediately and directly or mediately and indirectly, the duties prescribed to us by law are either *immediate* or *mediate*.

2. The immediate duties directly express the sentiment due to God, and insofar as they are prescribed by natural law, they are recognized as tending to signify that sentiment directly, or in their very notion. Such are the du-

---

1. Supplement II, and notes from bk. I, ch. 3, "On Natural Law."
2. Supplement II.

ties surveyed by our author in chapter 4 [Pufendorf, *On the Duty of Man and Citizen,* I.4], and all of them may be summed up in this one precept, which we lay down as the *first precept,* that *God is to be worshipped.*

3. In the mediate duties, i.e., those which are directed not immediately toward God but toward created things, the same sentiment is declared to be due to God. The sum of these duties consists in this, that *each man should treat the universal system of rational creatures with benevolence subordinated to love and reverence for God; and therefore each man should attempt to promote the common good of these creatures so far as his strength permits, and so long as he has no knowledge that it may interfere with the illustration of the divine glory.* When we speak of rational creatures we mean creatures which are endowed not only with some capacity to reason, but with that kind of reason whose right use enables them to rise to knowledge of the great and good God and of their obligation to him. For rational creatures bear the image of their Creator in a special way. And in the divine dispensation toward them, there shine out those perfections of God, whose illustration is the aim of all divine works. Toward rational creatures God has dispensed the effects of his goodness with so generous a hand that, after the illustration of his own glories, he seems particularly to have intended their happiness, so far as they bear themselves with due subordination to him. Therefore, just as love toward the head of a household is shown through effective benevolence toward his servants, so devout affection for God, whom we cannot benefit or harm, is appropriately shown by exercising the greatest benevolence and beneficence we can toward his rational creatures, so far as they bear his image and are not contrary to him.

4. But, to bring this rule closer to practice, we must note two things. First, no consideration suggests that there are other rational creatures apart from men, whom men by any actions of theirs can either help or harm; much less can any loss or harm be inflicted on these others by the greatest happiness which men can procure for other men. Hence it follows, in the rule or summary of mediate duties given above, that for *the universal system of rational creatures* we may substitute *the whole human race.* We note, secondly, that there is no consideration which suggests that the greatest benefits which men can procure for men oppose the illustration of divine glory. For although the facts themselves proclaim only too obviously that the hu-

man race has fallen away from God, and has rendered itself liable to his righteous retribution, yet the whole series of divine dispensations toward the human race seems to prove that men are still in a state of probation and have not yet been thrust into the eternal abyss of the penal state while they live on earth. Furthermore, the good things which attend man's state on this earth far exceed the ills mixed in with them (apart from sin), and would exceed them much more if individual men did not fail themselves and other men. So individuals, by doing the duties of which they are capable, will afford to themselves and to other men a richer use of the good things which the divine kindness has placed in their power, and will also obtain the best hope they can have of future goods. And thus far from hindering the manifestation of divine glory, they must very much contribute to proclaiming the praises of the wisdom and munificence of God.

5. Thus we deduce the *second* fundamental precept of Natural Law which embraces mediate duties (as the first embraced immediate duties). It is that *each man should promote, so far as it is in his power, the common good of the whole human race, and, so far as this allows, the private good of individuals.*

6. To answer the more particular question, by what actions one may promote the interests of the human race, one must split the second general precept into two which are directly subordinate to it. For in the first place there are certain things a man can do which benefit him or others but do not hurt anyone else's interests; there is no room for doubt that such actions contribute to the common good of the human race. For what is of benefit to one part of the system, without harm or loss to any other part, is undoubtedly of benefit to the whole system. Since innumerable duties belong specifically to this class, which each man has a daily opportunity of doing for himself; and since duties which are to be done to others in any case can without difficulty be assigned to the precept of sociability, it is enough to say that the precepts given above entail the first subordinate precept which lays down that *each man should take care to promote his own interest without harming others.* Here belong the duties expounded at chapter 7, pp. 59 ff., which includes Supplement III.

7. But it happens often enough that the interests of different men, including our own and those of others, conflict, so that we are not able to

do good to all men at the same time. In this case, it may not be quite clear what kind of action is more useful for the human race as a whole. There is a place therefore for the reasoning which Pufendorf uses in his third chapter. Pufendorf argues that the nature of men is so constituted that, on the one hand, individuals need the help of others (1) to preserve their lives (and every individual has an acute concern and anxious devotion to his own life), and (2) to lead their lives agreeably (on this compare Cicero, *On Duties,* bk. II, ch. 3 and 4).[3] On the other hand, men are endowed, above all other animals, with the ability to be of assistance to others and are at the same time disposed to do so (see Cumberland, *On the Laws of Nature,* ch. II, sec. 23 ff.).[4]

By the same token, the constitution of human nature is such that men can abuse all these prerogatives of their nature to hurt each other in a very effective manner, and are liable to attacks of provocation which incite them to do so. It follows from this that it is necessary for the safety of the human race that it be *sociable,* that is, that men readily unite with one another, and behave with due consideration not for self alone but also for others. And by this union, individuals, insofar as it is in them, may obtain and encourage mutual benevolence and mutual trust. These are the two hinges on which depends the willing performance of all those mutual duties which tend to the preservation of human life and the improvement of its advantages.

8. So, from the general precept of *promoting the common good of the human race,* this second subordinate precept is deduced: *sociability is to be cultivated and preserved by every man, so far as in him lies;* that is, social inclination and social life are to be encouraged and promoted by every man, so far as it is in his power, both in himself toward others, and in others toward himself, and in all men toward each other mutually.

9. By this train of reasoning, *sociability* is not subordinated to *self-love.* It is not necessary to consider here whether the objection which Titius[5] makes against Pufendorf is right or wrong. For we do not say that each

---

3. Cicero, *De Officiis* [On Duties], II.[iii and iv]. 11–15.

4. Cumberland, *De Legibus Naturae* (1672); references are to *A Treatise of the Laws of Nature,* pp. 143 ff.

5. Titius, *Observationes,* no. 78.

man ought to live sociably only because he cannot otherwise be secure. We say that because social life is necessary to the safety and preservation from harm of the human race as a whole, and every violation of it tends to its harm, therefore each man ought to do his part, so far as he can, to encourage and strengthen it.

10. Our method makes it unnecessary to give a lengthy argument for the divine authority of these precepts. For we have shown above that it pertains to the showing of love and veneration toward God that *each man should try to benefit the human race so far as he can.* And it is likewise convincingly shown that *innocuous care for oneself* and *sociability* make for the common good of the human race. And therefore it is quite evident that God requires both from men as a sign of due sentiment toward him and that he intends to reward performance of the relevant duties, or at least punish their neglect and violation. Moreover since we learn these things from the nature which God has made for man's contemplation, by using the reason which He has also given us, it is clear that the same considerations by which we argued for the divine authority of natural law in general (p. 28) are abundantly evident in these general precepts, and consequently in all the derivations from them.

11. Furthermore, that there is a sanction to these precepts is proven not only by those general reasons by which, at pp. 21–24, we demonstrated that it is in a man's highest interest to obey every precept derived from the Divine Law, but also because reason and daily experience confirm the special rewards which flow from the observation of these precepts and the penalties which naturally flow from their violation. It is unnecessary to point these out in the case of a man's *duties toward himself.* As for the *social duties* which we do for others, they are naturally followed by *serenity of mind and a healthy state of the body* (which even apart from consideration of moral good, usually accompanies kindly and agreeable sentiments), *benevolence to other men,* and the *security* which frequently arises from it. The contrary actions are frequently succeeded by perpetual *anxiety* (which is accompanied by emotions which even *undermine the health of the body*), by *contempt* or *hatred* for other men, and by the innumerable *dangers* that arise from them. Consult Cicero, *On Duties,* book II, where he inculcates these points at length. And because these sentiments are connected by a

kind of natural entailment with observation of or contempt for the law of sociability, they have the same status as rewards or punishments seeing that this natural connection itself was established by God, the author both of nature and of the natural law.

12. As the basis of the natural laws we place not one fundamental precept, as Pufendorf does, but three: that *God is to be worshipped;* that *each man should pursue his own interest without harming others;* and that *sociability should be cultivated.* To the first of these we refer the duties which are to be performed directly toward God; to the second those duties of man toward himself which do not conflict with the interest of any other person; and to the third, all the duties of a man toward other men, as well as such duties toward himself as a man should only do after he has fully satisfied the demands of sociability, as they are prejudicial to the claims of certain other men.

13. To understand the use and application of the precept on *cultivating sociability* more clearly, we think that one should take note of three points which define the limits of what should be done and what not done in cases in which men's differing interests seem to prompt them to different courses.

14. In the first place we note that there are certain *advantages* or *pleasures* which men can get either from their own actions or from external objects or from the actions of other men, and which it is to the interest of human society to secure to them in certain circumstances, and which should not be obstructed, withdrawn, or intercepted, since they contribute to preserving and strengthening social inclination and social life among men. This is why these advantages and pleasures are fortified by the general precept of *cultivating sociability,* and become *rights,* either perfect or imperfect, according as they are necessary for preserving sociability or merely conduce to strengthening it.

15. Secondly, we note that these rights are *equal* for all in similar circumstances; hence, if they are given by nature, they belong to all men equally so far as they have not forfeited them; or if they are acquired by means of some human act, they can be acquired equally by all in similar circumstances, by means of similar acts.

16. Thirdly, we note that it is not contrary to the nature of social life but

is essential for sustaining it, even in cases where men's interests conflict, that each man *should take a certain particular care of himself and his own, though subordinate to the cultivation of sociability.* If this were not so, there would be massive general confusion, since most men would rely on someone else to help them, while idling their time away and neglecting to cultivate the resources which nature had given them. Hence, from the other point of view, it would follow that no one could have a firm expectation of anything from other people or count on their help in advancing his own claims.

17. We conclude, therefore, that the right cultivation of *social life* consists in *each man protecting his own right with due consideration for every man's right,* perfect or imperfect, *in accordance with the assumption of the natural equality which belongs to every other man.* It follows that, in order to define the duty which is incumbent on each man with respect to other men, we cannot pursue a better course than to weigh carefully, in due order, the various rights which belong or may belong to individuals, to groups of men, or even to the human race as a whole, and the different foundations on which each rests. For it will be immediately evident what obligations correspond to each right.

18. In the appendix[6] we have given a general idea of the method which we think should be followed in doing this; it is rather different from that of Pufendorf.

Worship of God the first law of nature[7]

It is clear from what we have said that Pufendorf's method of deducing our duties toward God [i.e., indirectly from sociability] ought by no means to satisfy us. On the contrary, it is a prior and more evident principle that *God is to be worshipped* than that *one should live sociably with men.* This is particularly so since, as the distinguished author admits at section 10 of this chapter, for the precept on *cultivating sociability* to obtain the force of law, one must necessarily presuppose *that there is a God, and*

---

6. See ch. 23, pp. 211–17.
7. From the notes to bk. I, ch. 3, "On Natural Law."

that he rules all things by his Providence. And it is not true, as the author adds here, *that reason alone can progress no further in religion than so far as it serves to promote the peace and sociability of this life.* For even though the religion which effectively procures the salvation of souls originates in a particular divine revelation, yet reason itself teaches that in worshipping God and offering universal obedience to the divine laws, one must have before one's eyes something more than the good things of the present life, especially if these good things are only regarded as flowing by a certain natural consequence from the performance of those duties. See pp. 22 and 24 and compare p. 30. [I.3.13.i]

Care of self the second law of nature

There is no reason to deduce *care of self* from *sociability,* for any man would be bound to care for himself even though he were alone in the world. Similarly there seems to be no better reason why *care for self* should be deduced from *religion* in the narrow sense more than *sociability* should. Obviously duties of both kinds must be performed with regard for God; but despite that, all duties, apart from direct worship of God, are appropriately deduced from their own principles established above. Thus one must admit that there is such a close bond between the duties of man toward *God,* toward *himself,* and toward *other men* that there will always be a temptation to change the order and try to deduce them from any one of the three principles given above.[8] [I.3.13.ii]

8. It was a persistent theme of Carmichael's jurisprudence that one should avoid attempts to reduce duties to God, self, and others to the cultivation of sociability. See below, *Philosophical Theses,* 1699, "On directing the mind to lasting happiness," sec. 30, pp. 348–49, and on sociability, pp. 73 ff.

CHAPTER 6

On Duty to God[1]

Among the duties owed to God, our author is right to give first place to correct beliefs about him. Beneath the first elements of moral doctrine we must set a sure and certain knowledge of God, of his attributes, and of the dependence of all things upon him. (In this sense the distinguished Gerard de Vries in the last paragraph of the final chapter of his *Pneumatological Determinations,* section 3,[2] has rightly observed that the end of pneumatology is the beginning of moral philosophy.) Consequently these beliefs are not put forward here so much to establish their truth as to emphasize every man's duty of supporting and protecting them. [I.4.1.i]

The older writers may profitably be read on this argument [to the existence of God from "reflection on the fabric of the universe"]; we will realize that nature clearly confessed its author even before it was explored. But we should give particular attention to those who have recently written on this question: for the greater the progress that has been made in the science of nature, the more brightly the signs of the Divine Workman shine.[3] [I.4.2.i]

Conviction of the existence and providence of the Supreme Deity

---

1. From the notes to bk. I, ch. 4, "On the Duty of Man toward God, or on Natural Religion."

2. See *De Natura Dei,* p. 89.

3. Carmichael identifies the more recent writers at *Synopsis,* I.5, pp. 241–42, below. The "older writers" are the Augustinian scholastics (Anselm, Peter Lombard) and the Reformed theologians (Wendelinus, the elder Turretini), whom Carmichael followed particularly in *Synopsis,* chs. 2 and 3. De Vries continued the older tradition of Reformed theology in his *Pneumatological Determinations,* sec. III, "De Deo."

should be planted deep in our minds as the immovable foundation of all religion and morality. And therefore, we must very much beware of those who oppose this belief and must root them out of our midst, as they have an utterly destructive effect on men's very morals.

Particularly pernicious in this way (apart from atheism and Epicureanism, both of which, as the author notes, equally attack in a very direct way all religion and morality) is the opinion of those ancients, whether philosophers or poets, who taught that all things and actions are necessarily determined by a certain inevitable fate, antecedent to the determination of the divine will; they subjected even Jove to fate.

Nor is it a correct understanding of the absolute dominion of God to think that the network of secondary causes and effects is so firm and inviolable that even God himself could not abolish it once he had established the original frame of things, or suspend it in a particular case. Innumerable examples of miracles fully prove the falseness of this doctrine. It is a mistake to object, as our author does at *Of the Law of Nature and Nations*, II.IV.4, that if you accept this belief, you seem to destroy the effect of prayers, penitence, and moral reform. For God could connect the moral actions of men with these moral effects both by his decree and also, if he willed, by the pre-established harmony of things. And it is reasonable to believe that this is the case, since experience proves that divine providence often reveals its splendor in attuning the outcome of events to our moral actions, even when there is no reason to believe that a miracle has occurred. Others may wish to argue for a physical concatenation of causes and effects in order to exclude the moral connection of which we have spoken, but we cannot readily accept this error, which has quite pernicious consequences, so far as morals are concerned. Those who attribute an insuperable efficacy of this kind over the good or ill events which happen to individuals, to the aspects of the stars or other imaginary causes which have no connection with them, add insanity to impiety by tormenting themselves with an anxiety which is as vain as it is irreligious.

But none have a more unworthy conception of divine providence than those who think that evil spirits are permitted to control human affairs so that one can only get or keep one's health and safety in this life by showing some fear or reverence for them in one's words or actions. Akin to this is the impious, or shall I say, fatuous, superstition of those who, although they reject the malice of evil spirits and the pernicious arts of sorcerers, yet themselves employ absurd, idolatrous, and diabolical practices which rest on no sound reason, no experience of intelligent men, nor on any revelation except perhaps from the devil, but which find their strength in the mere stupid and fatuous credulity of the ignorant people. The pernicious effect of all these superstitions shows itself not only in inspiring groundless anxiety and terror, but above all because those whose minds have once been taken over by these ravings show no concern thereafter to conform their actions to the norm of the divine law, whether in performing their duties toward God himself or toward men, since they have placed all their hope and salvation, and thus all their religion and morality, in the observance of these follies. [I.4.4.i]

Spiritual, or thinking, nature cannot be at all reconciled with extension, since the latter includes a real diversity of parts; and therefore the infinitude of the former does not lie in infinite extension, nor its finitude in figure or in the termination of extension. Therefore, figure is to be denied to God, not only because it involves the limits of a thing having figure or an outline, but also because it presupposes extension, which, precisely because it is constituted of finite parts, cannot be an attribute of an infinitely perfect Being. And for the same reason, not only can God not be fully comprehended by *imagination* properly so called, he cannot be reached to any degree at all by this means. [I.4.5.i]

I would think that a distinction absolutely must be made here. For since what is understood by the term *sensation* and its individual kinds, taken strictly, involves a passive state and hence includes dependence in its very idea, it must certainly not be attributed to God. But we must speak differently of the terms *intellect, will,* and *knowledge* (provided the last is not restricted to dianoetic knowledge). For although they denote things which in men really are imperfect, yet those imperfections are not at all involved in the abstract idea itself which is associated with these terms. For it is not true that intellection or cognition of the truth in themselves involve a passive state or that willing as such implies lack of an appropriate object. On the contrary he would have an utterly unworthy conception of God, who did not conceive of him as understanding as well as willing in the most perfect manner. Our author agrees with this at *Of the Law of Nature and Nations,* II.4.3, and elsewhere. [I.4.5.v]

[Pufendorf had reduced the terms applicable to the attributes of God to two kinds, negative and indefinite. Carmichael would add a third:]

When indefinite terms such as *good, just,* and the like are attributed to God in an eminent degree, they are in this case equivalent to superlatives. I would think therefore that one should add *relative* terms as a third class, such as those the author mentions later, *Creator, King, Lord,* etc.

From what has been said it is clear that not only must all imperfections be far removed from the Supreme Deity, as happens particularly in the case of his *incommunicable attributes,*[4] but we must also constantly attribute to him also all the pure perfections and in particular those proper to rational agents, which are usually called the *communicable attributes* of the Deity,[5] and insist that they are possessed by him in the most perfect, and consequently incommunicable, manner. We must also attribute to him every activity concerned with created things, especially rational creatures, which is worthy of those perfections. That is, God must be conceived as *infinitely wise, powerful, just,* and *holy.* From him, as from an intelligent and free cause, other things have their origin and the principle of their motion. And as he governs all things by *physical* authority, so he governs rational things, particularly men, by moral authority. By this authority he requires duties from them; observation of duties pleases him, violation and contempt of duties displeases him; and in their name he will exact an account from all incorruptibly, without respect for persons. For recognition of the moral authority of God and of the moral perfections he displays contributes in a certain special way to duly regulate men's moral behavior; hence those who oppose this belief should be carefully watched and kept far away.

Such are the fantasies of those who imagine that the Supreme Deity strikes bargains about the sins of men. That is, that he accepts the offering of gifts or of any kind of rituals (especially those devised by men's puny

---

4. See *Synopsis,* ch. 2, pp. 248–56.
5. *Synopsis,* ch. 3, pp. 257–69.

minds) in satisfaction for wrongs which men have committed, or are about to commit; or that a man can be freed, by any satisfaction offered for sin, from the obligation to perform the duties of piety and goodness in the future. Even more detestable is the insanity of those who hold that the Deity favors certain sins and treats them as jokes—as the old pagans imagined that the gods smiled at the perjuries of lovers; they even established different gods as patrons of nearly every different kind of crime. One must also outlaw the impiety of those who dare to hope that their wicked prayers will find favor with God, by which they seek to bring down some undeserved evil on others for their own benefit, or that a religion will be pleasing to him whose teachings tend to subvert the common laws of sociability, as when they teach for example that faith is not to be kept with men who differ from them in religion, that nothing is forbidden in the propagation of a religion, and so on. These, I say, and similar monstrous doctrines, as alike contumelious to God and his authority and inimical to all religion and moral goodness among men, are to be thoroughly detested by all good men. [I.4.5.vi]

[Pufendorf is considering "the usefulness of religion in human life" as "the ultimate and the strongest bond of human society." Carmichael comments:]

By the term *religion* here, of which these things are said, we are not so much to understand the narrow sense of the direct worship of God, as that universal respect for Him as Supreme Lord and Judge which should be involved in all obedience to law, upon whose removal, ideas of moral good and evil become empty noises. Some, including Grotius himself, *Rights of War and Peace,* Prolegomena, sec. 12, have rashly taken up a contrary opinion; and some have championed it in our time with an ulterior motive, namely, to conceal the hideous features of atheism under whatever disguise they can. But this matter requires a fuller discussion than the plan of this course allows: see the remarks of the distinguished Barbeyrac against the censure of Anonymous (i.e., the celebrated Leibniz), secs. 13 ff.[6] [I.4.9.i]

6. Barbeyrac, "Jugement d'un Anonyme," secs. 13 ff.

CHAPTER 7

On Duty to Oneself[1]

It is not a superfluous obligation for a man to take care of himself with regard for the law and for the superior who has made the law. We have discussed the grounds on which a man is obliged by the law to look after himself at p. 53. [I.5.1.i]

Pufendorf passes too lightly over the *cultivation of the mind,* a subject which has an important place among the duties which natural law prescribes. This seems to be virtually the only thing which some recent writers understand by *ethics* when they opt to distinguish ethics from natural jurisprudence. In various editions of this treatise several commentators have corrected this defect from the author himself by placing the material from *Of the Law of Nature and Nations,* II.IV, in their text or in footnotes or appendices. We decided to insert the following supplement here, which is largely excerpted from that source,[2] as we indicated in the preface. [I.5.2.i]

On the duties of a man toward his own mind[3]

The cultivation of the mind consists particularly in these things: *to fill it with sound opinions in matters relating to duties; to learn how to judge rightly*

---

1. From the notes to bk. I, ch. 5, "On the Duty of Man toward Himself"; and Supplement III.

2. Carmichael's account of the duties of a man toward his own mind is an adaptation of Pufendorf's treatment in *Of the Law of Nature and Nations,* II.IV, pp. 151–80, which ignores Pufendorf's many classical allusions and recasts the discussion in accordance with Carmichael's moral psychology. His discussion is also indebted to Locke's *Essay,* as he acknowledges below, p. 67.

3. Supplement III.

of the objects which commonly stimulate human desire; to be accustomed to
command the passions by the norm of reason; and to be duly instructed in some
honest skill appropriate to one's conditions and manner of life.

1. Among the opinions or beliefs with which the mind must be filled, the most important is a sure and firm conviction of the topics surveyed in *Of the Law of Nature and Nations,* II.IV, on *God as the Creator, Preserver and Governor of this Universe.* This conviction not only implies a specific human duty (which that chapter impresses upon us), but is also the foundation of a kind of joyful peace, which pervades the human mind; it is also the mainstay of the practice of all integrity toward other men. Hence a right conviction about the existence and providence of the Deity is a duty, in different respects, toward *God,* toward *ourselves,* and toward *other men.*

2. After the knowledge of *God,* it is of the greatest possible value to every man that he properly *know himself,* as he relates to God and to other men. In the former respect, each man should know that he was created by God, and depends wholly on his effective providence; and he is thus held by a most sacred bond to worship him, and to conduct himself with God in view in all things, however contrary this may be to his own or other men's desires. He ought also to know that he has been endowed by his Creator with a rational faculty, whose right use requires that he should not be carried along by blind impulse, like an animal; but should set before himself an end worthy of his nature, and should use means fitly chosen for its achievement; and thus not wander through this world but proceed purposefully, which is the prerogative of a wise man. With respect to other men, each man should recognize that, however great he seems to himself, he is but a small part of the human race; in which every other man naturally plays an equal part: and therefore, since sound reason teaches us *to make similar judgments about similar things,* he must permit to others in similar circumstances everything that he claims for himself; and should no more prefer his private convenience to the common good of the human race, than he would privilege the comfort of his smallest limb over the health of his whole body.

3. Next, what is relevant to a man's due knowledge of himself is that he should have taken the measure of his own *strength* and the effect which his individual actions can produce on external things. He who has duly

weighed this will readily acknowledge that there are some things which cannot be promoted or prevented by his own actions; others, which seem to depend somewhat on the influence of his own actions, but in such a way that innumerable other causes may intervene and frustrate his efforts; others finally which depend wholly on the determination of his will, and such are every man's free actions. A man should give particular attention to the last, to bring them into line with the norm of sound reason, since they alone in themselves, can be imputed to him, for praise or blame, reward or punishment.

4. A man should give due attention to the things which do not wholly depend on human will, provided that they do not altogether exceed the influence of his actions, and if they tend toward his legitimate end and deserve to receive his attention. Everything else should be committed to divine providence; nor ought anyone to disturb himself on account of evils which have befallen him, or may befall him, without his fault. This eliminates no small part of human cares. And just as in those things which give scope to human foresight, we should not blindly entrust the matter to a throw of the dice, as it were, so, if we do what it is in our power to do, for the rest we cannot control an outcome which is unforeseen and not dependent on our direction. And just as it is the part of a wise man not only to see what is immediately before him, but also to foresee what will be, so far as the human condition allows, and constantly to pursue a policy duly formed by this consideration, so it is also the part of a wise man that he not easily allow himself to be turned away either by fear or by enticement of present pleasure. On the other hand, it is characteristic of a stolidly obstinate person to struggle against the stream, and not adapt to things when he cannot adapt them to himself. Finally, since the outcome of future events is uncertain, one must not have too secure a confidence in the present nor anticipate the future with too anxious concern; arrogance in prosperity and despair in adversity are to be equally eschewed.

5. We have said that it is also relevant to the right cultivation of the mind that each man should accustom himself *to judge rightly of those things which commonly stimulate men's desires.* In the forefront of these is *reputation,* which has always been valued by men of good character, men who are made of the right stuff. Every man should take the greatest care to pre-

serve, so far as he can, his simple reputation,[4] that is, the character and report of being *an honest man*. If it should be assailed by slander, he should do everything he can to restore its luster. But if, after every effort, an unfavorable opinion prevails with the public, a good man may be satisfied with the consciousness of his own innocence, whose witness is God. A wise man should not seek an intensive reputation, which is founded in special honors and marks of honor, except so far as it arises from a distinguished ancestry or opens a wider field to illustrious action by which he will deserve well of the human race. When honor is won, he should not boast of it arrogantly, much less should he canvass for undeserved honors; least of all should he intrigue for them by evil and shameful practices. And if we should not win honors equal to our merits, our spirit should not be cast down, nor the zeal for doing well abandoned.

6. In addition various *external objects* are necessary to the support of life; and duty sometimes also obliges us to provide them for others. And so we are right to strive to obtain them, so far as strength, opportunity, and honesty permit. But here every man must remember that a finite, even a small store of these things is enough for his own use and his family's, so that he should learn not to give too much scope to his desires and ambitions. What we have acquired should be considered as supports for our needs and material for doing good to others, not as things we may pile up without end to gratify our imagination. One must also remember that nature does not cease to be fertile in things which are useful to men. Likewise, what we lay away against the future is liable to all kinds of accidents, so that a restless anxiety often tortures men as much in the protection of their goods as in their acquisition. And everything must be abandoned when we die. So just as one should not neglect an opportunity of justly acquiring external things, so too one ought not to lose heart if they are stolen or lost. And just as they should be expended readily, if duty requires, so they are not to be wasted beyond necessity; for it would be equally stupid to withhold them from a use for which they were intended, as prodigally to consume them in unsuitable and superfluous ways.

4. For Pufendorf's account of "simple reputation," see *On the Duty of Man and Citizen,* II.14; see also below, ch. 21 (iii), p. 194.

7. Next we turn to the *pleasures* of the senses which also entice men's appetites, and the *pains* appended to them. So far as possible we should avoid unnecessary pains, since they harm the body's health, at least in some part, and by engrossing the mind's capacity, make it less capable of performing its functions. We should welcome objects that please the senses, at least to some degree; for when these are used with moderation, they conduce both to health of body and to the mind's ability to perform its functions. Exquisite sensual pleasures, however, should not be cultivated, since they weaken the strength of the body and stifle the vigor of the mind, and commonly make it useless for doing any serious business at all, as well as using up time meant for better purposes, and wasting the stock of external goods which are necessary for living life comfortably; and in other ways are often associated with sin. Therefore just as it would be close to insane to give oneself unnecessary pains, so it is the part of a wise man rather to sip modestly at the pleasures of the senses than to drink deeply of them. Above all one must beware of allowing oneself to fall into a violation of duty for the sake of pleasure.

8. We have pointed out above that it belongs to the cultivation of the mind, to *accustom ourselves to be restrained in our passions.* For if they shake off the rein of reason, and become excessive, they waste the vigor of both mind and body, blunt the edge of the judgment, and drive one headlong into innumerable deviations from duty. Here it would be useful to offer a more detailed discussion.

9. It is widely known that *love* and *hatred* are the springs of all the *passions;* hence the moderation of all the passions depends on governing them rightly. The rightness of love and hatred may be said to consist in two points: (1) their direction to appropriate objects; (2) the appropriateness of their intensity to the value and importance of their objects. But since love and hatred, in a certain special way, are directed toward persons, it is important to know that in the love of persons, an apt distinction is commonly made between the love which consists in *benevolence,* by which we intend the welfare of others, and the love of *sexual attraction,* by which we seek to enjoy the company of others in whatever way we can. In the former kind of love, indeed we do not so easily stray beyond the olive trees, provided we submit the interests of others, equally as our own, to the dispen-

sation of divine providence, and do not wish upon them false and imaginary rather than true goods. But one must be careful to direct the love of sexual attraction to a worthy object, so that it does not develop into "chambering and wantonness," nor interfere with other duties or degenerate into disease. And finally if we aspire to the enjoyment of an object which we cannot get or keep, we must be careful that our love is not so intense that if the object is withdrawn or lost, the mind will completely collapse.

Similarly hatred of persons is either the hatred of *malevolence* or the hatred of *aversion.* Hatred of the former kind is always bad; and one must strive against it with all one's strength as a most destructive mental disease. But the hatred of aversion, by which we avoid the company or even the mention of a person, is also quite a disturbing emotion to anyone who suffers from it. We should therefore get control of it, and not direct it toward someone who does not deserve to be avoided, and not let it lead us to hurt anyone contrary to duty. We should also free ourselves from it by simple neglect, by avoiding the mention or company of any person whom we properly avoid rather than by frequent repeating of any act of hatred. However much a person may deserve to be hated we should not draw the poison into ourselves in this way.

10. From what has been said it is readily apparent what the moderation of the individual passions consists in. In the first place, *desire,* which is nothing other than love or hatred exercising itself with respect to future time, is kept within just limits, if the simple love or hatred, from which it is born, keeps proportion with the dignity of the object. When desire settles on an object which can be stolen or lost from without, it is essential to the tranquillity of life not to allow the mind to be too fixed in the contemplation of that object; nor to permit it to turn into a sickness by repeating too anxiously the act of desire; for if we should be deprived of the desired object, it will end eventually in the worst of all the passions. I mean *sadness,* which, as an enemy to our nature, we can scarcely too much resist; except so far as piety demands that we grieve for sins committed by us or by others, and humanity that we grieve for calamities befalling other men. Most to be detested is the sadness brought on by inappropriate causes, as, for example, by the prosperity of others; whence arises the sadness called

envy, which often produces pernicious effects both in others and in the envious man himself; for the envious man is corroded by his own character as iron is by rust.

Related to sadness is *fear,* a passion as painful as it is pernicious and destructive of the mind's capacity to act; and therefore only to be indulged so far as it prompts us to take timely measures to ward off imminent danger, so far as we can; anything beyond such precaution is useless and harmful. *Anger* too belongs among the gloomy passions: it is a violent passion, the Stoics called it a *short insanity.*[5] We do not go so far as to condemn it altogether, but we think it is plainly wasted labor to celebrate its usefulness, as some have done; how many people need a spur here rather than a rein? Certainly, it is very difficult to keep anger within just bounds, and an excess of it must be regarded as one of the things which most of all makes human life unsocial, and has pernicious effects for the human race. Thus we can scarcely be too diligent in restraining our anger. But we must take especial care not to do anything in a state of blazing wrath which will bring a long train of consequences after it; if we cannot wholly rid ourselves of the sickness of anger, which in itself is sufficiently serious, at least we need not bring on ourselves or others its pernicious consequences.

11. The leader of the chorus of the kinder emotions is *cheerfulness,* a friendly passion indeed to human nature. But it must be under control, so that it does not show itself at the wrong times, or for unsuitable reasons (especially for the misfortunes of others) nor degenerate into frivolity nor destroy our sense of the evils to which we are still subject or liable; and that it does not exclude thoughtful care for the future. Related to *cheerfulness* is *hope,* which, however agreeable, must be held in check so that the mind does not suffer by it. For in busily embracing objects which are vain, uncertain, or beyond our powers, we may wear ourselves out for nothing; and hope, prolonged to infinity, may impede our capacity to enjoy the good things we already have.

12. To counter all the immoderate assaults of the passions, we must make careful and intelligent inquiry about the things which come before us with a particular significance for ourselves (for these are the only things

5. Horace, *Epistles,* I.2.62.

that have the power to excite the passions in us). We should refrain a while
from passing judgment on them, if the case allows, until the hot assault of
passion cools down at least to the point where it does not refuse to admit
the governance of sound reason. To this end, our thoughts should be di-
verted elsewhere for a while, until time and quiet shall have soothed to
some extent the commotion of the blood and the animal spirits. But if the
passion presses, and the nature of the situation before us does not admit
delay in action, contrary considerations should be suggested to the mind,
so that the impulse of passion may drive us from the straight path as little
as possible. Even if they are of too little significance to determine the
mind's direction altogether, they will be able to blunt the former impulse,
and set the mind as it were in equilibrium, and so make it more fit to perceive the real dictates of sound reason. If by these and other means (on
which there is no time to dwell) our passions are reduced to a reasonable
temperature and subjected to the power of reason, it cannot be denied that
they acquire an admirable utility, as they alert both mind and body to
speedily obey and expeditiously perform what reason prescribes.

13. But all this and everything else that aims at the moral cultivation of
the mind, has the particular purpose of filling the mind with love of the
right and with the proper disposition to perform every duty. This cannot
be achieved in this depraved state of the human race without the special
assistance of the Deity, and all genuine dispositions of this kind assume a
sound and rightly founded conviction of the sure means of obtaining the
favor of God and the supreme happiness which lies in him. And this conviction, in corrupt men, can only rest on a really firm foundation through
a special revelation of the divine will. It is therefore evident that each man
is bound by the prescription of natural law to seek that revelation at all
costs, and to fashion his conduct by it when found; and thus natural religion itself in a certain way leads to revealed religion.

14. A final point: since with regard to his own cultivation every man also
has the duty *to make a timely choice of some manner of life which is honorable, advantageous, and suited to his capacity and fortune,* he is also bound
to apply his mind at an early age to learning what will be useful in the kind
of life he intends. Those whom a kinder fortune allows to live their lives
without earning their income by their own labors, may not regard them-

selves as completely exempted from this obligation. For although they do not seem to be obliged by law to practice a skill for the sake of an income, they are nevertheless not only obliged to take good care of their property and to administer it prudently (and this cannot be done without some education), but they must also apply themselves to promote in some way the advantages and benefits of human society, and especially of the country to which they belong and of the men with whom they have to do. It would be exceedingly unworthy in men of great fortune, who claim higher reputation and greater authority than others, to offer no benefits to the human race, to be useless burdens on the earth, drones born to feed off the fruits of other men's labors. To the contrary, the more they expect to be held in esteem above others, the more they should be anxious to deserve that special honor by conferring exceptional benefits on their dependents, their country, and the human race; otherwise their claim to honor for themselves on the ground of birth or fortune would be empty indeed. Since therefore their own happy position gives men of superior fortune, more leisure and the other prerequisites of study than other men have, and also offers them an opportunity to perform duties of greater importance to their country (duties which cannot be properly discharged without a variety of knowledge), it cannot be doubted (provided nature has not denied them the intelligence which few will admit to not having) that such men should aspire to achieve a wide range of knowledge. See Locke, *Essay*, IV.XX.6.

The right of self-defense

[Pufendorf says: "Despite the dictum that one is not justified in resorting to killing when the danger can be averted in a milder manner, it is not usual to be scrupulous about details because of the mental turmoil caused by imminent danger." Carmichael comments:]

The distinguished Titius rightly observes that the doctrine of this paragraph should apparently refer especially to the civil state, which the author had been discussing in the previous paragraph.[6] But several provisos

6. Titius, *Observationes*, no. 134.

which are introduced here for restricting the license of violent defense, may well be applied to both states, provided they are properly explained. For not even in the natural state is it *right* (at least by the law of charity) to rush precipitately into killing when the danger, both present and future, may be deflected by a more appropriate means. Hence in that state too it is rash to descend from a safe place to meet a challenger, when the provocation comes from a sudden attack which will perhaps soon disappear, or when there is hope that the aggression of the attacker will be checked later with less danger to ourselves or others.

Finally, the hatefulness of duels asserted by the author at the end of this paragraph is largely valid in both states, both against the challenger and against a man who has been challenged and voluntarily stands firm and *obstinately remains in the same mind.* Even in the natural state a declared contest is not a completely acceptable mode of asserting one's right and may only be excused by necessity (see Grotius, *Rights of War and Peace,* III.XX.43). And likewise so-called injuries, in the proper meaning of that word (*injuriae*), i.e., the insults which normally involve fellow citizens in duels with each other (for duels which are entered upon to settle a doubtful question, or claim an object which is not due by perfect right, are manifestly unjust); insults, I say, do not afford a just cause for extreme violence even in natural liberty. For it is utterly abhorrent to equity, to humanity, and to justice itself to attempt to repel or vindicate them in that manner. That is, the restoration of an injured reputation, which they usually say is the point of this ferocious avenging of injuries, is a pure and unadulterated fantasy in the minds of men of outrageous vanity. Such men need to learn that true reputation (which is nothing but the opinion of one's excellence on the part of other men, particularly of good and sensible men) can be neither got nor kept except by doing good and deserving well of human society; and that it cannot be weakened by insults, except so far as they raise a suspicion that one deserved to be so badly treated; hence reputation can only be restored and renewed by measures which altogether remove that suspicion. No one but a madman could convince himself that violence leveled by private assault against the author of the insult would contribute to this one little bit. By this sacrilegious attack therefore, they deliberately profane two most sacred words: they are not ashamed to proclaim their wicked customs as *laws of honor*. But these customs are diametrically opposed to divine and human laws, and have been transmitted to us from barbarian peoples and centuries, to the great dishonor of human nature, to say nothing of the Christian name. [I.5.13.i]

Apart from what the author mentions, the victim can require nothing else by his own right from the attacker. But it is a good question whether, even in the state of natural liberty and equality, physical punishment cannot be inflicted on those who have openly violated the law of nature, in the name of the human race, so to speak, as a measure pertaining to its common security. With Grotius (*Rights of War and Peace*, II.XX.40 ff.) and Locke (*Second Treatise of Government*, ch. 2), we think this question should be answered emphatically in the positive, at least in the case of the more atrocious crimes, which have been committed with malice. However great moderation should be shown here. For punishment should not be inflicted suddenly or secretly, in case greater disturbances arise in a society and make the remedy more disastrous than the disease. In particular one must be careful to prevent the injured man himself, still seething with anger, from trying to keep on punishing and using force to assert his right.

Here the author ends his discussion of defense against unjust aggression, but prematurely; he should first have made a clear statement on the nature of human *rights* and on the foundations on which they rest before discussing the license permitted in their defense. This is the point that Titius (*Observationes*, no. 119) seems to suggest in his own way, when he points out that the precepts of self-love and sociability should be treated separately before they can be compared with each other. Thus one should add the teaching about the prosecution of one's right to the teaching on the defense of one's right. Pufendorf could not have referred less appropriately to this passage. For (as we said above at p. 45) we not only have a right to do something or hold it simply, but often also have a right to require something of another person. As the former right is properly asserted in resisting someone who unjustly attacks us or our property, so the latter right is no less properly asserted, in the natural state, by forcibly seizing what is ours or due to us from someone who is refusing to offer it of his own accord. Therefore in the former case a violent *defense* of one's own right, in the latter case a violent prosecution of it (always assuming appropriate circumstances), is a duty which a man owes to himself. We should add a few points about this.

It is clear in the first place that as a violent defense of right in the civil state is restricted to rather narrow limits, so a violent prosecution of it is utterly forbidden to individual citizens, as plainly repugnant to nature and the end of civil society. It is appropriate on a regular basis only in the natural state in which, when just cause requires, it is to be exercised with the same force against persons, as far as they oppose the satisfaction of our right, as Pufendorf rightly teaches that the natural state permits in its defense. Moreover, since in this case, something of ours or something which is owed to us and not freely tendered, is presumed to give grounds for war, we not only rightly take possession of our own property, if it can be done, but also appropriate something that belongs to another person; if a particular object is owed to us, we seize that; if the debt is nonspecific, we seize as much as is owed. For want of these things, we can appropriate any property belonging to the enemy in compensation for the debt. Further, since neither defensive nor offensive war can be waged without expense and multiple loss, we rightly demand from an unjust enemy restitution for this, and rightly claim in compensation for them whatever is taken from him. However, all these things ought to be understood as due *without detriment to the right of the innocent.* Beyond these limits (although it cannot be denied that infinite license is permitted against an enemy who perseveres in wrongdoing, of devastating his property, and of taking it away, especially if it may be useful in war), we have no right to acquire anything, however just our cause in fighting, and to retain the advantage we derive from it, after the enemy has agreed to peace terms (and we may understand from this the nature of the peace terms). See Locke, *Second Treatise of Government,* chapter 16. However we may retain some of the property of an enemy in our custody, as a means to guarantee against the launching of similar attacks in the future, but it must be in such a way that the fruits and profits of the property, beyond what is spent on its custody, are preserved for the owner, as long as he keeps the peace. From the point of view of bare natural right, the situation is the same, whether it is two men living in natural liberty who are in conflict with each other or two states.[7] [I.5.17.i]

The rights of extreme necessity

[Pufendorf has explained that "the case of necessity is not included in the general scope of the law." Carmichael comments:]

But the two general laws of *worshipping God* and of *promoting the interests of the human race* admit of no exception; they are themselves the foundation of such exception as is to be admitted in the more particular laws. This is not to be taken to mean that there is no necessity which might rightly draw us away from any particular act of divine worship, especially external worship, which otherwise would have to be performed, but that one may not in any case undertake an act which is contrary to worship, an act, that is, which would betray contempt or hatred of God. Such acts are *denial of God, blasphemy, idolatrous worship,* and (here the distinguished Titius vainly and wrongly resists) *the giving of a promissory oath without the intention to put oneself under an obligation.*[8] I add that the positive obligation of the precept about worshiping God is so far universal that man may not in any case completely abandon direct worship of God, or suspend it for so long that he ceases to have Him habitually before his eyes, or even intermit a particular act of external worship when the intermission would be taken as a denial of God (cf. *Daniel* 6.10). It is quite evident that neither the precept on *promoting the common interests of the human race* nor the two directly subordinate to it on *every man's seeking his own innocent advantage* and on *furthering sociability,* as we have explained them above,[9] can admit any exception of *necessity.* Hence we reject the conflict between

---

7. Carmichael considered his reasons for the right of self-defense important enough to be regarded as a supplement. See below, appendix, sec. 20, p. 215. While his argument (against Pufendorf) was indebted to Locke's *Second Treatise of Government,* his primary concern was not, as with Locke, defense of property. Carmichael's emphasis was defense of the liberty of individuals and of societies. See below, p. 142 and n. 6, and p. 179, nn. 6, 7.

8. Titius, *Observationes,* no. 141.

9. See Supplement II.5–8, pp. 48–49.

self-love and sociability which Titius so frequently teaches.[10] For all the cases in which that distinguished man finds this conflict are to be explained merely on the basis of the law of sociability. For according to the variety of circumstances, this law assigns more to an individual's own benefit in one case, more to that of others in another, and thus determines which particular precepts admit the exception of necessity, and in what cases. [I.5.18.i]

One should say rather with Grotius (who treats this whole matter at II.II.6–10) that an extreme necessity which can be met in no other way, makes a perfect right; i.e., in this case it revives, for this purpose, the right of primitive community. However this is not in virtue of an agreement (as Grotius teaches, in conformity with his false hypothesis about the origin of ownership, on which see below),[11] but because of the very nature of the case and the manifest interest of human society. The arguments brought against this by our author at *Of the Law of Nature and Nations*, II.VI.6, are excessively weak.[12] [I.5.23.iii]

10. On the conflict between self-love and sociability in the natural law theory of Titius, see above, p. xiv.

11. See below, pp. 92–96; see also p. 97.

12. Pufendorf distinguished, as Carmichael did not, between relief of necessity as a duty of humanity and relief of necessity as an obligation under the law of nature. In *On the Duty of Man and Citizen*, p. 55, Pufendorf declared that "a rich man ought to help someone in . . . necessity as a duty of humanity." In *Of the Law of Nature and Nations*, II.VI.8, he described admission of a necessitous man to one's estate or house as conduct which is "not such as can be fairly defended on the Grounds of Natural Law" (p. 210). Carmichael's treatment of duties of humanity as rights and obligations under the law of nature (in the case of extreme necessity as perfect rights) was a frequent point of contention between Barbeyrac (who agreed with Pufendorf) and himself. See below, p. 179, n. 6.

CHAPTER 8

On Duty to Others, or Sociability[1]

On not harming others

[In expounding our duty not to harm others, Pufendorf raised the question of exercising due care and diligence in our activities, the obligation to make restitution, and the exemption from the duty not to harm others in various particular activities such as fighting. Carmichael briefly summarizes and comments on these points.]

We are always bound to employ the most *scrupulous* diligence that the nature of the business admits, to avoid causing harm or loss to others. The different degrees of diligence which are required in different contracts concern the custody or care due to someone else's property by virtue of these contracts. Their effect is not only that the object not be harmed by us, but that it not be harmed in any way so far as we can prevent it by use of the requisite diligence. Moreover, using the most scrupulous diligence *that the nature of the business allows* in order not to do harm to another does not always exempt us from the obligation of making good his loss. For sociability forbids us ever to undertake any business which threatens loss to another, unless we are prompted by a serious necessity, and even then we are obligated to compensate for the loss which may occur by that means, unless the necessity is communal, as may easily be understood from what the author himself has taught at the end of the previous paragraph. The reason

1. From the notes to bk. I, ch. 6, "On the Duty of Every Man to Every Man, and First of Not Harming Others"; ch. 7, "On Acknowledging the Natural Equality of Men"; and ch. 8, "On the Common Duties of Humanity."

therefore why a soldier is not liable, when brandishing his weapons in the heat of battle, for the harm which he does to the person who happens to be standing next to him, is not only that the nature of the business does not allow him to be more careful, but that both common and individual necessity require that it be done. We allow that the obligation for making good a loss inflicted by necessity does not arise from delict, which is assumed not to be present, but from quasi contract; or if not from quasi contract, as is sometimes the case, then from a true contract, for example by the inclusion of an express provision on the subject. [I.6.9.i]

Natural equality

The natural equality of men includes: (1) that each man is equally a man, and consequently is subject to a moral obligation from which no human being can exempt him; and has certain rights belonging to him, which are valid against all men; (2) that with whatever gifts of mind or body a man may by nature be endowed above other men, he may not for that reason claim by his own right any power over others or a greater share of things available in common, since nature permits the acquisition both of ownership and of power to all by the same means and on the same conditions.

It is not worth discussing whether what Aristotle so labors to teach in the first book of the *Politics*[2] on the nature of master and slave, is altogether in agreement with this natural liberty. The philosopher's teaching is thoroughly ambiguous on the subject, and has given rise to the just suspicion that he was flattering the vanity of his fellow countrymen, who imagined that nature had given them the right to rule barbarians. And this suspicion has not been completely dispelled by the celebrated Daniel Heinsius in a prolix dissertation (Rutgers's *Various Readings*, IV.3),[3] in that he seems, by the opinion he holds, following Aristotle, to attribute no other natural liberty to men as a whole than what belongs to birds and fish which have not yet been captured by anyone; as if men's natural liberty did not

2. Aristotle, *Politics* I.3–7. Carmichael's major discussion (and denunciation) of slavery is in chapter 16, "On Masters and Servants."

3. Rutgersius, *Variarum Lectionum Libri*. Daniel Heinsius, a Dutch classical scholar, published an edition of Aristotle's *Politics* in 1618.

include the right (which does not exist among birds and fish) not to be hauled away into slavery without a prior act on their own part. [I.7.2.i]

[Pufendorf derives from equality the rule "that no one require for himself more than he allows others, unless he has acquired some special right to do so, but allow others to enjoy their right equally with him." Carmichael comments:]

This comes to the same thing as that golden and universal rule taught by our Lord, *as ye would that men should do to you, do ye also to them likewise.*[4] But this rule must be understood as tacitly limited by a twofold assumption of *similar circumstances on both sides* and a *right will conforming to reason.* It ought therefore not to be regarded as a principle from which, when applied to the individual actions of life, a sure distinction between right and wrong is to be deduced. Rather it should be regarded as an indication of an appropriate remedy to free the mind from the command of self-love and the assaults of the passions, to set it in equilibrium, and as it were, restore it to itself, so that it may be free to attend to the careful weighing of the importance of the arguments on either side. [I.7.3.i]

Harmless pursuit of self-interest and the rights of humanity

Grotius discusses the benefits of pursuing one's own interests without harming others at *Rights of War and Peace,* II.II.11 ff., where he teaches that such things may be demanded as due by perfect right, and gives several instances of this category. But see the examination and some corrections of these by our author at *Of the Law of Nature and Nations,* III.III.[5] In general I would think that the claim of *harmless self-interest* should not be boldly advanced as a foundation of a perfect right unless there is also a

---

4. Matthew 7.12, Luke 6.31.

5. Rights of humanity, whether derived from necessity or from harmless utility, were considered perfect rights (by Carmichael, as well as by Grotius and Pufendorf) only in the state of nature; in civil society, these rights are considered imperfect rights, incapable of enforcement by governments. See below, ch. 9, p. 82. Francis Hutcheson attached particular importance to these rights: see *A Short Introduction to Moral Philosophy,* II.IV.5, pp. 144–45, and *A System of Moral Philosophy,* II.XVI.8, pp. 111–12.

claim of *necessity*. The latter is often sufficient in itself and is considerably strengthened by the former. [I.8.4.ii]

This is where we should speak of the humanity which shipwrecked men receive from all who have not divested themselves of their human nature. The reason why inhuman cruelty has sometimes taken its place is the irrational custom, which has gained the force of law among various peoples, of *surrendering to the public treasury the goods of shipwrecks, so long as no living person has made it to shore from the ship*. The absence of this limitation would have contributed to the saving of many lives.[6] But it would be far better to revive among all Christians the constitution of Constantine, which survives at *Codex*, XI.5; a rescript of Antoninus had anticipated the example of its equity, as we are told at *Digest*, XLVII.9, at the last line.[7] [I.8.4.iii]

Beneficence and friendship

See the more extensive treatment of these subjects in Cicero, *On Duties*, I.xiv–xviii,[8] in which he treats beneficence at length. It is our author's source for the best part of this and the preceding section. This is also where the rights of friendship belong. See the lucid exposition of these rights which Cicero puts into the mouth of Laelius in the book of that name. But the great man seems to allow too much to friendship, when he allows in chapter xvii that *if by chance it should happen that we have to lend support to a friend's less than honest designs, we should diverge from the straight path so long as we do not incur too deep a disgrace*.[9] Aristotle too discusses friendship at length in the *Nicomachean Ethics*, books VIII and IX. [I.8.5.i]

6. This refers to "wrecking," the practice of luring ships onto a rocky coast and plundering them, after first killing any survivors in order to satisfy the legal requirement that the ships' goods might only be taken if there were no survivors.

7. This must be a reference to Justinian, *Codex*, XI.6, "De naufragiis" (rather than XI.5). It is a law of the emperor Constantine forbidding the practice of "wrecking." Justinian, *Digest* XLVII.9.10, records a pronouncement of the emperor Antoninus to similar effect.

8. Cicero, *De Officiis* [On Duties], I.[xiv–xviii].42–60.

9. Cicero, *Laelius de Amicitia* [Laelius: On friendship], [xvii].61. Carmichael omits a qualifying clause which Cicero has after "designs": "in which his life or his reputation is at stake."

Natural Rights and Agreements[1]

[Pufendorf distinguished between absolute duties which every man owes to every man (not to harm others, to recognize others as equals, and to be useful to others, so far as it is convenient) and hypothetical duties, which presuppose particular conditions or arrangements. Carmichael comments:]

Our author's method relies heavily on the distinction [between "absolute" and "hypothetical" duties]. But he does not explain it with sufficient clarity nor apply it at all skillfully. And since there is the same variety of obligations or duties as of rights to which they correspond, in place of this distinction one may substitute the analysis which we give in the next note [I.9.1.i] and again in the appendix annexed to this treatise.[2] [I.6.1.i]

Kinds and creation of rights

To achieve a clearer conception of the nature of agreements, we must argue some central points on a broader basis. In the first place we must recognize that perfect rights which belong or may belong to individual men, are either *natural* or *adventitious,* depending on the foundations on which they rest. Nature herself has endowed each man with natural rights; adventitious rights arise from some human action or other event. Among natural rights are the right of *life,* the right of *physical integrity,* the right of

---

1. From the notes to bk. I, ch. 9, "On the Duty of Parties to Agreements in General"; bk. I, ch. 10, "On the Duty of Men in the Use of Language"; and bk. I, ch. 11, "On the Duties Involved in Taking an Oath."
2. See ch. 23, below.

chastity, and the right of *simple reputation;* I mean the right to have all these things. I add the *liberty,* or power, of ordering one's actions as one pleases within the broad limits of the common divine laws, as well as the closely related *ability to use in common* things which are by nature positively *common,* as also of acquiring any other *adventitious rights* by appropriate means. All of these are sanctioned by the general precept of natural law, by which every man is *forbidden from violating any of these rights in another,* that is, of attacking without a special foundation of right any of the good things given above which belong to someone else.

Adventitious rights are either *real* or *personal.* Real rights are concerned with having, possessing, using, etc., some thing (*rem*); personal rights, with obtaining some thing or service from another person. To real rights, equally as to natural rights, there corresponds from the other side an *unlimited* obligation not to disturb the owners of these rights in the exercise of them. And ᴗ personal rights there correspond *limited* obligations to render to individuals those things or services which they have a right to require of us.

Both real and personal rights are created, transferred, and abolished in various ways. Among the many ways by which personal rights are created or abolished, and by which rights of both kinds are transferred from one man to another, one stands out as particularly prominent. This is *mutual consent on the part of the person by whom a right is transferred and on the part of the person by whom it is acquired, both being signified by appropriate signs.* I say *is transferred,* because the actual creation and abolition of a personal right lies in a kind of *transfer.*

For a perfect personal right (which is the only thing that we are speaking of here)[3] is simply a certain particle of a man's natural liberty which is transferred to another man by some act or event, and takes on the character in this man of a *personal right* valid against the other, by force of which he may require him to do or not to do anything which, in his judgment, it is in his power to do or not to do. That same right, when it returns

---

3. It will be argued in the following chapter that *real* rights (rights to property) are perfect rights which are *not* created by agreement or individual consent: see below, ch. 10, pp. 92–96.

to its natural subject and is consolidated with the rest of his natural right, loses its character as a *personal right* and recovers the name of *natural liberty.* Thus personal rights are said to be *created* by those actions by which men begin to be obligated in a particular way by the transfer of some particle of their natural liberty to others; and are equally correctly said to be *abolished* by the opposite actions, by which men cease to be obligated in that way, when the particle of liberty which they had alienated is restored to them.

We therefore had good reason to say that the creation and abolition of personal rights *as such,* no less than their transmission in the same kind (as also in the case of real rights), lies in a form of *transfer.* And, apart from some modes of transfer which are irrelevant to the present subject, every transfer is very naturally initiated, as we have said, by *mutual consent,* by a declaration of appropriate signs on the part of the transferor and of the recipient of the right.

This *mutual act* seems to take *four* different forms, depending on the type of right which is being transferred or its circumstances. In the case of *real* rights, it is always one and the same, carrying in itself from one subject to another the mere transmission of the rights which relate to its immediate object on both sides (see however what we say below at pp. 101–2).[4] In the case of *personal* rights, it may produce three possible effects: (1) a right which was previously contained in the natural liberty of the *transferor* has been transferred to another man and now belongs to him as a personal right against the first party; in this case a new personal right and corresponding obligation are *created* for the first time. Or, (2) a personal right which previously belonged to the transferor against a third party has been transferred to someone else and now belongs to him against the same third party; here we see the *transfer* of a personal right of that particular kind. Or, (3) a personal right which previously belonged to the transferor against the recipient is transferred, or rather restored, to him and consolidated with his natural liberty; and in this case the personal right, as such, and the corresponding obligation are *extinguished.*

Each of these acts can be performed either *unilaterally,* with the effect

4. In his discussion of "rights over the property of another."

that a right is transferred from one party and merely acquired by the other, or *reciprocally,* with the effect that a right is transferred by both parties and received by both of them against each other, and the transfer would not be understood to be fully and validly effected without the other. Thus from these various combinations of acts of the same or of different kinds, arise several kinds of reciprocal acts; some of these have specific names given them in law and popular usage, while others have not.

As for the term *pactum,* or "agreement," this stands for a variety of ideas which do not all have the same extension. The definition of *pactum* given by Ulpian, *Digest,* II.14.1.2[5] is *the concurrence of two or more persons in the same intent;* Ulpian also appends to the same law (sec. 3) that the explanation of the term *conventio* is that men *from different motions of the mind consent to one thing,* i.e., *arrive at one opinion.* If we look at the proper meanings of the words, both these definitions seem to apply to all the types of mutual acts we have just enumerated. But we admit that the commonest usage is to apply the term *pactum,* or "agreement," almost exclusively to acts which are obligatory on at least one side, i.e., acts by which a new personal right is given, as we explained above; and that is how our author seems to understand it.

Titius defines *pactum,* or "agreement," as something done by the *consent of two or more, given for the purpose of licitly creating or abolishing an obligation;* and therefore includes under the term "agreement" not only acts consisting in the mutual consent by which personal rights are created, but also those by which they are abolished.[6] But I do not think that we apply the word "agreements" to acts by which personal rights and corresponding obligations are abolished, more than to acts by which rights, whether real or personal, are transmitted from one person to another. It is irrelevant to our purpose as being a matter merely of arbitrary law, that the Roman jurisconsults and their interpreters used this term almost exclusively of acts which create by themselves only a natural and not also a civil obligation unless confirmed by a civil law, and on this ground distinguished them from contracts. [I.9.1.i]

5. Justinian, *Digest,* II.14.1.2 (an opinion of the jurist Ulpian).
6. Titius, *Observationes,* no. 198.

Promises and agreements; two senses of agreement

We have just said that in his first paragraph[7] our author understands by the term *pactum,* or "agreement," an act consisting in mutual consent which is obligatory on at least one side. Now in this paragraph[8] he restricts the word to one species within that genus, namely, that which is obligatory on both sides. However it should be noted, that if by the division here proposed a distinction is made in the case of *an act obligatory by mutual consent,* between one which creates obligation *on one side only* and one which creates obligation on both sides, the former is not well named a *gratuitous promise.* For there are acts which are obligatory on one party only, and which nevertheless, can by no means be called *gratuitous promises,* since they include from the other party, either some transmission of right, as in *loan for consumption (mutuum)* (where the term implies that the receiving party in this transaction is obligating himself to the giver, because the latter is at the same time transferring to him the ownership of the money given by *mutuum*), or the cession or remission of a right which was previously valid against the party creating the obligation, as is often the case in transactions.[9] However if you are willing to understand by the term *pactum,* or "agreement," in its narrower sense, a mutual act by which an obligation is contracted by at least one party (or, which is the same thing, by which a man transfers a personal right to be valid against himself), and in return a right of some kind is transferred by the other party, then *pactum,* or "agreement," in its broader sense is rightly divided into *gratuitous promise* and *pactum in the special sense.* [I.9.5.i]

---

7. Pufendorf, *On the Duty of Man and Citizen,* I.9.1, p. 68.
8. Ibid., I.9.5, p. 69.
9. Barbeyrac objected that in such transactions there is a mixture of gratuitous promise and agreement, and so the term free or gratuitous promise should be retained: Pufendorf, *Of the Law of Nature and Nations,* III.V.i, n. 1, p. 267. His difference with Carmichael on the subject is linked to their disagreement concerning the relevance of the moral content of promises and agreements. Carmichael thought that agreements, including "gratuitous promises," continue to oblige if the content of such agreements was morally desirable (consistent with the laws of nature). Barbeyrac considered the content of agreements of no relevance to jurists, natural or civil.

[Grotius distinguished agreements based upon mere declarations of intent and the necessity of keeping faith from perfect agreements, where there is a clear sign that a right is to be conferred (Grotius, *Rights of War and Peace,* II.XI, p. 281 ff). Pufendorf applied this distinction specifically to promising (Pufendorf, *Of the Law of Nature and Nations,* III.V.6, p. 269; Pufendorf, *On the Duty of Man and Citizen,* I.9.6, pp. 69–70). Carmichael comments:]

The authors apply this distinction of *perfect* and *imperfect* to *promises* rather than to agreements in general, perhaps because every reciprocal agreement is perfect in the state of nature. I say, in *the state of nature;* for in civil society, only those agreements and promises which may be enforced in the courts by an action taken under civil law are considered perfect. And just as a perfect promise confers a perfect right, I do not see why an imperfect right should not follow from an imperfect obligation. [I.9.6.i and ii]

"Error" in promises and agreements

[In Roman law promises and agreements are frustrated by various forms of error, fraud, or force which occur in the making of them. In all these categories Carmichael allows fewer circumstances to void an agreement than Pufendorf.

Pufendorf's first category is: "When in promising I have assumed something as a condition, without regard to which I would not have made the promise, there will naturally be no force in the promising." Carmichael comments as follows:]

This is to be allowed only in the following sense: If I have either expressly declared this assumption on my part as a condition of the promise, or if I thought in good faith that it was understood by the promisee from the nature of the transaction. For my own silent thoughts which I cannot reasonably believe will be understood by the party I am addressing, do not alter the sense of what I say, nor consequently its moral effect. [I.9.12.i]

[Secondly, Pufendorf says: "If I have been impelled by error to make an agreement or a contract and I discover it when the matter is whole and nothing has yet been performed, it would be perfectly fair that the privilege of changing my mind be allowed to me." Carmichael comments:]

Yet this privilege cannot be claimed by perfect right, unless the error concerns something which the person who was in error at least thought was assumed as a condition on both sides. And in reciprocal agreements, an event which is not explicitly put as a condition is not easily understood to be such, unless it is either affirmed in the article itself actually to exist by the other party to the transaction, or it is such that without the condition which it is agreed the promisor cannot perform, it would be manifestly impossible or absurd to fulfill the promise, or finally unless it concerns the actual object or matter which is the subject of the agreement, its valuable qualities or lack of them.

But if he who has made an error in an agreement says that he tacitly assumed that the event about which he was mistaken was understood on both sides to be a condition of the agreement, despite the fact that the other party did not and reasonably could not understand that the agreement was limited by that condition, the claim of error is still not completely excluded even in this case, provided that the claimant proves by proper evidence that he really understood the situation the way he says he did (for even in natural liberty the same judgment holds about what does not appear and what does not exist, as far as the external forum is concerned), and provided that he is prepared to reimburse any loss the other party may have incurred, in accordance with what we shall argue below at pp. 84–85. [I.9.12.ii]

[Pufendorf gives as his third form of "error": "When a mistake has occurred concerning the actual object of the agreement, the agreement is defective, not so much because of the mistake, but because it has failed to satisfy the conditions of an agreement." Carmichael has two notes on this:]

That is, as may be understood from what has been said before, that one of the parties to the agreement not only supposed that the object was of a different kind, or of different valuable qualities, than is in fact the case, but thought in good faith that this supposition of his and the will to make a contract on such an object was understood on both sides. [I.9.12.iii]

The celebrated Titius correctly observes here that the author was not right to make the distinction he does make, since the reason why this kind of agreement does not satisfy the terms of an agreement is that it is not being made about the proposed object as it really is.[10] [I.9.12.iv]

[Carmichael concludes:]

The nature of the object of the agreement and its valuable qualities or lack of them, which may be thought to have had some weight in determining either of the contracting parties to make a contract which he would not otherwise have made, are naturally understood to belong to the essence of the actual contract. Hence an error committed in any of these matters, by natural law, vitiates the contract as long as no performance has been made by either party; if discovered after the contract has been wholly or in part fulfilled, it gives a right to the injured party to withdraw from it, and to require that any performance be restored on both sides. But if the error in question concerns only the external value of the object or other qualities without regard for which the party in error would clearly have made the contract though with different conditions, it is at the discretion of the other party, provided he is clear of fraud, either to release him from the contract or to make up the value to him.

Here we must note that in every case in which a contract is voided for error, if fault on the part of one party to the agreement (whether the party making the claim for error or the other party) has given cause for error concerning either the object itself or the circumstance on which the claim is based or concerning the deception of one party by the other, and if the other party will suffer loss as a result of the voiding of the contract, then the former is obliged to compensate the latter for his loss; he must ensure that he is in no worse situation than if he had not entered into the agreement. And if one of the parties to the agreement recognizes the other's error with regard to the object or its qualities, and fraudulently claims that the other had accepted it, he ought also to pay *what the other lost thereby*, i.e., the benefit which the deceived party would have got if the agreement had been fulfilled, in accordance with his expectation and intention; for this is what he seems to have committed himself to by his consent. These positions are not far from what is laid down in Roman law on these cases,

10. Titius, *Observationes*, no. 220.

provided we remember that the distinction between things which void an action in their own right and those which give rise to a claim or an action by which it may be quashed, are a subtlety of the courts which has no place in the simplicity of natural law. [I.9.12.v]

Force and agreements

[Pufendorf argues that in general agreements made under compulsion are invalid. Once again, as in the case of promises or agreements made in error, Carmichael takes a more restrictive line.]

Our opinion on this much discussed point will be clear from the three following propositions.

1. Agreements extorted by unjustified force give no right to the extortionist which he may legitimately use against anyone; nor by mere natural law do they bind the conscience of those who succeed to the position of the person who was subjected to force, to justify them in refusing performance, or if it has already been made, in demanding compensation for damage inflicted by unjust force. These points we grant to the considerations adduced by the author.

2. Nevertheless, the promisor is bound in conscience, on the ground of truthfulness and good faith, if he has promised anything that may be lawfully offered and therefore lawfully promised, in order to preserve life or avert serious loss (even though the most unjustified force by the other party imposed on him the need to make the promise). For he seems to have promised that he will not make use of the counterclaim of *force and fear,* even though it is quite evident, I suppose, in the very nature of the action.

3. Grotius aptly observes (II.XVII.19) that it seems to have been accepted by the consent of nations that the claim of *force and fear* cannot be brought against agreements extorted by the success of declared wars or by fear of them, whether by the parties to a treaty or by their successors, lest public disputes should never have an end. To declared wars however I think that one should add (for this purpose alone) all other actions done publicly, deliberately, and as it were, in the eyes of the world, and which are ended by agreements which have not been suddenly or secretly ex-

torted. The purpose is that the conditions of peace established by these agreements, whether between princes and subjects or between different factions of citizens after a civil war, should be held sacred and inviolable. If the thing were otherwise, it is not clear that there would be any use in treaties restoring peace, or that old disputes, about which wars had been fought in the past, would not always be open to further conflict. For individuals enter into agreements to end disputes on the basis which the fortune of war has given to their side.[11] [I.9.15.ii]

[Carmichael later adds that, while such a promise is valid in itself, the addition of an oath to it provides a further ground for respecting it.][12]

We said in the previous note that the extortion of a promise by unjustified force does not prevent the promisor from being bound in conscience to perform it, if the thing promised may be legitimately performed. If it were not so, it is not at all clear how in good faith one could buy off with an onerous promise a threat of greater evil leveled unjustly at oneself by another person. What is certain is that it would be horribly impious to try to give such a promise the sanction of an oath, believing that it would still be invalid even with this sanction. Grotius indeed contends that a promise extorted by unjust fear is invalid by itself, but acquires force from the addition of an oath, and adds an inappropriate argument which our author refutes at *Of the Law of Nature and Nations,* IV.II.8. [I.11.6.3]

[Consideration of error, fraud, and force in the formation of agreements leads to a discussion of truthfulness and falsehood in the use of language in general.]

---

11. Carmichael's argument that promises made under duress may oblige in conscience, even though such promises have no power to oblige under natural law, may be compared with the position taken by Hutcheson, who thought that while public peace might require honoring a treaty made under compulsion, forced promises should never oblige private individuals (*Short Introduction,* II.IX.9, pp. 189–91). Adam Smith, on the other hand, distinguished, as Carmichael did, between the requirements of natural jurisprudence and the demands of conscience or casuistry. He held that conscience may require one to keep promises which are forced upon one, even though such promises should be considered void in natural jurisprudence (*Theory of Moral Sentiments,* VII.IV.8–14, pp. 330–33).

12. From bk. I, ch. 11, "On the Duties Involved in Taking an Oath."

Language as signs

To understand this whole matter clearly one must recollect from logic that two kinds of signs need to be distinguished. One kind, by reason of nature or convention, signifies something without any regard to the supposed intention of the sign-user as to what is to be signified. The other kind of sign signifies precisely because it is assumed to be employed by a rational agent of his own accord to signify his thoughts to another person. And this is achieved either by some prior explicit convention about their significance, or (in the absence of an explicit convention about their use) because of some accompanying tacit convention about using the signs employed in the sense which either their nature or accepted usage indicates. This distinction by no means coincides with the commonly accepted distinction between natural and arbitrary signs. For natural and arbitrary signs are found equally in both of the categories we propose. It is however in fact the same as Grotius gives at *Rights of War and Peace,* III.I.8, n. 2, and following him our author at *Of the Law of Nature and Nations,* IV.I.12, and the use of this distinction in this matter is obvious. For the rule [of non-deception] should be understood of signs not of the former kind but of the latter (among which are words and other signs which perform the same function). Truthfulness consists in making these true as falsehood consists in making them false. [I.10.1.i]

Truthfulness

[Pufendorf says that the use of language requires that "users of any given language must employ the same words for the same objects following the usage of that language." Carmichael comments:]

Truthfulness lies in the fulfilment of this obligation and falsehood in its violation, provided that in the phrase *employing words in a certain sense* you also include, *to make true speech according to that sense of the words,* where *true* means conforming to the view of the speaker. In eliminating the obligation contained in this paragraph, the distinguished Titius seems to be making a highly unfortunate attempt to remove all distinction between truth-speaking and falsehood and to expel truthfulness from the catalogue of the virtues. But one may still ask, whence arises this virtue? And if it derives from convention, when and how do men enter into that convention? It would not be absurd to say that this obligation quite evidently arises from the very nature of the thing and from the obvious indispensability of the duty here prescribed for effecting the use of speech, and consequently for cultivating social life among men. I fully agree that a convention is not to be denied in this question: the only difficulty about it is, when and by what means the convention was entered into. For it can scarcely be maintained that the convention is entered into by individuals by some one single act, which establishes the norm for all future acts of speaking by everybody. One must rather say that each man, in addressing another person, particularly when he attempts to narrate something to him, makes a tacit agreement with him to use words in the sense which he thinks will be understood by him with the help of reason. He has to accept that the sense which normally goes with such words in similar cases will be the one understood (if it has not been otherwise defined by any special convention). The same is to be said of any other signs which perform the same function. The only exception is signs which are suited by their nature to signify some particular thing, where no other intervening use or express agreement has determined their signification otherwise; in their case, the sense to be reasonably understood, and for the preservation of which a tacit convention is made, is the sense which the nature of each sign suggests. It is agreed therefore that this obligation of which we are speaking is inviolable, and cannot be destroyed by any case or event, since a man would have to make a new contract every time he opened his mouth to speak. If this obligation were not assumed, the use of speech, particularly descriptive speech, would be eliminated from human life. It would be useless to tell anybody anything, and equally absurd to listen to anyone telling you anything. [I.10.2.i]

The limits of prevarication

[Pufendorf says that "I may shape what I say to express something other than what I have in mind" under certain conditions. Carmichael comments:]

Here the author begins to desert the sound principles which he had established earlier.[13] One must be very careful about exceptions of this kind. For although people do not in general have the right to learn our thoughts on any matter whatever, yet a person does have the right *not to be deceived by speech or by other signs which he may justifiably believe are being used to express those thoughts.* That is, we should not use signs which we judge that the other person will justifiably interpret as intended to signify something to him which is not true, or at least which we do not think to be true. As was said above, we have bound ourselves by a tacit convention to make the signs which we use, on any reasonable interpretation, consonant with our thoughts.[14] [I.10.5.i]

[Pufendorf says: "In these cases, therefore, we may make use of a dissembling and specious language. . . ." Carmichael comments on this principle and some of its applications:]

I am tempted to say that the author uses such language here. In any case if he means speech which by the most reasonable interpretation signifies something different from the sentiment of the speaker, we must apply the well-known and correct rule, *Do not do evil that good may result,* especially since the universal loss which arises from the weakening of good faith among men, that is, from the relaxation of the common bond of human society, cannot be made up for by any private gain. [I.10.6.i]

In educating children one must often use very crude metaphors. But the effect of speaking untruths is nowhere more pernicious than here. The result often is that children not only learn to disbelieve true lessons, but

13. Carmichael is referring here to Pufendorf, *On the Duty of Man and Citizen,* I.10.1–2, pp. 77–78.

14. It is reported by one of Carmichael's students that he was particularly adamant in his insistence that one never deceive others by words or signs; that "he often differs from Puffendorf. Particularly when he makes the end of the Law of Nature to be confined to this Life . . . and where he allows persons to express themselves contrary to what they think, when they may profit themselves and wrong none, to which Mr. C. answers, if we are not obliged to tell the truth, we should hold our peace, or give a generall answer, never forgetting the universall and unexceptionable Law of nature. That none deceive others, either by words or signs, which in Philosophy may be justly taken for expressions of our conceptions" (letter of Jonathan Woodsworth to the Rev. Peter Walkden, 1 July 1715).

also acquire a wicked habit of lying. In this matter, they think themselves justified by the authority and example of their teachers. [I.10.9.i]

Nor should we allow that we may tell lies to an enemy. The author himself acknowledges at *On the Duty of Man and Citizen*, II.16.5, that an enemy is not to be deceived by fraudulent promises or agreements. And we showed above (pp. 87–88) that a sort of tacit convention about using signs properly, appropriate to the occasion and the subject matter, accompanies every use of speech. He therefore who purports to say something to an enemy in all seriousness, while the enemy in his turn listens to him in the belief that he is telling him something in all seriousness, by that very fact contracts as it were the same obligation anew, despite the situation of enmity. It is quite wrong to class false stories with stratagems, since our author himself, following Grotius, specifically recognizes that in the former case a convention takes place, in the latter not. On both, see the references given above on p. 87. [I.10.9.ii]

CHAPTER 10

On the Right of Property[1]

The divine origin of property

Surely there is a purpose in God having given man a life which cannot be preserved without the use of external things, and in his creation of things which cannot be imagined to have any use as worthy of Divine Wisdom as this, and among them things which are suitable for use in themselves but which would soon perish uselessly if not so employed. [I.12.1.i]

Human property rights not shared with animals

Animals are not endowed with reason (see above, p. 47); no sharing of right can exist between animals and men; and God does not command men to hold any society with them. For there are many things which are suited to serve the different purposes of both animals and men, and there are also many ways in which men can receive benefit or suffer harm from animals, and can themselves either save or destroy them; yet nature has not given us a way to become familiar or share thoughts with them so that we could make agreements with them, as we do with other men, about mutually sharing things and services or at least about not hurting each other. The author of nature would clearly have made provision for this, if he had wished the human race to cultivate society with the families of animals. No right therefore belongs to animals either over themselves or over other

---

1. From the notes to bk. I, ch. 12, "On Duty in Acquiring Ownership of Things"; and bk. I, ch. 13, "On the Duties Arising from Ownership."

things which would limit the universal authority of the human race over external things or prevent men from using them in whatever way would make them most useful to men as a whole. [I.12.1.ii]

How things become property

It is quite certain that external things are not assigned by nature to one man rather than to another. Unless therefore we assume an express donation by God (of the conferring of which on anyone alive today whether directly or indirectly, no trace that we know of can be seen), no particular right in any external object can belong to one man or to one part of the human race more than to another, before it is secured by some human action. But there is no similar agreement as to what are the human actions by which rights of that kind can be acquired. It seems that we must seek an answer to this question in the nature of the community (*communio*) to which earthly things are thought to have been subject in their original state.

According to our author (*Of the Law of Nature and Nations,* IV.IV), community of property may be either *positive* or *negative*. Positive community is simply *ownership (dominium) of a thing which belongs without division to more than one person;* negative community is *the condition of things which are publicly available to anybody.* The effect of positive community is that the common thing is either to be held in common, or to be proportionally divided whether by agreement between the associates who share the common right, or, occasionally, by the judgment of a third party. The effect of negative community is that any of those to whom the things are available, may take from the common store what he can use for himself and apply them to his own purposes, provided only that in so doing he does not prevent the rest from enjoying the use of the things that they need. If this were not the effect of negative community, i.e., if any of those to whom the things are available could not, without the consent of the rest, acquire for himself separate possession of the things that lie in negative community, or make use of them, or even consume them, *negative* community would be no different from *positive* community; and the effect on all the things that God had granted to the human race in positive community would be that each thing would remain thus common until by universal agreement it should either become someone's property or be conceded to someone to occupy.

There is no merit in Pufendorf's objection that a common right of this kind cannot be called *positive community*, on the ground that neither ownership nor positive community can be understood when there exist no others against whom those rights are valid.[2] In reply to this, *first,* even when other men do not exist, it is possible for a right to exist which would be valid against others if they did exist; hence there is no reason why one man, even if he were alone in the world, might not have ownership of certain things. *Second,* positive community is a right belonging to a whole society, not only against outsiders lest they take for themselves a share in a thing which does not belong to them, but also against individual members of the society lest any of them should claim for himself any part of the common property without consulting the society, or even appropriate a part which exceeds his due portion. And yet the doctrine of the author obviously assumes that in the primitive state this right against individuals belongs to the human race.

We conclude therefore that separate ownership could only have been introduced by means of such agreements as the author describes here, if things had been subject to positive community from the beginning. But if things were available to all in negative community, it would suffice for the acquisition of ownership to occupy the thing so available with the intention of keeping it for oneself, without any agreement. Therefore the celebrated author is scarcely consistent, when he denies that the primitive community was positive, while contending that separate ownership of things could not be established without agreements.

But whether external things were from the beginning subject to positive or to negative community, must be determined from the condition of the human race and of the things which have been granted for its use. For the same benevolent author of nature, who has given men the capacity to use and enjoy external things, should also be thought to make the use of this capacity conduce as effectively as possible to the security and benefit of the

2. Pufendorf, *Of the Law of Nature and Nations,* IV.IV.3, p. 365.

whole human race. And most earthly things which are useful to man can provide little or no use to several men at the same time, and many of them are consumed by use; but they can be developed, and they need to be developed, by human labor and more closely adapted to human purposes.

For things of this kind to be of service to men in the use for which they are granted, they need to be specially appropriated and adapted to the purposes of the appropriator or of others to whom he concedes them. This appropriation should be accompanied by a valid right against other men. For if other men attempt to take away a thing so occupied from the occupier or prevent him from using it for his own purposes, and at the same time deny it to others for all of whom together it would not be adequate, they would be stealing the fruit of his labor, and this would be a wrong. At the same time they would be frustrating, so far as they could, the purpose for which such things have been given to men by a benevolent creator. For it would be pointless for a man to appropriate a thing which had been available to all and use it for his own purposes, if it were equally right for others to take away what he had so appropriated and frustrate the purposes of the appropriator. It is therefore essential that the occupation of such things should confer on the occupier a right of using them for his own purposes in perpetuity or until they have been consumed, of barring others from random use of them, and of disposing of them in favor of whomever he wants. And since the whole effect of ownership is contained in these points, it is obvious that, in certain things at least, the acquisition of ownership consists in an act of the acquirer alone, and should not therefore be made dependent, as the author contends, on a general human agreement. In other words, these things have been subject from the beginning not to a positive but to a negative community.[3]

3. Carmichael's argument that the right of property had its origin in the appropriation of things by human labor, not by agreement, as Pufendorf had contended, is clearly indebted to Locke's *Second Treatise of Government,* ch. 5, secs. 27–30. Barbeyrac also maintained, against Pufendorf, that the right of property had its origin in labor, as Locke had argued (Pufendorf, *Of the Law of Nature and Nations,* IV.IV.4, n. 2, p. 366). Both authors may be said to have been particularly responsible for the interpretation of Locke's labor theory of property as a theory of occupation of a world

And it is clear that this is the case, *first,* in things which give man immediate, present use, whether for the moment, like food, or on a continuing basis, like clothes and housing; these are things that we cannot use properly unless we appropriate them for our purposes. If anyone could rightly take any of them away from us, he could by the same right take anything similar from us; and to admit this would be to frustrate the purpose for which their use has been given to men.

Second, since nature has taught man to be provident of the future, the same right seems to extend to the appropriation and preservation of things related to a man's likely purposes in the future, provided he does not allow any amount of natural goods to perish with him unused or frustrate the opportunity for others to acquire goods which their own use requires.

But, *third,* this applies not only to things, moveable or self-moving, which are directly useful to men in themselves, but also to things, moveable or immoveable, which serve human purposes with their fruits or services. For the same consideration of utility drawn from future uses also holds here, and there is the same foundation of right in the labor spent in appropriating a thing which was common before, in subduing it, cultivating it, or making it better suited to serve human purposes in any way— these being precisely the means by which one obtains the right of disposing of the thing so acquired and of barring others from random use of it.

Fourth, and finally, the further expenditure of labor and industry which the interest of human society requires in the way of competition in cultivating the things of the earth, is likely to achieve a greater stock of a certain kind of thing than our own personal use requires. In return for these we can acquire, by the use of agreements, other things which are useful to us. This further fruit of our labor should not be taken from us, provided we got it without fraudulent and unfair oppression of others, who should al-

---

not yet occupied, i.e., a negative community. See Moore and Silverthorne, "Gershom Carmichael and the Natural Jurisprudence Tradition," pp. 80–83. It is remarkable that in the translation of Cumberland's *A Treatise of the Laws of Nature* the translator, John Maxwell, refers not to Locke on the origin of property but invites the reader instead to "see Carmichael's and Barbeyrack's Puffendorf upon this Head of the original of Dominion upon which our Author is very General" (p. 315).

ways be left the opportunity to get what their own use requires under fair conditions.

We conclude therefore that in all the cases mentioned, private ownership of things which have limited use can be acquired solely by the expenditure of labor in appropriating them or in preparing them for use, with the intention of keeping them for oneself; we need not ask or await the suffrages of others. For a more thorough discussion of this matter, read the celebrated Locke, *Second Treatise of Government,* chapter 5. [I.12.2.i]

Things which cannot be acquired[4]

[Things which are not consumed by use, e.g., air, are to be used] *in such a way that they may be available for all the purposes of all men,* particularly since another characteristic attached by an almost indissoluble bond to this quality is that these things can be cultivated or better applied to human uses without human labor. Thus nature itself makes these things positively common, we might say, to the whole human race, just as nature has made all other things negatively common, even those which can be drawn from a positively common store (contrary to the celebrated Barbeyrac's first note on this paragraph).[5] Nor can things be fundamentally changed by human agreement from either of these states in which nature has placed them. For although in adventitious rights transmitted from ancestors to descendants, a renunciation on the part of the former may easily be prejudicial to the latter, yet those yet to be born cannot be excluded by any act, however universal, of men now alive, from the exercise of rights which nature herself has granted to individuals. Such are the right of making communal use of things of unlimited abundance, and the right of appro-

---

4. Having given a "natural law" justification of property, Carmichael continues his exposition by taking the topics on property largely in the order in which they were normally discussed in treatises of Roman law, e.g., in Justinian's *Institutes,* bk. II: occupation, accession, servitudes or rights over the property of others, usucapion, or prescription. In several cases he amends Roman law doctrines in the light of his understanding of natural law.

5. Barbeyrac, *Devoirs,* p. 306, considered that the reason some things are left in negative community is that these are things that either cannot be possessed or cannot be defended from others.

priating for one's own use anything of the other kind, provided that no one else has occupied it before. [I.12.4.i]

As for the opinion of Grotius (II.II.12) about a river, that, so far as it is a river, or a mass of water contained within certain bounds, it may be privately owned, despite the fact that the individual flowing drops are common, the same could be said without absurdity about the air, and about light itself, insofar as they exist within certain bounds. But like the vast ocean in places remote from shore, so the even vaster atmosphere and the sun's rays which permeate it in regions high above the surface of the earth, are without doubt positively common. *Flowing water* however is inaccurately classified by our author, following the Roman jurists, among things positively common, since the community of individual drops of water is not positive but negative, inasmuch as they can be drawn from the common store by anyone and by being drawn made private property. [I.12.4.ii]

Original modes of acquisition

i. Occupation of territory

If a tract of land, not exceeding the extent which supplies the needs of the occupier or of those for whom he is obliged to provide or in whose name he takes occupation, is defined by natural limits, there is no need to set other limits; in this case, entry on the place with a declared intention of occupying it is sufficient. Furthermore, he who undertakes to fix his home in some larger tract of land which is still vacant, by that very fact acquires the right of extending his boundaries in due time to the extent necessary to his purposes. In doing so he should not be hindered by the lawless aggression of later arrivals. [I.12.6.iii]

ii. Occupation of moveables: game laws

[In discussing occupation as a means of acquiring ownership of wild animals, Pufendorf had said that we may acquire wild beasts and such like by occupation, "provided that the civil power does not forbid the casual taking of such things. . . ." Carmichael comments:]

I would prefer that our author had said, *provided that prior occupation of the place has not preceded the acquisition there of things of that kind.* It is undoubtedly true that anyone who has acquired a piece of land by right of occupation does not immediately become owner of everything that exists within the bounds of that land (even of things which have been appropriated to no one else); in particular he does not become owner of animals which of their own will can slip away to another place. Nevertheless, he has acquired the right, if he so wishes, to prevent others from taking those things in his territory or of making them their own by taking. The author concedes this with respect to princes at *Of the Law of Nature and Nations,* IV.VI.7. But neither prince nor people acquire, by the occupation of a wide region, any more right in it against outsiders than any man in the natural state would acquire in any little parcel of land he had acquired. Therefore a people which has occupied some region in its entirety is simply making use of the right of an owner in permitting or forbidding within its territory, either directly or through a governor, the casual taking of moving or moveable things. The same is true if in the latter case it assigns distinct parcels of land to private citizens, either with or without the right of seizing certain things in the parcel of land. But if private owners of parcels of land hold them by original right and have not derived them from a people or a prince, the sovereign is defending the natural right of owners in preventing for the benefit of the owner the casual taking of things of that kind on another man's land, or rendering it ineffective. But if he upholds such taking, and denies owners a claim on things so taken (as happened among the Romans), or if he claims the taking of certain things for the public treasury, he is making use of the right of civil government which individual citizens had conceded to him against themselves. Therefore it is the license to take moveable things on another man's land rather than prohibition of that license which it seems we should assign to the civil power and the positive laws. Cf. Grotius, *The Rights of War and Peace,* II.II.5, and II.III.5; consult Grotius also on the occupation of moveable things (Ibid., chs. VIII, I–7). [I.12.6.v]

Moveable objects, especially animals, may be taken not only by hand but also sometimes with appropriate instruments. That is, we acquire them naturally when we catch or trap them so that they cannot get away

by the use of instruments which we have put or set in a place where we
have the right to take them. This we think, with Grotius (II.VIII.2), is
what should be said about animals which are kept within the limits, however ample, of a place subject to our ownership, e.g., in pools or well-
fenced woods. But also things which by their nature are not able to move
from a place at least temporarily, and which have to remain in the same
place for a time while they mature, can be taken and acquired even though
they do not move from the place, provided that a permanent sign is put
up, indicating the special care spent on them and the intention to catch
them, so that they will not be taken by others subsequently. But we cannot
at all agree with the distinguished scholars, who recently published the
paradox that a declaration of will alone suffices for acquiring ownership of
a thing which belongs to no one, without any taking whether direct or
indirect: see Barbeyrac, note 1, on this section.[6] Moreover this doctrine in
no way fits Locke's principle of the origin of ownership, which in other
respects the distinguished commentator seems to embrace, since no labor
is spent on a common object in simply making a declaration of will. Their
other point about the consent of others who renounce their own right of
occupying a certain thing in favor of a certain other man, has effect only
against those who are renouncing the right. Cf. Grotius, II.II.15. [I.12.6.vi]

iii. Accession and merger

The rule [of accession] can perhaps be set out more clearly in this way: *all
fruits, all additions, all improvements, which accede to my property without
involving the property or labor of other men, are wholly acquired by me, except
so far as another man, by contract or other means, has acquired for himself any
right by which my ownership of my property is limited.*

There is a more difficult question, which our author should not have

6. Ibid., p. 308; see also Pufendorf, *Of the Law of Nature and Nations,* IV.VI.2, n. 2,
where Barbeyrac attempts to defend this opinion (that a declaration of will may sometimes suffice to establish occupancy), which he asserts is also Titius's view (*Observationes,* no. 292), by allowing that the moment one neglects to act upon this declaration,
one renounces the right one had begun to acquire. He took this to be a sufficient
answer to "Mr. Carmichael's Objection" (p. 386).

completely ignored: if things belonging to two or more people have merged or mingled to form a new compound object, in such a way that they cannot be told apart or separated, at least without expense; or if a new artifact has been formed from one man's material and another man's expert art and industry, how are we to decide in these cases about the ownership of the compound or artifact? On this question, in general, it seems that no opinion is more in line with natural equity than Grotius's verdict at II.VIII.8 ff.: *where the property or labor of several persons has combined to produce some whole, this whole, by natural law, is acquired by those several persons in common, in the proportion of things or labor that each contributed to it.* This is to be understood with the proviso that he who has mixed his property or labor with the property of another, did so in good faith, or at least without fraud, and with the intention of acquiring for himself and not of transferring his property or labor.

But if the common thing cannot be held in common or divided without expense, it was fiercely disputed among the ancient jurists,[7] to which owner it should preferably go, and there were distinct cases of various kinds contained under this head. The decisions of individual cases presented in the law of Justinian on the basis of their disputes are quite arbitrary and mutually inconsistent. In place of all these, the simplicity of natural law merely commends to us the rule given by our author (*Of the Law of Nature and Nations*, IV.VII.10): *whoever can best sustain the loss of the thing which is now common, is obliged to yield to one who is in desperate need, and should receive fair compensation for his portion of ownership in that object.* If the issue is in doubt, there is a need, in the natural state, for the intervention of the judgment of a good man.

The question of the person who, by fault or fraud, has mingled his property or labor with someone else's property, is also quite intricate. One thing at least seems clear, that if my property is mixed or modified by fault or fraud on the part of someone else and made unsuitable for my purposes, he should pay me the full value of it while retaining the thing itself. On the other hand, he who has made something from a thing of mine by de-

7. The two schools of thought among Roman jurists on this question went under the names Proculian and Sabinian.

liberate fraud, or has mixed it with his own property, acquires no right in my property on that ground, and cannot claim from me the full value of his property or labor above the amount by which I believe myself to be enriched, that is, the amount by which I judge that the mixed or modified property has appreciated beyond my estimate of the value of my original property. If on the other hand I estimate that it is less than it was originally and yet I still prefer to keep it, despite its mixed or modified state, rather than exchange it for another of the same kind, the fraudulent appropriator is obliged to reimburse to me the amount by which it has been devalued. See *Of the Law of Nature and Nations,* IV.VII.10. [I.12.7.i]

iv. Rights over the property of another

Full ownership of a thing, as it arises from the modes of acquiring reviewed above, combines several rights which may be regarded as distinct, since it is capable of producing several different effects. Any of these may be separated from the complex (which will still retain the name of ownership) by one of the acts by which rights are transferred from one man to another, with the effect that it will belong to someone other than the owner of the thing. Such distinct rights are *real rights* in the full sense, since they terminate in the thing itself and so are valid against any possessor of it. Moreover, they are normally known by that title precisely when they have been separated from ownership, as we have said, and are distinguished from ownership and among themselves by their own particular names. Whether these rights inhere in the owner or in another person, they equally regard their immediate object, i.e., the thing itself, and so must be said to be born and to die with ownership itself. Nevertheless, since they are marked by those particular names only when they are separated from ownership (as we have said), they are commonly said to be created or constituted precisely when they are separated from the ownership, and are said to be abolished at the point when they are again consolidated with it. In this sense much the same thing can be said about these real rights, in comparison with ownership, as we said above about personal rights compared with natural liberty (pp. 77–80): both the constitution and the abolition of them as rights is effected by some kind of transfer, and thus their transfer gives rise to a triple division, and so on.

Some writers reckon these separate real rights as four (see Titius, *Observations on Lauterbach*, 32): (1) *possession,* or the right that belongs to the legitimate possessor, against anyone else who does not have a better title; (2) *hereditary right,* and under this name we include not only the right of the nearest heir to the inheritance in question (i.e., this hardly differs from ownership insofar as it relates to physical property contained in the inheritance), but in particular the right of substituted heirs, which, in the case of property in land, often has a much wider scope in our country than among the Romans; (3) *pledge;* and (4) *servitude.* [I.12.8.i]

Derivative modes of acquisition

[Pufendorf says: "Among the derivative modes of acquisition, there are some by which a thing is passed to another by disposition of the law, others by a prior act of the owner." Carmichael comments:]

[Pufendorf's] distinction [among the derivative modes of acquisition] is not expressed in quite the right words: for all rights, all obligations, in a word, all moral qualities, are derived from some law, natural or positive, divine or human, and therefore there is no ownership or transfer of ownership except by the disposition of some law. On the other hand, rarely or never does a law transfer ownership without assuming some act, or omission of some act, on the part of the previous owner. What our author means is that ownership is sometimes transferred by the explicit will of the owner to transfer it, and sometimes by the disposition of the law without an explicit will of this kind, on the assumption of some other act or omission on the part of the previous owner. With this clarification the distinction is correct. [I.12.9.i]

i. Succession

A. INTESTATE. [Natural law] itself in the natural state regularly confers the estate of an intestate on those whom he is presumed to have held most dear, in accordance with common human feeling and duty. Incidentally, two things should be noticed about succession in the natural state: (1) since there is no positive law in place, considerable weight has to be given to the accepted custom first of the intestate's family, if that is adequately known, and then of the neighboring families. He is rightly presumed to have intended to follow this custom. (2) The same weight as a testament is naturally to be given to any declaration of the will of the deceased about the succession to his property, if the reliability of any such declaration can be proved to others and if there is no reasonable evidence to show that it had been revoked. [I.12.10.i]

B. BY WILL. Here finally it should be noted that the will of the deceased, whether express or tacit, transfers both ownership and the other rights, both real and personal (particularly the latter), that were not limited to the person or life of the deceased himself. Lack of acceptance of the inheritance by a certain time is not a bar; since the deceased cannot revoke his will, it is reasonable for it to be accepted after an interval of time. [from I.12.12.iv]

ii. Transfer "among the living"

This kind of transfer occurs naturally when there is concurrent consent on the part of both giver and receiver (according to our doctrine at pp. 79–80) about the object to be transferred; for this effect natural law does not require either actual delivery (see Grotius, *The Rights of War and Peace*, II.VI.1 and 2) or previous binding consent. But since this previous consent frequently occurs earlier, and since the civil law requires for the actual transfer of ownership in these cases the delivery of the thing, the distinction has arisen which is familiar to jurists between acquisition of the *title* and the conveyance. By the simplicity of the natural law these two things may easily coincide, and even in the civil law they are not always found separated, as is obvious for instance in a spontaneous donation, in which the wish to give is signified and the thing is handed over at one and the same time.

But the distinction which the author adds here between the *gratuitous* transfer of ownership and transfer by means of a contract, has to be interpreted differently depending on whether or not a previous obligation to transfer is assumed to precede the transfer itself. If no obligation precedes, it is said to be a *gratuitous* transfer, and takes place by a single act, i.e., by an act which does not involve the reciprocal transfer of any right from the other party. A *nongratuitous* transfer is one which takes place by a reciprocal act, or by an act which involves such a transfer. Even if there is a preceding obligation to transfer ownership, the thing is still said *to be given* if that obligation was based on a gratuitous promise of giving; in the Roman jurists the promise itself comes under the name of *donation* (see Justinian, *Institutes,* II.7.2). However if the obligation is based on any other cause, whether contract, quasi contract, or delict, the thing is said to be transferred with a *burdened* title.[8] [I.12.13.i]

iii. Transfer without consent

Ownership of things (as well as of other rights on occasion) may also be transferred, against the will of the previous owner, by the disposition of the natural law though with the intervention of some human act, in order to satisfy a right which already belongs to the acquirer against the owner and which he has refused to satisfy of his own accord. This is in line with our doctrine at pp. 69–71 [on the right to punish in the state of nature]. This natural justice is also the foundation of the legal execution, by which in civil societies the property of debtors, whatever their title, is applied to pay their debts to their creditors, provided a judge so authorizes; and is also the foundation of all acquisition in war which can be considered licit and just. Furthermore, in civil societies property is transferred as a penalty for delicts. [I.12.14.i part]

iv. Usucapion or prescription

Here the author describes *Usucapion* as it obtained among the Romans, which is recognized as originating in the civil law by Justinian, *Institutes,*

---

8. Carmichael discusses contracts, quasi contracts, and, to some extent, delicts in chapter 11, below.

II.5.6. But there is something analogous to usucapion or prescription in the acquisition of a thing, after presumed abandonment by the former owner, especially if acquired in good faith; such acquisition is valid by the natural law itself (see Grotius, II.IV). And we surely know no other prescription properly based in this right than that which relies on the presumption of tacit abandonment or on tacitly accepted alienation. This presumption necessarily assumes not only that the owner has not made a claim to the thing, but also that he has been given a proper opportunity to do so. The simple passage of a long period of time does not in itself guarantee that there has been such an opportunity. However I do not think it is incumbent on a possessor to prove by positive evidence that the owner has had a proper opportunity to claim. I would say rather, in this as in certain other cases, that men who live in a natural state with each other must have recourse to arbitration by a good man; and he, after duly weighing the length of time passed, and the other circumstances of things and persons, is to determine (by the evidence we referred to in the note just cited) whether or not the former owner appears to have abandoned his property or to have tacitly accepted it as alienated. This is surely the rule which we recognize in natural liberty for ending the dispute between possessor and a former owner. In civil societies however no one will readily deny that a certain period of time is rightly established as the criterion for ending such a difficult dispute. One should add in passing that, when a possessor is relying on occupation confirmed by abandonment by the former owner, it makes little difference whether the occupation took place before or after the former owner had given adequate indications of his will to abandon it. In the latter case, the abandoned property was truly available for occupation at the time when it was occupied; in the former case, occupation seems to have been granted by the will of the owner to anyone whose possession of it is legal in other respects. [I.12.15.i]

Contracts and Quasi Contracts[1]

i. Contracts

[At p. 107 below, Carmichael rejects the distinction which Pufendorf offers between "agreements" (*pacta*) and "contracts" (*contractus*) according to which "contracts" are agreements which "deal with things and actions of commercial significance and which consequently rest on a presupposition of ownership and value in things" (Pufendorf, *On the Duty of Man and Citizen*, I.15.1, p. 97). Carmichael therefore merely makes some incidental remarks on value before proceeding to discuss contracts in detail. In discussing contracts he follows the order of exposition which was usual in accounts of this branch of Roman law, while amending specific doctrines in the light of natural law.]

For a thing to have value, the first requisite is this *suitability,* either real or imaginary ["to make a direct or indirect contribution to the needs of human life and to render it fuller and more agreeable" (Pufendorf)]; however the justification of the value is not the same as the reason for the suitability, as the author himself properly points out later. In general it can be said here that the value of things rests on two grounds, *scarcity* and *difficulty of acquisition.* And scarcity is estimated on the basis of two factors, the *number* of competitors for an object or service and its *suitability* to contribute to the use or pleasure of human life. See Grotius, II.XII.14. [I.14.3.i]

This method of defining value ["by men's common valuation and as-

---

1. From the notes to bk. I, ch. 14, "On Value"; and bk. I, ch. 15, "On Contracts Which Presuppose Value in Things and on the Duties They Involve"; also Supplement IV, "On Quasi Contracts."

sessment, or by the usage of the market together with the consent of those who are dealing with each other" (Pufendorf)] holds no less in the natural state than in the civil state, i.e., in both cases the value of things is determined on the one hand directly by an agreement between contracting individuals, on the other hand, unless a law of the commonwealth forbids it, by the usage of the marketplace. [I.14.5.i]

Agreements and contracts

[Pufendorf says: "In its general sense an agreement (*pactum*) is the consent and concurrence of two or more men to the same intent (*placitum*)." Carmichael comments:]

On this definition of Ulpian's we have said enough on p. 80, where we have also pointed out that the term *agreement (pactum)* is usually used in the stricter sense for an act which consists of mutual consent and is obligatory on at least one side. We have also noted (at p. 81) that the same term is there taken in the strictest sense for an act which is obligatory on both sides, or at least for an act which is obligatory on at least one party and transfers some right from both parties. It is in this last mentioned sense that the term *agreement* should be taken, so that, in the division of the *mutual obligatory act,* it is directly opposed to *free promise;* here too it is most aptly taken in this sense. [I.15.1.i]

[Carmichael rejects Pufendorf's distinction "between simple agreements and contracts."]

The author could safely have omitted this distinction since, as it is understood by the jurists, it arises from a superfluous subtlety of Roman law, and (as Titius says) it obviously smells of the notary's art.[2] The author evidently felt this and does not explain the difference between these two things according to the maxims of Roman jurisprudence but rather by natural reason, though he seems to think that they come to more or less the same thing. But even as explained by the author the distinction is not of much use in itself, and does not square properly with the accepted appli-

2. Titius, *Observationes*, no. 354.

cation of these terms among the Roman jurists (for there may be innumerable agreements about things or actions occurring in commerce, which would not be called *contracts* by the nomenclature of the Romans, for example exchange of things by consent alone). Thus it seems more satisfactory to drop the distinction between *bare agreements* and *contracts* from natural jurisprudence altogether; under the influence of equity, the distinction has been eliminated in our day from the moral systems of most nations. [I.15.1.ii]

[Pufendorf classifies contracts as "gratuitous" and "onerous."]

The author rightly expounds the differences between contracts as they are founded in nature, and drops the [Roman] distinctions of *nominate* and *innominate* contracts, as well as of contracts which are made by *things,* by *words,* by *writing,* and by *consent alone.*[3] Once one removes the contrast between *bare agreements* and *contracts,* all these finicky distinctions converge of their own accord. Compare Grotius, II.XII.1–13. [I.15.2.i]

Remarks on specific contracts

[Carmichael comments on one type of "gratuitous contract," namely, "loan for use," typically going behind the legal technicalities to the principles of natural law:]

In accordance with the various definitions of the term various views are taken as to whether a *loan for use (commodatum)* should be said to be contracted only by the actual delivery of the object loaned or by the promise to deliver it; in either case this implies the obligation to return the object of the loan undamaged, and also involves the question whether a *loan for use* is a *real* or a *consensual* contract. We wish to apply the same question to the other contracts which the jurists call *real contracts.*[4] It is in any case certain that by natural law mere consent, even without delivery, strictly

---

3. For these distinctions see Justinian, *Institutes,* III.13 ff; and Pufendorf, *Of the Law of Nature and Nations,* V.II.6–7, pp. 473–74.

4. The four so-called real contracts are loans for use, for consumption, for deposit, and for pledge.

binds the party giving the service to make the first performance, not only in the case of loans for use but also in the case of deposits and loans for consumption, i.e., it obligates the lender for use and the lender for consumption to deliver the object, and binds the depositee to accept the deposit. But mere consent produces no obligation to make subsequent performances, unless the other party shall have got the promised benefit, i.e., where the party taking the object for use or the borrower for consumption has accepted the object, or the depositor has delivered it. We are assuming here that the parties are entering into *beneficial* contracts properly so-called; the non-interest-bearing loan (*mutuum*) is usually of this kind, though the author applies this term indiscriminately also to the *onerous* kind of loan.[5] For on the other hand, if the advantage of both parties is in view from the beginning, as in the case in which there is an agreement in the loan about paying interest, or if, as sometimes happens, it is a mixed transaction, of loan for use and deposit, or of loan for consumption and irregular deposit,[6] both of the contracting parties can be obligated by mere consent. [I.15.6.i]

[“If the object loaned should be destroyed while in the hands of the borrower,” Pufendorf says, “it seems fair that the borrower should pay the value of the thing.” Carmichael characteristically broadens the scope of the issue:]

This seems rather fairer than that the whole risk arising from pure chance of the object loaned should lie with the owner (as the civil laws hold, *Institutes*, III.15.2).[7] For we should not readily assume that the owner intended his kindness to involve him in loss beyond what the nature of the contract requires. We must in any case reject the view of the celebrated Wernher, who argues, in his *Elements of the Law of Nature and of Nations*,[8] that this question does not belong to natural law, and that many other questions about cases which occur frequently in human life and can easily

---

5. A *mutuum* is a "loan for consumption" (e.g., an apple), as distinct from a *commodatum*, "loan for use" (e.g., a tool). Both are essentially noninterest bearing.

6. An "irregular" deposit is a deposit in which the depositee has the right to make use of the object.

7. Apparently a reference to Justinian, *Institutes*, II.14.2.

8. J. B. von Wernher, *Elementa Iuris Naturae et Gentium.*

happen in places where they are defined neither by positive laws nor by conventions, do not belong to the law of nature. For one may not believe that where men are in a state of nature with each other, God has not given them a rule by which disputes of this kind may be settled, but has left them to be decided by force of arms on both sides. We admit however that most questions of this kind about the interpretation of contracts, where it is not satisfactorily defined either by positive law or by accepted custom, are most suitably met by the contracting parties themselves by means of an explicit agreement on those articles. [I.15.6.iii]

Legitimate chance and gambling

[Pufendorf: "there are several contracts which involve chance." Carmichael comments:]

These too are usually "onerous." Some of them yield certain expectations and some uncertain expectations; the latter may be brought closer to the former so that they will not deserve the reproach of unfairness.

But it is for other reasons, I think, that we should condemn contracts in which the only effect is to make something which was not previously an object of doubtful dispute dependent on the simple hazard of chance. For above all they bring no benefit to mankind and daily give rise to many evils, and take men away from more honorable methods of increasing their estate which would be more useful to the country and less risky for themselves. And of course, as it is vile and dishonorable to set out to enrich oneself at others' expense without deserving it, so the ingenious author of the *Art of Thinking*, IV.16, has rightly noted how deceptive and vain is the hope that entices men into making contracts of this kind.[9] It is proper therefore that gambling (and all games in which the contest is for a stake) should be moderate, so that the stake is proportionate to the ability of the parties to pay, and the object of the bet is such that the outcome may be directed, or at least foreseen with probability, on the basis of the strength or skill of the contestants. [I.15.13.i]

9. A. Arnauld and P. Nicole, *La Logique ou l'art de penser*. See part IV, ch. XVI.

Debt in natural law and theology

[In this section on one man's standing as surety for another man's borrowing, Pufendorf says that the surety is "more strictly bound than the principal debtor." Carmichael illustrates this:]

A surety, for example, may be held to the pledges he has given in the court *of the land* or by his oath in the court *of heaven,* even though the principal debtor may perhaps not be bound in either way. But insofar as he owes more than the principal debtor either in amount or time or place or cause, he is not properly a surety. Hence I cannot agree with the note of the celebrated Barbeyrac on this passage.[10] [I.15.14.i]

Among theologians who have crossed the boundaries of jurisprudence and among jurists who have returned the favor to theology, the question has been much debated, whether, before the price of redemption had been paid, Christ our Lord had the position simply of a *surety* (*fidejussor*) or whether it was actually that of a substitute debtor (*expromissor*).[11] The second alternative has been proved by most lucid arguments to be correct by, among many others, the celebrated Ulrich Huber, much missed in the world of learning, in his golden treatise *On the Rights of Civil Society.*[12] [I.15.14.ii]

10. *Devoirs,* pp. 373–74, and Pufendorf, *Of the Law of Nature and Nations,* V.X.10–11. Barbeyrac contended that the principal debtor remained obliged to repay his debt; that the surety remained such even if he had contracted to pay more than the debtor; for the creditor might not have agreed to the contract without this assurance. Both Barbeyrac and Carmichael were reacting, on grounds of natural law, against those Roman jurists who held that if the surety had contracted for a sum larger than the amount of the principal debt, the obligation of the surety might be voided (Pufendorf, *Of the Law of Nature and Nations,* V.X.9, n. 9).

11. A surety (*fidejussor*) guarantees the debt of a debtor; a substitute debtor (*expromissor*) takes the debt upon himself, thus releasing the original debtor from obligation toward the creditor.

12. Huber, *De Jure Civitatis,* I.IV.6, pp. 127–38, argued that if Christ were merely surety (*fidejussor*) for the debt owed to God, he would not be God; as substitute debtor (*expromissor*), he has himself made the promise (of redemption) and thus reveals himself to be God. See Moore and Silverthorne, "Protestant Theologies," p. 185.

The standards of care

[Pufendorf says that a creditor must treat a pledge with "no less care than he gives to his own property." Carmichael takes the opportunity to expound a standard topic of Roman law:]

That is, no less than he *owes* to his own property. The creditor is therefore bound to look after the object pledged in the manner of a good and diligent head of a household. He should do so in accordance with the rule affirmed by natural no less than civil law: *where a contract, by force of which a thing is in the custody,* or natural possession, *of another person, is for the advantage of both parties,* as in rental and pledge, *moderate care is required* of the kind which any diligent head of a household is accustomed to bestow on his own property, and the corresponding *light fault* is applicable. *Where a contract is for the advantage only of the possessor,* as in loan for consumption, *the most scrupulous diligence is required,* and consequently in this case *lightest fault,* which corresponds to that degree of diligence, should be applied. *Where* finally, *a contract is for the advantage not of the possessor but of the other party,* as in deposit, *a less strict diligence is adequate, provided it is as great as the possessor is accustomed to give to his own similar property,* or (as the civil jurists have determined, because this definition has difficulties) as much diligence as sensible people are accustomed to show to their own property; and here therefore, apart from fraud which is applicable in every contract, only *gross fault* needs to be applied; *gross fault* corresponds to the lowest degree of diligence and is equivalent to fraud. [I.15.15.iii]

ii. On quasi contracts[13]

[There is a brief treatment of the Roman doctrine of quasi contracts at Justinian, *Institutes,* III.27. Quasi contracts are essentially situations in which one party has an obligation to another party not on the ground of a prior agreement. In Roman law such an obligation would arise, for example, if a person incurred expense in protecting another's property in an emergency without his knowledge; the obligation to compensate him was said to be *quasi ex contractu.* Another kind of case was the obligation to return something if it was paid to you by someone who

---

13. Supplement IV.

mistakenly believed that he owed it to you. Quasi contract was a restricted category in Roman law of miscellaneous cases, where there was obviously an obligation but which did not rise from a contract: it was "like a contract," though not actually a contract. Carmichael's treatment follows the restricted Roman understanding of quasi contracts and distinguishes them carefully from tacit contracts.

There is another kind of obligation which some Romanists and natural law writers seem to have included in quasi contract in early modern times, namely the obligation to make compensation or even pay a penalty for delictual activity, where the compensation or penalty is seen as payment of a debt incurred by the wrongdoer. Carmichael does not give quasi contracts such a wide scope.]

1. In the note at pp. 77–80 above, we said that the particularly natural mode of contracting obligations, or, what is the same thing, of *creating personal rights,* is the *mutual consent* of the person who is obligated and of the person by whom the corresponding personal right is acquired. But this is not the only means by which obligations and their corresponding rights are created. This is clear from what was said above on *compensation for loss* (pp. 73–74), which comes to be due simply by the infliction of damage; on *the right* of harming *unjust aggressors and those who oppose the satisfaction of our right* (pp. 69–71), which is founded in the continuing wrong itself; on *the obligation to return an object,* which arises from present possession of another person's property, *and the obligation to restore residual benefits,* which arises from past possession of another's property.

2. In addition to these, there are also other acts by which, without the concurrent consent of both parties, obligations can be and are commonly made. These are obligations which are founded in an obvious equity which it is presumed that the parties who benefit do not repudiate or at least would not repudiate, if they were aware of the situation. They are usually classified by jurists as *quasi contracts.* Quasi contracts must not be confused with *tacit* contracts. In tacit contracts consent is argued to have occurred in actual fact on the basis of some action or nonaction; but in quasi contracts consent is pretended for the sake of equity.[14]

---

14. In contrast to Carmichael, Barbeyrac found no place at all for quasi contracts in his jurisprudence: "This sort of Consent is of no use nor necessity in Civil Life; and

3. Obligations of this kind can pretty well be reduced to two classes: they are contracted either *by involving oneself in someone else's affairs as such or in affairs which involve obligation to another in some way, or by obtaining some substantial benefit at someone else's expense which was neither given nor agreed.*

4. In the *former* class, if a man has *managed the property* of someone who is *absent* and unaware of his action or of someone who is present but by some defect of judgment *incapable of giving consent, he incurs the obligation to give an account to the owner of what he has done, and to restore any property of his that he holds,* and also *to compensate for loss inflicted by his own fault* (which will be differently estimated according to the circumstances); the relevant actions in civil law are the *direct* actions for *management of affairs* and *guardianship.*

5. To the same class belongs the obligation by which an heir, after entering explicitly or implicitly upon his inheritance, *is bound to satisfy the creditors and legatees of the deceased,* to the extent of the inherited estate. It is no objection that the civil jurists include only the obligation of the heir toward the legatees under *quasi contract,* considering that the heir with respect to the *creditors* is the same person with the deceased. This, I say, is no objection to what has been said, so long as the heir, because he maintains the person of the deceased, is bound to fulfill his obligations from the estate; i.e., the creditors gain no right against the heir from any other source than from his entering upon the inheritance.

6. In the *latter* class we include the obligation by which, when someone has incurred necessary expenses for preserving in their proper condition the property or rights of a person who is absent or unable to consent because of defect of judgment, that person is bound to give full reimbursement to the other of those expenses. (These expenses naturally include losses suffered in his own property for this reason.) And the other party must really possess those things or use those rights, for whose preservation the expenses were incurred. He is also obliged to refund expenses *usefully*

---

the lawyers invented it only to found certain Obligations upon, for which they could not see any true Principles" (Pufendorf, *Of the Law of Nature and Nations,* III.VI.2, n. 3 [1717 edition], cited in Birks and McLeod, "Implied Contract Theory of Quasi-Contract," p. 67).

spent by another on his property, to the extent that he has become richer by it. The *counteractions of administration of affairs and of guardianship* are available for enforcing this obligation (which has been applied in different cases, variously enlarged or restricted, as the interest of society has been thought to require). In the case of *guardianship*, this obligation is based not only on the common consideration of equity, which is equally applicable in *administration of affairs,* but also in the explicit or presumed will of the person who passed the property to the ward, in which the ward seems to acquiesce when he becomes an adult by entering into possession of the property. The ward is also obliged to indemnify others with whom the guardian has contracted in the ward's name, at least indirectly, insofar as he is bound to indemnify the guardian for anything that he has done which is useful. Moreover the ward is obligated to the guardian not only for what he has properly and prudently spent on his *property,* but also for his outlays on his *person,* i.e., expenses incurred in feeding the ward and giving him a suitable education. This applies also to retarded or insane persons with respect to their caregivers for the cost of their maintenance and, I would add, their supervision.

7. But what obligation shall we say is due from a *dependent*[15] to the *person who raised him,* from whom he received sustenance and a suitable education in his early years when he had nothing of his own. I find that this obligation has up to now been very differently regarded in different cases in both positive law and custom. In the case of *free-born persons* it has almost no effect, except that *children* (for we count children, when brought up by their parents, as *alumni*) are commanded by the civil laws to *look after destitute parents.* On the other hand it is quite wrong to extend this obligation to the case of *slaves born in the household,* to keep them in perpetual servitude; for it will be made clear below (pp. 143–45) that this is the only ground that can plausibly serve as a pretext for perpetual hereditary servitude. Subject to the opinion of wiser men, I think that this obligation (perfect by natural law) is based on the ground of refunding the

---

15. "Dependent" represents *alumnus,* which is used by Carmichael here for a child, whether slave or free, who is being raised by an adult, who may or may not be his biological parent.

necessary expenses of maintaining an *alumnus* through his early years and of educating him to be a fit member of human society. I say *necessary*, since exaggerated expenditure, made for reasons of rank or show, should not be included. Thus on the one hand it is quite out of line with the love and duty expected of parents to enter into a strict calculation of accounts with their children, unless they were utterly ungrateful, since, as well as giving them a suitable education, they should do what parents normally do and establish their fortunes as far as their resources allow, and bequeath to them, as their nearest and dearest, what remains to them of their property when they die (unless there is a special reason not to). But at the same time I would think that even when children receive no other patrimony from their parents, it is still a kind of free and unselfish gift that they are not required to refund the expenses which had to be made for their upbringing and education. In the case of slaves born in the household the obligation to refund expenses extends no further, as I shall make clear below (pp. 143–45), and does not provide a foundation for perpetual servitude.

8. The obligation of someone who has used *the privilege of necessity* in the case of another man's property also belongs to this same second class (which our author discusses at *On the Duty of Man and Citizen,* I.5.23 and 24). So does the obligation of someone who *has accepted something which was not owed as if it were owed,* or (which is the same thing by natural law) has accepted something on the basis of an agreement to which a legitimate counterclaim could be opposed, or finally, *has accepted something on condition of his paying a thing or doing a service which he did not subsequently honor.* Thus all of these are equally obligated to make restitution.

9. Where the property of several persons has been made common without a contract, mutual obligations arise from the fact that one person alone has managed the common property or alone incurred necessary expenses on it. The obligation of this man toward the others seems to belong to the former of the two classes mentioned above, while the obligation of the rest toward him seem to belong to the latter class. But the obligation to accept a division, which arises by itself from the actual holding in common of a thing which is really not suited to be held in common, seems to have its own rather different character.

10. Finally, obligations which bind *someone other than the person through*

whom they were contracted (which are discussed at Justinian, *Institutes,* IV.7) so far as they are part of natural law, are to be resolved either into a *true contract,* if someone has made a contract by *the order of and in the name of another,* or, if not, into a case of *management of affairs.* There are exceptions in certain cases in which the obligations should rather be said to concern the party with whom the other has contracted only indirectly, insofar as the person who is ultimately obligated is bound on the basis of mandate or of management of affairs[16] to restore the losses of the other party through whom the obligation was contracted.[17]

16. Mandate (*mandatum*) was an actual contract, not a quasi contract: it was "a consensual contract, by which one party gratuitously undertook a commission for the other"; however, "management of affairs" (*negotiorum gestio*) was a quasi contract.

17. Carmichael's Supplement on quasi contracts was taken up by later philosophers of the Scottish enlightenment in a variety of contexts. Francis Hutcheson employed this idea to expand upon the obligations of children to their parents, of orphans to their adoptive parents, and of later generations of citizens to the original contract of government entered into by their ancestors (Hutcheson, *A Short Introduction,* II.14, pp. 223–27; III.2, pp. 269–70, and III.5, pp. 286–87). Thomas Reid used the notion of implied contract to explain a wide range of social obligations, including the relationship which ought to prevail between citizens and governments (*Practical Ethics,* pp. 70 ff., 237–46, 401–8).

Dissolution of Obligations[1]

The principle of dissolution

Several of the means [of dissolving obligations] which are reviewed here may also dissolve other obligations than those that arise from agreements. The *dissolution of an obligation* (as may be understood from our observation on p. 79 is simply the reversion of the corresponding personal right to its original subject, and its consolidation with his natural liberty. By this agreement the *personal right* itself is said to be abolished because he no longer has a reason for such a right. [I.16.1.i]

Modes of dissolution

Just as an obligation is constituted by the perfectly natural mode of *mutual consent* on the part of the person who obligates himself and of the person to whom he is obligated, so it is no less naturally dissolved by *a contrary will on both sides*. I say *on both sides*. For just as in a simple promise when a particle of natural liberty is transferred to another person by the consent of a future debtor, so in a simple *renunciation,* when that particle of liberty reverts, by the will of the creditor, to its natural subject, the *consent* of its *acquirer* needs to be given as well as that of the *transferor.* The obligation is dissolved by the concurrent consent of the creditor, in this case the transferor, and of the debtor (the acquirer), either *gratis*—in which case it is

---

1. From the notes to bk. I, ch. 16, "How Obligations Arising from Agreements Are Dissolved."

properly said to be *renounced*—or *for onerous cause,* i.e., in view of some other thing or service. The personal thing or service may be either performed at that very moment or promised for later; it may be either the assignment of a right against a third party (for example, by *delegation,* see I.16.9.i) or the reciprocal remission of some other obligation by which the creditor himself has been obligated to his debtor. For this reason reciprocal obligations are said to be dissolved on both sides by *mutual dissent,* as our author says in his next paragraph.[2] [I.16.3.i]

The duration of an obligation may be said *to depend upon a point of time* in *two senses.* Either it is meant that *the performance which could be required before a certain date cannot be demanded after it,* or the sense is that *performance may be required at certain intervals up to a certain end-date, but not after it.* In the *former* case, it is obvious that the obligation is understood to be conditional, i.e., one is only obliged to perform, if required to do so within a certain time. If this condition is not met, the obligation disappears, not because of the mere lapse of time but because the condition is lacking. In the *latter* case, the end-date by which the performances are to be required is either *definite* or *indefinite.* If the end-date is *definite,* the obligation requiring performance after that date does not so much expire as never existed. If the end-date is *indefinite,* because it depends on some event the date of whose occurrence is unknown, in this case the obligation to seek performance by any given end-date is conditional, i.e., *provided the event in question did not occur before.* If this condition, which relates to future time after the existence of this event, is not fulfilled, then performance is no longer required. In either case the obligation to do any particular thing before the end-date has passed, is only removed by fulfilment or some equivalent mode. This is true also in the first case, if the performance is demanded before the passing of the end-date. [I.16.7.i]

The grounds on which these obligations [which are "essentially rooted

2. Barbeyrac differed from Carmichael on the mutuality required to dissolve an obligation. In the case of a loan, in his view, the obligation is dissolved when the creditor releases the debtor from his obligation. It is not necessary for the debtor to agree as well: "It is in vain that Mr. Carmichael makes what is necessary to contract an obligation equally necessary to cancel it" (Pufendorf, *On the Law of Nature and Nations,* V.XI.7, p. 531, n. 4).

in a man's person" (Pufendorf)] are said to be dissolved by *death,* may be understood from what was said in the *previous paragraph* about obligations which expire with time, particularly an indefinite time. These obligations are to be regarded as *rooted in a person.* This is indicated either by the actual words of the agreement or testament on which they are based or by the nature of the transaction. On this question the correct position seems to be as follows: (1) Every obligation deriving *from an onerous cause is transmitted to heirs and against heirs,* unless it happens to concern some special service where it obviously matters to the creditor which person performs it, or it matters to the debtor to whom the payment is made. For the obligation of the former is understood to be rooted in the person of the debtor, of the latter in the person of the creditor. And here anything which was given in expectation of a service which had not yet been performed when the obligation expired, ought to be returned, unless there was a stay against its performance from the creditor himself. (2) All obligations arising *from beneficial cause,* concerned with merely *personal services,* are naturally understood to be *rooted in the person* both of the debtor and of the creditor, so that they disappear with the death of either of them. (3) Obligations flowing *from discretionary cause* for paying some *object* or *quantity* at fixed *intervals* of time, or for permitting *continuous use* of a *thing,* when *no end-date* is given, seem naturally to *be rooted in the person of the creditor but not of the debtor;* this is still more the case if something has been expressly given to someone *for so long as he shall live.* But obligations, though *from beneficial cause,* to give something *once,* or on repeated occasions *at intervals,* or for conceding the use of a thing *to some definite end-date,* which we suppose to be neither the death of the debtor nor of the creditor, are rooted in the person of neither, but naturally *pass to the heirs and against the heirs.* I say *naturally* because there is no doubt that obligations of this kind may be extended or restricted by positive laws or customs. In all these cases the death of the debtor or the creditor does not cause the expiration of the obligations to the burdens whose time of payment has already passed, provided that their payment is made from the property of the debtor, either directly or in subsidiary manner. (4) An obligation *to corporal punishment* does not *go beyond the person* of the delinquent. But a pecuniary penalty owes its origin to the civil laws and so passes to the heirs or not, as the laws may determine. [I.16.8.i]

What our author here describes as *delegation,* is actually the cession of an action against a third party which a debtor makes to his creditor, thus transferring his obligation to the third party. It counts therefore as the dissolution of an obligation for the debtor who has ceded the action and thus obtains immunity from the obligation by which he was previously bound, but not for the third party whose obligation is merely transferred and not dissolved (see above pp. 118–19). *Delegation* as the Romans described it is actually the *substitution of another debtor* (*expromissio:* see above p. 111). In natural law *expromissio* is only necessary when someone is delegated on behalf of a person to whom he had no previous obligation of a kind which the creditor has a right to transfer. *Novation* in its special sense our author rightly treats as one of the excessive subtleties of the civil law. In the civil law a novation is the abolition of a prior obligation when a new obligation is contracted among the same persons on the same matter. For the novation which conforms to the simplicity of natural law is the addition or removal of something by a new agreement while the old obligation remains intact in other respects. The mere formal change [in the Roman system] to a stipulation from another form of contract is merely a matter of civil law. However if a nonliquid obligation arising from the infliction of damage or a similar cause is changed by agreement to a liquid obligation, this relates to what we said above at pp. 118–19.

Thus all the modes of dissolving obligations so far surveyed may be reduced to three, viz., *dissolution, cession* by the creditor in favor of the debtor (whether done *gratis* or from onerous cause), and *failure of the condition. Compensation* naturally reduces itself to the first; all *transactions, delegations,* etc., are obviously contained in the second, according to our observations at pp. 118–19; under the last head we find *perfidy* of the other party, *change of status, lapse of time,* and *death* (to which must be added the *perishing of the specific object* owed) whenever the obligation expires for any of these reasons. A peculiar mode of abolishing an obligation is *confusio,* i.e., when a creditor succeeds to a debtor, or a debtor to a creditor. [I.16.9.i]

A note on the interpretation of laws

I see no good reason why the distinguished Titius and Barbeyrac thought that this rule ["interpret favorable expressions more broadly, invidious expressions more strictly" (Pufendorf)], needed criticism, since it is so natural, and almost everyone would approve it. Universal common sense dictates that there is a distinction among things: some things are more desirable in themselves than others; or rather, there are some aspects of things from which they should be considered *desirable,* others from which they should be seen *to be avoided,* so that it is useless to look for clear definitions of *favorable* and *invidious* or *odious* here. But it is still very clear that this distinction should have some weight in interpreting an ambiguous utterance, so that we recognize, so far as the usage of words and other circumstances permit, that this or that was the intention of the speaker.

They criticize the instances of favorable and odious things adduced by Grotius and our author as inconsistent with each other; since what is to the common interest is said to be favorable, and anything that contains a penalty is said to be invidious, despite the fact, they say, that the imposition of penalties is in the common interest. But this instance simply proves what the author himself admits, that certain things are *mixed qualities* which contain in themselves something favorable and something invidious. The infliction of penalties is odious in itself, insofar as it involves suffering and pain on the part of the man penalized. But it is favorable insofar as it is in the public interest; and the favorableness of this consideration, where it actually is relevant, absorbs the odiousness of the other consideration. Therefore as the pain inflicted on a man tends to the public advantage (though not simply and in itself but within limits and in certain situations), so insofar as the pain is odious in itself, it is to be regarded as desired for that purpose or enjoined by the legislator only because obvious reasons or clear indications of his will have shown the need for it. The aforesaid rule is not therefore a "wax nose," however much those who have not thought about it or are swayed by the power of their feelings, may distort it, as they may distort all the best rules, by applying it badly. [I.17.9.ii]

[Barbeyrac responded to Carmichael's observations on interpretation at length, in his notes on Grotius, *Rights of War and Peace,* II.XVI.10, n. 1, pp. 356–57: "I shall at present only add some reflections, occasioned by what I have lately observed in a new Edition of the Abridgment of Pufendorf . . . printed at Glasgow in 1718, under the direction of Mr. Carmichael, Professor of philosophy in that University. That able Man, who has added a Volume of Notes and Supplements, larger than that of the Text, says, in his Remarks on Bk. I, Chap. XVII, that the Difference of Favourable and Odious, which I have rejected after others is founded in the very Nature of things; . . . To this, I answer, first, that not one of those who have rejected the Distinction under Consideration, ever thought of denying that some things are more desirable than others; but the Question is, whether that Quality can be of service here for settling sure Rules of Interpretation. Now I am not convinced that it can." Barbeyrac goes on to specify his reasons for skepticism concerning the relevance of this distinction. The same thing may appear more favorable or odious depending on how it is perceived. The two qualities are often inextricably mixed together. One may interpret laws without applying this distinction.

The differences between Carmichael and Barbeyrac on this subject were fundamental. For Carmichael's understanding of natural law requires one always to consider the spirit or disposition of an action or a positive law: whether it is consistent with reverence for God and for God's creation, with respect for the rights of self and others. Barbeyrac considered Carmichael's concerns on this subject to be beyond the scope of natural jurisprudence. See also *Devoirs,* I.XVII, I, n. 1, where Barbeyrac reminds Carmichael that Pufendorf consistently opposed the human court or forum (the proper sphere of natural law) to the divine forum or tribunal of conscience. This was precisely the dualism that Carmichael sought to overcome.]

The State of Nature[1]

Natural and adventitious states

A state [status] is *a condition of man considered morally,* that is, a condition which involves certain rights and obligations, and which does so not merely with respect to an isolated act or omission but to a whole series of acts. In the previous book and in our notes to it, we outlined all the general sources of rights and obligations. The duties we present in this book are not inconsistent with those, but some of them have a special definition when they arise from the use of some of the sources surveyed to form a particular association or adventitious state. [II.1.1.i]

The *natural* state may be understood by the method of *abstraction* in which it is consistent with all adventitious states, or by the method of *negation* in which it is in some degree distinct from any and every adventitious state. Pufendorf's discussion [of the state of nature] is badly confused by the lack of any such distinction. [II.1.2.i]

This twofold distinction applies to all three aspects of the state of nature enumerated in the last paragraph [i.e., with respect to God, to ourselves, and to other men]. Pufendorf is not correct therefore in employing only the method of *abstraction* in conceiving the natural state with respect to *God,* while he employs only the method of *negation* in considering each man's relationship to *himself* and to *others.* It would be more correct to describe the natural state of man according to the method of abstraction (which can be described in general as a state of *humanity* as opposed to the

---

1. From the notes to bk. II, ch. 1, "On the Natural State of Man."

life and condition of animals) as, in relation to God, a state of *dependence,* by which he is bound to acknowledge and worship him as his author. In relation to *himself* it is a state of normal *self-love,* by which each is bound to look after himself and to seek his own harmless advantage. In relation to *other men* it is a state of *sociability* in which each is bound to cherish the social inclination and a social life with other men.

If on the other hand, we understand the natural state by the method of *negation,* we must exclude from consideration some or perhaps all adventitious states. In this respect man's relation to God in the state of nature is the condition of those whose knowledge of God is confined to natural means. More broadly, it is the condition of those in whom the innate evil of the soul has not been redeemed by divine grace. This is the meaning of the natural state which has been taken up by theologians.[2] And though, so understood, it includes the evil which is adventitious to human nature, this state may be called natural inasmuch as it is with every man from his birth. The state of nature as it applies to man's relationship to himself and to other men according to the method of negation is described by Pufendorf himself [in the following paragraphs].[3] [II.1.3.i]

Titius remarks that the state of *solitude* is quite improperly called *natural,* that in fact such a condition is supernatural inasmuch as God has destined man for sociability. But *natural* is not meant here in the sense in which it coincides with *connatural* and is thus opposed to *supernatural,* but in the sense in which it is contrary to *adventitious,* and in particular excludes any assistance from other men or, extraordinarily, from God, toward a man's development and cultivation.[4] [II.1.4.i]

---

2. In the theology of the Reformed in this era, the state of nature or fallen state followed the state of innocence and was succeeded by the state of grace and the eternal state. See, e.g., Boston, *Human Nature in Its Fourfold State.*

3. The condition of man in the state of nature, deprived of family, household, and civil society, was perceived by Pufendorf as above all a condition of weakness and poverty in the absence of any arrangements for mutual assistance. The condition of man in relation to other men was a condition of independence, with no subjection to a husband, a master, or a ruler, but also none of the benefits or the injuries which those adventitious arrangements provide (Pufendorf, *On the Duty of Man and Citizen,* II.1.4 and 5, pp. 115–16).

4. Titius, *Observationes,* no. 452.

The emergence of the state of nature
from the Adamic state

As long as the children remained in the paternal household [of Adam], even after they had attained the mature use of reason, it is credible to suppose that they agreed, expressly or tacitly, to prolong the father's authority. [II.1.7.i]

[The emergence of the natural state] showed itself by obvious effects. It could not have failed to exist, unless abolished or prevented by some human act, and *state of nature* implies nothing more. It must have come about in the following way. When children were born to our first parents and to the patriarchs who succeeded them, they were incapable of directing their own actions precisely because they were infants. Although they were endowed with the same right of natural liberty as their parents, they were not able immediately to make use of it. As long as their reason remained immature, they needed to be directed by the intelligence and guided by the will of their parents. And when they reached maturity, so long as they remained in the father's house or on his land (or even, from a sense of duty toward him, simply in the neighborhood), they could not have avoided giving him, by express or tacit consent, such government over themselves as at the time it seemed essential to place in someone's hands over everybody, in order to preserve peace and provide security against enemies. Cf. Locke, *Second Treatise of Government,* secs. 73 ff.[5]

But that unity was dissolved when the father died, either because it had depended on a common owner (*dominus*) of lands which were now divided among many, or because it was rooted in some other way in the person of the father. Or, as was more often the case, the unity was dissolved by the sons' leaving the parental home to make new homes for themselves, which they did not choose to subject to another man's government, especially if they were far away. In either case, that was when the natural liberty of the sons began to assert itself, and that is how independent human societies appeared. [II.1.7.ii]

5. Locke's narrative of how it was possible "for the Father of the Family to become the Prince of it" is presented in the *Second Treatise of Government,* ch. 6, "Of Paternal Power," p. 318.

In the following passage [on the "nastiness" and "barbarity" of the state of nature] Pufendorf follows Hobbes, perhaps too boldly; certainly he has been criticized on this account by the distinguished Titius and Barbeyrac. I would not want to make my own criticism of this passage more severe than theirs; much less would I doubt that the condition of citizens under a government that is not utterly evil (for I dare not affirm more) is much preferable to the condition of individual men or even of individual families living in the natural state. But one should not conceal from the reader, as the Hobbesian words which Pufendorf adopts do, that the worst condition of the natural state is being compared with the civil state as it ought to be, rather than with the civil state as we find it all around us in man's present fallen condition.[6] [II.1.9.ii]

6. Titius, *Observationes,* nos. 460, 461; Barbeyrac, in Pufendorf, *Of the Law of Nature and Nations,* II.II.2, nn. 6–16. Francis Hutcheson clearly had all of these references (and more) in mind when he declared that "not only Hobbes but Pufendorf himself has paid a penalty [for his views on the state of nature] at the hands of distinguished men, Titius, Barbeyrac, Cumberland, Carmichael, and above all the most elegant Earl of Shaftesbury" (*Inaugural Lecture,* p. 7).

On the Rights of Husbands and Wives[1]

[The first or most elementary form of social life according to Pufendorf is married life, or the conjugal state. He described it as an adventitious state, since its beginnings depend upon a human act, an agreement or contract between two persons to live together. But the conjugal state is also a natural state, inasmuch as men and women are made by God to live together. And they have been endowed by God with a sexual instinct which makes them naturally inclined to propagate and have children. Thus marriage is the nursery or "seminary" of the human race. It follows that any indulgence of the sexual instinct outside marriage is contrary to natural law. Bestiality and homosexuality are also clearly opposed to the law of nature. Carmichael's discussion proceeds from the last of these observations.]

It is obvious that none of these pollutions have anything whatsoever to do with the procreation of human offspring; they are contrary to the order of nature and are accordingly condemned by natural law. The law of sociability also requires men to temper the natural union of the sexes for the good of human society. For the interest of society is not so much the unlimited growth of human population as the proper mental and physical training of those who are born, so that they may come on to the stage of the world as educated men and women. It follows that the only honorable manner of procreation is one which permits a suitable education and formation for each of the children. To this end, a matrimonial contract may be required, such as the one described below. [II.2.2.i]

Those who would unite their bodies in an appropriate manner are required to enter into *marriage*. By this term we mean the agreement which

---

1. From the notes to bk. II, ch. 2, "On the Duties of Married Life."

we are about to describe, or rather the association which results from that agreement. There is indeed no general consensus on the articles of the *matrimonial agreement* according to the law of nature. And in no other part of natural law do natural duties fall further below Christian morality than in this matter of married life. But perhaps the difference will not seem so wide if we give due weight to the reflection that nature itself requires that the propagation of the human race be undertaken only on terms and conditions which are consistent with the rational and social nature of the parents, and which are likely to ensure that their offspring will be duly trained to observe the natural law. This is the object of the conditions of the matrimonial agreement, as we describe them in this and the following sections. [II.2.4.i]

Whether the contract is initiated by the man or the woman, both are to be regarded as seeking to have their own children. In any case the duty to preserve and raise the children falls on both parents, and that requires the united efforts of both parents, as shown below. [II.2.4.i]

The father must know that the offspring are truly his, if he is to perform his duties as a father with a father's love. And therefore he must be sure that his wife is his and no other's, at least for that period. For this reason, and particularly for the raising of the children they share, those who unite their bodies must form one family and live in the same household from the time of their first coming together, at least as long as there are children to be raised. And just as it is obviously inconsistent with the character of this society that the woman should go with other men, it is no less appropriate that the spouses should maintain their physical relations with each other, especially as the woman is able to give birth to several children before the first comes to an age when he can look after himself. Compare Locke, *Second Treatise of Government,* secs. 78–80.[2]

So far therefore we understand by the very law of nature that there should be in the *matrimonial contract a mutual promise to live together in the same family, and to continue to do so at least as long as the care due to their*

---

2. Locke considered it evidence of Divine Providence that the union of man and wife should be longer lasting than that of other creatures so that families would be more industrious and provide for the future of their offspring.

offspring requires it, and to allow sexual intercourse with each other during that time; there must also be a promise on the part of the woman that she will not give enjoyment of her body to anyone other than her husband. Whether it is also part of a just marriage according to natural law that the man should promise not to have a relationship with any other woman will be discussed in the next section. [II.2.4.iii]

Since spouses coalesce into one family, and so constitute as it were one moral person, it is necessary that this moral person be subject to one direction. This can only happen between two people if the will of one is subject to the will of the other in running the family they share. In the absence of positive laws, this subjection can only be guaranteed by an agreement between the spouses. The natural law seems to have determined no part of this agreement except that authority over the family should be conferred (positive laws and customs apart) on the more prudent spouse. And since the custom of all ages and nations has assigned this prerogative to the man, it would not be appropriate even for those in natural liberty, and however ignorant they might be of the Divine Law (from which the universal custom seems to derive), to consent to a marriage agreement on some different condition. [II.2.4.iv]

Since, as shown above, a woman is restricted, by the character and end of the marital society so long as it lasts, to association with one man, natural equality requires that *the man* too *should be content with the bed of one woman.* This is particularly so since men and women are more or less equal in number, and therefore *simultaneous polygamy,* instead of *monogamy,* does not tend to increase the human race, as experience testifies. On the contrary, it contains a most iniquitous oppression, not only of wives, who are told to be content with just a little bit as it were of the marital partnership, but also of other men, very many of whom are compelled for this reason to do without wives. And it specially implies oppression of the children, since one father's care is not adequate to provide a proper upbringing when there are so many of them. Consequently, such license is almost bound to occasion widespread indifference on the part of fathers, ingratitude on the part of children, and quarrels and adultery on the part of wives. [II.2.5.i]

It is beyond question that the necessity of raising children utterly forbids dissolution of the marital association for trivial everyday reasons. We therefore are to enter this association on the understanding that its duration does not depend upon any discretionary condition, except a condition which would frustrate the chief end of entering it; much less does it depend on the lack of some nonessential condition, so long as there are shared children to be raised.

But what if the bond which springs from the obligation to rear the common children should happen to fail or cease, either because there have been no children, or because the children have died or grown up, and no others have come along nor perhaps are expected? Many wonder whether at that point, where the positive law does not teach otherwise, a marriage may be ended.[3]

It would be too tedious to review separately the variety of cases which arise here, and to argue one by one the reasons which in each case favor the stability of marriage. In general we note that the close union, of hearts no less than of bodies, which is requisite for the purpose of this association, does not allow either that it be entered upon for a time, or that its duration depend on conditions which are beyond human nature to satisfy. The chief purpose, and the one which we should normally assume to be intended, we suppose to be the birth and rearing of children together. But what if sometimes the attainment of this end is not expected, because of the advanced age of one or both of the spouses? Legislators can determine to what extent such marriages, especially those of the former kind, ought to be tolerated in a state; this was the object (to quote an example from the past) of an article of the *Lex Julia et Papia*.[4] But if they are tolerated at all, the dignity of human nature requires that they be vested with the same sanctity that should be brought to more regular unions, as we showed above. Finally, because of the nature of the marital association, it is not easy to preserve it at the will of one of the spouses, when the other is discontented and complaining. In man's present depraved condition one should try to ensure that a marriage is not subject to constant disturbance,

3. Locke, *Second Treatise*, ch. 7, p. 321.
4. The *Lex Julia de maritandis ordinibus* (18 B.C.) and the *Lex Papia Poppaea* (A.D. 9) are both parts of the emperor Augustus's marriage legislation.

that it does not rest on too fragile a foundation. Consequently, it should be protected not only by the usual conditions on which people make agreements with each other, but also by being indissoluble even by the mutual consent of the spouses themselves, or if you prefer, by their dissent. Even if the positive law of God did not supply this sanction, the parties to the agreement should create it for themselves by formally declaring their matrimonial agreement before God in the form of a vow.

From the course of the argument so far, therefore, it is established that *matrimony,* which by the natural law itself is needed for the legitimate propagation of the human race, is a *union of a man and a woman which entails an exclusive habit of life together.* This is the definition given by the Emperor (Justinian, *Institutes,* I.9.1); it is rightly approved by the celebrated Huber in preference to the one which Grotius gives in accordance with his laxer assumptions on this topic.[5] [II.2.6.i]

Our author is right to follow Grotius in deriving from natural law itself the prohibition of marriage between *ascendants* and *descendants* to infinity. The reason is that the love and physical expression of marriage utterly differ from and cannot coexist with the respectful modesty which is required between *parents* and *children* in whatever degree by the nature of this relationship and its resulting duties. This is how I understand the doctrine of Grotius (II.V.12), which our author explains rather than corrects at *Of the Law of Nature and Nations,* VI.I.32. [II.2.8.i]

On the one hand it matters to human society in general that individuals be restrained from promiscuous and illicit intercourse; on the other hand it matters to individual spouses, that each be strengthened by the help of others against the infidelity (should it happen) of their partner. Both ends require that a matrimonial vow be made in the presence of appropriate witnesses. Each citizen is bound to conform to whatever other legal solemnities the civil laws of different places require, particularly those which are necessary to ensure that a marriage is valid in its essential effects in the civil courts. Anyone who neglects these solemnities incurs the disgrace of illicit intercourse. However ceremonies which are

5. Huber, *De Jure Civitatis,* II.II.6; Grotius, *Rights of War and Peace,* II.V.8.

not a matter of command, but pertain only to certain inessential effects, e.g., to the dignity of the spouse or the children, the patrimony and such things, can be performed or omitted at pleasure. Hence what is called *secondary marriage,* which is quite foreign to our customs, is not to be confused with *concubinage.*[6] [II.2.9.i]

6. Pufendorf described secondary marriages at *Of the Law of Nature and Nations,* VI.I.36, as marriages, otherwise legal, between husbands and wives of unequal condition who are not able to claim the same rights for their children as other lawful mothers.

CHAPTER 15

On the Rights of Parents and Children[1]

Since everyone obviously needs the care and protection of others because of the condition in which he enters the world, it is appropriate that the persons who were the authors of his taking his first breath should provide him with the necessities of life. But they should not only supply what is necessary for the preservation of animal life; they should also form the minds and the morals of their children, so that the life they gave them will not be lost nor turn out to be a burden to others and painful and shaming for themselves. This obligation [to our children] flows necessarily from the act of begetting itself, whether or not we assume with Titius that the begetter consented to it.[2] And since this obligation is an indissolubly integral part of parental power, nothing prevents us from saying, with Grotius, that this power too is founded on begetting. Cf. Locke, *Second Treatise of Government*, chapter 6.[3] [II.3.2.i]

[Pufendorf asserted that the right and obligation to bring up a child devolved upon the father in any formal marriage (inasmuch as the marriage contract must be supposed to have been initiated by him and he is normally the head of the

---

1. From the notes to bk. II, ch. 3, "On the Duties of Parents and Children."
2. Titius, *Observationes*, no. 502.
3. Grotius, *Rights of War and Peace*, II.V.1–7, pp. 185–88; Locke, *Second Treatise*, ch. 6, "Of Paternal Power." Locke's emphasis was different from Carmichael's: Locke was concerned to underline (against Filmer) the role of mothers in the generation of children and the continuing authority of mothers in the family (*Second Treatise*, ch. 6, secs. 52, 53). It was also to affirm that no child should be understood to be the creation of his parents; children are the workmanship of God alone (sec. 55, and *First Treatise*, ch. 6, secs. 52–54).

household), but on the mother if the child was born out of wedlock. Carmichael stresses the right and the obligation of the father to share in the raising of the children in all possible circumstances.]

Even outside a regular marriage, agreements may settle this question, as often happens in concubinage (cf. *Of the Law of Nature and Nations,* VI.II.5). In fact even without an agreement, if the father is somehow known, there is no reason why we should not say that the parental right and obligation is shared between the parents. We may ignore the nonsense of Hobbes about the origin of the mother's right in occupation:[4] even if a human life were a suitable object of ownership (the contrary of which will appear below),[5] it should still be noted that it would be a case of the accession of an object belonging to someone else. [II.3.3.i]

Apart from the civil law, however, the positive law of God awards a prerogative power to the man in matrimony and a particular right over legitimate offspring. [II.3.3.ii]

Because husbands are the heads of their families, civil societies are usually constituted by such heads of families not *vice versa.* The prerogatives of husbands are therefore older than civil societies. [II.3.3.iii]

[Pufendorf says that when the father dies, the right over a child (not yet adult) goes to the mother. Carmichael comments:]

This must be understood [only] of the *parental right,* strictly so called, because its aim is the rearing of the children. It is not to be understood of the right which belongs in the natural state to the head of a separate family as such, and which passes to his heir with the ownership of the land, nor of the right which was granted specially to the father by the civil laws of several peoples, particularly the Romans, and which dies with the father. [from II.3.3.iv]

[Pufendorf distinguished between the power which the father has as such, and his power as head of the family, and between the power of the father in families

---

4. Hobbes, *On the Citizen,* 9.2–3, pp. 108–9; cf. *Leviathan* (1946), ch. 20, pp. 130–31.
    5. See below, pp. 139–40.

living apart and the power of fathers of families in civil society. Carmichael observes that:]

> . . . the power of the *father* as *such* is the same [whether he is considered as the begetter of the child or as the father of a family]. But the power of the father as *head of his family* takes different forms, depending on whether the family is *separate from* or *subject to a civil power*. [from II.3.4.i]

Grotius (II.V.2 ff.) distinguishes three periods in a child's life: first when his judgment is unformed; second, when the judgment is formed but the son remains part of the family of the parents; third, after he has left the family.[6] [I.3.5.i]

The division of paternal power [into the power of the father as such and the power of the father as head of the family] belongs in a very particular manner to the second period [distinguished by Grotius]. For the power of the father *as head of the family* is not at all relevant to the third period, and while the first period lasts, it is absorbed in the properly parental power. [II.3.6.i]

The power of the father *as begetter* in the second period is nothing other than that parental *authority*, in the etymological sense of the Latin word, as the "author" of their being, which children are bound to acknowledge and revere to the very last breath of life. And in truth the *power* of the parent, properly so called, which affects grown-up sons who still remain in the family, and which is accordingly characteristic of the second period rather than the third, is posterior to the power which belongs to the parent as *head of his family*. [II.3.6.ii]

This is not the place to determine what the emperor Justinian meant by his statement (*Institutes*, I.9.2) that *the right of authority which the Romans had over their children was a right peculiar to Roman citizens*[7] or whether this statement was in fact true. But we may see in what sense it could be true *de jure*, if we note two points. First, since children are subject to government and the civil law only through the mediation of their parents, the power granted by law to the father over his children cannot be

---

6. Grotius, *Rights of War and Peace*, II.V.2.

7. *Patria potestas* is said at Justinian, *Institutes*, I.9.2, to be "a right peculiar to Roman citizens."

greater than the power given him by nature. Second, a father of a separate family can rightly demand that neither grown-up children nor anyone else should remain in his family, or even on his territory, unless they are willing to recognize his government (*imperium*). Accordingly, in a larger state the supreme ruler (*summus imperans*) who has the power to appoint lesser magistrates could grant to fathers of families a subordinate civil government (*civile imperium*) over their own grown-up children and members of their household. This government, which was very broad among the Romans, was gradually weakened subsequently and has finally been abolished by more modern sentiment. Today, the father is left with only a modest coercion, enough to preserve proper order in the family, its ultimate recourse being expulsion from the family if the need should arise. [II.3.7.i]

Filial obligation should be the more sacred and extensive, the more the father has shown diligence and affection in caring for his children. A parent who has played no more than a minimal part in bringing up his children seems to have done his duty badly. [II.3.8.i]

A parent may not transfer to someone else any right to profit from the property or labor of a child, beyond what is rightfully due to the parent himself; the limits of this have been explained at pp. 115–16. The father should see to it that the purchaser [of his son's property or labor] has no excuse for stretching his right beyond the modest limits which I describe there. In this connection, the parent should ask less from the purchaser than what the child owes him for his past maintenance, since the child's life and health are uncertain. And perhaps the father should require nothing at all, if the son is far removed from the age at which he can earn his daily bread by daily labor. But more on this matter in the next chapter. [II.3.9.i]

CHAPTER 16

On the Rights of Masters and Servants[1]

It is quite likely that the earliest servitude (*servitus*) arose from voluntary contracts.[2] But whether, in the beginning, slaves or servants (*servi*)[3] bound themselves in perpetuity or for a limited period, it is not possible to determine, and it makes no difference to know. [II.4.1.i]

Among most Europeans today, slavery has been abolished. And it has been the universal practice of Christians, when war has arisen among them, not to make slaves of their prisoners in a way that would allow them to be sold and forced to work and made to endure the other sufferings of slaves, as Grotius points out at III.VII (*final paragraph*). [II.4.1.iii]

[Pufendorf observed that there are different degrees of servitude, and that the power of the master and the condition of the slave or servant varies accordingly. Carmichael concurs with the judgment that the first of these kinds of servant, the wage earner hired for a specific length of time, cannot be subjected to grievous bodily harm, much less death, by the master, and investigates the reasons why.]

Why not [subject a hired servant to severe punishment] also when he disturbs the decency and quiet of the family? The right permitted a master to punish a slave or servant, whether in an independent household, or in one which is subject to the civil power, can be judged from what we have said above (pp. 136–37) about the authority of *the head of the family*. But

1. From the notes to bk. II, ch. 4, "On the Duties of Masters and Slaves."
2. As Pufendorf argued at *Of the Law of Nature and Nations,* VI.III.4; and *On the Duty of Man and Citizen,* II.4, pp. 129–31.
3. Carmichael, like Pufendorf, uses the term *servi* to cover "servants," "serfs," and "slaves."

sensible masters and mistresses of households will use corporal punishment very sparingly, especially on adults hired for a limited time, particularly if they are of a different sex. For if their behavior displeases, a milder remedy will soon be available in the form of dismissal from the family after the agreed term has expired. [II.4.2.i]

[Commenting on Pufendorf's second category, the servant "bound . . . of his own free will for perpetual servitude," Carmichael says:]

Titius rightly observes that the association between master and servant includes the same rights and the same obligations, whether it is forever or for a limited time, except that in the one case the rights are temporary, in the other perpetual.[4] [II.4.3.i]

A servant who is hired for a limited time or in perpetuity may bind himself either to services of a particular kind or to perform whatever services the master imposes upon him, provided these are just and licit. [II.4.3.ii]

[On Pufendorf's third category, "slaves captured in war":]

In nothing have the nations so strayed from the law of sociability than in their assessment of the right of *war* with regard to the introduction of *slavery.* It makes one wonder that the human race should so forget its worth, and willingly conspire to bring upon itself endless outrageous indignities, abuses, and afflictions. It will be readily agreed, to be sure, from the principles laid down above, that *anyone who cannot repay a debt* incurred by contract or by committing an offense or for any reason whatsoever, *is obliged by the law of nature to offer his services to his creditor or victim.* And *anyone who has inflicted an atrocious offense,* such as one who has violently attacked the life and fortune of another in a war conducted without even probable cause, *can find himself rightly reduced to servile status as punishment less severe than another which might be inflicted.*

Nonetheless, (1) capture in war confers no right upon the captor where there was no antecedent right; therefore anyone who makes war unjustly has no right to enslave anyone. (2) Physical punishment can only be in-

---

4. Titius, *Observationes,* nos. 529–30.

flicted on men who have committed violent offenses; therefore, he who is waging even a just war cannot impose slavery as a punishment on those who have contributed nothing either by assistance or advice, to an unjust war waged by another party. (3) Even those who wage just wars must set limits on their demands; nor can anyone make claims beyond the limits which we specified at pp. 69–71. (4) Whatever may be due from the prince and people whose citizens have been captured in a just war, it is not clear that an ordinary citizen who has enjoyed no advantage from the war and has not involved himself in it by his own volition should be bound to suffer personal enslavement. (5) If a man should be enslaved as a punishment or because the rights of another require it, this does not mean that he has fallen from the class of person into the class of things. There is to be sure a common right to punish criminals; see pp. 69–71. But a man is never to be considered among the goods of his creditor, whatever thing or service he may owe him or a criminal may owe society. For men are not among the objects over which God has allowed the human race to enjoy dominion. Indeed it seems absurd (to make a small change in the words of Justinian)[5] that *man should be classed among things, since nature has supplied all things for the sake of man.* [II.4.4.i]

Even if the victor may rightfully require servile services from the vanquished (which it will be agreed from what has just been said, is very rarely the case), still no one readily allows that the cause he was defending was unjust, much less that he is obliged to suffer punishment when he can avoid it. And therefore, if the captor wishes to enjoy securely the services of the captive, it is up to him to guarantee his life and safety, while stipulating in return obedience and faithful service; which being done, hostility ceases. And the agreement should be made by explicit provisions. But I do not deny that if the captor spares the captive's life and holds him without bonds or imprisonment, this fact seems to form a tacit agreement which prevents the former from killing the latter without fresh cause and which

5. Justinian, *Institutes,* II.1.37. Carmichael substitutes "things" for Justinian's word "fruit," thus converting a point about usufruct into a general statement against the ownership of human beings.

prevents the latter from using this opportunity to launch hostilities. [II.4.4.ii]

We have shown above that the bodies of slaves cannot be considered as merchandise. But this does not prevent the transfer of the right to require the services of the slave, which have their origin in the causes described above, to another person at the discretion of the creditor. For the right to the service of a slave is an alienable right, and the agreement which fixes the relationship does not permit any other interpretation. And he who subjects himself and his property to a victor, so far as he may, in order to avoid the death penalty, is understood to have made whatever agreement he could make, and thus he must be supposed to have transferred the alienable right [to his services] to the victor [in a just war].

But no one who has wrongfully taken someone into slavery or holds him in that condition has any title to transfer to another person any right which would be valid against the captive or prisoner. Even good faith cannot be pleaded in this case. For benefit of the doubt does not apply to possession by force; and good faith cannot transfer the burden of proof of a right from a violent possessor to a claimant from whom the thing was taken by force. Above all if the claimant can prove, against any possessor at all, that the object he claims once was his, this is enough to compel the possessor to show that the thing had been subsequently alienated or abandoned by the claimant or lost in some legal way. Everyone is naturally the owner of his own liberty or of the right of determining his own actions; and therefore no one can in good faith claim that this right has passed to him, unless he can show that it has passed out of the hands of its natural subject, and further unless he can prove that it has been transferred to him. For freedom is not open to occupation. In fact the right against any man's liberty which may belong to another man, is not an *owner's* right properly so called, but a *creditor's* right, as we have shown above at pp. 139–40.

I know that however consistent these principles may be with both *civil* and *natural* law, this did not prevent the *Romans* (apart from a few privileges in favor of liberty), as well as all the barbarian nations, from going astray from the truth on this point. They all cherished the prejudice so deeply ingrained in most people today, as well as in former times, that *in*

war the occupying power acquires ownership indiscriminately over the persons
and property of the enemy and of anyone subject to his rule. How alien this is
to reason and how contrary to natural law may be observed from the preceding paragraph and is made particularly clear in the celebrated Locke's
Second Treatise of Government, chapter 16.[6] I do not deny that the *external*
right, to use Grotius's phrase, which arises from the consent of nations,
has some validity in respect to things captured in war and transferred to
another who is not an enemy (see the notes at pp. 204–5). But this [exter-
nal right] cannot deprive innocent citizens of their *personal liberty,* since
the right of the state over its citizens does not extend so far. Nor can this
external right apply in any way satisfactory to conscience, in cases that admit of *recovery of civil rights* (which the laws of all nations allow to free men
taken captive in war). It cannot take from the original proprietor the capacity to recover his rights; at most it may prevent him from obtaining
restitution in a certain place, or rather beyond the limits of a certain place.
[II.4.5.i]

Justinian has rightly taught us (*Institutes,* II.1.37) that it *seems absurd*
that man should be classed among products since nature has supplied all prod-
ucts for the use of man.[7] But if, for this reason, as the emperor intended, the
offspring of a slave girl does not belong to the *usufruct,* it is also obvious
that it cannot belong to the owner of the property as a product of something he owns; at pp. 139–40 we used the same argument as Justinian to
show that a man cannot be in the *ownership* strictly, so called, of another

---

6. Although Carmichael cites Locke in support of his denunciation of slavery, the
gravamen of his critique is different from Locke's. Locke thought that conquerors had
a right to enslave enemies captured in a just war; he was concerned to deny to conquerors the right to occupy the property of these men; their property might be needed
to preserve the wife, children, and servants of the conquered man (Locke, *Second*
Treatise, ch. 16, secs. 178 ff.). Carmichael's primary concern was not deprivation of the
land or property; it was the loss of personal liberty. See also Hutcheson, *Philosophia*
Moralis (1745), III.3, p. 282, who urged his students to consult both Carmichael and
Locke on the subject of slavery. The translator of Hutcheson's work has misplaced
both the note and the reference to Locke in *A Short Introduction to Moral Philosophy,*
p. 275n.
7. Here Carmichael quotes this passage verbatim; see n. 5, above.

man. I add that since the soul, the nobler part of man, is not derived from the parents, it is fitting that it should draw the more ignoble part to itself. [II.4.6.i]

It is obvious from what we have said so far that the only pretext which remains for hereditary slavery is that the slave who is born in his master's house is indebted to the master to the amount of the expense incurred in feeding and raising him. I remarked above (pp. 115–16) that the child too is indebted to his parents by whom he is nourished. But there is a difference: it is abhorrent to the natural affections and duties of parents to require payment of this debt from their children, at least when they have no external source of income, unless the parents suffer from extreme poverty, in which case it would be ungrateful for the children not to help them. Nothing prevents masters, however, from requiring compensation from their born slaves, and since born slaves are assumed to be incapable of repayment otherwise than by offering their services, they are obliged to offer the master their services up to the value of what it cost to rear them, in accordance with the doctrine expounded above (see pp. 139–40). It does not follow, however, that born slaves owe a perpetual debt for their upbringing, since a man endowed with even mediocre gifts of mind and body can pay off this debt in a much shorter time than the span of his whole life.

It follows from these principles that if a third party wants to take and raise a born slave from birth, or decides later to pay off the slave's debt to his owner in order to improve the slave's condition or to enable him as an adult to seek his own transfer, then the owner of the mother of the slave can require nothing more. It also follows that anything that comes to the slave from elsewhere, accrues to the slave himself and not to the owner of his mother, and thus may be used for his liberation. In a word, it follows from these principles that the condition of the born slave should be no worse than that of a Roman citizen who had been bought back from the enemy and held as a pledge until the price was paid (see *Codex*, VIII. 51).[8]

And the slave's debt should not be increased on the ground that the

8. Justinian, *Codex*, VIII.50 (51).2, p. 360.

master did not know whether the slave would survive or be able to pay back the amount of his expenses, as if the uncertainty of the situation should be compensated by the amount of profit to be made through the slave. For to every man coming into the world *necessity* gives a right to what he needs for his preservation and for forming him to be a useful member of human society. Furthermore in claiming for himself the labors by which the parent would otherwise be able to look after himself and his offspring, the master owes maintenance, to the child no less than to the parent, under the burden of repayment, if the slave can ever repay it; but if not, without it. We must make the same point here as in other cases in which the necessities of life are allowed to those who suffer from extreme poverty. For this reason, everyone allows that by strict right repayment should be made whenever it can be; but no one in his right mind would say that in this case a profit was due because of the high risk involved, as if it were a *nautical loan.* Finally, it is not correct to cite human laws in support of this obligation; for before men can do anything themselves, they are subject to the civil laws only through the mediation of parents or guardians, and until they consent to them themselves, these laws cannot make the power of parents or guardians greater than nature herself has made it.[9]

I have treated the matter of these last three sections at some length because this usurped right of *owning* slaves like cattle, as it existed among the ancients, is exercised today by men who profess to be Christians, to the great shame of that holy name, with greater tyranny perhaps than it was by the ancient pagans. It is not practiced to be sure *by Christians among*

---

9. Carmichael's forceful denunciation of slavery on grounds of natural law may be contrasted with Barbeyrac's position on this matter. In notes added to the fifth edition of Pufendorf, *Of the Law of Nature and Nations* (1734), VI.III.9, nn. 1–4 (English translation 1749, p. 617), Barbeyrac invoked the authority of Grotius and of Pufendorf to defend the rights of masters in opposition to Carmichael's reasoning. Barbeyrac found nothing absurd in considering persons as property; he considered it just that children born of a slave mother should remain the property of the owner; he thought it very unlikely that a slave would ever be able to discharge the debt owed to his master for his upbringing or that a third party might secure the release of the slave. As for Carmichael's argument that the soul, the nobler part of man, is not derived from the parents but from God, Barbeyrac remarks, "I own I cannot see the Force of this Argument, or, if it has any, it is very remote from the Subject."

themselves nor do we find it *in most parts of Europe,* but we do find it in other parts of the world. I am deeply convinced that its existence, to use the apt expression of Titius, is *a sure sign of the death of sociability.*[10]

If anyone objects that this right is assumed in various precepts of the Mosaic Law, let him consider whether the same thing should not be said about this (and about the precepts that assume polygamy for that matter), as was said about the law which permitted divorce in the external court: i.e., *that the Hebrews were allowed these things for the hardness of their hearts,*[11] especially since one of the precepts [of the Mosaic Law] provides for external permission for divorce (*Exodus* 21.3–4). I may add that one right was permitted to the Hebrews over Hebrew slaves, and a different one (as a punishment, it seems) over foreign idolaters, at least in the external court; but nowadays that fraternity which the Hebrews were encouraged by the letter of the Mosaic Law to foster among themselves, has been extended to all men by the dictates of natural law and by the teachings of the Gospel. Cf. *Leviticus* 19.18 and *Luke* 10.36–7. [II.4.6.iii]

---

10. Titius, *Observationes,* no. 535.
11. Matthew 19.8; Mark 10.5.

On the Origin of Civil Society,
or the Original Contract[1]

I do not know why the distinguished jurists Titius and Barbeyrac reject
the fundamental cause of the *origin of civil society* given by Pufendorf;[2] certainly they put nothing equally probable in its place.[3] I do not doubt that
crafty and ambitious men used their arts to promote the institution of new
societies, no doubt promising themselves leading places in it. But I ask
what arts they could have used, and with what success, if they were not
able to give reasons for their schemes which seemed persuasive to the people? In fact nothing can be more probable than what has been advanced
by Pufendorf on this subject. Let those who talk of *force* as the origin of

---

1. From the notes to bk. II, ch. 5, "On the Impulsive Cause of Constituting Civil
Society"; and bk II, ch. 6, "On the Internal Structure of Civil Societies."

2. ". . . the true and principal cause why heads of households abandoned their natural liberty and had recourse to the constitution of states was to build protection around
themselves against the evils that threaten from man to man" (Pufendorf, *On the Duty
of Man and Citizen*, II.5.7, pp. 133–34). The heads of households achieved this by
making a series of agreements with each other (ibid., II.6.5–9, pp. 136–37).

3. Titius (*Observationes*, nos. 547 and 555) and Barbeyrac (Pufendorf, *On the Law
of Nature and Nations*, VII.I.6, n. 1) disputed Pufendorf's account of the origin of civil
societies. They opined that the earliest societies were not established by covenant or
by general agreement; that they first "plainly owe their rise to the Cunning and Management of some ambitious Mind, supported by force" (Barbeyrac, ibid. [1729],
VII.II.8, n. 2). In this light, the first and second of the three contracts which Pufendorf
found at the origin of societies were of little importance; it was the third contract
between sovereign and subjects which properly constituted a state. Carmichael's defense of the original contract in this chapter was in large part a response to this revi-
sionist position.

society consider whether they are not assuming the existence of the very thing whose origins they are seeking, namely a *civil society,* and one, at that, *which is strong enough to conquer its neighbors and bring them into subjection.* This is an error which they should be particularly careful to avoid as they have accused our author of committing it. And surely it is easier to conceive that before societies had been formed at all, men might be constantly harassed by troublesome neighbors, beaten, robbed of their property, and thus compelled to form civil societies as the most certain refuge against these evils, than to suppose that a permanent yoke could be imposed upon them against the will of most of them. What the distinguished commentators find incredible and without foundation in history—that in the beginning a great crowd of men assembled together, promptly debated the evils of their condition and the most effective means of escape, and finally came to a unanimous decision that *they must make a civil society,* of whose character and regular shape they already had a perfectly clear idea— none of this is required by Pufendorf's doctrine. He never dreamt that those first specimens of civil society would be complete and finished in every respect, with a full complement of citizens, a regular form, and appropriate laws. See Locke, *Second Treatise of Government,* chapter 9. [II.5.7.i]

The process of agreement

In order to establish a *civil society* and institute a *civil government,* it is abundantly clear from the principles set out above that the consent of the citizens is required. But it is legitimate to doubt whether this consent must always be given in the order described.[4] And the author himself did not wish to insist on it. If one would establish a complete *civil society* (*civitas*) in a way which provides some guarantee that it will last, I admit that it can only be constituted by a *double obligation,* one, of *the citizens with one another,* the other *a mutual obligation of the ruler and his subjects.* And these

---

4. The process is described by Pufendorf at *On the Duty of Man and Citizen,* II.6.7– 9: first an agreement to become fellow-citizens, then a decision or decree on the form of government, and thirdly an agreement between the citizens and the government.

obligations are in this case independent of each other. The *first agreement* (*pactum*) described above is particularly relevant to producing the first obligation; the *second* produces the second obligation (but presupposes an *intermediate decree,* when preceded by a bare first agreement). I therefore acknowledge that no such civil society can be instituted without some action which would have the force and the efficacy of *the three acts* just mentioned.

But this can be done in two ways: either quite explicitly, by three successive actions in the order described by the author; or, more summarily, by one act which has the force of all the actions described above in generating the two obligations. In the former case it is evident that each of the agreements produces its own obligation and does so permanently. Thus the distinguished commentators whom we have so often cited, have little reason to say that the first agreement is to the second merely as a temporary platform or scaffolding is to the construction of a building.[5] The author puts it much better when he attributes to the permanent efficacy of the first agreement the fact that when the king dies in an elective monarchy, or the royal family becomes extinct in a hereditary monarchy, the subjects remain bound by the civil bond which obliges them to manage the arrangements for their own safety and security with their own collective wisdom and initiative. But it is also possible, as we have said, that both obligations can be formed by one agreement,[6] and that a complete civil society can be instituted in this way. The author concedes to be sure in his work *Of the Law of Nature and Nations,* VII.II.8, that in a popular republic the second agreement is not so evident; but he argues that even here the second agreement needs to be fully acknowledged as the basis of the obligation by which individual citizens are bound not only to obey the orders and regulations which issue from the collective assembly (though this might have been inferred from the first agreement), but they are also bound (by the second agreement) to preserve the republic to the best of their abilities. But why should it not be equally the case that individuals

5. See below, n. 7.

6. Carmichael normally uses the word *pactum* for any kind of "agreement" (see pp. 77–80); at pp. 107–8 he also indicates that he will not make a distinction between *pactum* and *contractus* ("contract").

enter into an agreement with one another in founding a republic in such a way that each subjects his will to the will of all and each also undertakes to hold public office when required? In this way a complete *democracy* might be formed by a single contract, or at least by a contract of a single kind.

Moreover Pufendorf himself recognizes in the passage cited above that a *monarchy* can be instituted without any prior agreement among the citizens themselves by means of a single agreement, that is, by an agreement made between the monarch and his future subjects. Yet in order to establish by this means a civil society which will have a long duration, the prince should be considered as requiring from each individual subject for the sake of the new state not only allegiance to himself as ruler but also allegiance to his fellow subjects and to the whole state (*civitas*) so that it may serve the ends of civil society (*civilis societas*). In this case the single contract which the ruler enters into with his subjects has the force of both the first and the second agreements described by Pufendorf. This corresponds to the procedure, recognized by everyone, whereby in a state already established, new citizens are admitted by just such a single agreement made with the sovereign, tacitly or expressly, which obliges the newcomer not only to the sovereign but to the whole state and to each of his fellow citizens.

A complete civil society (*civitas perfecta*) can therefore be instituted in either of these two ways: by means of two agreements with an intermediate decree which could also be included in the first agreement, or by means of a single agreement. In the former case the citizens are obligated, first as individuals to each other, then all together as a body to the sovereign; in the latter case individuals are obligated to the sovereign at the same time as they are obligated to each other. Some version of the former may seem most natural, at least when it is a government of one or of a few which is being instituted. For just as government can scarcely be conferred by separate individuals upon a few men, unless those few men are united with each other by a previous agreement, so it is not easy to understand how government is conferred by separate individuals upon one man, unless he already has or is on the point of having a suitable number of subjects. If he is said already to have subjects, the state is assumed to be already instituted, but our inquiry is precisely about its earliest institution. If on the other hand he is supposed to be merely on the point of having subjects, we shall get a more accurate view if we ask what factors his expectation could be based on and what those factors should be thought to have contributed to the acquisition of civil government.

First, inasmuch as the regular and peaceful condition even of a simple *family* requires that those who live in it do not settle their differences by force when a dispute arises among themselves, and do not defend their rights individually when disputes arise with outsiders, it follows that anyone who enters a domestic society (even though he enters that society not so much to protect his rights as to satisfy his needs) seems to allow to the head of the household something akin to *civil government* to be exercised over himself and on his behalf. Further, since one household is incapable of defending itself against outside forces, and since a head of a household does not seem to be intending to share his right with others simply by admitting them to his family, newcomers are understood to be agreeing, so long as they remain in the family, to subject themselves to the civil government to which the head of the household chooses to subject himself and his property. Much more so when a household is already subject to a civil government, anyone who enters such a family or remains in it as an adult, is understood to subject himself by his own consent to the same government. In their turn, in all these cases, they stipulate for protection from the government to which they have subjected themselves.

Second, such ownership of things as derives from the original modes of acquisition includes the power to dispose of them as one pleases, provided they serve the uses for which God has granted them to men. Thus anyone who acquires full and unimpaired *ownership of land* (*dominium soli*) can rightly require that no one may live on that land unless he is willing to recognize its ownership as his own sovereign civil government. Further, any landowner may transfer this right, which is called *government of land* (*imperium soli*), to someone else, while retaining ownership in other respects. When such a transfer has been made, neither the owner nor anyone else can rightly live on that land or possess it without conducting himself as a subject of that other person. And someone who is an owner with full

right can transfer the *vulgar ownership,* as they call it, to others while retaining the government to himself.

Hence we may see how provision is made for the strength of societies
and the duration of civil governments notwithstanding the natural liberty
of individual men. For the use of the land to which men are connected by
different sorts of obligations is closely related to the ties of civil obligation.
And anyone who is born in a land and remains there as an adult, and anyone who comes to live in a land, excepting those who come declaring war,
must be understood to have given their tacit consent to that obligation.

Thus we may understand very easily how even before larger societies
were formed for common defense, one head of household could stand out
among his neighbors, because of the *number of his dependents* and the *extent of his estates,* and seem to be marked as the most suitable leader and
sovereign to submit to, and to entrust their own safety and the security of
their goods to him, provided he was not deficient in a sense of justice, and
particularly if he possessed superior endowments of mind and body. It is
unlikely, to be sure, that all these qualities, so far as they could be found
in this dispersed condition of mankind, would be sufficient to persuade
any head of a household to submit to another before provision was made
by agreement that other heads of households who might also enjoy the
benefits of entering civil society would do likewise. Therefore it does not
seem far from the truth that *in laying the first foundations of civil societies,
an appropriate number of heads of households first bound themselves together
and then jointly conferred the government on the one whom they wished to
adopt as their sovereign.* Thus the earliest specimens of monarchical government may be said to have been produced by two contracts rather than just
one. But the decree whose purpose was to determine not only the form of
government but also the person of the ruler could easily have been included in the first agreement.

I cannot then conceal my astonishment that those distinguished men,
Titius and Barbeyrac, should have described such a formation of the original civil societies as a myth, even though they generously allow that new
civil societies can be and indeed must be established in the manner described by our author. I am certainly unable to discover any difference be-

tween the first and subsequent civil societies in this respect, except perhaps that it seems more credible to apply what the eminent men say about *force* to the formation of any state other than the first. The appeal to the evidence of history in this case is beside the point, since the first examples we read of, of the use of that kind of force, presuppose large multitudes of men already united under civil government.

However this may be, the conclusion is clear. *Mutual obligations between citizens themselves or between a sovereign and his subjects can only be founded in consent, given expressly or tacitly, directly or indirectly, in one or in several stages.* And consequently, those who set about to prove from the records of history that a *legitimate* civil government can be established without the consent of the citizens are playing a silly game and setting themselves up for deserved ridicule. For in every example which can be adduced, they must either allow that this consent must have been given in some manner, although perhaps not noticed by historians, or they must acknowledge that the government was unjustly usurped. Unless they advance some other legitimate title in which civil government may be founded! And this they will never be able to do.[7] For it is clear from what has been said above that neither the *power of the father* (*patria potestas*) nor *seizure in war* can provide such a title. One must be careful then to keep in mind the distinction between civil government (*imperium civile*) properly so called, which is government over men, and *government of land or territory* (*imperium soli*), which, as we said above, naturally inheres in land ownership and can be transferred by consent of the owner. On this whole

7. Barbeyrac himself was finally persuaded to abandon his objections to the original contract as Pufendorf had outlined it. In the fifth edition of Pufendorf, *Of the Law of Nature and Nations* (1734), he acknowledged that whatever difficulties the original contract might present for historians, one might suppose that something like the three agreements had "expressly and successively" occurred in order to ensure that civil societies continue to exist during an interregnum, or when the succession in a monarchy is uncertain. He concluded: "I therefore freely retract ("j'abandonne de bon coeur") what I said, after Mr. Titius (*Observationes,* no. 555) in the preceding Editions, that this Convention is only, with regard to the second, what Scaffolding is with respect to the building, for whose Construction it was erected." He refers the reader to Carmichael's notes on this chapter and to the annotations of Everard Otto (of Utrecht), who followed Carmichael very closely in his own commentary on Pufendorf's *De Officio Hominis et Civis* (1728), p. 3, *passim,* and on the original contract, pp. 342 ff.

argument see Locke, *Second Treatise of Government,* chapter 8, and Grotius, *On the Rights of War and Peace,* I.III. [II.6.9.i]

[Pufendorf defined a civil society or state (*civitas*) as a "compound moral person" whose will is constituted by a union of wills (in the tripartite original contract outlined above), and this will must be considered the will of all. Accordingly, it may employ the powers and capacities of all its subjects to secure peace and security (II.6.10; cf. Pufendorf, *Of the Law of Nature and Nations,* VII.II.13, n. 1, p. 641). Carmichael comments:]

The illustrious Titius makes an unwarranted criticism of this definition on the grounds that it confuses *civil society with the sovereign ruler.*[8] But it is certain that the will of the sovereign is itself the will of the civil society when the sovereign acts within the limits of the power granted to him on matters consistent with the ends of civil government. In fact the will of a civil society as a source of public actions expresses itself through the sovereign. Thus it is not surprising that [Pufendorf] attributes to the will of society what the illustrious Titius allows to be true of the will of the sovereign. A civil society therefore, may be defined, more briefly and no less aptly, as *an appropriate number of men, joined in a union of their wills and resources under one supreme ruler, for their mutual protection and security.* [II.6.10.i]

[The will of the sovereign power may be exercised by one man or by an assembly, depending on the institution in which sovereign power has been invested (by the original contract). Thus Pufendorf observed that, where sovereignty is invested in a council or assembly, the will of a society is determined by a majority of the members of that assembly. And when the votes of those members are equally divided then nothing is done. Carmichael elaborates upon these procedures:]

When the question is simply whether something should be done or not done, and the votes are equally divided, then the negative opinion prevails, at least for the time being. Such a determination does not have the force of a decree, however, and would not prevent the same question from being deliberated in the same council anew and decisively. Similarly, in judg-

8. Titius, *Observationes,* no. 557.

ments [made in courts of law] it is normally accepted that the defendant
has been acquitted when the votes of the judges are split equally. Once
acquitted he may henceforth oppose a claim of *judgment given* against the
same action or accusation. From these considerations it may be understood why, when one question is included in another, and both questions
propose something positive, then the lesser proposal prevails, when the
votes are equally divided (see Justinian, *Digest,* XLIV.1.38). But in most
courts and assemblies in our country, an equality of votes is avoided in the
accepted manner, by allowing the president to cast a deciding vote, when
the votes are split equally. [II.6.12.i]

[If there are several proposals before an assembly, that proposal will prevail which has a plurality of votes] despite the fact that it may have fewer
votes than the rest taken together. But Grotius rightly advises that when
part of a proposal is contained in another, different opinions should be
taken together in those parts on which they agree (II.V.19). Moreover,
when none of the opinions is contained in another, one may take the precaution of resolving a question which consists of several parts into several
two-part questions, so that no decision which is not agreeable to the majority may be regarded as a decree of the assembly. [II.6.12.ii]

[Pufendorf had observed (1) that the supreme ruler of a society may be called
a monarch, a senate, or a free people; (2) that the rest are called subjects or citizens; and (3) that citizens may be either native or naturalized. Carmichael's comments on these terms are as follows:]

1. There are various honorary appellations and epithets by which these
[holders of sovereign power] can be distinguished. Insofar as they denote
a supreme and independent ruler any one of them may be assumed, without detriment to the right of the civil society. Nor can anyone rightly argue
about the use of these terms so understood. But insofar as a certain order
is supposed among princes and people, or different degrees of dignity are
indicated by those terms, they can only be derived from the consent, express or tacit, of the citizens. It is absurd that any one man, whether Pope
or Emperor, should claim the power to confer or refuse these titles, even
when this has an adverse effect on those who do not depend on him.
[II.6.13.i]

2. In a monarchy, all men except the monarch are subjects. In other states, individuals taken separately are subjects. Even those who have the right of voting in a supreme council are subjects, including even the president of such a council, who thus holds the highest office in such a republic. [II.6.13.ii]

3. The distinction [between native and naturalized citizens] is not of great importance, especially in a state of long standing, as Titius rightly observes.[9] But it is still more to the point to remark that it is not everywhere that all fathers of families who have settled their fortunes in a state are regarded as citizens, properly so called. Other conditions may be required before a man enjoys the rights of the original citizens. So that men who have fixed their residence in a state and have even been born there are still considered *aliens*. [II.6.13.iii]

Nature herself requires us to ascribe to God the *authorship of civil government* for three reasons: (1) Inasmuch as God has granted to man those natural rights whose transfer in part to a ruler constitutes civil government. (2) God has instructed men by the nature of things interpreted by the dictates of right reason that it is a necessary condition of the dignity, peace, and security of the human race when grown to a multitude, that, by the circumscription of their liberty in some respects, they should gather together into states and submit themselves to civil governments. And he has enjoined civil government by the law of nature itself as a mean to these ends. (3) Finally, by the same law, God has defined the obligations which follow from the establishment of civil government among men, and has commanded that faith be religiously observed, especially with respect to the mutual duties of rulers and subjects. For the safety and security of human society depends particularly on these duties. In these three respects, I say, civil government is rightly ascribed to the authorship of God, even while it is constituted directly by men. As has been declared by two of the apostles, government is "the ordinance of God" (Epistle to the Romans 13.2), and it is also a "human creation" (I Peter 2.13).[10] Some may prefer to say with Titius that God is the immediate *efficient* cause of sovereign

9. Ibid., no. 564.
10. Carmichael gives both quotations in Greek.

power, and that the agreement is its *sine qua non* or *occasion*.[11] It comes to the same thing. For the efficacy of the law's commands, which we have referred to in the third point made above [in this note], is attributed to God by the illustrious commentator's own admission with regard to *government* in the same way as to any other *moral entity*. Indeed every right and every obligation, whether derived from an agreement, or from human law, or from any other source, should be resolved ultimately into a command of the *divine law*, as we have already observed above at p. 28.

Some object unskillfully that sovereign power cannot be constituted by agreements in the same way as other rights, because *one cannot grant to another what one does not have oneself*. And neither individual men, they say, nor a dissociated multitude has *majesty* or supreme civil power. We freely acknowledge that neither any one man nor all men together could have had *joint* possession of this power as *one moral person*, as it exists in a sovereign, until they were united by some agreement. Nevertheless it can be safely affirmed that the seeds of that power lay scattered as it were in the *natural liberty* of individuals. And when it was conferred by one or several agreements on a sovereign ruler (*summus imperans*), it came to be called sovereign civil government (*summum civile imperium*). This will become clearer when we survey the various parts of sovereign power with our author in the following chapter. [II.6.14.i]

---

11. Titius, *Observationes,* no. 567.

On the Constitution of
Civil Government[1]

The celebrated Locke (*Second Treatise of Government,* ch. 12)[2] neatly reduces all the parts of sovereign power to three: *legislative* (as it is commonly, though improperly, called),[3] *executive,* and *federative.* It belongs to
the *legislative* power not only to command what is to be done and not
done, but also to say what penalty is to be inflicted on him who omits the
one or does the other. Pufendorf explicates the *executive* power and the
judicial power which facilitates its exercise, and finally discusses the *federative* power. Also the power of making magistrates and ministers (of which
Pufendorf gives an independent account) belongs either to the executive
or to the federative powers, according as the subordinate acts of the one or
the other are entrusted to such magistrates or ministers. As for the power

1. From the notes to bk. II, ch. 7, "On the Functions of the Sovereign Power"; and
bk. II, ch. 8, "On the Forms of Government."

2. Carmichael interpreted Locke's presentation in chapter 12 of the *Second Treatise
of Government* in the way he read other chapters of the *Second Treatise,* as a commentary
on Pufendorf's jurisprudence. Pufendorf had distinguished seven ways in which the
sovereign powers of government may be exercised: they were powers of legislation; of
vindication (or execution); of the judiciary; of making war and peace (federative
power); of appointing magistrates; of levying taxes and of examining doctrines (*Of the
Law of Nature and Nations,* VII.IV.1–8). Carmichael demonstrates how these seven
ways of exercising the powers of civil government may be reduced to the three powers
specified by Locke.

3. See p. 45, above, where Carmichael insists that the legislators of ancient Greece
and Rome were so called only because they were the authors of laws which derived
their legitimacy from the votes or enactments of the people.

of raising revenue, one could easily refer their imposition to the legislative, the actual collection to the executive. Finally, it is obvious that both of these powers are concerned with doctrine.

It is also easily shown that *all these divisions of the supreme power are derived from the consenting will of the subjects.* For civil power, by commanding and prohibiting, by imposing fines or handing down sentences, or, finally, by making treaties with foreign powers, *obliges* the citizens to do, omit, or suffer what, in the state of nature, it would be in their own power to do, omit, or prevent. Manifestly therefore civil power is founded in the consent of those *against whom* it is exercised. A man's right of disposing of his actions and therefore of his property so far as that depends on his actions, is called *freedom* (*libertas*) while he remains in the state of nature; this same right becomes *government* (*imperium*) when it is transferred, with each man's consent, as the end of civil society requires, to a sovereign. On the other hand when civil power *defends the rights* of citizens against their fellow citizens or against foreigners, it acts with the consent of those *for whose benefit* it is exercised. For civil power is in fact nothing but the right which belonged to individuals in the state of nature to claim what was their own or what was due to them, and which has been conferred upon the same ruler for the sake of civil peace. In this category belongs the power of inflicting *corporal punishment* on the guilty, except that since this power belongs naturally to all men, it ought not to be said to be *conferred* upon the sovereign power, so much as *restricted* to him, while the rest of the citizens forbid themselves its use. [II.7.1.i]

The power of establishing *universities* and supporting them with laws and adorning them with privileges is a power which political writers usually include among the lesser rights of majesty (the greater rights are the essential parts of sovereign power described above). This authority naturally comes under the *executive* power, as do most of the other so-called *lesser rights of majesty*, where they exist: such as the power of *conferring dignities, of coining money, of granting fairs and holidays, of legitimating children, of restoring reputation, of granting the pardon of age, of remitting the customary penalties of the laws, of granting forgiveness to debtors, etc.* Some of these rights can be conceded to subordinate magistrates; some can be omitted altogether, without damage to the state or to civil government.

And other rights of this kind, such as *the acquisition of forfeits for the treasury, the occupation of unowned objects to the exclusion of other people, and so on,* are not so much parts of the sovereign power as rights of convenience, which are conceded to the sovereign power, by the laws of many states, to maintain its dignity.

If Pufendorf's teaching in this section is understood to apply to doctors of the church, it leads to the vexed question of the right of the sovereign power in sacred matters. Whether this right provides for the regulation of the form of worship favored by the laws of the state, or for the suppression or toleration of those who dissent from it, is a question which in both respects requires a deep and careful investigation which the plan of our course does not allow us even to broach here.[4] [II.7.8.i]

One can scarcely avoid acknowledging, for the reasons given by Pufendorf,[5] that the operations of the state will be awkward and poorly coordinated if the various parts of the sovereign power are vested in quite different offices. But there is nothing difficult about the prince or senate exercising alone some parts of the supreme power, such as the executive and federative powers, while the other power, the legislative, can act only with the consent of the various orders of the state. See below, pp. 169–72. [II.7.9.i]

The forms of government

[Pufendorf distinguished between regular governments and irregular governments. In the former, government was united in a single will; in the latter, government was distributed or divided in such a way that no single body or institu-

---

4. It is remarkable that Carmichael should have chosen to say nothing at all about the government of the church in his writings. The orthodox position of the Reformed theologians and of the Westminster Confession of Faith, which Carmichael had sworn to uphold as a condition of appointment to the University of Glasgow, was that civil governments have the duty to enforce the doctrines of the established church (i.e., the Presbyterian Church of Scotland). Carmichael's silence on this subject may indicate some sympathy with the more tolerant position taken by Locke, whose political ideas he endorsed, albeit in his own manner.

5. See *Of the Law of Nature and Nations,* VII.IV.10.

tion exercised sovereign power. He also described systems of states, where different sovereign states were united under a common king or by a treaty.]

[A regular government locates the sovereign power in one body], that is in one man or in one assembly of men, united in the exercise of government. [II.8.2.i]

[There are three forms of regular government: monarchy, where the sovereign power is vested in one man; aristocracy, where it is exercised by a council of select citizens; thirdly, democracy, where it is housed in an assembly composed of all the fathers of families. Carmichael observes:]

The noblest example of the [aristocratic] form [of government] furnished by the ancient world was the *Lacedaemonian*. In the modern world it is provided by the *Venetian* Republic. The discussion here is about simple governments [not systems of states]. [II.8.3.i]

The [democratic] form of government was most conspicuous in the ancient *Athenian* republic. The Roman republic is referred to below, in section 12 [II.8.12.i]. The examples [of democracy] which exist today are found mainly in minor states especially among the *Germans*. In these states also the people are rarely convened; most business is entrusted to the Senate and the Magistrates, who exercise power, albeit dependently. The government of the individual provinces of the *Netherlands* is not democratic, as is attested by their own jurists. [II.8.3.ii]

An example of an irregular government is the *Roman* Republic, as described by Pufendorf in a Select Dissertation entitled *On the Form of the Roman Republic*. [II.8.12.i]

An example of another kind of irregular government [where the nobility have so increased their power that they have become unequal partners of the king] is provided by Pufendorf in his treatise *On the State of the German Empire,* published under the pseudonym of Severinus de Monzambano.[6] He justifies the interpretation [of the German Empire] which he gives there in a Select Dissertation entitled *On Irregular Governments*.[7] Ti-

---

6. Severinus de Monzambano [Pufendorf], *De Statu Imperii Germanici.*
7. Pufendorf, "De republica irregulari."

tius however contends that the Empire is not a simple government but a *system* [of states] albeit *irregular.* [II.8.12.ii]

See also Pufendorf's dissertation, *On Systems of States.*[8] [II.8.13.i]

The British kingdoms furnished Pufendorf with an example of [a system of states united under a common king] when he was writing the Select Dissertation cited above. But for a system to be formed by a common king, it is necessary for the king to have free exercise of the power of *war and peace,* so that he may use the forces of either kingdom to defend and promote the rights of the other. However if the king can exercise all parts of the sovereign power at his own discretion, it is easy for a system of that kind to degenerate into a single kingdom. [II.8.14.i]

We have examples of this kind [of systems of states, united by treaty] before us in the federated *Belgic* provinces and in the federated cantons of the *Swiss.* [II.8.15.1]

---

8. Pufendorf, "De systematibus civitatum." It was Pufendorf's view that the government of the German empire ought to be reconstituted as a system of states; in its unamended form, he considered it a monstrosity. See Moore and Silverthorne, "Protestant Theologies," pp. 178–84.

On the Limits of Sovereign Power and the Right of Resistance[1]

[Pufendorf contended that the government of any state, whatever its form, must be sovereign, that its actions cannot be rescinded by a superior, inasmuch as there is no body in a civil society superior to the sovereign. Carmichael comments:]

The author has not included the words *by a superior* without a purpose. For while sovereign power is indeed derived from the consent of the citizens, once it has been conferred it makes the person on whom it has been conferred truly superior to the rest of the citizens not only as individuals but as a whole. Hence it readily follows that the acts of the sovereign cannot be *rendered void* by anyone, *as by a superior.* But this does not prevent his actions from being rightly *held to be void* on some occasions, if it happens that he has clearly exceeded the limits of the power conferred on him, as defined by the very nature of civil government or by fundamental laws. [II.9.1.i]

A sovereign is not liable to human penalties nor to coercion as proceeding from a *superior.* Nor is there anyone to whom he is accountable. Further, the *internal* acts of governments, that is, those which terminate within the state itself, must carry a presumption of justice, when this presumption is not manifestly ruled out by signs to the contrary. Certainly no *power* in the state can be said without contradiction to have equal or su-

---

1. From the notes to bk. II, ch. 9, "On the Characteristics of Civil Government."

perior force to the sovereign power. Yet the sovereign is nonetheless
obliged to administer the government in such a way that no occasion will
arise for his subjects to think that he is deviating from the public interest
or exceeding the bounds of legitimate power. Hence, if public necessity
demands from time to time even the appearance of such a deviation, it will
also be necessary to explain the reason for that appearance, at the earliest
moment. Much more should appropriate justifying reasons be made
known to all in the case of *external* acts of government, in which the state
clashes with neighboring states in war, at any rate in offensive war; for, in
that case, the presumption of justice, which we spoke of above, is wanting.
[II.9.2.i]

In any state, the sovereign has no superior who can impose an obligation on him, and as he cannot obligate himself by means of a *law* (i.e., by
means of a *superior*), it follows clearly that the acts of a sovereign cannot
fall within the jurisdiction of the civil laws. But notwithstanding [the logic
of sovereign power]:

1. There can be no doubt that the sovereign is bound by the *divine laws*,
both natural and positive, provided that they have been declared to him.
And he is so bound not only as a *man*, in respect of the duties he shares in
common with other men, but also as a *sovereign*, to administer the government in accordance with those laws.

2. He is also bound by the *agreement* in accordance with which government was conferred upon him and accepted by him, to exercise his government in the way that will most effectively provide for the safety and
security of the people and the promotion of their advantage. Special articles concerning the manner and limits of the exercise of sovereignty may
be included in this agreement from the beginning, or subsequently added
by mutual consent of sovereign and subjects. Such articles are commonly
called *fundamental laws*. The sovereign will be bound by these, too, not as
laws issuing from a superior (although such public acts on the part of a
state or sovereign are frequently given the name of *laws* inasmuch as they
establish a rule of procedure) but as *agreements* into which he has entered.
Furthermore, although we would not imagine a sovereign contracting an
obligation (which would be quite absurd) but simply accepting the gov-

ernment on the terms on which it was offered to him, yet the sovereign
would not be right to extend his power beyond the limits of the rights
granted him.

3. It is consistent with this [limitation] that the sovereign be obliged to
set limits on *the acts of subjects* and the consequences of such actions, in
accordance with *the laws in force* in the state at the time. This restraint
should be extended even to sovereigns who have the full exercise of legislative power, since new laws are to be applied to future, not to past, cases.

4. The consequences of the *private actions* of the sovereign, as of anyone
else, are to be judged in accordance with the laws concerning such actions
which are accepted in the state; unless the sovereign has declared, or circumstances reveal, that it has pleased him to exempt his actions from the
force of those laws (as Grotius rightly remarked at II.XIV.2 and 5).

5. In all civil laws which contribute to the good morals of the state,
whose content is relevant to the sovereign, Pufendorf gives useful advice at
the end of this paragraph [that the sovereign be willing to comply with
these laws in his own conduct].[2] [II.9.3.i]

[It was Pufendorf's judgment that citizens should patiently bear the severities
of harsh government, that individuals ought to flee the country to escape misfor-
tune rather than take up arms against their government. Carmichael commented
at some length on this opinion:]

The author distinguishes *individuals* in this passage from *the whole,* or
the greater part, of the people. This doctrine of *individuals* is further modified by Grotius (I.IV.7) and by Pufendorf in his larger work (VII.VIII.7).
But Grotius also alleges in the same work that the right [of resistance]
granted by nature has been abolished by Christian moral teaching.[3] Quite
rightly this view does not find favor with the distinguished Huber (*On the
Rights of Civil Society,* I.9.3.33 and 43 ff.), nor with the illustrious Rev-

2. It was a persistent theme of the natural law theories of Samuel Pufendorf, Ulrich
Huber, and Gershom Carmichael that government could be sovereign and also limited.
For discussion of their theories of limited sovereignty and its application to the governments of their own countries, see Moore and Silverthorne, "Protestant Theologies,"
pp. 171–97.

3. *Rights of War and Peace,* I.III.7 ff.

erend B. Hoadly (Bishop of Hereford, formerly of Bangor): see his treatise published in English under the title, *The Measures of Submission to the Civil Magistrate Consider'd.*[4] On the question of resistance itself, this seems certain: that no man has an unlimited right against another man, and consequently, *where the right of one man over another ends, injury begins, and with it, the right of resistance,* if we consider only *expletive* justice as it may be applied to the man who inflicted the injury; consult the remarks of Locke in the *Treatise* we have often cited, sec. 202.[5]

In these cases one must consider not only what one can do to defend oneself when a ruler manifestly exceeds the limits of the power conferred upon him, one must also consider one's duty to one's native land and one's obligation to ensure the safety and security of many innocent citizens. For this reason it would be both wicked and stupid to attempt to involve the state in the calamities of civil war for an injury, however atrocious, which only one man, or a few men, had actually suffered. Certainly it does not seem that anyone of sound mind would lightly initiate a *resistance* which had that aim, unless he expected that the great mass of citizens would support him. And he could scarcely expect such support, however he might delude himself with vain hopes, if in such a case he spoke of injuries which were either tolerable, or which had not yet directly affected the great majority of the people. See again the *Treatise* of Locke, sec. 208.

But there are cases where the attacks of the sovereign do injury not so much to the *private rights* of individuals as to *public rights,* i.e., those rights which are understood to be transferred by individuals to civil government when they enter civil society. If for example a king who is limited by laws behaves like an absolute monarch, it is within the power of the civil society to defend these rights, although violent resistance should not be offered on these grounds before clear signs have shown that the people or the majority of the people wish it. When I use the word *people,* I mean the citizens

4. Hoadly, *The Measures of Submission.*

5. For *expletive* justice, see above, pp. 43–44. Locke's and Carmichael's justification of the right to resist tyranny was not a right of retribution so much as a right of restraint and reparation, consistent with Locke's theory of the right to punish as described in the *Second Treatise of Government,* ch. 2, secs. 8–11, pp. 272–74; and by Carmichael in ch. 7 above, pp. 69–71. See also below, pp. 275 ff.

who are so called in a more eminent sense, more or less as Pufendorf describes them above (*On the Duty of Man and Citizen,* II.6.13), i.e., those who by direct consent and agreement made with the sovereign himself, originally instituted the state, and those who have succeeded to the rights they possessed relating to their public position. But who are to be included in this number? We have pointed out that not all heads of households qualify (pp. 154–55). The composition of the body of citizens, properly so called, is to be inferred from the fundamental laws and customs of each state. It must also be determined, by those laws and customs, whether the citizens are to be counted as individuals, or by certain divisions, as members of which they have the right of casting a vote in public assemblies through delegates. However, in order that their will to resist may become known in such a case, it is not always necessary for them to declare their will gathered in assembly. For it sometimes happens that assemblies in which the genuine will of the state could express itself in a regular manner cannot be held without first offering violent resistance. In this case necessity requires that the public will be inferred from other signs, which are usually apparent, as was the case in the *British* Kingdoms in 1688, when under the providence of God, the happy liberator of these islands delivered them from the jaws of papal tyranny when they were all but devoured.

If, in addition to those grave causes which arouse just and necessary public resistance, there is a pertinacious cunning which manifestly intends to devise similar injuries in future, so far as situation and opportunity permit, the people are no longer bound to leave the guardianship of their rights to one who has by his actions openly declared himself an enemy of those rights.[6] For nothing is more absurd than that the right of government should come into collision with the end of government. Further, anyone who assumes a duty on another's behalf, and then proclaims by

---

6. Barbeyrac also defended, against Pufendorf and other commentators on the work of Pufendorf, the right of subjects to defend themselves against a government that violated the natural rights of the subjects. He concluded his comprehensive rebuttal of other jurists on this subject by observing with pleasure that Carmichael had followed the opinions of Grotius and Locke on the right of resistance, and not allowed himself to be misled by Pufendorf (*Of the Law of Nature and Nations,* VIII.III.4, n. 8, pp. 762–63).

words or deeds that he refuses to perform it within the conditions under which and for which it was entrusted to him, should by that very fact be considered to have renounced it.

However, not even in cases of this kind can a government which has once been legitimately established be completely rejected or abjured before the will of the people has been solemnly declared. It is true that the dissolution of the obligation toward a ruler is not to be sought so much in the decision of the people (as if this alone could deprive a sovereign of power in the way that a lower magistrate is deprived by decision of a higher magistrate) as from the evidence of the situation itself; that is, from the fact that the sovereign has notoriously and persistently exceeded the limits of the power conferred upon him, has abused it to bring disaster on the civil society, and has sufficiently revealed his intention of abusing it in future. Yet even granted the abuse, which ought to be manifest in itself, it is still for the people to determine what particular means are appropriate for public precaution against future abuse. They must decide whether it should be by curtailing the resources of the sovereign ruler or by entrusting the government to someone else. Therefore even in those extreme cases which demand an extraordinary remedy, nothing more should be permitted to individuals than to repel present force by force, and to ensure that there is opportunity for the state to provide against the common danger by common counsel.

Much less is it right for individuals to punish a sovereign, however delinquent. It is certainly obvious that this is not permitted, so long as he retains the government; and in most monarchies, it is accepted by law or custom that the *person* of the king be considered *sacrosanct*. But once he has fallen from power, power devolves upon the civil society, and it is there therefore that the capacity lies to make a decision in so grave a matter as the punishment of one who recently held sovereign power. There is further the question of the penalty to be inflicted in this case by the people themselves or by his successor in government, a particularly difficult and dangerous question, as the distinguished Huber recognizes (*On the Rights of Civil Society,* I.9.4.40 ff.). For it seems absurd even to suppose, as Huber warns us, that he who has once held a legitimately acquired kingship should be brought to judgment by those who have been his subjects, be compelled to plead his cause, and submit to condemnation and punishment; it cannot but move men's indignation; it is unheard of in any age, except in the example which a furious faction gave in this island in the last century, a faction which had previously oppressed the state itself with armed violence. But even in a case of this kind it is a no less outrageous species of crime secretly to kill or to overwhelm by popular attack one who is already stripped of the power to do harm. Hence the author we have just cited rightly concludes that the better counsel is with those who wish to protect the public security by restricting the punishment of a deposed king to simple exile or perpetual imprisonment.[7] In addition there is no doubt that it is right to use his wealth and resources to repair the harm he did to the society or to individuals.

As far as concerns the seven cases surveyed by Grotius (I.IV.8–14), it may be questioned whether the kind of resistance justified above, which was also adopted in the happy Revolution of these Kingdoms, falls under any or all of these cases, as they are understood by that eminent man. However, I have no doubt that this resistance can be defended on the basis of some of them for an obviously similar reason. For it is not only the man who openly professes himself an enemy of the whole people who is to be considered as *bent on the destruction of a people, and as having the intention to ruin it* (sec. 11); but also he whose administration tends notoriously and persistently to bring disaster on the people (compare Locke's *Treatise,* sec. 210). Moreover a government, like a marriage, can be regarded as a *trust* (see Grotius, sec. 12) in which the essential articles of the agreement on which it was founded have been violated, and the end for which it was established frustrated; even if a *trust clause* was not expressly included. So too he who confers on another a right against himself, within certain limits and for a specific purpose, need not add that *he will be allowed to resist* (see Grotius, sec. 14) if the other should make demands that obviously exceed the prescribed limits, or manifestly deviates from the intended purpose. Hence, in particular, a king's power may be circumscribed by the explicit limitation that *he may not alter the laws, or make new laws, unless the people*

7. Huber, *De Jure Civitas,* p. 263; and Moore and Silverthorne, "Protestant Theologies," pp. 196–97.

consents, either directly or through its delegates meeting in assemblies. Whether this arrangement should be called, according to the view of Grotius (sec. 13), a *division of sovereignty between king and people* or not, at any rate it includes a right in the people not to be compelled to observe laws to which it has not given its consent. It therefore includes also the capacity to resist any force which attempts to violate this right of the people, i.e., the right to demand the observance of such laws or to take action against those who do not observe them. For no conception of a *perfect right,* and this applies particularly to *the power of government,* can fail to include the capacity to protect that right; nor should this capacity be thought to have been abolished by the Gospel, whether in respect of other rights or above all in respect of government. Therefore it was not without reason that the doctrine of this section (Grotius, sec. 13) was considered to be applicable to the case we are discussing here by the noble Stanhope, distinguished in the arts of peace and war alike, whose *death was lamented by good men* everywhere, in his public case against Sacheverell.[8]

I feel that this disquisition has expanded further than the plan of our work required. But I am not afraid that fair judges will find it inappropriate in the reign of an excellent king, against whom no resistance from his subjects ever was or is to be feared, except by partisans of the doctrine which condemns all resistance indiscriminately. That their designs, which have in the past been utterly crushed, may finally cease or always be in vain, may God ensure in his providential care for the religion and liberty of the British peoples. [II.9.4.i]

Here we must be careful that we do not confound things which are distinct; many people go wildly astray on this subject. For a *limited* government does not cease to be *sovereign,* nor should a *limited monarchy* be confused with a mere *principate.* In the former the prince truly enjoys *sovereign*

---

8. The speech given by the secretary of state, Sir James Stanhope, one of the six managers of the impeachment of the High Tory clergyman Dr. Henry Sacheverell for sedition and subversion of "her Majesty's government and the Protestant succession as by law established . . ." (Articles of Impeachment, Preamble) before the House of Lords in 1710 went furthest in proclaiming an original contract and the right of resistance to be the basis of civil government. The speech is printed in *The Tryal of Dr. Henry Sacheverell,* pp. 71–77. See Holmes, *The Trial of Dr. Sacheverell,* pp. 139–40.

power, even though he exercises it within certain limits established in the conferral of power, and may require the consent of the people to exercise some part of it. In the latter the prince is only a distinguished *magistrate* whose acts can be declared null and void by the senate and people by force of their superior authority. Also *absolute* government provided it is understood as *civil* government must not be confused with *despotism.* For *civil* government is only the authority to rule others for their common safety and the preservation of their liberty and property. And an *absolute* government differs from a *limited* government only in the means employed by the sovereign to pursue those ends. Whereas a limited monarch governs for the benefit of civil society within prescribed limits and with the consent of others to use means of certain kinds, an absolute monarch pursues the same objectives guided only by his own judgment and by taking whatever measures seem best to him. In contrast [to these forms of civil government] a *despotic* government employs the services and property of his subjects at his pleasure and for the benefit of himself alone. Such governments cannot be acquired by right, I would say, over any entire people, nor can they be maintained through successive generations. For I have shown above (pp. 139–40) that the justification of the imposition of servitude on men against their will applies only to a few individuals, never to an entire existing people, and therefore even less to its future members. And there are certainly far fewer people who would want to consent to this condition of their own will.

Nor can the use of the land for the sake of which civil government is established forever, as we said above (pp. 150–53), be linked with an obligation of servile subjection. The owner of the land certainly has the right to dispose of his property as he wishes, but it must be in such a way that his property serves the natural uses for the sake of which property was granted to men by God. Hence the owner of a large tract of land, sufficient for the habitation of many men, or many households, cannot rightly require that anyone who may live on that land must be willing to submit to the yoke of his own despotic government; nor can he transfer to anyone else the right to impose such a condition. For men could not tolerate this iniquitous condition, hence it would tend to subvert the working out of the divine plan by which the surface of the earth has been granted to the human race for habitation.

Nevertheless, civil government may rightly be established over entire peoples, in both its *limited* and its *absolute* forms, and over certain individual men also in its *despotic* form. Some governments however qualify as tyrannical: a government assumed by someone to whom it does not belong by right, or a limited government assumed by someone to whom it belongs within certain limits, but exercised beyond those limits notoriously and persistently. Hence limited government, if exercised as absolute, and absolute civil government, if exercised as despotic, and despotic government itself, if exercised with brutal and intolerable cruelty to the person of the slave, is to be branded with the stigma of *tyranny.* For it is obvious from what has been said, that every human government over other men has its bounds and limits. And there is no government which does not admit of some abuses to which a just resistance may be opposed. As for the right of putting a man to death for a capital crime (which, as we taught above,[9] belongs in the natural state to each man individually), it would be quite improper to call it a power of government. And yet it would be possible to threaten a man whom one had the right to kill, with injuries which he could not only resist legitimately but which he ought to resist; thus even in this case the license of one man against another would have its limits.

I cannot imagine what Master Spavan had in mind, in his *English* epitome of Pufendorf's work *Of the Law of Nature and Nations,*[10] illustrated with notes which he drew, as he himself says, from the storehouse of Barbeyrac, when he chose to gloss these words of the author (which Barbeyrac does not annotate) with a paragraph from the *Jus Regium* of our countryman Mackenzie, which begins with these words, *I cannot but highly praise our ancestors who so prudently chose absolute monarchy,* etc.[11] I pass over the question, whether by these words Mackenzie has contradicted himself by

9. See above, pp. 69–71.

10. J. Spavan, *Pufendorf's Law of Nature and Nations,* vol. II, pp. 219–21, n. (b). Spavan's commentary on Pufendorf was studied in dissenting academies in England. See MacLachlan, *English Education under the Test Acts,* p. 132.

11. Mackenzie, *Jus Regium,* p. 42.

deriving absolute monarchy from the choice of the people, since he elsewhere carefully insists that it was established by God himself and by Nature. But it cannot be accepted that he should describe the monarchy of
the Scots as absolute, without adding any qualifications. For among the
Scots it was never in the power of the king either to make laws or to impose
taxes, unless the orders of the kingdom agreed. And it is well known that
political writers refer to such a government not as an absolute but as a limited monarchy. As for the curious reasons which Mackenzie offers in the
passage cited and elsewhere in the same book, in his effort to disparage the
familiar constitution of his native country, these reasons, by his own admission, had no more weight than the authority of the decrees which had
been published shortly before by his patrons (the *Oxford* men) and signally
deserved to go up in smoke in the same flames. (See the Dedicatory Epistle
in that book, and compare the last part of the "Judgement against Sacheverell.")[12] However, I would not like this to be taken to imply that I do
not myself equally detest a good many of the propositions condemned by
those decrees, or that I would in any way detract from the wholly justified
reputation which that most ancient and distinguished university enjoys
among all those who cultivate letters. As Oxford has always flourished in
esteem for every kind of learning, so has it not failed from time to time to
assert the just cause of liberty, nor will it cherish forever (we believe) sentiments hostile to that cause. [II.9.5.i]

It may be understood from the observations contained in the above
paragraphs that these [limitations] are not *laws* properly so called nor precepts that proceed as from a *superior.* They are *agreements,* or rather *articles*
of the *fundamental agreement* by which government is conferred. One may
readily draw the following conclusions.

1. Civil government, even at its most extensive, is said to be *absolute,*
not simply but in a *qualified* sense, i.e., it does not exclude *all* limitations,
but only *specifically expressed* limitations, which do not flow of their own
nature from the end for which civil society is established.

2. *Specific,* as well as *general, limitations* might be valid, even if the sov-

---

12. Ibid., pp. i–iii; and *The Tryal of Dr. Henry Sacheverell,* pp. 261 and 327.

ereign were assumed to have taken no *obligation* upon himself. For in order not to owe obedience beyond certain limits, it is enough not to have
obligated oneself beyond those limits. And yet it is entirely abhorrent to
the end for which civil government is instituted to believe that individuals
or groups confer its exercise over themselves on someone who is not in
turn obliged to conduct his government within the limits and according
to the ends for which it was established. And certainly an obligation of this
kind, as it applies to the positive acts [of a sovereign], can be constituted
only by an agreement.

3. Neither an *agreement* nor any *special limitations* on government established by agreement, invests the *government* in the *people,* as distinct
from the ruler (not even if the agreement includes a provision that the
ruler can only perform certain acts of government with the consent of the
people). Even less may such agreements permit the people to exercise government over the king himself.

4. In order to justify *resistance* against a ruler in certain extreme circumstances, there is no need to take refuge in an *agreement* by which the ruler
obligated himself, nor to assume *special limitations* of power, nor to ascribe
government or a part of it to the *people* itself. It is enough that he has manifestly exceeded the limitations which may be satisfactorily inferred simply
from the purpose of establishing a civil society. However I do not deny
that this judgment comes much more easily, and provides much readier
means of protecting liberty, when special limits have been set to government by some positive *constitution,* or by a uniformly accepted custom.
Hence there is no doubt that the public safety is better guarded in a monarchy or aristocracy if it is limited than if it is absolute.

5. In every state properly so called it is the normal situation, as the author points out (*Of the Law of Nature and Nations,* VII.VI.7, *toward the
end*), that there is an *absolute power, habitually* at least, if not always in
practice, since what a *king* or *senate* may lack with respect to absolute
power is understood to be in the hands of the *people,* and can be furnished
by it. For it is not easy in practice for *individuals* entering the civil state to
add special limitations or exceptions to the agreement by which each subjects his own will to the will of all; yet if it were agreed that they had been
added, there is no doubt that they would be valid. Hence it is not at all

abhorrent to reason, that when two *independent states* move to amalgamate into one, they may each insist that certain *particular rights,* which would otherwise be at the discretion of the civil government, are rights which they do not submit to the judgment either of the prince or of the whole state which has been made from the union of the two. It would be absurd to object here that *reservations* of this kind are no more than laws which later laws might abrogate; for it is quite clear that they are the means by which one or other section of the united state acquires, or rather retains, a *right* which cannot rightly be taken from it against its will. And yet this section is not regarded as deciding this either by the will of the whole or of a majority, because it is a matter which it intended explicitly to exempt from the discretion of the majority. Rights therefore which are reserved in this manner at the time of the union of the states are as valid for either section of the state against the whole as the rights received in the transfer of a limited monarchy are valid for the people itself against the king; and it is for the same reason, namely the internal quality of the consent by which the government is conferred. [II.9.6.i]

CHAPTER 20

On Conquest and Patrimonial Kingdoms[1]

[Pufendorf had argued that, while all legitimate governments must be derived from the consent of subjects, this consent is not always elicited in the same manner. For subjects are sometimes forced to consent to a government that is imposed upon them by a conqueror following a war. The subjects of an occupying power are justly required to consent to such a government which has, after all, spared the lives of the conquered people. Moreover, the subjugated people must have understood that in making war they had risked their lives and fortunes at the gaming table of Mars. And they had therefore consented tacitly to whatever conditions might issue from the war. Carmichael offers the following observations on this argument:]

Many opinions are current on this question of the acquisition of power or government. They need to be carefully scrutinized. It has been established above[2] that whatever is owed by the vanquished even to a just victor, beyond the fact that he had given cause for war, is owed either as *compensation* or as a *guarantee* for the future or as *punishment.* To begin with the last, only those who actually do *harm* are liable to *punishment;* for Grotius has rightly noted that the civil association between ruler and citizens does not entail that innocent citizens may be punished in the human court for the crimes of the ruler (II.XXI.17; see also III.XI.2). But in the case of an unjust war, its being waged by a state usually means that it is waged by the sovereign and the soldiers under his command. The vast majority of citizens have made no contribution at all, whether of wealth or counsel, and

---

1. From the notes to bk. II, ch. 10, "On the Ways of Acquiring Power, Particularly Monarchical."

2. See above, pp. 139–42.

are therefore totally exempt from punishment, however wickedly the war was waged. The first justification, therefore, which Pufendorf gives for the acquisition of power by force, that *if the victor had wished to make strict use of the rights of war, he could have taken the lives of the vanquished,* is applicable only to a small portion of the conquered state—on the assumption that one understands by the strict rights of war not what is done by inhuman and unjust victors, but what may be done rightfully. For once enemies are defeated, the only justification for taking away their lives is as *punishment,* in the same way that in the state of nature only physical punishments are applicable. I omit to inquire whether the common soldiers deserve any mitigation of punishment on the ground of justice, because they were lured or even pressed into war by the authority of the ruler, and because specious pretexts often cloak unjust wars. I also ignore the question whether they have a worthy conception of civil government who think that men who have deserved extreme penalties should be compelled to enter military service as their punishment.

On *compensation for loss,* the following seems certain. (1) It rarely, if ever, happens that the loss which the inhabitants of a well-cultivated territory wrongly inflict on another people or prince equals the value of any distinct part of the region which the wrongdoers possess. It also rarely happens that the aggressor is not both willing and able, when it has to make the choice, to compensate for the damage otherwise than by ceding any part of its territory. In which case the injured party has no excuse for holding this territory, much less for suppressing the liberty of innocent citizens.

(2) Whatever is due to the victor as compensation for loss, need not (it seems) be paid by innocent citizens in a way that would also deprive them of the continued use and enjoyment of the *civil government* for whose sake they are assumed to have incurred the obligation. For the only justification of the obligation by which citizens need to make restitution for public wrongdoing seems to be the same as that which in private law underlies *noxal actions* and *the action de pauperie.*[3] Thus it would be considered fair

---

3. Noxal actions and actions *de pauperie* are actions in Roman law for compensation for damage committed by slaves and animals, respectively; essentially, the owner of the slave or animal either made good the loss or surrendered him or his services to the injured party.

that *those who have taken certain means to procure profit or pleasure for themselves as a result of which others have suffered loss through no fault of their own should either make good the loss or cede to the injured party the piece of their property which caused the loss to the injured party.* This rule has to be modified in the light of a stricter equity, as I have explained above,[4] but as it stands, a prince or people which has suffered loss from the *civil government* of another people cannot claim *the power to govern* if it obtains any other compensation; and if it does succeed in taking *power,* it cannot claim any other compensation from the innocent citizens.

(3) It is consistent with this, that, however just a war may be, the only thing that the victor can rightly claim from the innocent citizens of a conquered people is *government of the land (imperium soli)*, if, as rarely happens, he cannot get any other compensation for his loss.[5] This does not prevent innocent citizens from maintaining all their rights in other respects, whether they prefer to remain in the territory and live as subjects of the government established there, or to take their possessions and go elsewhere.

But if the victor has himself taken compensation in moveables for the loss he suffered beyond what was due to him at the beginning, or if he is offered such compensation in peace negotiations, it follows from what we have said that the seizure he has made by means of war is not sufficient

---

4. Noxal damage and *pauperies* had been explained by Carmichael at I.6.11.ii and at I.6.12.i and ii. There he recalled "the civil law of the Romans (cf. Justinian, *Institutes,* IV.8 and 9), though many scholars wonder to what extent these judgments are also valid in natural law. As far as concerns a servant by whom a loss has been caused, his master seems to be wholly obligated either to make up the loss or to surrender the servant, unless in either case the master himself sustains a loss in that servant; in this case, I would think that the loss should be prorated as is done among the creditors of a debtor bound to service." [I.6.11.ii]

"Not all the revenue which comes to a master from his animal is to be regarded as profit; but only that which exceeds the price given for him, together with the expenses laid out on keeping him. Hence I would think that this judgment should have the same limits as the previous one. For the Hebrew laws on this question, see *Exodus* 21.28 and 35." [I.6.12.i]

"This obligation ceases if the injured party is at fault as regards the loss; as for instance if he provoked the animal." [I.6.12.ii]

5. On *imperium soli,* see above, pp. 150–53.

ground for asserting either *dominion* or *government* over the territory itself
or any part of it. We did indeed say above (pp. 70–71) that any enemy
property which we have seized may become ours in compensation for
what is owed to us; but we also stressed that one must not infringe on the
rights of innocent people. Now it is obviously in the interest of each state
and of each individual citizen (most of whom are rightly presumed to be
innocent in such a case) that the *government of its territory* be kept intact.
Compensation for loss, therefore, or reparation for any similar debt,
should be made from moveables, at least where the *government* is not patrimonial.

Finally, the *guarantee:* it is clear that it is usually possible for the injured
party to obtain a guarantee for the future in the same way as he may obtain
satisfaction for loss inflicted up to that point. [And he may obtain such
guarantees and satisfactions] even if he is not permitted to take over the
government either of the people who were the source of the injury or even
of the territory they inhabit.

There is no objection to this in the second justification which our author gives of seizure of government by force, viz., that *in going to war with
one whom he has previously harmed and to whom he has refused to give reasonable satisfaction, he puts all his fortunes on the gaming table of Mars,* etc.
This may perhaps be plausibly urged against one who takes the initiative
in invading the rights of some weaker party without any pretext of right,
relying solely on the force of arms, but it would seem difficult to accept
against one who professes (with truth) that he thinks his own cause just
and that he is waging war not simply because he is confident in his power
to do so, but with the intention of protecting and advancing his own
rights. Further, no one would be willing to accept the condition our author imposes unless the enemy did so too. And our author himself admits
that such acceptance cannot be presumed on the part of one who goes to
war for a just and necessary cause after gentler means of protecting his
rights have been tried in vain. Compare *Of the Law of Nature and Nations,*
VIII.VIII.1, where our author in this case goes to the opposite extreme, as
I point out at p. 209, below.

Clearly therefore it rarely happens that the victor even in the most righteous war is justified in claiming for himself the government of the terri-

tory of a conquered people, far less absolute dominion over it. Nor is he justified in preventing them from keeping their property intact after their country has been conquered, whether they prefer to stay or to emigrate. It follows that he is not justified in using the threat of extreme measures (as our author would have it, ibid., sec. 3) in compelling them to consent to his government.[6] See above all, Locke's *Second Treatise of Government,* chapter 16, which we cited above.[7]

If the victor has extorted such consent by unjustified force (too often employed even in wars begun for just causes), it is not completely void, as we have indicated above (pp. 85–86). In fact, any citizen may validly bind himself, by a promise extorted by extreme violence, not to use force against an invader in defense of the legitimate ruler, even though the right of the ruler, as well as of the rest of the citizens, remains valid in other respects. But in no case is a citizen justified in obeying an invader against a legitimate ruler, since one must not serve even a legitimate prince in an unjust cause. The famous *English* law of Henry VII offers only external immunity.[8]

Further, since the very idea of a promise made to an unjust aggressor is

6. Carmichael's arguments against Grotius and Pufendorf that conquest and enforced consent never provide justifiable grounds for allegiance were challenged by Barbeyrac, who insisted that "we must here distinguish between what the *Rigours of the Law* demand, and what the Rules of *Humanity* and *Equity* require, . . . by this means, all the objections vanish, which Mr. Carmichael brings against our Author. . . . For with regard to the external Effect, the Injustice of war, on the Side of the Conqueror, no ways hinders the vanquish'd from being oblig'd to keep the Agreement, tho' forc'd, by which he is brought under subjection. This is what the peace of Mankind requires. . . ." (Pufendorf, *Of the Law of Nature and Nations,* VII.VII. 3, n. 5, p. 506). See also Barbeyrac's notes on Grotius, *Rights of War and Peace,* III.VIII.1, p. 608.

7. Hutcheson concurred with Carmichael and Locke on the subject of the "much celebrated *right of conquest*": "upon this subject, see *Locke on Government;* whose reasonings are well abridged in Mr. Carmichael's notes on Pufendorf's smaller book" (*A Short Introduction to Moral Philosophy,* III.7, pp. 309–10: this note does not appear in *Philosophia Moralis* [1745]).

8. 11 Henry VII (1495), c. 1, which provided immunity for activities in support of the King "for the time being," and thus offered amnesty to former opponents of Henry prior to his coming to the throne (Elton, *The Tudor Constitution,* pp. 2, 4–5). According to Elton, Francis Bacon had started a tradition of mistakenly reading into this law a distinction between a *de facto* and a *de jure* king.

offensive, it needs the clearest evidence to validate its existence, and is not
to be extended at all. Mere intermission of resistance should not be taken
as an indication of binding consent, among citizens reduced to such a condition that they cannot even open their mouths against him without the
most pressing danger. Yet an intermission of resistance does have the consequence that arms should not to be taken up again lightly, without ascer-
taining the will of the people or of their rightful ruler, and without a new
declaration of hostilities. And when active hostilities cease, although the
right of the former ruler and of the people itself is maintained against the
invader, yet individual citizens are obliged, for the public interest and because of the presumed will of the rightful ruler himself and of the whole
state, to obey for the time being the present possessor of government in
matters which affect the daily peace, and do not pertain to the contro-
verted right of ruling.

On the other hand, it also sometimes happens that an unjust invader
administers a territory with such fairness that all the citizens cordially wish
him for their ruler, and constantly declare their genuine consent to his rule
by repeated signs, quite spontaneously. In this case, the fault of the acquisition is purged with the proviso that it does not impede the right of the
former ruler, as if it had been abolished by death or by express or tacit abdication.

Now according to the author's doctrine in the final paragraph of the last
chapter,[9] the holding of a kingdom in patrimony *belongs especially to those
who have acquired a kingdom by arms and have made a people for themselves.*
One may therefore infer from what I have said, that *patrimonial kingdoms
scarcely ever have a just beginning;* especially since what is held by occupation in war (if by chance the cause of acquisition is just, as rarely happens)
should be considered most often as having been acquired as the patrimony
of the victorious people rather than of the prince. The reason for this is
not merely the reason that Grotius rejects (I.III.12.3), that *these acquisitions
have been achieved by the blood and sweat of the citizens,* but above all because *they have been made to satisfy some other right which belongs to the people more than to the prince.* I admit that this reason does not always hold,

---

9. Pufendorf, *On the Duty of Man and Citizen,* II.9.7, p. 147.

nor the other rejected by Grotius; yet they are rarely both wanting, unless the conqueror already held some other kingdom in his patrimony.

One must not deny that it may happen, though rarely, that a patrimonial kingdom is established by other than violent means and by some other pretext than that of satisfying some other right. A man may, for instance, with the help of servants or other hired men, occupy some vacant territory, sufficient for the settlement of a normal society; he may accept an appropriate number of settlers, and impose upon them, among other terms, the condition of *civil subjection;* or he may offer other inducements to invite men to become citizens in a society dependent on himself; or finally, a king may succeed to the immoveable property of individual citizens (which scarcely ever happens). It is plain that, if the king is granted the right in such cases not only of *alienation* but also of *division,* this very fact implies that there is not that firm *union* of the citizens with each other, independent of the actual ruler, which we showed above (pp. 147 ff.) is requisite to a normal and stable society, and which, as we noted there, is normally formed by a prior agreement but can also be established by one single pact entered into with a supreme ruler. Though we admit that when the first foundations of a state are laid by means of one single pact entered into with a king, the citizens are usually to be considered not as being united with each other by its means, but rather as subject to the supreme ruler in such a way that their future union depends on his discretion, if no further bond occurs subsequently. By this means only an imperfect state is constituted; and almost all the patrimonial kingdoms that exist are imperfect states. [II.10.2.i]

We can understand from pp. 151–53 what reason there might be, as is commonly claimed, for this distinction [between patrimonial kingdoms, which are supposed to be divisible and alienable, and kingdoms instituted by the will of the people, which cannot be divided in these ways]. For when a king is understood to have once acquired dominion over a whole region, and once his subjects confer upon him whatever right they have over its individual parts, a *patrimonial* kingdom is assumed to have been established. This is understood to be achieved by *one agreement,* by which the individual citizens who settle in that region subject themselves and their successors in the beneficial ownership or other use of that land to the civil power of the said king and of his rightful successors, who are the supreme lords of that land; in return they claim the protection of the government and use of their acquired rights in that land.

By contrast, when parts of a region are owned by individuals, and the common power over that region is transferred to a king by these owners, it is best to regard this as the establishment of a *nonpatrimonial* kingdom. This is often done by means of a *second agreement,* i.e., a second agreement by the original citizens who are the owners of the individual estates and who had been previously united by the *first agreement* into one perpetual association. In conferring the government on this man they are understood to be moved by consideration of the person himself, hence we should not regard them as granting the right of transmitting it to his descendants, unless they have expressly said so; in which case it is also their right to define the order of succession. The facts themselves show that this manner of constituting a state and a civil power is particularly consonant with its nature and end. We have discussed above[10] by what right, or by what wrong, one man can acquire that universal ownership or dominion over a region which is supposed to be the foundation of a patrimonial government. Meanwhile we note that even assuming such ownership, he owns only the territory in his patrimony and the right of collecting the ample revenues which are consequent on ownership; this does not include civil government over the people. His right is not to be confused with civil power, however much it may be combined with it. For the former looks to the particular advantage of the ruler, the latter, to the advantage of all and everyone, since the rights of individuals, though perhaps narrower here than under certain other forms of government, are yet equally valid, and equally to be scrupulously observed by the ruler. Indeed no one is a suitable object of civil government except so far as he has certain rights which are valid against all men. So far does *civil* government, however absolute, differ from *despotic* government. [II.9.7.i]

If the kings under discussion here hold their kingdom only to the end of life, and may not transmit it to their [descendants], they are to that extent comparable to *usufructuaries.* But if they can transmit it to their de-

10. See above, pp. 180 ff.

scendants, in a fixed order, they have similar rights to *feudataries,* because they cannot alienate the kingdom at their discretion, nor change the order of succession, nor burden the succession to the kingship as such with their own private debts. For as in the former case the order of succession has been set by a *superior,* so in the latter case it has been set by the people. But this analogy should not to be extended further, as if the supremacy and dignity of the royal power were diminished by not being contained in the Patrimony. [II.9.7.iii]

When *free consent* is spoken of [in the election of a monarch], a free consent which is given by *a people in process of formation or already formed,* it is opposed not only to consent *extorted by force,* but also to the kind of consent which *is elicited from individuals* with respect to government over a territory which has been previously acquired by a king, where people have established or are beginning to establish their homes, and which he has given them to use precisely for that purpose or for the enjoyment of any similar advantage he offers to induce them to enter a civil association depending on him. [II.10.3.i]

By a people *which has been formed* one must understand a people which has become *a complete state* by the erection of a civil government. But a people *in process of formation* is one which has coalesced into some rudimentary form of state by means of the first pact alone; this is also the condition into which a monarchical state relapses (as the author says in the following paragraph) when, after the death of the former king, there is occasion for a new election. There are two kinds of election. An election held by a *formed* people is any election held by the combined citizens even if they are only united by the first pact. But an election held by a people *in process of formation* is one which is included in the first pact, as we have said sometimes happens (pp. 147–53). [II.10.3.ii]

An election may be held, though it is not a common event, under an absolute monarchy, either in the particular kind of monarchy called elective, in the event of the death of the reigning monarch, or in a hereditary monarchy, in the event of the extinction of the ruling family. An election may also be held, though this also rarely happens, in a completely aristocratic or democratic state, in changing by election to a monarchy without any intermission of the actual government; to say nothing of the election which takes place by means of the first agreement in a state not yet fully formed, in which the actual government has not yet been established. [II.10.4.i]

Our author explains at length the form of the state during an interregnum and the bonds by which it is maintained in one of his *Select Dissertations* entitled "On Interregna."[11] It is to no avail that the celebrated Titius dissents here, contending that the union of the citizens in an interregnum, when no previous arrangement has been made about who will administer the country on a vacancy of the throne, does not rest on a previous agreement but on a new agreement expressly or tacitly made at the very time of the interregnum.[12] For if this is admitted, it follows, contrary to what that distinguished scholar wishes to maintain, that the state dissolves into a disunited multitude at the very moment when the previous king dies. Nor is this consequence preempted by their continued living together, for such living does not imply a moral union, however much it may afford the opportunity to restore such a union. Therefore it would be more correct to agree with Pufendorf that *civil union* is preserved in an interregnum by the force of the *original agreement,* by which the union had been established in the beginning. And this union includes not only a *simple obligation* between citizens, such as Titius wants, but also a *bond of government.* For it is certain that during the period when there is free power to determine a government, for that time preeminently *government* itself still exists. Thus Pufendorf rightly declared[13] that *interregna have the character of a temporary democracy,* which the people, at its discretion, can either establish forever or change into any other form of government it likes. Nor does it matter that nothing had actually been settled previously about the administration of the government after the death of the king. For in this case, the state is presumed to will that the magistrates who are at the time in charge should continue in the exercise of their functions, simply for the sake of preserving peace; and that the most eminent among

11. Pufendorf, "De interregnis."
12. Titius, *Observationes,* no. 609.
13. Pufendorf, "De interregnis," sec. 7, pp. 274–77.

them should at the first opportunity call the citizens together to take counsel for their country. [II.10.4.ii]

It is certain that in this case [where the succession in a monarchy instituted by the people is in dispute] no more suitable arbitrator can be employed than the people. For since the people is regarded as morally the
same as it had been in any previous century, it knows well how to make its
mind known even if previously, it is supposed, it had not declared it with
sufficient clarity. A declaration of this kind, however, is no more a judicial
opinion (as the author cautions in the final paragraph of this volume of
the *Law of Nature and Nations*)[14] than an interpretation made by a donor
of his own obscure and ambiguous words.

Even though there may be no dispute over the natural order of succession, it may be clear that the person favored by the accident of birth holds
opinions which will inevitably lead him to govern in such a way that he
endangers the public safety. If such a course is actually pursued and obstinately maintained, the people may (as shown above)[15] rightly remove the
king from power, however justified his accession may have been. The people is not acting as interpreter of law, but is taking necessary measures for
its own preservation. By the same right, then, when a people has obvious
indications beforehand that such an administration is likely, it may exclude from the succession the heir designated by the chance of birth.
Among such signs none is more obvious than the profession of any *religion*
whose teachings tend to undermine the sacred and civil rights of citizens
and to eradicate any consciousness of obligation among them.

Furthermore, when manifest abuse of power gives cause for removing
someone from the throne, or when a deliberate fault such as we have described above provokes grounds for excluding him from the succession,
such abuse equally excludes from the throne at the same time all his posterity, or at least those born after he has given such cause. For both have
the same force as *abdication* (*renunciatio*), since it makes no difference
whether one simply refuses to rule or whether one refuses to rule in such
a way as to achieve the end of government. The right of a successor in a

14. *Of the Law of Nature and Nations*, VII.VII.15, pp. 715–16.
15. See above, pp. 164–69.

nonpatrimonial kingdom does not depend simply on the designation of an heir by his predecessor at his own discretion, who may institute anyone as heir or even disinherit someone with the effect of barring him from the succession, against the people's will. Rather, the right of succession, so far as it is valid against the people itself, is transmitted from the monarch who was first entrusted with the kingship to his distant descendants only through persons intermediate in a direct line. Nevertheless, any possessor of a kingdom or, in a certain case, his lineal successor, can remit his right to the people if they so will, and renounce it in their favor, and this enables them rightly to divert the succession from all his descendants or at least from those born after the abdication (Grotius agrees with this at II.VII.26, *at the end*). *This will involve no loss to collateral heirs.* For the right of succession is transmitted to them not through the abdicating king but through his ancestors in the direct line. Grotius and others want to apply this principle also in favor of *descendants* of the abdicating king *who were born before the abdication.*[16] But to tell the truth, no argument convinces us that the right is acquired by the child by mere birth, without any subsequent act, against the unanimous will of those who by their consent could have taken the right away from him before he was born.

Whatever the position of children born before the abdication, it is obvious from what we have said that a *deliberate incapacity* of the sort we have described above also *bars the transmission of the right to the descendants.* It follows that, in any kingdom where the profession of the reformed religion is established by law, and where the people has striven to secure a perfect right to the perpetual stability of those laws, the profession of the *Pontifical religion* has the effect that not only the individuals who make such a profession, in whatever order they are designated successors to the kingship by the lot of birth, but also their children, or at least those born after the contraction of that incapacity, and their descendants forever, can rightly be prohibited from the succession by the people, in their zealous (and reasonable) care for their religion and their liberty. In this case the government is rightly conferred on the next collateral in line, to be transmitted also to his descendants.

16. *Rights of War and Peace*, II.VII.28, pp. 243–44.

It was therefore a salutary counsel, and no less consistent with the principles of universal law, by which the *British* nations, after excluding all who
had surrendered themselves to the Roman Pontificate, conferred the succession of government among themselves on that most illustrious family,
pointed out by the finger of Heaven to save them from destruction, a family which has given us the most Serene King George, today happily ruling
over us, and which will continue to afford a line of pious Kings, who will
endure, if *Britain's* prayers prevail, as long as the sun and the moon.
[II.10.12.i]

On the Rights of Citizens[1]

i. Citizens under the civil law

There are in general two kinds of *civil* laws (and the same may be said of *natural* laws, so far as they are reduced to definite propositions enunciated in words). Some expressly *prescribe* what is *to be done* or *not to be done,* often with the explicit addition of a *penal sanction,* though the latter is quite commonly left to be tacitly understood. Others simply *define* what is each man's *own,* and what is *another's;* by what agreement each right is *constituted, transferred, or abolished,* etc. Although the latter do not contain an express *precept,* much less a *penal sanction,* they do nevertheless teach or forbid something (see pp. 39–40), since a corresponding obligation is attached to every right. The equivalent more or less of the penal sanction in these laws is a permission of civil *action* or *execution,* by which each man is to prosecute and obtain his right. *Criminal* cases derive from the *first* kind of laws, *civil* cases from the *second.* [II.12.4.i]

The author seems here and in the *previous* section to have before his eyes the same two kinds of laws that we have just distinguished. There he showed how the strength of civil society is added to natural laws in both cases; here he explains how natural laws are more specifically defined by civil laws.

Here arises the familiar and important question, whether civil laws

---

1. From the notes to bk. II, ch. 12, "On Civil Laws in Particular"; bk. II, ch. 13, "On the Right of Life and Death"; bk. II, ch. 15, "On the Power of Sovereign Authority over Property within the State"; bk. II, ch. 11, "On the Duty of Sovereigns"; and bk. II, ch. 18, "On the Duties of Citizens."

which set other limits of right and wrong than those set by the natural laws, offer immunity of *conscience* to a person whom they support, if he requires something not due by natural right, or fails to perform something due by natural law. The *negative* side is championed by, among others, Ames, *On Conscience,* book V.41.10, etc.,[2] the *affirmative* by Huber, *On the Rights of Civil Society,* book III.1.3.[3] To take a middle way between an outstanding theologian and a learned jurist, I acknowledge that by the act by which one enters civil society, one gives a right to his fellow citizens, in matters relating to the patrimony and within probable limits, to require of him what the laws of the state define as due, and not to give him what the laws do not make due. I also acknowledge that, barring special reasons, everyone who has conceded the same thing to others against himself may rightly have the benefit of this law.

Nevertheless I maintain that there may be reasons of *equity, humanity,* or *good faith* which suggest that the rigor of *expletive justice*[4] as defined by the natural law should be tempered at times, and these reasons should have equal weight in mitigating the rigor of the civil laws. This consideration is to be maintained with particular care *in the case of a promise,* even when it does not suffice to produce a civil obligation, unless there is a countervailing circumstance which would annul the force of the promise even in the natural state. By duly applying these principles we can arrive at a judgment about the duty of an heir in an intestacy to challenge a will which is invalid in civil law or not; of a son of a family in the matter of pleading the senatorial decree *Macedonianum,*[5] and that of a woman in pleading the so-called *Velleian* decree;[6] of a minor, with regard to seeking *restitution,* and so on. See above all on this subject the elegant discussions of the celebrated Barbeyrac published in *French,* on *The Permission and Benefit of Laws.*[7] [II.12.7.i]

---

2. Amesius, *De Conscientia et eius jure.*

3. Huber, *De Jure Civitatis,* pp. 487–94.

4. *justitia expletrix:* for this term, see above, pp. 43–44.

5. This law restricted or prevented the bringing of an action for payment of a loan made to a son of a family.

6. This law forbade women to undertake liability for others, e.g., in standing surety for loans.

7. Barbeyrac, *Discours sur la permission des loix,* and *Discours sur le bénéfice des loix.*

Moreover, if they [the civil laws] really do conflict [with the divine law], the citizens should not obey them, even if perhaps the conflict is not completely open and beyond all shadow of doubt. For every doubt about the meaning of the divine law which has been revealed to us is to be attributed in the court of God at least to a certain culpable weakness. See our remarks above, at pp. 32–33. [I.1.5.iii] But if the question is about what can most safely be done while the doubt remains, it seems that the only general rule which can be suggested is that one should incline to the side which is supported by the stronger arguments and where the danger of sin appears smaller. But if the arguments look equal on both sides, even when the authority of the civil ruler is included in the calculation, and the considerations which his authority implies (considerations which do not always prevail in these cases), see the author's discussion at *On the Duty of Man and Citizen*, I.1.6. Hobbes's comment is absurd, that *the civil laws cannot conflict with natural law, at least in those matters which regard men's rights*,[8] as if men, while subjecting their rights, both adventitious and natural, to the civil government for protection, could and would let the ruler deal with them as he pleases. [II.12.8.i]

I have no doubt that many things may rightly be done by subordinates which it would be wrong for superiors to do because they are contrary to the law of prudence or humanity, especially as the judgment to be given about them often depends on particular facts which superiors are presumed to have studied, and of which subordinates are invincibly ignorant. I contend nevertheless that an action done by a subordinate under whatever authority, does not cease to be imputable to him, if in doing it he exercises the power of his own will. And therefore no instruction from a superior legitimizes on the part of a subordinate any of the actions which I said at pp. 37–38 cannot be excused by the second type of coercion. This also settles the view we should hold of the example Pufendorf gives of the citizen who bears arms in an unjust war (see also on this, Grotius, book II, final chapter: much better argued than by Pufendorf).[9] It is clumsy to ob-

Both tracts were bound with Barbeyrac's translation of Pufendorf's *Les devoirs de l'homme et du citoyen* (1718; 1735).

8. Hobbes, *On the Citizen*, XIV.10, p. 159; *Leviathan* (1946), ch. 26, pp. 174–75.

9. Grotius, *Rights of War and Peace*, II.XXVI.1–6, pp. 507–15; and Pufendorf, *Of*

ject that a judgment cannot be given on this matter except by those who are present at the secret councils of a prince; for the *justice* of a war is to be judged not by the *persuasive* causes, which may indeed be secret, but by the *justifying* causes, that is, those which are published to the whole world to assert the justice of the war undertaken. [II.12.9.i]

ii. On punishment

[Pufendorf says: "A punishment is an evil one suffers, inflicted in return for an evil one has done; in other words, some painful evil imposed by authority as a means of coercion in view of a past offense." Carmichael comments:]

Both definitions used here are wrong, in that they ignore the *purpose* of inflicting punishment (for this is all that we are discussing here). It is its purpose which distinguishes a *punishment* properly so called from *parental correction, from compensation for loss wrongfully caused, from guarantee for the future, and from the evils of war;* for these too should only be inflicted directly on *wrongdoers,* i.e., on those who invade our right or prevent us from obtaining it. A better definition of punishment might be, *an evil which is rightly inflicted on a wrongdoer because of the wrong he has done, for the purpose of providing security to human society against the commission of similar wrongs in the future on the part of the same man or of others by his example.* And since there has to be a *right* in the punisher to exact the penalty, this certainly implies that there is an *obligation* on the part of the person punished, if not of active cooperation, at least of nonresistance, to a deserved punishment. It is no objection to this that the penalty is to be inflicted against his will, since even a man who submits to it from consciousness of moral obligation may recoil in horror from the actual punishment as dreadful and painful to him. [II.13.4.i]

It is not always necessary for a penalty to be exacted in the exercise of authority, as may be understood from our remarks at pp. 69–71 and from the passages of Grotius and Locke cited there. [II.13.4.ii]

---

the *Law of Nature and Nations,* VIII.I.6. Barbeyrac devoted a long note to Pufendorf's discussion, arguing forcefully that citizens cannot execute iniquitous orders "without making themselves Accomplices of the Iniquity of him that gives them" (n. 2, pp. 750–51).

Sufferings inflicted in the course of fighting in war or battle do not have the nature of *punishment*. This is not because they are not inflicted *in the exercise of authority* (see the previous note), but because they are not inflicted specifically *to provide security for human society in the future*. They are inflicted as necessary means for defending or pursuing the right of an injured party, against those who attack that right or hinder its satisfaction. [II.13.4.iii]

On the right to inflict punishment in the state of nature, see pp. 69–71. We spoke above (p. 158) about the origin of the power which belongs to the civil ruler in a state to inflict physical punishment on the guilty. At *Of the Law of Nature and Nations,* VIII.3.1, Pufendorf rightly derives this power of government as exercised against a criminal, not so much from the consent of the criminal himself as of the rest of the citizens. He does not however adequately explain the character and effect of this consent when he says there that it is the act *by which individuals oblige themselves not only not to defend, but also to lend their strength, if need be, against anyone whom the ruler of the state is to punish,* while at the same time denying that the right of punishment belongs to individuals in the natural state. For these arguments do not prove that *the right of punishment* itself belongs in the civil state to the supreme ruler and his delegates (the main point in question here), but that he has the *right to make use of other men's strength* in inflicting a punishment, assuming that he has the right to punish.

I see no way to clear this matter up except by arguing that the right to inflict punishment on flagrant violators of the natural laws as an unavoidable way of protecting the safety of the human race is indeed common to all men in the natural state (though not equally so to wrongdoers), but that it is devolved by those who subject themselves to civil government on the supreme ruler to exercise on their behalf. In vain would you say, with Titius, that the fact that a person can be punished derives from the *crime,* if there was no one who could inflict a penalty appropriate to the crime before the *agreement* of the criminal himself.[10] But if individuals may do this in the natural state, then the agreement of the person against whom

---

10. Titius, *Observationes,* no. 643.

the right is valid does no more harm in the case of punishment than in the case of other rights, to those who naturally have these rights and have not made an agreement to submit the exercise of them to the same civil government. The reason therefore why criminals should be punished only by a magistrate is not to be found in the consent of the criminals, as the celebrated commentator suggests, but in the consent of the rest of the citizens. This is the only thing that *government of territory* gives against outsiders, that outsiders may not rightly exact by force either a punishment or anything else that may be due to them from those who live within its boundaries, without first invoking the cognizance of the *civil ruler of* the territory, in order not to disturb the public peace with unnecessary violence.[II.13.5.i]

The question of the punishment of corporations (*universitas*) is difficult and complicated. For on the one hand, the author has properly explained that a private penalty cannot be imposed on someone against his will for a public crime, and so nothing can be taken from him which he did not hold in the name and for the benefit of the corporation. On the other hand, it is not equally clear by what right the state as such may be liable to punishment; for states too count as corporations on this view. For as Grotius, and Pufendorf following him, acknowledge, *merit* and *demerit* belong to the class of things which are predicated of a corporation, not directly in themselves, but by abstraction from individuals, exactly as we say that a corporation which has many learned or brave individuals is itself *learned* or *brave.* For this reason too, as they both recognize, when the men who gave their consent and cooperation to a public crime are dead, the crime too, and the debt of punishment likewise, are extinguished. Thus it seems consonant with these points to speak of the penalty properly so called as owed not by the corporation itself as by the delinquent individuals. There is also the point that the chief purpose for imposing punishment among men, i.e., *the terror of the example,* is irrelevant, since criminals tend to be deterred from crimes by fear of evils to be inflicted on their persons, not on the corporation of which they are members. It would suffice therefore, at the most, when a public crime has been committed, that the guilty individuals should be punished and the loss be made good by the state itself and that a guarantee for the future be given to the injured party, the corporation's right being left unimpaired in other respects to the nonguilty. But I do not deny that when a state has shown an intention to harm not one state or another but all states indiscriminately with whom it is not associated by treaty, such a state is rightly outlawed, for the common security of mankind, if the guilty cannot be separated from the innocent.

For crimes committed or duties omitted by common counsel, subordinate corporations are normally deprived of certain privileges or sometimes of their very status as *corporations*. This seems to have the character of a *conventional penalty*, since corporations are assumed to be constituted, explicitly or tacitly, on that condition by the supreme ruler. [II.13.19.i]

iii. On reputation

[Pufendorf distinguishes between "simple reputation" and "intensive reputation" (or "reputation by distinction" in Barbeyrac's phrase). The former belongs to the morally good or law-abiding man; the latter is recognized by honor from other men. Carmichael is chiefly concerned to stress the moral foundation of both kinds of reputation. For example, even slaves may have simple reputation:]

It is inhuman and contrary to reason that simple reputation in civil society should be thought lacking in anyone on account of a condition [slavery] which contains no moral turpitude. [II.14.8.i]

[But he is chiefly concerned to stress that the conventional system of honors has a moral basis even where it seems not to:]

Titius carefully points out here that intensive reputation should be divided into two: one is *absolute* or *ethical*, and consists of true excellence, either conforming or conformable to the laws, and commands a genuine feeling of honor; the other is *hypothetical*, or *civil*, is based on an agreement or law, and produces only external effects in civil life.[11] Now we are all aware that these two are different, and do not normally go together. However the abuse of civil reputation should not be confused with its original use and scope, so that one would come to believe that it has nothing in common with true excellence. Here is the way we should look at it. It is

---

11. Ibid., no. 666.

natural that those who are regarded as making a greater contribution to promoting the interest and splendor of human society should be honored above the rest and distinguished with greater honors. But if judgments about the application of this prerogative and the distribution of external signs of honor in accordance with it were given from the facts themselves, men would inevitably disagree with each other, and from that disagreement more serious evils would arise to disturb human society more than if precedence were completely neglected. To avoid this situation, the custom has been introduced, and confirmed among citizens by laws, with foreigners by treaties, that as this whole thing pertains to certain external effects in human life, it should be defined by external criteria that have an impact on the senses. For this reason no one who is not totally ignorant of the character of human affairs will be surprised that the actual distinctions made do not coincide exactly with the truth of the matter. That it strays such an immense distance from the truth, is to be attributed to the notable depravity and corruption of men; yet in this matter its effects ought to be tolerated, since they cannot be corrected without more serious disadvantages. [II.14.11.i]

[Similarly Carmichael assigns a moral gradation to Pufendorf's miscellaneous list of human qualities:]

The qualities surveyed here are not all to be given equal value. Some are material for praise in themselves, for example, the *moral virtues* and their exercise. Others recommend a man, either because they are not acquired without laudable diligence or because they at least make their possessor more inclined to do good. *Intellectual endowments* are among these. Others simply bring a man the esteem of providing the means or opportunity for promoting more effectively the interests of the human race; in this category we place *the goods of body and of fortune.* From this it is clear what qualities have most power to excite a sincere feeling of honor among intelligent men, though in distributing the external marks of honor, almost greater account is usually taken of the things that strike the senses, and especially of the goods of fortune. This is not only because of agreements and laws which ground a perfect right to those distinctions, but also because of the influence of the prevailing manners, on which an imperfect right is often founded. Manners may scarcely be neglected without a stain of boorishness, whether among citizens or between those who live in mutual natural liberty. [II.14.13.1]

iv. On virtues[12]

The virtues which are particularly relevant here are reviewed by the celebrated Barbeyrac as follows: 1. *Piety to God.* 2. *Justice and love of equity.* 3. *Fortitude tempered with prudence.* 4. *Discretion.* 5. *Moderation of desires.* 6. *Kindness and mercy.* 7. *Generosity.* The learned commentator illustrates each of these and several other things that Pufendorf says in this chapter with very appropriate reflections of his own and some which he has borrowed from writers of the highest genius. Prominent among these are Montaigne, Charron, La Bruyère, and, above all, the perceptive author of the noble tale *Of the Deeds of Telemachus,* the whole of which, indeed, from beginning to end, is an elegant and copious commentary on this chapter. See also Buddeus, *Practical Philosophy,* part III, ch. 5, secs. 3 ff.[13] [II.11.2.i]

[Pufendorf gives a summary account of the professions, to which Carmichael adds the following paragraphs in praise of lawyers and doctors[14] beginning with this comment:]

12. From the notes to bk. II, ch. 11, "On the Duty of Sovereigns"; and bk. II, ch. 18, "On the Duties of Citizens."

13. Barbeyrac's extensive discussion of the virtues that should be cultivated by sovereigns is set out in notes to Pufendorf, *Of the Law of Nature and Nations,* VII.IX.1–4 (pp. 731–38). All of the references to the authors mentioned by Carmichael may be found there. The Spavan abridgement (1716) contains an adaptation of the same discussion at vol. II, pp. 249–73. Carmichael's perfunctory treatment of the subject is consistent with his view that virtues are best understood as corollaries of the various rights and obligations of men and citizens. See above, pp. 18 and 43. It is not surprising on the other hand that Barbeyrac should have been more receptive to skeptical and humanistic writing on the virtues; while Barbeyrac maintained that natural law theories were the best antidote to skepticism, he frequently attempted, as we have seen, to incorporate the insights of skeptical authors in his exposition. See p. xv and 146, n. 3.

14. Loosely summarized from Quintilian, *Education of the Orator,* 12.7 ff.

No one will take it amiss, I think, if I am reluctant to omit altogether from this list the two noble orders of the educated professions in one or other of which a good part of the youth of the university are expected to take their place one day. No one will take it amiss either that I have not chosen to separate advocates from judges; I have described their duties more in the words of their great teacher, Quintilian, than in my own, so that no one will complain that the subject is defined too rigidly. The evidence of truth itself forced from Cicero an acknowledgment of these duties though he did not always fulfill them. His words are quoted by Ammianus, book XXX, ch. 4, which the editors of the fragments have assigned to the fourth book of Cicero, *On the Commonwealth:*

> Since nothing in the republic should be so uncorrupted as the giving of a vote or the declaring of an opinion, I do not understand why he who has corrupted it with money is deserving of punishment while he who has corrupted it with eloquence is even rewarded with praise. Indeed he seems to me to do more harm who corrupts a judge with an oration than with money, because no one can corrupt a prudent man with money but one can corrupt him with words.[15]

Let those who devote themselves to pleading cases, the high priests of Justice, not open the safe harbor of their eloquence to pirates, but look at the merits of each case before they take it up. Once they have taken up a case, let them work at it faithfully; but let them never think that they should put their case above truth and justice; and let them not hesitate to drop a case which seemed good when they took it but which they recognize to be wicked as the process unfolds, simply because they have always spoken the truth to their client: for they are not to deceive a litigant with vain hopes nor knowingly maintain an unjust case before the judges, either by misrepresenting the truth of the facts or by not scrupling to assert about the state of the law what they would blush to pronounce if they were giving judgment from the bench or lecturing in the classroom. It will be no

---

15. This passage of Cicero, which is quoted by Ammianus Marcellinus, *Roman History,* XXX.4, is now assigned by editors to bk. 5 of Cicero, *On the Commonwealth* (*De republica,* 5.11, fr. 2).

impediment to the administration of justice but rather a help if the role of
the advocate is guided by religion.

Those who offer their skills for the healing of the sick should give serious and sustained attention to learning their art and always improving
their proficiency, as well as to investigating the case of each patient carefully; let them not take excessive fees by unduly prolonging the treatment,
but prescribe the best remedies for each case, the same remedies, in fact,
that they would apply to themselves in a similar case and give to their nearest and dearest.

CHAPTER 22

On the Rights of War and Peace[1]

War and the law of nations

This is not the place to put forward a general doctrine of *war*, which should be derived from *On the Duty of Man and Citizen*, I.5; although Pufendorf has only discussed *defense* there, we have added some notes to section 17 on the prosecution of one's rights by force which, we suggested, is relevant to the topic.[2] What we said there about self-defense or prosecution by force is equally true, whether the conflict is between individual men in a state of nature with each other or between multitudes of men, united either by the obligation of a simple agreement or by the bond of government. Hence too the genuine notion of *war*, as it is considered in the discipline of *natural right*, is abstracted from all variations of that kind.

War is therefore defined by Grotius (*Rights of War and Peace*, I.I.2) as *the state of those who are in violent conflict, so far as they are so*, and that would be adequate, if he had added *for the sake of rights*, so as to exclude conflicts undertaken for practice or profit. Titius, though including that distinguishing mark, has a definition of war that is too wide for another reason, *the state of those who are in dispute, in fact or intention, for the sake of rights*.[3] As if the general notion of war abstracted not only from the number of the disputants but also from *the violent manner of the dispute*,

---

1. From the notes to bk. II, ch. 16, "On War and Peace"; and bk. II, ch. 18, "On the Duties of Citizens." Carmichael makes no significant commentary on ch. 17, "On Treaties."

2. See above, pp. 67–71, on the right of self-defense.

3. Titius, *Observationes*, no. 684.

so that even legal disputes, not to mention verbal conflicts outside of court, would be included in the scope of war.

Since therefore war is not by its nature unique to states, the only things strictly relevant to this topic are those which concern the mutual obligation of a ruler and his subjects with regard to war or the sharing among them of the pertinent obligations, or finally the privileges voluntarily granted by the right of nations to those who with the performance of all due solemnities wage wars by the authority of sovereigns, in states which are known and recognized as such by neighboring nations. [II.16.1.i]

These [a demand for reparations and guarantee for the future] are contained in the affirmation *by which we assert our claim to what is due to us by others but has been denied.* That is, every just war presupposes a wrong, which comes about (as we noted above, p. 44) through an unjust action which violates some natural or real right, or through the omission of an action due, which constitutes a refusal to satisfy a personal right. Compare Grotius, II.I (*at the beginning*). [II.16.2.i]

A *declaration* (as Grotius rightly points out, III.III.7) is either a *conditional declaration,* which is associated with a demand for restoration of property and precedes the outbreak of war by some interval of time, or a *pure declaration,* which accompanies the actual commencement of hostilities. One must infer from the end and scope of either, the cases in which the one or the other is necessary by natural law. The aim of a *pure declaration* is to announce what right it is for whose protection or pursuit the war is being waged. The aim of a *conditional declaration* is to make known that what we claim as rightly ours or as owed to us, cannot be obtained without military force.

Hence it follows, (1) that no declaration on the part of the defending side is required by nature for a legitimate defense against an unjust aggression, if no declaration of cause preceded it, or if it was manifestly unjust or no time was allowed for a response. But when a plausible cause for starting a war has been declared, because it rests on facts which would suffice to justify aggression if they were true and their consequences could not be nullified by other facts, in that case I would think the defender obliged, at the earliest opportunity, either to deny those facts or to adduce other facts which nullify the claim of the aggressor (even though his facts may be true). And sometimes no reason may be given for an act of aggression, yet still, if the other party defends himself by offensive acts not only against the aggressor himself but also against his subjects, who did not share his violent act and perhaps were not aware of it (I have discussed the grounds on which they are obligated above at pp. 175–81), then in cases of this sort one is always obliged to make clear the reason for using force against the individuals on whom it is directly inflicted, and to allow them time to produce what one is claiming from them; the only exception is if force is being employed as a punishment, but innocent citizens are not liable to punishment for a public crime as is clear from what has been said.

It also follows, (2) that no conditional declaration is required when war is made on the guilty parties themselves, to inflict capital punishment on them. However a pure declaration is required. For force is never to be used against anyone without signifying the reason, unless it is quite clear from the situation itself. The same perhaps should be said about the forcible seizure of someone who shows by obvious signs that he designs to use force against us, i.e., in this case a pure declaration is required, accompanying the forcible seizure, not a conditional declaration preceding it, if this would be harmful to our situation.

(3) Finally it follows, that when war is made for some other reason, a prior or conditional declaration is required, so that one gives an adequate indication to the other party of what one is claiming before using force; and so that it may be clear that force has to be used to prosecute one's right in this respect because of neglect to settle the claim. I do not exempt the case in which one intends to seize one's own property, if by chance one cannot get hold of it without hurting those who are holding it.[4] When there has been an explicit conditional declaration, and the required restitution is not forthcoming, it is not necessary also to make a pure declara-

---

4. In *Rights of War and Peace*, III.III.6, no. 7, p. 554, Barbeyrac disputed Carmichael's opinion that a conditional declaration was required before using force to reclaim one's own possessions from persons not party to the war. He considered the retainers of such possessions to be "accomplices in the Injustice, [who] therefore deserve to be treated with no greater Tenderness than the principal Detainer."

tion; however this seems to be absolutely required, when there has been a merely implicit conditional declaration, i.e., a declaration concealed in the demand for what is due.

What we have said pertains to the justice of acts of war as defined by *natural right*. The account of *declaration* [of war], as it is required for the *formality* of war and for the effects of a formal war, is different, and is defined by what is specifically called the *law of nations*. Hence this topic also seems to require us to make some brief remarks on the *law of nations*, so far as it is distinguished, rightly or wrongly, from the *natural law*.[5]

The terms *natural* law and law *of nations* are sometimes used in a confused manner. They are often understood to indicate bodies of law which are wholly or partly distinct, but the distinction is differently explained by different authors. Some, including Hobbes, make the law of *nations* one of two branches of *natural* law, i.e., there is the natural law of men and the natural law of states, and they want to apply *law of nations* to the latter; this is the only meaning of the phrase that they recognize.[6] For most writers however the *law of nations* is a wider term than *natural law*. I will not waste time on those who include in the law of nations everything which they find introduced or approved in the civil customs of all or most nations, or at least the more civilized nations, since the only kind of law of nations relevant to this discussion is that which pertains to *the mutual association of nations with each other,* as Grotius says (II.VIII.I).

The philosophy of Ulpian is also irrelevant, in recognizing as natural law only that *which nature has taught all animals;* for natural law is to be judged not from the instinct of animals but from the dictation of reason, as almost everyone today agrees. More correctly several interpreters both of *natural* and of *civil* law explain the distinction between *natural* law and the law of *nations* specially so called, according to the two definitions of the *law of nations* which the Emperor gives at *Institutes,* I.2.1 and 2.[7] The first is the law of nations as defined at section 1 as *what natural reason has established among all men,* which is said by the interpreters to be the *pri-*

---

5. Grotius, *Rights of War and Peace,* III.III.6, pp. 553 ff.
6. Hobbes, *On the Citizen,* XIV.4, p. 156.
7. Justinian, *Institutes,* I.2.1 and 2.

mary law of nations and is actually *natural* law itself. The second is defined in section 2, i.e., *what human nations have established for themselves under the pressure of custom and human needs,* which is called by the same interpreters the *secondary* [law of nations], is actually the *law of nations* itself in its particular sense, and is called by Grotius the *voluntary* law of nations.

In this respect some of the most distinguished jurists seem to me to have gone astray (see Vinnius[8] on these paragraphs and Huber, *On the Rights of Civil Society,* I.I.5) in that they restrict the *primary* law of nations, which they recognize as identical with *natural* law, to what is *directly* known or, as they say, known by the *noetic* intellect; and they ascribe to the *secondary* law of nations whatever is discerned by the *dianoetic* intellect, i.e., the intellect that makes use of argumentation.[9] As if conclusions deduced from necessary principles which have immutable truth could be altered at men's discretion! Rather we should assert to the contrary that the truth of moral principles and the truth of the conclusions that flow from them are equally necessary and equally valid. I do not deny that these conclusions often presuppose certain human actions. Nonetheless it is necessarily and unalterably true that, given those actions, certain rights and certain corresponding obligations follow. For natural law deals not only with things which exist without the will of men, but also with many things which are consequent on the action of a human will, as Grotius rightly pointed out (I.I.10). And he is therefore right to ascribe to *natural* law whatever is known by nature to be prescribed or forbidden by God by the dictate of right reason, whether direct or indirect. To the *voluntary* law of *nations* belong only those things which have received their obligatory force from the will of all, or many, nations.

There is a major dispute about this *voluntary law of nations,* with regard to its *name* and to its *obligatory force.* Concerning its name, it is quite clear that as the *voluntary law of nations* does not proceed from a *superior* it cannot be called a law properly so called. The question of its *obligation* is more difficult, i.e., whether or not things which have been introduced into the customs of all or most nations, or at least of the more civilized nations who

---

8. Vinnius, *In quattuor libros,* I.2.1 and 2.
9. Huber, *De Jure Civitatis,* I.I.5, pp. 21–23.

interact with each other, have at least the force of an *agreement* which is
either *implicit* or tacitly concluded among those who have an interest in it,
and from which it would be wrong to withdraw. Here we feel we should
take a *middle* line, i.e., that rulers of individual states are so far obliged to
observe these customs, that they should not withdraw from them in order
to deceive other nations, that is, if the others have not been informed in
time, so far as their interest is concerned. This is the whole extent of the
obligation where there is no more particular, or explicit, agreement.

This is not the place to rehearse the details of what has been accepted
in the past or received today as included in this voluntary law of nations.
There will be an opportunity below to note in passing some particular
points which pertain to the *right of war,* and above all to the effects which
most nations have agreed to attribute to a *public and formal war.* To produce these effects, as Pufendorf points out in this paragraph,[10] it is required not only that the war be waged by the authority of sovereigns on
both sides, but also that it have been *publicly declared* or proclaimed, at
least by one of the parties. This *declaration,* as required by the law of
nations for such ends, has no other aim (as Grotius maintains at
III.III.11—see however the notes of Barbeyrac)[11] than *that it be absolutely
clear that the war is being waged not as a private enterprise but by the will of
both peoples or of their leaders.* It is consistent with this that it is not required (as indeed the peerless Grotius points out, ibid., sec. 13) that the
declaration of war be made some time before; and for a good reason, I
would add, so that it may explain the particular causes of the war; though
a proclamation of causes should be the special aim of a declaration that is
required for the justice of a war as defined by natural law. [II.16.7.i]

Grotius offers this *first* effect of a public and declared war according to
the voluntary law of nations at book III.IV.2 and 3 ff. But it would be to
the interest of the human race that such license or *external impunity* be
restricted in the following way. Even if men fighting under the banner of
a declared war could take up arms for any cause whatsoever, and indulge

---

10. *On the Duty of Man and Citizen,* I.16.6, p. 169.

11. In his note on Grotius at III.III.1 (*Rights of War and Peace,* p. 556), Barbeyrac
merely observes that wars may be declared in many ways: that an army appearing upon
a frontier may signal a state of war as effectively as a herald.

without purpose or moderation in the slaughter of enemy troops, and in plunder, arson, and looting against the enemy population at large, and get away with it, at least *deliberate slaughter of infants* and other obviously *innocent people, forcible rape and adultery,* and similar atrocious acts of cruelty and savage fury should not go unpunished among the civilized, particularly the Christian, nations. Compare Grotius, book III, ch. IV with ch. XI, also ch. V and ch. XII.[12] [II.16.12.i]

The *other* proper effect of a declared war according to the law of nations, which is discussed by Grotius at III.VI.2 ff., is *the acquisition of property captured in war.* So far as property is rightly captured in war by the natural law, and so far as it is acquired by being captured, I have said enough above (pp. 70–71). This right between enemies who are not bound by any more specific convention, of taking, keeping, or recovering things by war, seems to rest only on those natural foundations. But seizure which occurs in a public and declared war entails certain effects of quasi-law (called by Grotius, *external ownership*) in the eyes of most nations. These effects have usually been introduced for the benefit of states which have followed neither party in war into whose territories things taken in war have been transported, or for the benefit of private individuals who, not being themselves enemies, have acquired by legitimate title other people's property taken in war.

On the former: it may easily happen that moveable things captured in war are transported into the territory of a state which has followed neither party in the war, either by those who took them or by others who have acquired them under some title. If the objects taken were reclaimed by their former owners, and the ruler of that state were obliged to order their restoration on the hypothesis that they had been unjustly stolen, it would almost inevitably happen that every state would be involved, even against its will, in disputes with neighboring states. To avoid this, it has been decided that any war fought under the auspices of sovereign powers on both sides, and duly declared, should be considered just on both sides to the

---

12. In these chapters Grotius compares the right of killing enemies and of acquiring things taken in a declared war (ibid., III.IV, pp. 557 ff. and III.V, pp. 573 ff.) with what moderation requires in killing enemies and in laying waste (ibid., III.XI, pp. 650 ff.).

extent that if members of a nation which follows neither party in a war take things in such a war or acquire them by legitimate title and if the things are carried into their own country, they should be defended in their possession of them, as things acquired by right; nor would their repossession be permitted to their former owners on this ground.

But also, with respect to the *latter* cause, it has been decided to assign the same effect of capture in war, in the case of things of that kind, if by chance they are found on the high seas or in any other place which has no government, in the hands of a person who, though not an enemy himself, has acquired by legitimate title things captured by an enemy. Further it did not seem absurd either to the Romans or to other nations to grant an appearance of right to hostile seizure even within the limits of the state from which the things had been taken. However the effect of this was voided by the right of *postliminium*[13] in the case of captured men and immoveables as well as (originally) in the case of certain moveables. In the case of other things, and in our day when the right of *postliminium* no longer exists, in the case of moveables generally, the right of seizure in war is valid to the extent that former owners cannot succeed in a claim for such things seized in war against any nonhostile person, who has transported them to the territory of the same or of an allied state, whether they have been seized back from the enemy in the same war, or taken by some third party in another war, or even acquired in the course of commerce or for some other private reason. On captured men see pp. 207–9. [II.16.13.i]

[Pufendorf asserted that immoveable property is considered to be captured when it can no longer be effectively held. Carmichael comments:]

The usefulness of this definition relating to immoveable property may be denied on good grounds. For everyone admits that, between actual enemies, it makes no difference whether the thing is completely captured or not, since if the war continues, it may be recovered by the same right by which it was previously defended. But I do not find it agreed by the com-

---

13. *Postliminium,* recovery of rights by a returning Roman citizen who had been a prisoner of war. Grotius devoted a chapter to the right of *postliminium* (ibid., III.IX, pp. 611 ff.).

mon consent of nations, that the right of the former owner of immoveable property against a third party who has acquired it by some title from the enemy, is worse than against the enemy himself; provided that the former owner did not fail to assert his right to it, or at least gave no sign of an intention to abandon it. But if an immoveable thing has been restored to the jurisdiction of the same government, it is a matter of undoubted law that it is now restored to the former owner by the right of recovery.[14] The only direct effect of the seizure in war of immoveable property seems to be that those who have no interest in it, if by chance they owe any real servitude on the occupied estate, may rightly pay it to the new possessor, and should not be blamed by the former owner for doing so. I will note in *the following paragraphs* (pp. 207–8) that seizure of government has a similar effect but with wider application. [II.16.13.iii]

[Pufendorf says: "Rule over conquered peoples as over individuals is also won by war." Carmichael comments first on individuals and then on peoples.]

I have fully explained earlier (ch. 16, pp. 139–42) to what extent the captor obtains a right over his captive by nature; I have also explained that it is invalid to cite the consent of nations in defense of any license which goes beyond the limits allowed by natural law in this area (even allowing that one may see the consent of nations in depraved moral practices). But this question is of less importance among us, since the ancient custom of enslaving those captured in a declared war has long been abolished by reverence for the Christian name among Christians fighting each other. Furthermore though a Christian captured in war by infidels may be compelled to be a slave among them, yet he is not today thought to have changed his status in his own state any more than if he had been captured by robbers. Add Titius, *Observations on Lauterbach,* 1443;[15] see also on this whole subject, Grotius, III.VII, and compare ch. XIV.[16] [II.16.14.i]

14. Barbeyrac reinforced Carmichael's opinion on this subject, observing that whereas third parties or neutral countries in war may be ignorant of the proper owner of moveable goods, they could not be unaware of the proper ownership of land (note on ibid., III.VI.2, n. 1, p. 580).

15. Titius, *Observationum ratiocinantium.*

16. Grotius's discussion in *Rights of War and Peace,* III.XIV, pp. 661 ff., does not

I have given what seems to be the position of the law of nature on this question at pp. 175–81. As far as the law of nations is concerned, if it is a question of acquiring government over men themselves, this is no more valid against men generally than against individuals (see the previous note, and compare pp. 141–42). But if it is a question of acquiring *government over territory,* or of the right of requiring that no one remain on the land except under the law of civil subjection, I would not think that the voluntary law of nations is much more valid here than I argued that it was in the acquisition of immoveable objects (see above, pp. 205–6). For in spite of the immorality of belligerent nations, in spite of the sentiments of those who rejoice in superior force, it is not clear that there has ever been any common agreement among nations that a conquered prince or people, who have not consented in any way to the government of a conqueror (and for what is not to be considered as a sign of that consent, see pp. 179–81), has not as valid a right, against the enemy or against anyone deriving his title from him, to recover the government, as he had formerly to defend it. Furthermore, I would not think that even sovereigns who do not have patrimonial governments, could validly agree anything to the contrary, seeing that it would be no more than a transfer of government "in a certain contingency" and indeed to an "uncertain person."[17]

The one effect that the consensus of nations seems indubitably to have attributed to violent seizure of government over a people, or part of a people, by regular war, as well as to seizure of government over a whole people by internal sedition, is that foreigners who owe anything to a people or community, whose government has been seized by force, may rightly pay to an invader who demands it, what the legitimate ruler was able to demand rightfully, and by paying be discharged of the debt. And hence if the prince were restored to power or a people to its freedom, they could not claim a debt so paid. This is introduced for the reason indicated above, i.e., so that those who follow neither side in a war may not be unwillingly involved in other people's quarrels. Since this consideration does not ob-

_____

pertain specifically to Christians captured in battle. It is a plea for moderation with respect to all prisoners of war.

17. Legacies, as well as various other types of transaction, in favor of an "uncertain person" (*incertae personae*), were generally held to be invalid in Roman law (see, e.g., Justinian, *Institutes,* II.20.25).

tain in contracts entered into of one's own accord, I would not think that the same consideration should be extended to such people, and least of all to beneficiaries; hence *acceptilatio*[18] is not at all an adequate substitute for *payment* in this case. Concerning seizure of government, see Grotius, III.VIII, and compare ch. XVI, but above all Locke, *Second Treatise of Government*, ch. 16. [II.16.14.ii]

Concerning truces and other agreements made in the continuing course of a war, see Grotius, III.XXI.2 ff., but first read ch. XIX of the same book. The reasons by which our author at *Of the Law of Nature and Nations*, VIII.VII.2, seems to impugn the natural obligation of all agreements between enemies which do not remove the state of war are so trivial, and at the same time of such dangerous consequences, and for both reasons so unworthy of such a man, that we are ashamed to give them here, much less to spend time in discussing them. See the distinguished Barbeyrac's note on *the passage cited above*.[19] [II.16.15.i]

On agreements that restore peace, Grotius, III.XX, should be carefully read. The philosophy of Pufendorf on their validity, in cases where they have been extorted by unjust force, is too lax, and not sufficiently friendly to human society (*Of the Law of Nature and Nations*, VIII.8.1). Compare above, pp. 85–86. Further, just as preceding injuries are buried by the agreement which restores peace, so also subsequent injuries founded in some new pretext, while they afford a new cause for war, do not break the peace with the effect of reviving the old disputes: as Grotius rightly points out in the same chapter, sec. 27; Titius takes a different view in his note on this passage. [II.16.17.i]

Conquest and loss of citizenship

[Pufendorf observed that men cease to be citizens either when they leave a state with its express or tacit consent and settle with their fortune elsewhere, or when

18. *acceptilatio:* a formal release from an agreement.

19. Barbeyrac was of the opinion that agreements made with an enemy continue to oblige a nation until the terms of the agreement have expired or the enemy's violation of the agreement dispenses us from the obligation to adhere to it. Failure to honor such agreements must lead to perpetual jealousies and endless war (*Of the Law of Nature and Nations*, VIII.VII.2, n. 1, p. 853).

they have been deprived of the right of citizenship and have been driven into exile, or when they have been conquered by an enemy and have been obliged to submit to its government. Carmichael's reflection was prompted by the third and last alternative: his remarks recapitulate his earlier insistence on the rights of conquered people at pp. 164–72 and 207–9.]

[Men may be deprived of their citizenship violently] either as individuals, when they are captured in battle and taken away from their ancestral homes, or together, when the region or the city in which they have their homes is occupied in war. In the first case, the enslavement of men taken captive in war has been abolished among Christians, so that the country is not lost; and in the second case, that part of the country which has been occupied in war is not severed from the state: its relationship is merely kept in suspense until the conclusion of war. And in all the other ways [in which citizenship may be dissolved] which our author reviews in this section, no one may cease to be a citizen as long as the state itself remains, even though in the last case one's citizenship may be narrowly confined. Men cease to be citizens, to be sure, when the state itself is destroyed. In order to determine how this happens, see Pufendorf, *Of the Law of Nature and Nations,* VIII.XII.8–9, Grotius, II.IX.4–6, and also Locke, *Second Treatise of Government,* sec. 211. The authors cited also describe other changes in states which do not however dissolve the civil bond. I note in passing that the instance of the *Scots* which Pufendorf cites (sec. 8, *end*) is not an example [of the dissolution of a people]. For the Scots were not so scattered by Maximus *that they were no longer able to unite,* as subsequent events have shown.[20] [II.18.15.i]

---

20. Magnus Maximus, Roman emperor A.D. 383–88. During his command of the Roman forces in Britain, he fought successfully against Picts and Scots before being acclaimed as emperor by his troops. Maximus is said to have married a British chieftain's daughter and became a figure of legend in post-Roman Britain. It is noteworthy that Carmichael should have concluded his work with an affirmation of the continuity of the Scottish people, given his concern throughout to demonstrate that the consent of the people is the source of the legitimacy of the governments and that peoples have a right to resist tyranny and refuse consent to a conqueror. Barbeyrac accepted Carmichael's authority on the subject of the Scottish people (*Of the Law of Nature and Nations,* VIII.XII.9, n. 2, p. 882): "A very learned Scotchman (*un habile Ecossois*) . . . says, that the Sequel plainly shewed, the Scotch were never so totally defeated, but they could recover themselves."

CHAPTER 23

Appendix: The Rights and Duties of Men and Citizens

*In which concise ethical theses are succinctly set out in
the order which seems most natural for the study of
moral science*[1]

In almost every discipline, the evidence of the propositions taught depends on their connections with one another, with the principles on which
they are based, and therefore on the order in which they are presented.
Accordingly I concluded the first edition of this work with an appendix,
in which I made an attempt to set out the order which nature seems to
have directed us to follow in moral science, so far as it differs from that
given by Pufendorf. But I now believe that a clearer understanding of this
science can be achieved from an even shorter summary of the discipline
itself. And so I have attempted to offer a synopsis of moral science in the
following theses. The exercise may also be useful in another respect inasmuch as students may find sufficient matter for their disputations in these
theses which refer the reader to the relevant passages of Pufendorf
amended and amplified by the annotations and supplements supplied by
myself.[2]

I. A man can find the right road to that happiness to which he aspires
by the fundamental law of his nature only if he conducts himself in every

1. In this edition we have attempted to follow the order of topics outlined in this
appendix. See also the "Editorial Note," p. 7, above.

2. The page numbers cited in the text refer to pages in this edition.

one of his actions in a manner that exhibits love and veneration for the supreme being. And anything in his conduct which betrays hatred or neglect of the deity, he must scrupulously avoid: chapter 2, pp. 21–24 that is, he must act in conformity with the divine law or with that which is morally right: chapter 2, pp. 24–25.

II. All free actions and only free actions are within the scope of the divine law and are therefore capable of moral good and evil: chapter 2, pp. 25–26. These actions and their omissions are considered *moral* only when they fall within the compass of the divine law and may be imputed directly to an agent: chapter 2, p. 26.

III. We have considered the headings under which actions may be imputed to an agent in the court of God and of conscience in chapter 2, pp. 26–28. And Pufendorf[3] discusses the actions and outcomes imputed to us in the human court on the ground that they are connected with our actions.

IV. Although it is the divine law alone which obligates us, so that the morality of all our actions is ultimately to be referred to it, yet it may be useful to consider what is taught about law in general and about the qualities of actions derived from the law and the propositions that are put forward there for discussion. See chapter 4, pp. 39 ff.

V. The divine law is made known to us not only by positive signs [as in revealed theology], but it is in great part signified by nature herself. And when the divine law is so indicated it is called *natural law.* And the study of the precepts of natural law is the proper business of ethics, which for this reason is nothing but *natural jurisprudence:* chapter 2, pp. 28–29.

VI. The duties prescribed for us by natural law are either immediate or mediate. In our immediate duties we express our affection or lack of it to God directly; in our mediate duties this expression of affection is indirect: chapter 5, p. 46.

VII. All the *immediate* duties of the law of nature which are explained in Pufendorf's fourth chapter,[4] may be comprehended summarily under

3. Pufendorf, *On the Duty of Man and Citizen,* I.1.18–27, pp. 23–26.
4. Ibid., I.4, pp. 39–45.

the precept of the law of nature which we have put *first,* that *God must be worshipped:* chapter 5, pp. 46–47.

VIII. The *mediate* duties of the law of nature consist basically in this, that *each man should promote, so far as he is able, the common good of the whole human race and, so far as it may be consistent with the common good, the particular good of individuals.* This is shown in chapter 5, pp. 47–48.

IX. Further, all those actions in which a man brings good to himself or to another in such a way that he harms no one else contribute manifestly to the common good of the human race; therefore it follows as the *second* precept of the law of nature that *each man should pursue every man's interests but especially his own, provided he does no harm to anyone.* For each man can secure more harmless advantages for himself than for others, and the duties owed to others can always be deduced under the [third] precept [of the law of nature], the precept of *sociability:* chapter 5, p. 48, and also chapter 7.

X. Because the interests of men often conflict with one another, one must consider, in securing different interests, what is best, in general, for the human race. And given the character and condition of men on this earth, as described by Pufendorf,[5] it follows that for the human race to be safe, it must be *sociable.* Thus the *third* precept of natural law, which must be employed as the common criterion of all the duties that pertain to conflicts of interest or advantage is that *every man so far as he can must cultivate and preserve sociability:* chapter 5, pp. 48–51.

XI. The cultivation of social life consists in this, that each man should defend his own right in a manner that duly acknowledges the right of other men according to the hypothesis of natural equality: this follows from the reasons given at chapter 5, pp. 51 ff. We may infer then that the best method of defining the duties which apply to men with respect to other men is to set out the various *rights* which belong to men, jointly and separately, from which the corresponding *obligations* will become clear of their own accord.

---

5. Ibid., I.3.1–6, pp. 33–35, where Pufendorf describes the natural condition of mankind as a condition of weakness, poverty, and malice. See also Pufendorf, *Of the Law of Nature and Nations,* II.II.II, pp. 99–102.

XII. Rights are either *perfect* or *imperfect:* chapter 4, pp. 43–44, above and may belong either to *individual men* (or to groups, which do not need to be considered here separately since they result from a combining of the rights of individuals) or to *the whole human race.*

XIII. Perfect rights of individual men are *natural* or *adventitious.* Perfect *natural* rights are reviewed by us in chapter 9, pp. 77 ff.; and Pufendorf instructs us that an unlimited obligation is attached to them.[6]

XIV. *Adventitious* rights may be *real* or *personal.* Among real rights *ownership* is preeminent, and when it is unimpaired, as it is when it results from the original modes of acquisition, it comprehends all rights of this kind; see chap. 10, pp. 92–96. Moreover, Pufendorf shows that the same unlimited obligation adheres to real rights as to natural rights.[7]

XV. *Personal* rights (whose nature and origin are expounded at length in chapter 9, pp. 78–90) are constituted in various ways but particularly by *agreement* or by mutual consent declared by appropriate signs on the part of the person who acquires the right and on the part of the person against whom the right is acquired.

XVI. The obligation to tell the truth is directly related to the obligation of agreements; it derives from at least a tacit agreement: see chapter 9, pp. 87–88.

XVII. In both agreements and assertions the greatest consideration is given to *oaths:* see chapter 9, pp. 85–86.

XVIII. Agreements concerning things or services which enter into commerce and so come to acquire a definite value are called *contracts* by Pufendorf (see chapter 11, pp. 106–8).[8] The common types of contract have their own particular names, also discussed in chapter 11, pp. 108 ff.

XIX. *Personal* rights are also constituted in various ways other than by agreement (and often by the action of him alone against whom some claim may be imputed) as by the *possession of someone else's property* (chapter 10, pp. 101–2) and from those diverse causes which fall under the rubric of *quasi contracts:* chapter 11, pp. 112–17.

6. Pufendorf, *On the Duty of Man and Citizen,* I.6.2, p. 56.
7. Ibid., I.6.3, pp. 56–57; and I.13.1, p. 90.
8. Ibid., I.13, pp. 90–92.

XX. These latter rights commonly arise from a delict. The delict may lie in the past and insofar as damage resulted from it, the injured party has a right to reparation: chapter 8, pp. 73–74. (If the damage was inflicted by fraud, the person who caused the damage may also be required to give an undertaking to desist from such conduct in the future.) The delict may also be in the *present* inasmuch as damage is clearly intended or a debt is not acknowledged; in order to prevent the one or secure the other, force may be necessary. See chapter 7, and particularly pp. 67–71, which may be considered as a Supplement.

XXI. *Personal* rights, especially those constituted by agreement, may be abolished in the various ways reviewed in chapter 12, pp. 118–21. This does not apply to those personal rights reviewed in theses XIX and XX above; their duration is discussed in chapter 7, pp. 65–67.

XXII. There are also certain rights, partly real, partly personal, but more often for the most part real, which are founded, extraordinarily, in some individual necessity: chapter 7, pp. 71–72.

XXIII. There are also certain perfect rights which are common (as was said above, thesis XII) to the *human race* considered collectively and as a person which endures through successive generations. These rights of the human race are protected by God in the state of nature, and most of them are also enjoined upon men in civil society. Among these perfect rights are *the right of preventing* anyone from killing or mutilating himself or another (even though he may be willing) without just cause; the right of preventing anyone from enjoying an illicit or merely transient sexual union, chapter 14, pp. 128–31; the right to prevent anyone from needlessly spoiling things provided by nature for human use, particularly if others might enjoy long use of the thing in question; and the right to prevent anyone from inflicting obvious damage in any other way whatsoever on the living or on posterity or from violating the reverence which is due to the dead. Finally, there remains the perfect right to inflict physical *punishment* on violent criminals, a right which devolves in civil society from individuals to the ruler: see chapter 7, pp. 67–71, and chapter 21, pp. 191–94.[9]

9. On perfect rights that are common to mankind, compare Hutcheson, *A Short Introduction to Moral Philosophy,* pp. 246–47, and at greater length on somewhat different grounds, *A System of Moral Philosophy,* vol. II, pp. 104–6.

XXIV. There are also *imperfect* rights; these may be *unlimited* or *limited*.[10]

XXV. Most of the duties of men are defined either by positive laws or by agreements, and so they depend on a correct interpretation of the language used in those laws and agreements. Therefore *rules of interpretation* have a well-deserved place in natural jurisprudence. And these are explained in chapter 12, pp. 121–23.

XXVI. In addition to that *general* society in which nature has associated all men with one another there are also *particular* or narrower societies in which men are connected by necessity or utility almost always through certain actions on their part. And the ends of entering these societies demand that some must rule and others must obey. Moreover these societies are designed either for the satisfaction of needs or for the prevention of injuries: the former is achieved mainly in those lesser societies called *domestic* societies; the latter is for the most part secured in those larger societies commonly called *civil societies*. In both cases an *adventitious state* is superimposed upon a *natural* one: chapter 13, pp. 124–27.

XXVII. The first place among the particular or lesser societies must be given to *conjugal* society, which is the seedbed of the human race. Its laws and the duties which follow from them are described in chapter 14, pp. 128–33.

XXVIII. Conjugal society generates *offspring;* and the mutual obligations of parents and children are described in chapter 15, pp. 134–37.

XXIX. The different conditions of men brought about the introduction of *servants* into households (or domestic societies) by mutual agreements which reflected a concern for the convenience of both parties; while others were thrust into a servile condition against their will: how rarely this happens by right has been noted by us in chapter 16, pp. 138–45.

XXX. In spite of the fact that everything that is either useful or agreeable in human life could be obtained promptly and universally by the performance of general duties and of those particular duties which follow from the condition of domestic society, the common depravity of mortal men requires them to live in societies with laws of some severity which are

10. See above, pp. 75–76 and 80.

designed to keep them in check; and this is the reason for establishing *civil societies:* chapter 17, pp. 146–53.

XXXI. But such societies cannot be rightly established because of the natural equality of mankind unless prospective citizens give their *consent.* How this consent is obtained is explained in chapter 17, pp. 153–56.

XXXII. The supreme power in civil governments is composed of various *parts,* which may be reduced conveniently to three: *legislative, executive,* and *federative.* And there is not one of these parts which could not be derived from the concurrent consent of subjects, that is, of those for whom or even against whom any action is performed: chapter 18, pp. 157–59.

XXXIII. The *forms* of civil government vary according to whether supreme power is lodged in one man or in one assembly of a few or of all: chapter 18, pp. 159–61.

XXXIV. The sense in which the ruler is in all of these forms sovereign, *unaccountable* and superior to the laws and the sense in which he may be considered absolute and sacred is explained: chapter 19, pp. 162–74.

XXXV. On the various ways of instituting a ruler and of transmitting his right to rule to successors, particularly in monarchies: see chapter 20, pp. 175–87.

XXXVI. The power of making civil laws (the forms and uses of this power are described in chapter 21, part i, pp. 188–91) and the power of executing them extend (as do the limits of these powers) to the *lives* and *bodies* of the citizens (chapter 21, part ii, pp. 191–94), to their *reputations* (chapter 21, part iii, pp. 194–96), and to their properties.

XXXVII. Under the federative power is comprehended the capacity to declare war and make peace (chapter 22, pp. 199 ff.) and to enter into treaties for either purpose.

XXXVIII. The *duties* of sovereigns are described in chapter 18 and the general and particular duties of citizens in chapter 21.

THE END

To God Alone the Glory

Soli Deo Gloria

Natural Theology

The complete text of

A Synopsis of Natural Theology
or, the Knowledge of the existence,
attributes and operations of the Supreme
Deity, drawn from Nature itself

Suitable for the use of students

by Gershom Carmichael,

Professor of Philosophy
in the University of Glasgow

(Edinburgh 1729)

At the cost of John Paton, at whose premises
in Parliament Square copies may be purchased

CONTENTS

Preface. Natural Theology and the Foundations of
Morals   227

Chapter 1. On the Existence of God   234

Section i. In which it is demonstrated that an
independent being exists   234

Section ii. In which it is shown that the
independent being is a spirit, supremely perfect,
from whom all things have their being, that is, is
God   235

Section iii. In which it is shown that the physical
world cannot subsist without an immaterial
principle   237

Section iv. In which it is proved that the physical
world could not have been preserved forever, nor
ever originally brought forth, without some force
which operates above the laws of nature   239

Section v. In which it is shown from the structure of
the physical world that it is the work of an
intelligent and purposefully operating cause   240

Section vi. In which the existence of an immaterial
and essentially thinking principle is confirmed from
the thinking to be found in man, both as viewed in
itself and as combined with physical motions   242

Section vii. In which remarkable events are adduced
in support of the same conclusion   244

Section viii. In which universal human consent is
adduced to the same end, with some other
considerations   245

Section ix. On the arguments for proving the
existence of God made by the celebrated Descartes   246

Chapter 2. On the Attributes of God and First, on
the Incommunicable Attributes   248

Section i. On the attributes of God in general, and
their division   248

Section ii. On the necessary existence of God   249

Section iii. On the divine unity   250

Section iv. On the divine simplicity   251

Section v. On the divine immutability   252

Section vi. On the divine eternity   252

Section vii. On the divine immensity   253

Section viii. On the divine omnisufficiency   254

Section ix. On the divine incomprehensibility   255

Section x. On the divine admirability   256

Section xi. On the divine adorability   256

Chapter 3. On the Communicable Attributes of God   257

Section i. On the communicable attributes of God
in general   257

Section ii. On the divine ideas of things   258

Section iii. On the divine knowledge 259

Section iv. On the divine will 262

Section v. On the divine sanctity 266

Section vi. On the divine power 267

Section vii. On the dominion and majesty of God 268

Section viii. On the divine happiness 269

Chapter 4. On the Divine Operations, or Actions
Involving External Objects 270

Section i. In which the transition to this subject is
explained 270

Section ii. On the properties of divine operations 270

Section iii. On divine creation and preservation 271

Section iv. On divine government 274

Section v. Containing the epilogue of natural
theology and the transition to moral philosophy 280

Preface: Natural Theology and the Foundations of Morals

Greetings to the reader

I would not expect even my kindest readers to forgive me for putting before the public today this small and unpolished textbook on the most difficult and sublime of subjects, and I would certainly never forgive myself for publishing it, if I did not think that it was necessary to do so. I feel obliged to give a brief explanation.

Anyone who has any knowledge of the matter knows how valuable, indeed indispensable, it is, in teaching at the university level, to make use of a short system which sets out in an appropriate and natural order the main points of the subject which the instructor will explain to the students at greater length. The examples of the most learned professors in every faculty are surely good testimony to this, and it is amply borne out by the outrageous errors which teachers make on topics which they profess to know well and to dictate to others, when they reject this regular method of instruction and rely on their own native wit and miscellaneous reading.

For this purpose there were really only two such compends[1] available for teaching pneumatology, of which the discipline briefly outlined here is a part. Both came over from Holland in our own time and have been in use in our universities for some years now.[2] Neither is completely satisfac-

---

1. The treatises referred to are de Vries, *De Natura Dei,* and Le Clerc, *Ontologia.*

2. See below, pp. 381–82, in Carmichael's account of his teaching method (1712), how he substituted his own pneumatics for the third part of the pneumatology of de Vries. Francis Hutcheson employed a similar strategy when he composed his *Synopsis Metaphysicae* (1742): "I am sure it will match de Vries, and therefore I teach the 3rd. part of it *de Deo.*" Letter to Thomas Drenman, 29 October 1743 (Glasgow University Library MS. Gen. 1018, fol. 14).

tory; to explain why would be superfluous for the learned and useless to others.

I have long therefore wished that someone would prepare for the use of students a more suitable treatise of this kind, which would follow the lead of truth and not be out of line with the present state of philosophy. I had myself prepared a text which seemed to be quite suitable for explaining the second part of the subject; this was the treatise of the celebrated Pufendorf, *On the Duty of Man and Citizen,* on which I had published my own notes and commentary. But when a little while ago I obtained the Chair which limits my teaching of philosophy to an annual course in natural theology and moral philosophy, I was concerned that there was no text which I might prelect in covering the first part of the annual curriculum with equal ease and profit for my audience.

It seemed that nothing of this kind could be soon expected from anyone with more leisure and better qualifications in the subject. And since the state of my health would not allow me to take upon myself any heavier or longer labor, my only option was to take up again the very brief compendium of the subject which I had composed more than thirty years before for the pupils who attended my teaching at that time, when we still had the custom of using dictated systems. I had made no serious effort to revise it since then, except in some earlier sections of the first chapter, which I retouched a few years ago to bring them more closely into line with the current state of philosophy.

Both the style and the chain of argument in this compend bore various traces (which even now I am not quite convinced I have eliminated) of my youthfulness and inexperience at the time that I wrote them. However because it was quite short, it seemed it could be revised somehow with relatively little effort. But at the same time its very brevity was a problem, not only because I had to fill in various gaps here and there and explain some things at greater length, but also because as it was short, the reader would be unlikely to be willing to let me *nod off* occasionally, which, as Horace says, *may properly happen to a writer of a long work.*[3]

As I said then, I have carefully read this piece over, and so far as my

---

3. Horace, *The Art of Poetry,* ll. 359–60.

inadequate background and poor health permitted, I have revised it in some places and expanded it in others. I allow it to be published as you now see it, in the hope that it will be useful to young people, albeit with some danger to my reputation.

I have not however dared to forget what a grave and fearful theme it is which is treated here, and how scrupulously one should beware of publishing anything false about him whom (as the wise warned long ago) even to tell the truth is dangerous. It was far from my aim therefore to attempt to say anything new. If the evidence of truth, more powerful than any human authority, has seemed to require anything of me, even in the manner of explanation, which appears to be new, I am not so tenacious of my own opinions that I am not prepared willingly to follow anyone who shows a better way if I have committed any error. I am very aware of my own inadequacy, and of how readily I could slip into error, even when I most wished to avoid it.

I have never enslaved myself to any school of philosophers (nor of political writers either). I have always avoided the forms of speaking of the Aristotelian school, which are obscure, ambiguous, and, as it were, deliberately fashioned for deception; nor did I think they were made any more sacred because they had been blended into sacred matters, and for want of a better philosophy, applied to the explanation of the gravest topics of religion. Yet I cannot avoid confessing that if we look at the matter itself, in what is by far the gravest part of philosophy, and particularly in the articles concerning the unity of God, his simplicity, and the other incommunicable attributes which flow from them, as well as in those concerning the knowledge and decrees of God, and his providence in preservation and in government, the doctrines of the Scholastics,[4] or rather of the more ancient among them, seem to me much more correct and more consonant with sound reason, as well as with sacred scripture, than the doctrines which are opposed to them today, the opinions of certain quite recent

---

4. The scholastics to whom Carmichael refers are the Reformed scholastics of the late sixteenth and early seventeenth centuries: Lambert Daneau (the successor to Calvin and Beza at Geneva), the authors of the Leiden Synopsis, Gisbertus Voetius, Franciscus Turretinus, and others. For a systematic statement of their theology, see Heppe, *Reformed Dogmatics;* for historical background, Fatio, *Méthode et Théologie.*

learned men whose writings are very much in the hands of the students. Hence I have not been ashamed to develop on these issues certain views which have been hissed off the stage by recent writers as scholastic fictions. I have also felt no need to refrain from certain words and phrases proper to the scholastics, though they may perhaps grate on more delicate ears, when a more Latin manner of signifying the sense with equal precision did not occur to me.

The title adequately indicates that I will be expounding here only what is drawn from nature itself about God; and therefore what is known only by special divine revelation falls outside the limits of the subject I propose. And I have adequately shown in the Preface to Pufendorf, pp. x and xi,[5] that the use of this natural knowledge is not excluded, as some believe, but is on the contrary enlarged, by what is more clearly taught on the same matters in the Sacred Book.

There is just one thing left which I think in the interest of truth I should bring to the reader's notice.

I have asserted more than once in this little treatise that a genuine philosophy of morals must be built upon what I call a foundation of natural theology: every rightly founded distinction of moral good and evil in our actions and the sense of obligation that one must pursue the former and avoid the latter in all circumstances, ought to be deduced from the perceived relationship of those actions to God and from a knowledge of the existence, perfections, and providence of the Supreme Deity. I used the same method in laying the foundations of moral doctrine in the first and second Supplements to Pufendorf.[6]

But some have thought otherwise, so much so that in recent years schemes which utterly divorce morality from religion have been put before the public and commended to the world by a highly attractive combination of ingenuity and eloquence.[7] I wondered for some time whether it would be worthwhile to vindicate the doctrine I have given here and elsewhere by briefly examining the soundness of these hypotheses.

5. See above, pp. 30–31.
6. See above, pp. 21–29 (Supplement I) and pp. 46–52 (Supplement II).
7. Shaftesbury, *Characteristicks of Men, Manners, Opinions, Times;* and Hutcheson, *Inquiry.*

But at the same time I remarked that the foundation of moral obligation would be exposed only when *the immediate motive of the will,* which is always and everywhere common to all men, was established as the principle. For we ought in the last analysis always to do what we ought to judge is conducive to the end toward which we are directed by the fundamental law of nature. Now a universal motive of this kind is rejected by these authors, and the only motive which can with any likelihood of truth be called universal is not only criticized as sordid self-love by those ingenious writers I mentioned, but is also condemned for impiety by very grave men (who however go in quite different directions from the previous writers on the origin of moral obligation).[8] Therefore even if I had more leisure and strength, I could scarcely bear to involve myself in such squabbles (in which I see the cause of religion attacked from opposite sides).

I ask only that the learned in both camps who disagree would take a moment to reflect what it is they are doing when they hesitate between two proposed objects which pull the will in different directions; whether or not they then call in reason and judgment to advise them; and why they do this if it is not to disclose which direction is better, that is, which possesses a greater degree of that quality which, by the fundamental law of our nature, determines the will in the direction in which that quality is judged to preponderate; what likewise it is that they are doing when they attempt to lead others who are choosing and acting wrongly into a better way; whether they are not trying to correct their judgment by showing that the direction which they reject is better, or possesses a higher degree of the said quality.

And yet what opportunity could there be for all this, if there were not some common quality which always and everywhere determines our choice, in accordance with which all the other factors which enter into deliberation are compared among themselves? I freely grant to a recent ingenious writer, that no reason can suffice to determine our actions without the assumption of some instinct, i.e., some fundamental law, in accor-

---

8. The "very grave men" whom Carmichael had in mind may have been those Scottish hyper-Calvinist theologians (the so-called Marrow men), who denounced natural theology as legalism; they were in turn denounced as antinomians. See Lachman, *Marrow Controversy.*

dance with which a certain definite quality perceived in things immediately determines our choice.[9] But I contend that if more than one instinct of this kind is admitted, and thus more than one quality in things capable of moving the will with equal immediacy, no opportunity at all is left for reason to weigh them up and compare them with each other. But if they accept this, there is no apparent reason why in following this instinct or that anyone should be said to have acted better or worse.

Reflecting on all this, one may perhaps be permitted to ask one further question of those who have religious scruples about this. I ask whether they can conceive of anything more honorable to God or more worthy of a rational creature, than that God should direct each individual rational creature toward himself by the fundamental law implanted in its nature (by law I understand not a moral law but a physical law); so that the creature cannot fail to seek his happiness in God and pursue it by a series of actions which seek to illustrate the glory of God and testify to his esteem, love, and veneration for his supreme creator, without straying, by a shameful abuse of reason, from that end to which, by the said fundamental law, he cannot but aspire. But this is not the place to pursue this further.

At the College of Glasgow
May 12, 1729.

---

9. Hutcheson, *Inquiry*, and *Essay*, where a number of senses (or instincts as Carmichael puts it) are acknowledged.

On the Scope of Natural Theology

The knowledge of God which is drawn from nature itself is usually called *natural theology*. As it contemplates the most noble of all objects, so it greatly exceeds in the gravity and sublimity of the truths which it sets forth all other parts of human knowledge (excepting only the teaching which is divinely inspired and sealed by the sacred oracles). It also commends itself by its utility, since the whole of the philosophy of morals is built upon the principles of this knowledge; for no distinction of moral good and evil has a properly secure basis, unless it rests upon the great and good God, creator, Lord, and disposer of all things.

If we extend the term *natural theology* as far as the word *theology* is usually extended by theologians in the case of revealed theology (theology defined as the doctrine of acknowledging God and worshipping him, where the term "worship" implies obedience to all his commands),[1] moral doctrine, as we have said, will have to be considered as its second part. But the prevailing practice is to include under the name of *natural theology*, only the *theoretical* part, and to distinguish it from the *practical* part, which is to be taught separately. This is the subject of which we shall attempt to give a brief account, so far as our modest ability allows, under the guidance of the God we discuss. Our account will have four chapters: in the first we shall speak of the existence of God; in the second, of his incommunicable attributes; in the third, of his communicable attributes; and in the fourth, of his operations, or actions.[2]

1. This parenthesis was a footnote in Carmichael's text.
2. The distinction between the incommunicable and the communicable attributes of God is a characteristic feature of Reformed scholasticism. See Heppe, *Reformed Dogmatics,* pp. 58 ff.; and Fatio, *Méthode et théologie,* pp. 160–61.

On the Existence of God

SECTION I

In which it is demonstrated that an independent being exists

That something exists, we here assume as certain, and rightly so; for each man is intimately conscious to himself of at least his own existence as a thinking being; and hardly anyone doubts the existence of physical objects, perceived by sense. But that which is assumed to exist is either independent or dependent; that is, it is either sufficient to itself for existence, or it borrows its existence from elsewhere. If it is independent, we have what we aimed to demonstrate in the first place, so long as the properties of independent being, which we shall establish in the next Section, do not compel us to abandon this hypothesis and have recourse to another.

But if that whose existence is assumed is dependent, that on which it depends is either independent itself, or leads us, as we trace it back, to some first and independent cause; for in the subordination of causes, there can be no possibility of a circle or of a series running back to infinity. That the former is impossible, is clear by itself, but it is also clear that we should not admit the latter either. For the efficacy by whose power every particular effect exists, must necessarily be transmitted through all previous causes in a straight line; but no efficacy can be transmitted through an infinite series of causes, for the reason that infinity cannot be traversed; therefore no effect can depend on an infinite series of causes. The force of this argument will show more clearly, if we notice that every particular effect necessarily, so long as it exists, depends on some cause which is actually operative at the time; and it would be difficult to accept that there could be an infinite series of causes of this kind.

But it is most evidently clear that neither a circle nor an infinite series of dependent causes can exist without an independent cause; for either the whole range of dependent causes is itself dependent on something external, or it is not. If it is, we already have the independent cause which we are seeking, since it is distinct from the whole range of dependent causes. If it is not, then the whole mass of dependent causes will be independent; and nothing is more absurd than that. For since a whole includes every individual part, and its existence presupposes their existence, it is manifest that if none of the parts is sufficient to itself for existence, the whole cannot exist of itself either, but will still require an external cause. For an infinite number of effects will never be able to take the place of a cause, any more than an infinite series of weights, depending on each other, will be able to take the place of a fixed support. Necessarily therefore it must be conceded that there is an *independent being* which is prior and superior to particular dependent things.

SECTION II

In which it is shown that the independent being is a spirit, supremely perfect, from whom all things have their being, that is, is God

That which is independent must necessarily be supremely and infinitely perfect. For just as the perfection of any effect is measured either by the power or the will of the producing cause, so the measure of an independent being (if we may speak of measure) cannot be other than what is best for itself, i.e., a supreme and infinite measure. And as that which is sufficient to itself for existence, exists necessarily, so, by the same necessity, it enjoys every possible perfection. Hence the most perfect essence must be that which is possessed in the most perfect mode, and that is the independent mode.

Hence it follows (note this carefully) that anything which comes within the range of our sensation or reflection is dependent, by the very fact that it is not infinitely perfect but suffers from multiple defects.

But when we speak of something as supremely and infinitely perfect, we mean by that appellation to attribute to it every kind of pure and simple perfection and no imperfection. To put this in rather more technical language, it formally possesses absolutely every perfection, really pure as they exist in the object itself. The distinction that is taught in Ontology between *pure* perfections, or perfections simply so called, and *qualified* perfections, should be applied both to perfections absolutely regarded, as they exist in their own subject (in which sense only the divine perfections are pure and simply so called, all the rest being essentially limited and imperfect) and to perfections so far as they are represented by a given abstract idea. If the idea involves nothing in its comprehension which suggests defect or imperfection, it is said to represent a pure perfection, otherwise merely a qualified perfection. In this sense *thought,* as I go on to say, is a pure perfection, but *extension* is not.[1] It contains all the attributes of any possible things whatsoever in the manner in which they can be contained in the most perfect being. That is, it contains them virtually, as in the first and sufficient cause; and at the same time it contains them eminently, as in that to which should be attributed everything whose idea suggests pure perfection shorn of imperfections, and which is also negatively detached from all imperfections.

Hence we understand that though the perfection of the supreme being does not exclude the existence of finite beings dependent on itself (since finite perfections cannot be formally contained in an infinite being, and if they depend on it, are contained in it so far as they are able), yet it does exclude the existence of another independent, and therefore infinitely perfect, being. It also requires that every other being, and every state in which any being can be, depend so completely upon the supremely perfect being, that nothing exists or can exist without its *existence,* its *quality,* its *quantity,* and its *duration* being determined by the independent being. For if any-

---

1. The three sentences preceding, beginning "the distinction . . . ," were a footnote in Carmichael's text. De Vries, *De Natura Dei,* "Determinationes Ontologicae," ch. VIII, p. 121.

thing existed which was independent of this Being, it would not contain, either formally or virtually, the perfections of the other, and so would not be infinitely perfect.

Hence finally it necessarily follows that the Supreme Being, independent and infinitely perfect, is spirit or thinking thing (*res cogitativa*), since to have the use of thought is much better and more perfect than to be without it. It also follows that, as the creator of bodies no less than of spirits, it is not body; for the very idea of physical nature involves imperfection. By all these arguments we have afforded a demonstration of the existence of an *independent spirit, supremely perfect, from whom all things have their being*, that is, of *God* himself.

SECTION III

In which it is shown that the physical world cannot subsist without an immaterial principle

The general demonstration which we have given leads us from any finite, and therefore dependent, thing to an independent, and therefore infinite, cause; and from this in turn, as if a priori, it leads us to the spiritual nature of that cause, and its power of causing all other things there may be; and so on to whatever may be demonstrated of God. But there are also innumerable more particular reasons afforded by individual parts of the universe, which all conspire to prove that there is an *immaterial principle* of things, that it is *essentially a thinking* principle, and that it is wise, powerful, and benevolent beyond anything that we can conceive. Once these points are proven, the cause of atheism is overturned.

To make it clear that we must necessarily acknowledge an immaterial principle, we need not repeat once again that matter, since it is the lowest of all things that exist and contains perfection of the lowest order, is far from the supreme eminence of perfection which we have shown above to be necessarily involved in independent and necessary existence; and that matter therefore exists neither of itself nor necessarily, but presupposes a superior cause by which its existence is determined. Assuming that matter exists, it is indifferent with regard to motion or rest, and no individual piece of matter is destined by the necessity of its nature to the one rather than to the other. Moreover, since the varieties of possible direction are infinite, if matter is not set on one course rather than another by some external cause, it must necessarily be at rest forever. In order therefore that existing matter may be set in motion, having no principle of motion in itself, it stands in need of the influence of some external and superior principle.

If you prefer to suppose that matter is in motion rather than at rest from the beginning—apart from the fact that this supposition has been soundly refuted by what I have already said—it makes no difference. For just as matter at rest continues in a state of rest, so no less necessarily, matter in motion perseveres in a state of motion and uniformly in direction, except insofar as it is compelled to change that state by the application of forces; and since these forces are assumed to exist merely as bodies, they can be applied only by means of an impulse.

Yet it is no less certain, that continual changes occur in the motions of matter, that they are plainly required for sustaining the fabric of the physical universe, and that they cannot be derived from any physical impulse. This is so true that, if we assumed the existence of every particle of matter as well as of the compound bodies which are compacted from them, and if we assumed that they were arranged in the same order in which they are now arranged to compose this universe of physical things, and if too they were stirred by the same movements which actually do occur in them; if we assumed also that individual portions of matter could continue not only their existence, but also the motions which they have (however it may be that this happens) according to laws of nature known and proved by experience, or could even communicate these motions by contact with other parts; if all these things, I say, were assumed, still the fabric of the universe could not subsist even for one moment, if the motions of bodies did not undergo continual changes from an external source.

And since these changes do not proceed from the impact of other bodies, they can only come about by the unceasing application of forces from some immaterial principle in accordance with fixed laws. We see the evident effects of forces of this kind in the gravitation of terrestrial bodies toward earth, in the curving orbs of planets and comets, in the hardness and elasticity of bodies, in those wonderful phenomena of light recently detected by the celebrated Newton, and in other such things. None of them, as has been shown time and again, can be derived from the laws of a mechanism, much less are they produced by the essential forces of inert matter.

SECTION IV

In which it is proved that the physical world could not have been preserved forever, nor ever originally brought forth, without some force which operates above the laws of nature

The face of nature, as we now see it, could not have been preserved through infinite centuries, nor originally brought forth, by dint of those laws and applied forces by which today the fabric of the world is sustained.

The planets could not have turned for infinite centuries about the sun, without at last losing their projectile motion by one of those rare collisions of celestial matter, and rushing headlong by their own gravity into the sun once they had lost their motion; nor could the sun itself and the fixed stars have avoided the similar danger, by gravitation toward one another, of compacting, in the passage of infinite centuries, into a great immobile mass. Those flaming globes could not have emitted rays of light in every direction through infinite centuries without being at last exhausted of all light and heat. Finally, this globe itself, composed as it is of earth and water, could not have been irrigated by waters flowing down for infinite centuries, without its face being at last worn smooth, as the higher parts of the dry land were gradually carried down toward the sea.

But if physical nature, left to its own laws, could not have sustained itself forever in its own state, much less could it have arranged itself in the regular order which it has from any other state.

We may conclude therefore that the dry parts of the terraqueous globe were elevated above the surface of the waters, that the celestial bodies were placed at due distances from one another, that the sun and the other fixed stars were saturated with the most subtle fire, that the planets were propelled with great impetus, and so on, by some force and power which exceeds the laws of nature and is therefore without a doubt immaterial; even if we were to claim, contrary to all evidence of truth, that the said laws were essential to mater.

The propagation of animals and plants equally proclaims the same power. For it has been well known for a long time to all who are versed in these matters, that no new animal or plant could be formed by any laws of nature;[2] things which are commonly said to be generated have in fact been previously formed, and simply expand and unfold as the new fluids rise. Hence it follows that the generation of plants and animals cannot have continued through infinite centuries, unless we assume an infinite number of individuals of every single species and therefore an infinite number of wholes (which is supremely absurd). For however small the mass of each individual one was, it would necessarily have had to contain all the threads of life, that is, all the originally solid parts, and thus a specific quantity of matter. Therefore the bodies of all plants and animals were fabricated by some immaterial agent, and one who operates above the laws of nature.

SECTION V

In which is shown from the structure of the physical world that it is the work of an intelligent and purposefully operating cause

It is fully established by the arguments of the previous section that the physical world, from whatever direction we view it, betokens a creator, whose power is superior to the laws of nature; and he reveals himself as intelligent and free, as well as powerful, by the fact that, though he necessarily employed his power in the original creation of the world, he does not exercise it in the same way in its daily governance, but operates for the most part by means of fixed laws adequate to this end.

But an intelligent and purposefully operating creator of the universe is

---

2. Carmichael's note: See, among others, Archibald Pitcairn, an irreproachable witness, in his dissertation "On the Circulation of the Blood in Animals Born and Unborn," where he demonstrates this very point about at least the initial motion of fluids, even if all the organs of the animal are assumed to be formed and already filled with fluids ["Dissertatio de circulatione sanguinis . . ."].

more clearly attested by the overwhelming evidence of providential and benevolent design, which reveals itself in the apt disposition of all things, originally formed by that supernatural force and then preserved in accordance with fixed laws. So powerful is this evidence that it is much less conceivable that out of the infinite number of possible motions and combinations of motions, matter once set in motion formed of its own accord and without the direction of an intelligent principle, precisely that arrangement of things which we admire in this visible world, than that the whole *Aeneid* of Virgil could have been written in intelligible letters by the casual dripping of ink onto a page.

And here a vast store of things would suggest themselves to our thoughts (if our intention to be brief would allow it). Whether we contemplate the excellent order in which the various parts of the universe are laid out; or the striking beauty which shines out in individual things; or the marvellous utility found in all members of the creation and the exquisite adaptation of their structures to their specific ends, or the constant regularity of every individual thing in performing its operations; or the lavishly accumulated stock of all those things which make for the preservation of each kind of creature, and particularly of man; or finally the traces of thought, or even wisdom, which are perceptible in the operations of irrational agents: in all these things the evidence of infinite wisdom, power, and benevolence is more than manifest. But since I cannot spend time on this, anyone who wishes to see a large number of such phenomena surveyed and explained in detail, should consult *The Wisdom of God in the Works of Creation,* by the celebrated Ray, Pelling's *Discourse on the Existence of God,* Cheyne's *Philosophical Principles of Natural Religion,* Derham's *Physico-Theology* and *Astro-Theology,* Nieuwentijt's *Religious Philosopher,* and other books of the same tendency, which are widely available.[3]

---

3. Ray, *Wisdom of God;* Pelling, *Discourse;* Cheyne, *Philospohical Principles;* Derham, *Physico-Theology* and *Astro-Theology;* Nieuwentijt, *Religious Philosopher.* It is noteworthy that these texts (with the exception of Pelling's) were listed in the same order as items 353, 354, 355, 356, and 358 in the catalogue *The Physiological Library Begun by Mr. [Robert] Stewart.* For discussion, see Michael Barfoot, "Hume and the Culture of Science in the Early Eighteenth Century," in Stewart, *Studies,* pp. 151–90.

He should look at the older books but pay particular attention to the recent ones. For the greater the progress made in the knowledge of nature, the more indications emerge, and the more clearly, of the divine Artificer.

SECTION VI

In which the existence of an immaterial and essentially thinking principle is confirmed from the thinking to be found in man, both as viewed in itself and as combined with physical motions

But if the structure of the physical world points by such manifest signs to an immaterial and intelligent cause, how much more obvious are the signs we are obliged to recognize in the intellectual world. If matter cannot be brought into existence itself; if existing matter cannot move itself; if matter, however set in motion, is not sufficient to preserve the structure of the world for even a short while without the continuous application of new forces to it from elsewhere; if matter, together with those moving forces, whatever their source, by which we now see it impelled, is not adequate to give rise to the visible world or preserve it forever: much less could matter, by whatsoever means moved and by whatever forces impelled, acquire for itself the power of thinking.

Leaving aside arguments by which it has often been invincibly demonstrated that matter, however modified, cannot think, it is at least more than evident that thought does not belong essentially to matter, whatever motion or impulsion matter may undergo; as if matter could not be moved or impelled without immediately becoming conscious of itself. No matter under what conditions matter is moved or impelled, if (as atheists claim) it is the only vehicle of thought in man, it still needs the efficacy of a superior principle, and that an essentially thinking one, in order to be raised to a perfection that is not essentially appropriate to it. For thought cannot emerge by itself from things devoid of thought, especially if they are not mutually penetrable.

But if even thought of the lowest order cannot arise from matter however modified, much less can the nobler and more sublime modes of thought which the human mind experiences in itself. For often from the smallest and simplest principles, it arrives by long chains of reasoning at knowledge of the most recondite and abstract truths; it represents to itself at a glance not only things past and to come, but also infinite vistas of possible things; through earth and heaven it roams, yea, and ascends in its meditation beyond the bounds of both; it contemplates the idea of the most perfect being; it aspires to the beatific enjoyment of him, it recoils from his anger; and it is so strongly moved to obtain the former and avoid the latter that, without hesitation, it respects the divine precepts revealed to it, however contrary they may be to its desires, as the most sacred rules of morality which it may not violate with impunity.

Suppose we allowed the atheists to claim (yet no claim is more absurd) that there are certain distinct combinations of motions which, every time they happen to occur, necessarily give rise to thought. Since such a delicate combination of motions is required for such a singular effect (for out of an infinite number of equally possible combinations, scarcely one or two are suitable), it will certainly seem incredible that this combination occurs so frequently, is so constantly and regularly maintained and results in such remarkable effects. Certainly if no one ever dreamed that things which happen without purpose and by chance have their origin in men, much less should one think that the very power of taking thought from which such wonderful effects result, arose from a fortuitous concourse of atoms without the design of a superior cause.

Whatever then we suppose its inmost constitution to be, the mind gives evidence of some cause which is far superior to matter and also intelligent, and which (for the reasons given in the last section) possesses this intelligence essentially and independently, as well as all the other perfections to be found in the mind, so far as they are such.

This is also the strong implication of the wonderful phenomena of the union between the human mind and the body, that imperceptible reciprocity of thought and movement. When certain movements trouble the body, they are passed on by channels of which the mind itself is not aware, and are followed by certain perceptions in the mind which alert it to a timely concern for the body. In the other direction when the mind wishes to move a bodily limb, its decisions are taken up by specific motions of the animal spirits of which the mind is not conscious, which yet lead directly to the external motion whose execution it has itself commanded. Similar

evidence is afforded by the stupendous construction of the organs that
make this communication possible and by the imperceptible ties which
connect the human mind, by mediation of the body, with all the visible
parts of the world and especially with other men,[4] and which in turn incline man to enter society and cultivate peace with others of his kind,
which is the basis of the security of the human race on this earth and the
firm foundation of all government and order among men. All these things,
which cannot be thoroughly explained even by the most diligent and
skilled investigators of nature, man could certainly never have provided for
himself. Consequently if there was nothing existing in the world but the
human race, one would be utterly unworthy of the name of man if one
contended that man could be either created or preserved without the efficacy of the Deity.

SECTION VII

In which remarkable events are adduced in support of the same conclusion

Furthermore the creator and preserver who is proclaimed by the fixed order of things that stay the same or move in regular courses, is also revealed
as governor by extraordinary events which happen from time to time in
the world. Concealed crimes are uncovered in marvellous ways; the designs of the impious are frustrated by unexpected events; oppressed innocence is vindicated and set free by an unlooked for coincidence of various
accidents; contumacious sinners are afflicted with horrible punishments;
governments are transferred from one man to another because of the sins
of rulers and their subjects, with massive loss of life; while all the time,
government and, through government, order of some kind are preserved
in the world. If to all this we add miracles, which incontrovertible evidence
tells us have occurred for the benefit of man beyond the ordinary laws of

---

4. Carmichael's note: Compare what Malebranche says on this point at *The Search
after Truth*, bk. II, pt. 1, ch. 7, pp. 112 ff.

nature, and the no less wonderful predictions of future events, and revelation of the divine will by the testimony of both, no one in the face of all
these things will be able to resist the conclusion that there is a God who
judges justly, who has nature in his power and to whom all his works are
known from the beginning of the world.

SECTION VIII

In which universal human consent is adduced to the same end, with some other considerations

Finally a great deal of weight is added to the previous arguments by the
consent of almost all men, of every race and every age. However diverse
their opinions on the nature and properties of God, they have nevertheless
unanimously agreed that *there is a Supreme Deity.* Such universal agreement to a doctrine to which all the prejudices of the senses, the imagination, and the feelings are opposed, must necessarily be recognized as a native offspring of the reasoning faculties, as a seal which the divine hand has
impressed upon his work.

Various other considerations could be given here, based upon a comparison between the belief which denies divine existence and that which
affirms it. These include considerations of the great risk which the atheist
runs if he is wrong; of the horrid consequences of atheism, which will destroy all virtue, all order in human society; of the ineluctable difficulties in
which the atheist becomes involved in laboring to escape from certain difficulties in conceiving of the Deity; and of the weakness of the reasons
which the atheist puts forward compared with the reasons which establish
the opposite truth. But all this and much more that we must pass over,
which has the strongest tendency to confirm and illustrate this most important truth, may be read in the celebrated Master Jacques Abbadie's *On
the Truth of the Christian Religion,* volume I, section I.[5]

5. Abbadie, *Traité de la vérité,* pp. 1–151.

SECTION IX

On the arguments for proving the existence of God made by the celebrated Descartes

As no mention has been made above of the arguments which have been used to demonstrate the existence of the Deity by the celebrated Descartes in the third and fifth *Meditations,* the fame of the author and of his speculations seems to oblige us to explain this omission.[6]

In the third *Meditation* the celebrated author argues that any idea presupposes a cause of itself which has in itself so much reality and perfection, formally or eminently, as is contained in the idea itself objectively or by representation. Since therefore we have an idea which represents supreme and infinite perfection, it must necessarily be obtained from some cause which contains in itself all that perfection. I would consider this argument to be well-founded, if we were conceiving of God here in his own kind or, as the scholastics say, in his quiddity, such as one must believe the blessed inhabitants of heaven to enjoy, impressed upon them by the object itself, or by the exemplary cause. But since the idea of God which we have in this life is merely abstract, such an idea as can be formed, like other ideas, from simple sensations or reflections by variously separating or combining them, it is not obvious what can be inferred from this idea, more than from any other to be found in the mind.

You might perhaps argue that we can at least rightly infer from it that the first cause also of ourselves contains an idea of infinitely perfect being, and consequently that since it too has the power of actually possessing all the perfections of which it has the idea because it has the power of existing in itself, it is itself infinitely perfect. The celebrated author makes this argument toward the end of the same *Meditation.* I have myself shown above that being which exists by the internal necessity of its own nature, also possesses by the same necessity every perfection. But I do not see how it contributes to the elucidation of this question to say that the supreme

---

6. René Descartes, *Discourse on Method, Meditations on First Philosophy,* trans. Donald Guess (Indianapolis, Ind.: Hackett, 1993); pp. 70–81 and 88–93.

Being has the idea of infinite perfection, unless he is supposed, by some voluntary act of his own, to impart existence to himself and the perfection which he possesses; but this is certainly not acceptable.

Another argument which the same author uses in the fifth *Meditation,* which infers that God exists from the fact that necessary existence, as a perfection, is involved in the idea of an *absolutely perfect Being,* suffers from a more obvious fallacy. For from the fact that some attribute is involved in the idea of something, it only follows that this attribute belongs to that thing, if that thing exists, not that the thing having this attribute actually exists.

Anyone who wants to read more about these questions should consult the *Meditations* of Descartes cited above, with the supplements, objections, and replies. He should also read the teaching of the celebrated Gerard de Vries on this subject in his *Reasoned Discussions,* in the dissertation "On infinite extension" and "On innate ideas of things," and elsewhere.[7]

---

7. De Vries, *Exercitationes Rationales.*

On the Attributes of God and First, on the Incommunicable Attributes

SECTION I

On the attributes of God in general, and their division

In the last chapter we demonstrated *the existence of a Supreme Deity,* that is, *an independent spirit, supremely perfect, from whom all things have their being.* The next step is to give an outline, however briefly, of certain particular perfections of the Deity which are contained by necessary connection in the idea we have just explained and to demonstrate that they belong to the Deity. The perfections formally involved in this idea need no further work, since we have demonstrated above that God exists, when the idea of him is considered in its full comprehension. This was the result of the first two sections of the last chapter, where we proved from the evident series of causes that an independent being exists; then, that what is independent is infinitely perfect; that what is infinitely perfect contains in itself all the perfections of other things, and consequently all things depend upon it; and finally that this most perfect being is also a thinking being and is therefore spirit. Since, as I say, we have adequately demonstrated the existence of this Being which is represented by the idea of *God* just defined, we must now investigate the attributes which we infer are necessarily connected with that idea.[1]

---

1. Carmichael's exposition of the existence and attributes of God follows the method of the early (twelfth-century) scholastics, Anselm, Peter Lombard, and others, which

One part of this complex idea is generic, namely, that by which God is represented as *spirit,* or thinking substance; the second part is distinctive, by which God is represented as *infinitely perfect, independent, from whom all things depend.* Hence also arises a double order of secondary ideas, or attributes. Those which are a consequence of the generic concept, that is, *spirituality,* are called *communicable,* because they belong or may belong also to created spirit, at least in some degree. But those ideas which are a consequence of the distinctive concept, i.e., *infinite perfection, independence, and absolute primacy,* are normally called the *incommunicable* attributes of God.

We must speak briefly about both kinds of attribute, but first about the incommunicable attributes, both because they are by and large formed in our conception from the attributes common to every being by the removal of the imperfections or limitations which are found in every being except God, and because it is by adding incommunicable attributes that we are to give a particular description of the communicable attributes and in some measure elevate them in our thought in order to make our conceptions of them worthy of God. By this means other incommunicable attributes are generated from the combination of communicable and incommunicable attributes with each other. They designate in a manner appropriate to us the special mode in which otherwise communicable attributes belong to God. Thus infinitude added to knowledge constitutes omniscience, added to power, omnipotence, and so with the rest.

SECTION II

On the necessary existence of God

First, it is inferred from the divine independence that God *exists necessarily,* that is, by internal and absolute necessity, not (like all other things) in relation to some external principle.

---

was then adopted by the Reformed scholastics: of arguing from the order of the creation, or the *via causalitatis* (*Synopsis,* ch. 1); from those attributes of divinity which cannot be shared with mankind, or the *via negativa* (ibid., ch. 2); and from those attributes which are shared with mankind but are more perfectly possessed by God, or the *via eminentiae* (ibid., ch. 3). See Turretinus, *Institutio theologiae,* p. 196. For background, see Berkhof, *Systematic Theology,* p. 52.

However we do not therefore, as some do, consider the divine perfection as either the cause or reason of the divine existence. Perfection cannot be conceived as the reason for existence, unless existing perfection is meant; that is, unless we assume the very thing whose reason is supposed to be being explained, since existing perfection necessarily involves an existing subject to which it belongs.

We are correct therefore in saying that no cause or reason for the existence of the first and intrinsically necessary being ought to be sought or can be given. In truth it exists, *because it exists*. And therefore its existence does not have to be demonstrated by us *a priori*, but only *a posteriori*. However we do not deny that granted the existence of a deity, his infinite Perfection can be understood, to our way of thinking, as the reason why he cannot but exist in any case.

But from the fact that no reason can be given for first existence, it does not follow (as a certain learned man contends)[2] that the first being exists purely fortuitously. Intrinsically necessary existence is not less contrary to fortuitous existence, it is in fact much more contrary to it than it is to anything that follows by the strictest necessity from any principles whatever; and for this reason it cannot by any chance cease to exist.

SECTION III

On the divine unity

The infinity of God no less clearly entails his unity, or his uniqueness, which is utterly incompatible with the existence of several gods, several beings supremely and infinitely perfect.

For what is infinitely perfect essentially involves all pure and simple perfections; and so leaves no perfections of that kind (perfections, that is, from which every imperfection is absent) to be possessed by any other being whatsoever.

Likewise, all things depend on what is infinite, so that no room is left

2. Carmichael's note: S. Clarke in the "Letter on *a priori* argument," which is annexed to the most recent edition of the *Demonstration of God*, etc. [Samuel Clarke, *Demonstration of God*, 7th edition (London, 1728), pp. 497–504].

for any other independent being whatsoever. Divine perfection therefore utterly excludes any other being similar or equal to it.

Conversely, no finite being includes in the idea of itself any essential attribute which may not belong to anything at all.

SECTION IV

On the divine simplicity

Not only is God himself one, so that it is impossible that more than one God exists; but also whatever exists in God is one in such a way that it is plainly incompatible with the presence in him of several parts or perfections which are really distinct from each other or different from God himself.

For either the several things which are supposed to exist in God are finite and dependent, or they are infinite. If the former, they cannot belong to God, whose perfection does not allow that anything found in him be dependent or finite; if the latter, they imply a plurality of gods, a view refuted in the previous section.

The divine *simplicity* consists in this real identity of all things that exist in God, among themselves and within God himself. This not only precludes God from being composed of several things, that is, from drawing his existence from others; it also precludes him from being composed with several things, or entering as a part into the constitution of some whole. For this would prove that God does not contain all perfections in himself, but must borrow some by the addition of a component.

This is the point of the phrase of the Scholastics that God is *purest Act,*[3] by which they mean that in God there is nothing potential, that is, no passive power of receiving any perfection or quality whatsoever which is not contained in his essence itself.

---

3. Heppe, *Reformed Dogmatics,* p. 57, citing Daneau and others: "God is *actus purissimus et simplicissimus*" (purest and most simple act).

SECTION V

On the divine immutability

God's *immutability* necessarily flows from his simplicity.

Every change occurs either by a new arrangement of parts or by the addition of some new component, or by the removal of what had previously been a part. But none of these can occur to God, who, as we demonstrated in the previous section, admits neither parts nor components. Therefore the excellence of the divine nature utterly rejects any change whatsoever.

It is equally evident that all created things, being composed of several things or at least with several things, are liable to change.

SECTION VI

On the divine eternity

Because of this mutability of all created things and because of their contingency, they may not only possess perfections at one time and lack them at another, but also may exist at one moment and not exist at all at another. Further because of their finite natures and the frequent incompatibility of the properties which they may admit, they possess the various modifications of which they are capable only in succession. This is why we normally measure the existence of created creatures by time, that is, by the parts of succession with which they coexist.

By contrast, the uniform constancy (if one may put it this way) of the existence of God, who exists necessarily, and possesses immutably and therefore all together, all the perfections which can belong to a Supreme Being, and who contains all things by virtue of himself, is far above all those modes of measurement. Hence on the one hand it makes no difference to the essential perfection of the Deity whether succession itself exists and so whether God coexists with it, or not; and on the other hand the Supreme Deity could not lack any of the eternal constancy of existence which coexistence with a succession which was infinite on both sides would involve.

The ideas of divine eternity and immensity which we explain here may seem to some to be rather unusual. But we could not follow the philosophy of some recent writers[4] and accept succession and extension as properties of the Supreme Deity or regard them as anything but properties of contingent things, to which necessary existence is no more to be attributed for that reason than to the subjects in which they are. On the other hand we could not for that reason follow the unsubtle subtlety of the Scholastics,[5] who on the one hand declare that the whole idea of succession is so distinct from the concept of eternity that they do not seem to recognize any relation of one to the other, and yet by their very manner of speaking betray the fact that they secretly cherish in their minds the popular idea of eternity as a permanent coexistence with a certain infinite flux of moments, or a temporal space, so to speak; just as they do not conceal the fact that they conceive of immensity by means of presence (but without any extension on its own part) with infinite local space. At the same time, since they do not concede necessary existence either to succession or to *real* extension, they call both spaces *imaginary*, and thus attribute the properties of real entities to mere nothing. He who seriously reflects on this, will easily recognize that no other way is left than the one which we have attempted. [6]

God therefore is *eternal*, he is the one who, without succession in himself, transcends the whole order of successive things and embraces all succession in his own person, so that he can lengthen or shorten it, by the effective decree of his will, to whatever limits he wishes in either way, while he coexists with it all in the most perfect manner, neither adding anything to his existence, nor taking it away.

SECTION VII

On the divine immensity

Again, we are accustomed to define created things not only by times, or parts of succession with which they coexist, but also by places, or parts of extension with which they correspond.

---

4. More, *Enchiridion metaphysicum*, pp. 73 ff. Carmichael had made a similar objection in his early writings to More's claim that extension should be considered an attribute of spirit. See below, p. 342.

5. E.g., Turretinus, *Institutio theologiae*, p. 233.

6. This paragraph was a footnote in Carmichael's text.

Now the simplicity of the divine nature does not admit this kind of part any more than the other, nor does actual extension any more than succession belong to the essential perfection of the Deity (for the existence of both is contingent). It is a puerile sophism which some learned men have used in trying to demonstrate that real existence cannot be bounded by any furthest limits, much less not exist at all. That which is extended, they say, if it is finite, is either bounded (i.e., as they explain it, surrounded) by that which is extended or by that which is unextended or by nothing; if you say surrounded by nothing, you are, according to them, already attributing extension, which is a property of real being, to nothing. But what schoolboy does not see that the sense of the proposition by which it is said that *an extended thing is surrounded by nothing,* is negative, i.e., *it is not surrounded by any thing,* or not surrounded at all. For that every extended finite thing should be actually surrounded by something else (which necessarily posits a further extension) is an obvious *petitio principii.*[7] Yet it is certain that God cannot lack any amplitude which copresence with extension infinite in all dimensions would include.

We therefore conceive of God as *immense,* that is, as one who without extension in himself, transcends all extension and has it all within himself, so that by the effective decree of his will he may command it to be extended or circumscribed to whatever limits he pleases, being present himself to the whole of it in the most perfect manner, neither adding anything to himself nor taking it away.

SECTION VIII

On the divine omnisufficiency

From what has been said it is easily understood that God is *omnisufficient,* i.e., that both for himself, and for all others from himself, he is all in all.

That he is sufficient to himself, is quite obvious from his independence. But if God, the supremely perfect being, is sufficient to himself, much more must he be sufficient for other things which have no perfection at all

7. Part of this paragraph was a footnote in Carmichael's text.

in themselves, except so far as they carry some shadow of the divine perfections, whether for giving them existence and maintaining it, or affording them the highest perfection they can attain. This is particularly true of the dispensation of complete beatitude, perfect at every point, for rational creatures, not only for giving it to them from himself as the supreme provider, but also for exhibiting it in himself as omnisufficient object.

SECTION IX

On the divine incomprehensibility

From each and every one of the perfections explained so far, it obviously follows that the Supreme Deity is *incomprehensible,* that is, that he cannot be so thoroughly understood by any intelligence except his own that he is not infinitely more concealed than known.

This is not to be understood only in the sense in which it may be truly affirmed that no object of any kind can be comprehended by a finite intelligence, because any given thing has innumerable relations with other things, whether existing or possible, which no finite intellect could exhaustively enumerate. The divine incomprehensibility, I say, is not to be understood only in this sense. For not only does God have infinite relations with infinite external objects, but infinite in himself he also contains all their perfections within himself, and thus has infinitely more perfections than can be enumerated; which cannot be said of any other being.

In fact, though in some measure we do grasp the divine attributes which we conceive, yet in the manner in which they belong to God, each of them leads the mind as it were into an abyss which no finite mind has power to penetrate.

And yet this does not prevent the idea of God which with due attention we achieve, from being said to be *clear* and *distinct* in the sense intended by recent writers on logic.[8] For however inadequate it may be, and however much of the unknown it may contain, yet in itself it does strike the mind with sufficient vividness, and is easily distinguished from any other idea.

8. E.g., the authors of *The Art of Thinking.* See below, pp. 287 ff. and 380 ff.

Note too that the finite capacity of our minds implies not only that all the knowledge which we can have of God is quite inadequate in any case, but we cannot grasp it all in one go; we are compelled to present to ourselves the perfections which are plainly identical in God (as is clear from section iv) under various different notions.

But if God cannot be comprehended by the mind, much less can he be plainly expressed by the tongue; and thus he is *ineffable.*

SECTION X

On the divine admirability

From the divine incomprehensibility it follows that God is supremely *admirable,* since however long the mind persists in its contemplation of him, something new is always arising for its contemplation, even for eternity.

SECTION XI

On the divine adorability

Finally, from all the aforesaid prerogatives of Deity, his *adorability* necessarily flows; that is, the eminence of perfection on account of which every rational creature is bound to submit himself to God with the greatest mental devotion, and to order all his actions to celebrate his praises. This prerogative necessarily presupposes that God is a thinking agent, and is in truth the incommunicable acme of the divine *majesty,* of which we will speak in the next chapter.

On the Communicable Attributes of God

SECTION I

On the communicable attributes of God in general

It naturally tends to enhance our devotion to God to consider him as a *spirit,* a spirit in whom all the individual prerogatives of supreme Deity which we surveyed above are attached to each of the common properties of spirits. This attachment of incommunicable attributes to communicable attributes is neatly expressed by the reverend theologians of the *Synod of Westminster,* when in describing God in the *Westminster Catechism,* Question 4, they liken the incommunicable attributes to adjectives, the communicable to substantives which the adjectives modify.[1] In order to proceed properly in this train of thought, we should reflect on ourselves and on the modes of thinking which we experience in ourselves; we must then carefully distinguish in each mode what indicates a perfection and what indicates an imperfection. Our aim is to reject all imperfections, that is, all those conditions which derogate in any way from the divine prerogatives established in the last chapter, and to assign the remainder securely to the Deity, not only stripped of imperfections, but also negatively separated from them, or so elevated by the addition of incommunicable attributes, that the result is worthy of God and proper to him. We have explained

---

1. This sentence was a footnote in Carmichael's text. The reference is to Question 4 in "The Westminster Shorter Catechism": "What is God?" The Answer: "God is a Spirit, infinite, eternal, and unchangeable, in his being, wisdom, power, holiness, justice, goodness, and truth." *The Confession of Faith,* p. 288.

above (ch. 2, sec. i, *toward the end*) the way in which incommunicable attributes are formed from communicable attributes.[2]

But (to avoid repeating the same thing again and again later) we must make a cautionary point at the outset. We find an imperfection in all our modes of thinking: they are adventitious to our minds and different in reality both from the mind itself in which they inhere and among themselves, and they are only formed in us successively. But in God there is a completely different mode: all his thoughts are one most simple and eternal act which is in reality identical with his essence, as is quite clear from the simplicity and immutability which we previously asserted of the Deity.

Further, a consideration which we used above to form the notion of the simplicity of God in general is highlighted in a special way when we attribute the perfections of spirits to God. For, since the divine essence has necessarily to be recognized as most perfect in itself without addition of any distinct entity, it cannot be most perfect without actual knowledge, and that knowledge must be consistent with his most perfect nature, i.e., it must be infinite. Hence knowledge which is actually infinite belongs essentially to God, i.e., is identical with his nature. (The same thing is to be understood of an actual volition that conforms with the supreme reason, etc.) With this observation, we go on to particular points.

SECTION II

On the divine ideas of things

In the first place we experience in ourselves that we contemplate various ideas of various things or conceive of various objects; and since it denotes a perfection rather than an imperfection to conceive of objects or to apprehend them (because this is necessarily involved in every thought about them), there is no doubt that we should attribute the same to God.

But our mind has particular concepts of only a few things, and these are thoroughly imperfect and inadequate; and just as it views external things

2. See above, pp. 248–49.

only in ideas drawn from outside itself, so perhaps it does not know itself till it catches itself engaged with things other than itself.

By contrast God himself is the closest object of knowledge to God; thus while he comprehends himself in his omnisufficiency, he must also contemplate in the most perfect manner all possible things which are virtually contained in it. That God cannot comprehend himself without contemplating all possible things, since they are virtually and eminently contained within himself, is so far from convicting him of poverty (as Poiret foolishly fears) that on the contrary it is to be attributed to the infinite sufficiency of the Deity.[3]

But we must not attribute to the Deity the sensations and imaginations that are found in us, since they are not in themselves true representations of objects, but give evidence of passions and dependence on external things, and seem to have been given to us only to assist our weakness, i.e., so that external things, which would otherwise be hidden, may become known to us through their effect on our minds.

SECTION III

On the divine knowledge

We also observe in ourselves that we form opinions or judgments by comparing ideas with each other. As the knowledge of truth which consists in the sole act of judging is a great perfection of a thinking thing, without which simply having ideas by observation would be of little use to the mind, there is no doubt that judgment, understood in this sense, belongs also to God. We here use the term "judgment" as it is understood by logicians in describing acts of the mind. One must beware therefore of following the usage of our vernacular idiom and including anything in the idea of it which would derogate from the certainty of knowledge.[4]

But of the immense number of knowable truths our judgment extends

3. This sentence was a footnote in Carmichael's text. Pierre Poiret, *Cogitationes Rationales,* III.VII, p. 295.

4. The last two sentences were a footnote in Carmichael's text. On judgment, see below, pp. 298 ff.

only to a few, and is frequently uncertain even about these and quite often wrong. But the judgment of God bears on its face the highest evidence of truth in all things, and has the most absolute right to be called knowledge. It also embraces the whole range of truth in its scope; for only infinite knowledge is worthy of infinite Spirit. But to get a better grasp of these things so far as our means allow, we must distinguish between the different classes of truths to be known.

In the first place there is no doubt that God, however incomprehensible to every finite intellect, is wholly perspicuous to himself; he is conscious in the most perfect manner of his own existence and of his infinite perfections. For no other object of knowledge is either more intimate to infinite mind, or more worthy of it.

Further, since God in his omnisufficiency, as we said in the last section, contemplates all ideas of possible things whatsoever, he must be able to perceive all their possible relations, i.e., those hypothetical truths about the connections and oppositions between the attributes of things which, since they are the same at any point of time, are generally called *eternal,* and among which are all the things that we get to know by direct or indirect comparison of abstract ideas.

These hypothetical truths have this in common with the truths concerning the actual existence of God himself and the supreme perfections, that they are conceived as being as they are necessarily and independently of the decree of the divine will; hence both these kinds of knowledge in God are called the *knowledge of simple intelligence.*

With great effort and with no success the distinguished Poiret attempts to show that all truths, even purely hypothetical truths concerning the properties of finite things, have their origin in the free and indifferent decision of the divine will. In fact he seems to betray his case when he contends that in no way could those things be without those properties. But they could (he says) have been nothing. What is this? Not to exist? No one denies it. They could (he says) not have been possible. But no; for since they involve a contradiction, they could never have been possible for that reason. The learned man seems to have been misled by the fact that (following a scholastic prejudice on this issue) he considered the essences of nonexistent things as something *real;* nor has he fully recognized that whatever is affirmed of things which are not posited as actually existing, is only affirmed in view of the possible case that they exist. [5]

Again, God, who is intimately aware within himself of his eternal design, ever knows with supreme certainty the existence of all created things and all their actions and all the changes which may occur to them at any time, since these are all determined directly or indirectly by the decree of the divine will. Divine knowledge of truths of this kind, which he contemplates in the deliberation of his will, is called the *knowledge of vision.*

In knowing all these things, God does not depend on acquiring pieces of knowledge from external sources as we do, nor does he perceive them in their effects, but in the first cause of all things. Hence he does not make use of discursive thought, that is, he does not proceed from the known to things which were previously unknown. The supreme perfection of the divine intellect does not permit this successive mode of thought; its absolute simplicity and immutability does not suffer it; these individual perfections make it clear that the divine intellect surveys all truths in one eternal and simple act. But if our successive mode of knowing does not belong to God because it implies previous ignorance or doubt, still less does forgetfulness, which is subsequent ignorance, take place in him, not to mention the cruder imperfections of our intellect such as error and inconsistency in judgment.

God's knowledge is called *wisdom,* since it is concerned with what it is most worthy of divine perfection to effect and most fitting to illustrate his glory in a splendid manner. Since it is understood to embrace the whole system of things that might be created and thus assumes that nothing has yet been decreed, it belongs to the knowledge of simple intelligence.

Besides this double knowledge which we have shown to be rightly attributed to God, some of the Scholastics (namely those who, as we shall explain below, have denied to God the determination of the free actions performed by rational creatures) have concocted a third knowledge, which they call *mediate.* They were attempting to explain how God has foreknowledge from eternity of the free actions of creatures, though they have

---

5. This paragraph was a footnote in Carmichael's text. Poiret, *Cogitationes Rationales,* III.VII, p. 296.

not been at all determined by his decree. Mediate knowledge is the knowledge by which God is said to know what a rational creature would do, if he were placed in such and such circumstances; and thus God would know what the creature would actually do when he saw in his decree that the creature *would* be placed in such circumstances.[6]

But either the circumstances in which the creature is assumed to be placed have a necessary connection with the action which the creature is foreseen as likely to do in that case, or they do not. If the former, God knows the connection by the knowledge of simple intelligence, and by placing the creature in those circumstances, he determines it by that very fact to do the action necessarily connected with them. If the latter, the connection of the action with the circumstances supposed could neither occur nor be foreseen without an ordination of the divine will by which it would be determined, either in itself or in its cause (for nothing else can be credited with connecting things which are not linked by nature), and in this case God knows the said connection by the knowledge of vision. In both cases, the action of the creature cannot be known as absolutely going to occur except in those causes by which, when taken together as a whole, the exercise of the same action is determined. Nor could something which was to exist in time be foreknown from eternity, unless something also existed from eternity which determined its existence. And thus we are led to think about the divine will.

SECTION IV

On the divine will

We experience in ourselves that we will what seems compatible with ourselves and that we reject what seems incompatible with ourselves. Since

6. The notion of "mediate knowledge" (*scientia media*) was considered by some among the Reformed scholastics to be an invention of the Jesuits, adopted by the Arminians or Remonstrants, to reconcile divine foreknowledge (*scientia visionis*) with the human freedom to perform acts not determined by the divine will. Carmichael's argument against this position is consistent with the reasoning of Gisbertus Voetius and others, reviewed by Heppe, *Reformed Dogmatics,* pp. 77–81. For background on the lives and writings of Voetius, Turretinus, and others, see Trueman and Clark, *Protestant Scholasticism,* pp. 227–55.

this in itself shows no imperfection but on the contrary obvious perfection, it is certain that *will* is to be attributed to God. For we cannot understand the notion of a happiness in which the happy person does not acquiesce by willing it, and no action which is not done freely, i.e., by command of the will, is worthy of a most perfect being.

The difference is that men want what they will because it contributes in some manner to their felicity (which good men seek in God, and pursue in order to illustrate the divine glory). God, on the other hand, who is most happy in himself, as will be said below, first seeks, in whatever he wills outside himself, not the increase or preservation of his own felicity but the illustration of his infinite perfections (in which lies the felicity of rational creatures who seek their felicity in the manner which God commands). As we can conceive of no object outside God more worthy of conception by the divine will, so it is noteworthy that Holy Scripture everywhere favors this manner of conceiving him.[7]

What God's will is in other respects and with what objects it is concerned, can be understood to some extent from what has been said before.

Firstly, it is agreed that the divine will is utterly independent and cannot be moved or swayed properly speaking by external objects, since it is in reality the same as the divine essence and therefore is prior to all external things and eternal and immutable. As far as the objects are concerned, the divine will can be distinguished in much the same way as we distinguished divine knowledge in the previous section. First it is certain that God wills himself, wills his own existence and all his perfections; likewise he wills that the eternal and immutable relations of ideas, or what we have called hypothetical truths about the essential attributes of things, be always the same as they always are. But with respect to these, since the divine will, as far as our mode of conceiving goes, seems rather to presuppose than to precede the truth of the things themselves as it appears to the divine intellect, this will of God which is concerned with the objects of the knowledge of simple intelligence, is usually called *approving will.*

Secondly, God also wills that certain beings different from himself should exist, each in their own times; that they should have a certain fixed order and arrangement among themselves; that some things be born, some

7. This sentence was a footnote in Carmichael's text.

die, etc. As there seems to be no necessary reason in any of these things why it should be thus or otherwise antecedently to the ordination of the divine will, for this reason God is conceived (in our order of conceiving) as willing those things to be so, before the things themselves are conceived as such or known by God to be so. This will of God, which is concerned with the objects of the knowledge of vision (which is itself founded in that will, so far as our manner of conceiving it goes) has normally been called *deciding will* or *decree*.

And just as approving will extends to all necessary and immutable truths, so deciding will pertains to all truths which we normally call contingent, not only about things as absolutely going to be or not going to be, but also about connections made between things which are bound together with each other not in their natures but in the divine decree; knowledge of them, as we remarked above, belongs to the knowledge of vision.

For we understand here by necessary truths to which we extend the knowledge of simple intelligence and the approving will of God, only those truths whose ground, in our order of conceiving, does not seem to need to be sought in the divine will. Such truths, as we indicated above, include purely conditional truths, as well as the existence of God himself and his supreme perfections. By contingent truths, on the other hand, which we assign to the knowledge of vision and the deciding will, we understand all truths whose reason for being as they are should be sought in God's will. Such are all truths which are not purely conditional and abstract about created things as well as those which flow from the will of God and which we understand from the very idea of Deity as belonging to his most perfect nature.

Thus the distinction between the approving will and the deciding will in no way coincides with the distinction which some make between the necessary and the indifferent will of God. We assume, for example, that retributive justice is essential to God. On this assumption, it is certain that God necessarily wills that if sins have been committed, they should be punished; this however is the deciding will, and the knowledge by which God knows that sins will be punished is the knowledge of vision. For the reason why this will happen is to be sought in the divine will, and antecedently to the divine will there is no necessity for it internal to the effect itself, however necessarily that will (even in our ideas) is connected with divine perfection. Hence this necessity is not at all opposed to liberty rightly understood, since it does not prevent the effect being produced by God through the decision of his will.

The conclusion of the argument is that the will of God is the true cause of all real existence outside of God, since it completely depends on God and on his willing it. And since the divine decree is identical with God, it cannot depend on any cause which is really distinct from him, even though in our order of conceiving it (which is by analogy drawn from our mode of thinking) the decree presupposes the divine existence together with its essential perfections, as well as the knowledge of simple intelligence.

Furthermore by the mode of thinking with which we are familiar, one decree is normally thought of as presupposing another. For among men, what is last in execution of a set of effects bound to each other by constant connection, is normally first in intention; so in comparing the works of God (where what is last in execution seems to be superior in excellence, and its production seems to illustrate the divine perfections more clearly) it is natural for us to think of God as willing one thing first, then as willing other things so far as they are means to it. And indeed, when some creation of God's manifestly serves an excellent purpose worthy of the divine wisdom, it would be an absurd scruple, which would seriously insult the supreme craftsman, to doubt that the fitness of this creation to this use was appointed by the most wise counsel of God. And it is not only in the apt fitting of means to ends, but also of other things between which there is no physical connection (especially of moral actions with their moral effects) that the divine purpose so plainly appears that we cannot fail to recognize it without impiety.

Thus we prove that the successive mode of willing does not belong to God by employing the same considerations by which we showed in the previous section that discursive thought is not appropriate to him. The successive mode of willing is that by which we are led from intending an end to deciding on the use of means, or in general are led from a thing previously decided to deciding another which must be connected with it. Similarly it seems that we cannot find a more suitable way to think about the divine purposes from our narrow perspective than by representing God to ourselves as taking in at one glance the whole system of things, or even innumerable possible systems, or (as a certain recent excellent writer, Leibniz,[8] loved to say) infinite possible worlds, from which he chooses one, namely that system of things which are to exist at the time and place that has seemed to infinite wisdom to be most appropriate.

Since we see such a small part of this system (not to mention the infinite possible systems with which it is compared in the divine mind), the reasons for the divine purposes even in things which come within our view, are for the most part hidden from us.

Finally just as every vacillation and inconstancy is to be excluded from the divine will, so much more is every irregularity, though all too often found in our wills.

SECTION V

On the divine sanctity

And from here we move to consideration of the divine *sanctity*. The difficulty of conceiving it is all the greater because though it is a perfection in us to conform our will to the supreme rule, yet this implies the imperfection of assuming a superior whose will we are bound to respect; and to recognize a superior denotes a dependence which is as alien to the Supreme Deity as it is possible to be.

But one must reflect that the sanctity, or moral goodness, of a rational creature consists in his love and veneration of God, and in displaying these feelings by habitual will in all those actions which God determines to demand as evidences of them. And similarly the sanctity of God consists in the infinite love by which God embraces his infinite perfection, and in his immutable will to declare this love by all those dispensations toward creatures, and especially rational creatures, which eternal reason teaches most aptly serve this end. When we assert that the idea of *moral good* necessar-

8. Carmichael owned a copy of Leibniz's *Essais de Théodicée*. It was a gift from his student John MacLaurin, who became a respected Presbyterian clergyman; the copy is in Glasgow University Library.

ily has regard to God, we do not therefore abandon the idea of a moral goodness which is to be attributed to God himself, nor are we forced to turn it into something trivial, as some wrongly object.[9]

Here it is relevant that God is *truthful,* so that he is not able to contradict himself either by deceiving a creature by his testimony or by imposing a false proposition on him to be accepted by faith. It is also relevant that he is *benevolent,* or ready to do good to his creatures, especially his rational creatures, so far as they bear his image and are not opposed to him, and finally that he is *just,* i.e., he approves in a rational creature what is consistent with himself and rejects the inconsistent, and he wills that both be manifested by connecting the felicity of a creature with duly observed subordination to him, its misery with violation of that subordination.

God's will to interpret certain actions of a rational creature as tokens of due or undue feeling toward him or the preservation or violation of subordination and thus to connect it with the happiness or misery of the creature, this will, I say, when proclaimed to the creature by suitable signs, is called the *divine law.* No secret will of God is ever in conflict with this will so signified. For in its precepts God does not express absolutely what he wills or decrees that the creature should do, but what sort of deed on the part of a rational creature he will accept as an indication of love and veneration and connect with the happiness of the same creature; and what sort of deed, by contrast, he will hold as a sign of neglect or contempt for himself, and will connect with the misery of the creature. And the event always corresponds to this revealed will.

SECTION VI

On the divine power

We also experience in ourselves some power over external objects or at least a shadow of such power. This is the power by which in response to specific acts of our will, certain new motions are produced in our bodies and some-

9. This sentence was a footnote in Carmichael's text.

times also in external objects by means of bodily motions; and such motions could have been restrained or at least checked by contrary acts of will. Since power which is freely active (i.e., power that acts at the command of the will) argues no defect, but on the contrary denotes a perfection which is utterly worthy of the being who embraces all things by his own virtue, it is certain that freely acting *power* belongs to God, or that the will of God is efficacious in external objects.

But our power is quite limited and dependent; that is, it extends only to producing certain changes in things, a few small changes which are put within our power by the efficacy of a superior cause. These imperfections must be excluded from divine power. Only infinite power is to be attributed to an infinite being and only a wholly independent power to an independent being.

We are right to say therefore that God is *omnipotent;* by this title we imply that the efficacy of the divine will is such that God brings about outside of himself by the sheer command of his will whatever he wishes to exist, at the time and in the circumstances in which he wishes it to exist. He does so quite independently and irresistibly, so that in carrying out his will he does not depend on the influence of any superior or allied cause; nor is any other cause capable of putting an obstacle in his way.

By this kind of explanation, by which we conceive the power of God as the efficacy of the divine will, we neither confound the idea of power with the idea of will nor restrict the power itself. (Both of these objections are made and both are wrong.) We only restrict the exercise of it to objects which God actually wishes to exist.

SECTION VII

On the dominion and majesty of God

Since God, the creator of all things, ever seeks the illustration of his infinite perfections and of the infinite love with which he embraces them as eternal reason dictates, it cannot be doubted, that he both can and will, by most just right, dispose all things created by himself to that most excellent end. In the first place he can and will dispose those endowed with reason.

To them God shows himself a most worthy object of love and veneration in which alone they can be supremely happy, and at the same time declares that he wills with equally just right that happiness be connected with duly observed subordination to him, misery with the violation of subordination; and he is omnipotent to carry out this his will. It is evident that nothing is lacking to bind each rational creature by the most sacred ties to seek his happiness (to which he ever aspires by the fundamental law of his nature) in God, and to pursue it by a series of actions which God wills to require as symbols of love and veneration toward himself; and he rightly renders the creature which acts otherwise liable to supreme misery. And the sovereign right of the Supreme Deity, insofar as it affects all creatures indifferently, is his *dominion;* insofar as it regards rational creatures in particular, it is his *majesty* or authority.

SECTION VIII

On the divine happiness

Finally we have the experience from time to time of enjoying happiness or pleasure, but also sometimes are afflicted by misery or pain. And so we understand that our beatitude or misery does not depend wholly upon us, since we would wish to be always happy, never miserable. To be happy is indeed a great perfection of thinking substance, and therefore to be attributed to the Deity without reservation. But to depend on another for one's happiness, and to be capable of misery, are imperfections, which must therefore be excluded from God. As he is most perfectly conscious of his infinite perfection, he cannot but acquiesce in it with supreme complacency; he has from eternity infinite *beatitude* in the enjoyment of himself, to which no external thing can add or subtract anything.

On the Divine Operations, or Actions Involving External Objects[1]

SECTION I

In which the transition to this subject is explained

In the first chapter we demonstrated the existence of God from the visible operations of God. We should therefore look rather more closely at the modes and conditions of his operations. It is not necessary at this point to prove that all that exists outside of God owes its *being* to divine efficacy. We believe this has been adequately made out above where we demonstrated that God exists. For we included in the notion of God the idea that *all things depend upon him;* and in the same passage we also showed (to anticipate the objection that we are arbitrarily assuming such a universal principle) that this same thing is necessarily connected with the divine infinity and thus with the divine independence itself. Here we shall simply make a few small points about the mode of divine efficacy and its specific ways.

SECTION II

On the properties of divine operations

As to the manner of divine efficacy, it is certain in the first place that God is a *free* agent; that is, whatever he does, he does in accordance with a de-

---

1. The subject matter of this chapter falls under the heading of Providence of God in the systems of the Reformed dogmatists or scholastics, e.g., Turretinus, *Institutio theologiae,* pp. 526 ff.; and Heppe, *Reformed Dogmatics,* ch. XII, pp. 251 ff.

liberation of reason and a resolve of will. It is true that if God is to be formally called an *agent* or an *efficient,* an effect must exist outside of God, apart from his will which is eternal. And in this sense some kind of distinction can be made between the will of God and external action. Nevertheless we are right to say (despite objections in some quarters) that the manner in which God produces anything at all apart from himself is by *willing.* For one cannot conceive of any action intermediate between the efficacious will of God and the existence of the effect produced in its own time.

But God not only operates freely in all things, he also operates *independently,* so that he does not borrow from any other cause either sufficiency of willing or efficacy of will to produce an effect outside of himself. Hence it also follows that God is *irresistible* in his operations; what other cause can check the operation of him on whom all other causes absolutely depend, that is, from whom they draw both their existence and their active force?

SECTION III

On divine creation and preservation

We proceed to take note of the different kinds of divine operations. Every operation or efficacy either terminates in the actual being or existence of a created thing in that the thing exists rather than does not exist (is simply nothing), or it terminates in the introduction of some change in a permanent subject, whose existence it takes for granted.

Now since all the efficacy of which any trace is found in created agents is of the latter kind, we should not be surprised if we experience great difficulty in conceiving the other efficacy on which the very existence of continuing things depends, if it seems so incredible to men who are tied to their imaginations that any effect at all is produced from nothing; and if it seems still more incredible that an effect already produced cannot go on existing but will return to nothing, unless it is preserved in its existence by continuation of the same efficacy by which it was first produced.

These things (I say) are difficult to conceive, for the reason that we may not find any such thing in created agents open to our observation. For they produce nothing except from preexisting matter, nor effect anything other than a change in the arrangement of that matter or that subject by which it passes to a different state. This new state, though normally attributed to the influence of a mutative cause, persists after the action of that cause ceases; and in fact does not exist completely until the mutative action is finished. This is the origin of the common prejudice which conceives of an action as something which precedes the existence of an effect, and need only continue until the effect begins to exist; once the effect has been produced, it is assumed to exist thereafter of itself.

It is indeed not surprising that a cause whose only effect is the alteration of a given subject, is required to take no further action than the making of the change. Some argue that the need for continuous divine operation for the continued existence and activity of created things is removed by the fact that things continue to exist or operate after the created cause to which they attribute their continued existence and operation ceases.[2] It is clear that these people have not noticed how little is really due to the efficacy of created causes. For things which are said to be formed by them draw neither their substance nor their active force from them; just as a watch does not borrow from the craftsman either its material or the force of gravity or elasticity by which its wheels move.[3] But since the actual substances of things no less than the changes which occur in them, finite spirits no less than their thoughts, bodies no less than their movements, are at an infinite distance from supreme perfection, we conclude from what we said at ch. I., sec. ii, that they are no less distant from independence. And thus they are creatures, or effects, that is, things which need an external efficacy to determine them into existence, an efficacy which, as soon as it is exercised, makes at least the first existence of the effect contemporary with itself.

But if at any one instant these effects need the efficacy of an external cause to exist, there is no reason why they do not stand in equal need of

2. Heppe, *Reformed Dogmatics*, pp. 256 ff.; Malebranche, *The Search after Truth*, pp. 448 ff., 657 f.
3. The three sentences preceding were a footnote in Carmichael's text.

the same efficacy at all moments at which they exist thereafter. For however many effects are produced, they would never become independent or self-sufficient, and there is no necessary connection between the existence of an effect for this moment and its existence at a following moment. And you cannot argue that, once created, things exist until they are annihilated in a new action by God. For as annihilation does not have a positive outcome, it is not a positive action, and can only be conceived as a suspension of preserving action; such action therefore is necessary to the continued existence of a created thing.

The conclusion of all this is that every single thing accessible to our observation, whether spiritual or physical, derives its existence from the creative efficacy of God as long as it exists, and ceases to exist only when God no longer exercises that efficacy. We do not think it necessary to spend time on a fuller explanation of this, nor to pursue more carefully the distinction between creation and preservation. For the same action which terminates in the actual existence of a created thing, is called *creation* in the first moment of the effect's existing, *preservation* in subsequent moments.

I am aware that many writers on these subjects take pains to emphasize at this point that all finite things necessarily had some first moment of their existence, and thus were at some time created in the sense in which creation is distinguished from preservation. We believe by faith that the world and all that is contained therein had its beginning at a finite interval of time in the past; and it is self-evident that no dependent thing can be eternal, in the sense in which we have claimed this prerogative for God, that is, in such a way that in his essence he transcends all succession and embraces it all in his own virtue. But just as nothing seems to prevent God from bringing into being a permanent thing with which no succession coexists, in which case there is no room to distinguish between creation and preservation, so perhaps it has not been convincingly demonstrated that God cannot bring into existence a succession which is infinite in both directions and a permanent thing which is coexistent with the whole of it. It is enough to have proved that every single finite object, that is, every single thing that is other than God, has as much dependence on God as it has being at any time or place.

SECTION IV

On divine government

But if God is the first and original cause of all permanent things, we cannot doubt that all the changes that occur in things also take their origin from him. How the divine operation acts on them is given the general name of *government.*

The need to recognize his government and to allow that it extends to all events is quite clear from what we have said. For anything that happens implies an adequate cause by which it is determined to exist; but it cannot be determined into existence by something in which, antecedent to the existence of the effect itself, there is nothing which requires it to exist rather than not to exist. Anything therefore that is effected necessarily implies a cause which is antecedently determined to effect it, and the same has to be said about this cause itself and about its being determined to operate, until we ascend all the way to a first and independent cause. Either we must stop at God, who decides a given event, and thus determines it by the efficacy of his decision, or we must seek some other principle which is independent of this determination. For determination can no more arise from indifference than a thing can spring into being of its own accord from nothing.

Since therefore, as is clear from the demonstration above, there is no other principle which is independent of God, we must admit that all the changes which happen to things, no less than their actual substances, must be attributed to the efficacy of the divine will as first and adequate cause. If in producing these changes any created cause exercises, or seems to exercise, any efficacy, the efficacy of this created cause too, such as it is, must be sought in God as the first agent.

When the more sensible of the Scholastics recognized this *actual* dependence of all created causes, they thought that, to explain it, they needed to assert a double action of God in every single action of a creature, namely: *previous concurrence,* or (as it is more correctly called by others) *precursive concurrence,* by which God determines a creature to act; and *simultaneous concurrence,* by which he enters into a creature's action and advances it and produces an effect, the creature being the subordinate cause. *Government,* in the special sense of the term which some recent writers have introduced and by which God is said to dispose, with wisdom and power, all the actions of all creatures to ends predetermined by his eternal counsel, is not a particular action but the harmony of all divine operations.

But there were some among the ranks of the Scholastics who took the view that previous determination by a first cause could not be reconciled with the liberty of action of a second cause, and rejected previous concurrence in the free actions of rational creatures, admitting only simultaneous concurrence; while others, rejecting both, recognized only one form of dependence of a second cause on a first, namely its creation and preservation.[4]

But both parties are wasting their time. For even on the latter supposition, a creature can do nothing to which he is not determined by nature or by dispositions which are either directly or indirectly derived from the first cause, unless another independent principle is admitted, or (which is no less absurd) a causeless effect is imagined springing from nothing.

And on the former supposition, while the absolute primacy of divine operation is denied, the same absurd notions have to be swallowed, and at the same time the divine operation has to be said to be subordinated to the determination of the other independent principle or of some freakish accident. Some writers deny that God is the first Cause by which a creature is determined to the specific nature as well as the exercise of the action, but hold that God is determined by the creature so far as the former is concerned, in order to fit in his concurrence. These writers' speculations would be far more worthy of God, if they plainly denied any such concurrence; so that even if God were not lord over his creatures, he would at least not be subject to them. And indeed if a creature could be determined to an action by any other source than God, there is no reason why he should not also receive the power from some other source to carry out the action.

4. The manner in which God concurs in human actions, by initiating an act and by producing its effects, was debated by the Reformed scholastics. A number of theological opinions on this subject are reviewed in Heppe, *Reformed Dogmatics,* pp. 258–60.

But if we leave the subtleties of the Scholastics and attempt to follow the simplicity of nature in framing this question more plainly, it seems one should argue as follows.

From the beginning God produced various substances of various kinds, endowed with various modes or dispositions. He continues to preserve them and the modes with which they have been endowed, except so far as they are changed, either by God himself working according to the order of Nature or sometimes beyond it, or by themselves, or by other created causes. I say *by themselves or by other created causes,* because various changes naturally flow from the various created substances, variously modified and arranged (or at least they take them up in a regular manner). These may be changes in the substances themselves or in other substances of the same or of a different kind, to which they are duly applied. These substances are therefore said to effect those changes, or to be the causes of them, and we must not pretend that there is any intermediate action here between the cause itself as it is finally disposed and duly applied to a suitable subject (if this is different from the cause) and the effect, i.e., the change which is produced in the subject by the force of the cause so disposed.

As for how a created cause becomes effective, it is obviously requisite that at the very moment at which the effect, namely the change of a given subject, is to be produced, God should preserve the cause, together with all the dispositions of it which are needed for its operation, applied also to the subject, if that is external to it, in the manner we described. This action of God, so far as it relates to the action of the created cause which arises from it, is rightly called *predetermination* or *precurrence.*

Furthermore, for the effect to be actually produced, not only must God not place in the subject any obstacle to the change which flows naturally from the force of the cause so disposed, he must also preserve the Subject under that change. This action of God, in relation to the action of a created cause, may be called *concurrence.*

As these things are very simple, and abundantly obvious from the principles laid down above, I do not see what more needs to be said on this question, at least in the cases in which some true efficacy is allowed to created causes, or what we need to add to this doctrine to prove the dependence of the created cause on God in every way, as much in action as in existence. Thus we here assert a truly efficacious, and, if you like, a physical, determination, though we do not think that those new and peculiar actions of the first cause which the Scholastics imagine here, should be introduced, except in those actions of a created cause for which a fresh infusion of supernatural grace is required.

Many have been driven (I think) to devise these new and peculiar actions on the part of the first cause with regard to every single one of a creature's actions, because they have thought that the structure of a Creature is quite permanent, but its actions are momentary and soon passing, and not uniformly exhibited by creatures which have the same structures. But these people have given little thought to the fact that created minds are continually in flux, and every moment new thoughts are formed in them or new ideas imprinted upon them from outside, the traces of which remain in the mind and interact with ideas previously settled there, and dispose the mind to be continually initiating some new act.[5]

I have said that this is the situation when a true efficacy belongs to created causes; but one may suspect that such efficacy is much less common than is usually thought. It seems incontrovertible that in their internal actions (in which the subject is not different from the cause) created spirits exercise some true efficacy. But in the case of effects which are attributed to actions outside of themselves, whether they are actions of created spirits or of bodies, it is not equally clear whether they recognize any truly efficacious and properly so-called cause except God, operating in the regular circumstances of created things according to the laws of nature established by himself. There is no need to fear that on this hypothesis even the most ordinary effect will turn out to be miraculous. One should not speak of any causeless effect as miraculous except those which reveal themselves as above and beyond the general laws of nature, or for which no creature supplies the occasion in accordance with those laws. In fact since so many common effects of nature cannot be attributed, with any likelihood of truth, to the true efficacy of any created cause, the doctrine of occasional causes is by no means to be rejected.

But in the cases in which one should assert the true efficacy of a created

5. This paragraph was a footnote in Carmichael's text.

cause, particularly in the internal actions of created spirits, I am not afraid that any intelligent person will complain that too little is here attributed to the first cause. More trouble perhaps would be given by the difficulties raised by those who contend that when we apply the doctrine just taught to the evil actions of a creature, too little is attributed to the creature and too much to God. They ground the former criticism by arguing that the assumption of determination takes away the liberty which is needed to rightly impute an evil action to a rational creature and oblige him to render an account of it. They ground the latter criticism in the contention that the operation of God which was asserted above in general of all causes, scarcely seems able to be reconciled with the divine sanctity, when it is applied to evil actions on the part of created causes.

Enough has been said to clear up the former difficulty, I think, in our *Supplements and Observations* to Pufendorf, *On the Duty of Man and Citizen,* especially at pp. 35–36, above. But to show that we cast no aspersion on the divine sanctity by the doctrine given above, we will suggest three points for careful consideration.

1. God has given rational creatures such indications of duty and of the way to happiness that if they weighed them in a fair balance according to the rule of reason, they would choose what is pleasing to God and salutary for themselves. Now since God has never taught anyone that evil is to be done, nor urged it, nor commended it, i.e., since he has never signified to anyone that he wishes evil to be interpreted as a symbol of love and devoted affection toward himself or to be connected with the happiness of an agent, but has signified everything that is directly contrary to this, it is obvious that God cannot be called the *author* of any wicked action, according to the genuine sense of this word.

2. Insofar as providence which the doctrine given above attributes to God is related to evil actions by rational creatures, it is more permissive than effective; and it can be affirmed in a reasonable sense that God concurs in them negatively rather than positively. For God has endowed each rational creature with a certain unlimited appetite for happiness by which he continually aspires to the greatest pleasure which he can obtain and the most absolute immunity from pain. But he has also imprinted ideas on him by means of various objects, various pleasures, and the opposite pains,

some of which, though aroused by things of no particular significance, affect the mind quite vividly. There is no evil in this in itself: even though these ideas represent pleasures to be pursued or pains to be avoided which would run contrary to duty, yet they do not by themselves determine the mind to go in that direction. The mind is endowed with a faculty of reason; if it used it in a manner worthy of a rational nature, it would easily understand that the prospect of more excellent pleasures and the avoidance of more serious pains pull it in the opposite direction; and if the ideas of them were present to the mind with appropriate vividness, it would certainly choose the better direction. And yet so long as a mind which is finite and thus not incapable of error is left to itself by God, a mind, that is, which does not have sufficiently vivid ideas of the highest pleasures or pains impressed upon it by God's benevolence, it is held captive by lower ideas and enticed in the wrong direction.

3. It can also rightly be said that an action of a rational creature, however evil it may be, is not evil in so far as it proceeds from God; i.e., it is only on the part of the creature and not on the part of God that it involves neglect, contempt, or hatred of God himself (in which all moral evil consists). To the contrary, in whatever God determines that a creature do, he seeks to manifest the glory of his own infinite perfection, and thus gives evidence of his love and tender care for him in determining the very action by doing which the creature betrays his neglect or even hatred.

The reader will perhaps notice the absence of the solution which is invariably offered here by most of those who share our views in this matter, a solution that is derived from the distinction between a positive action and its evil, which is said to lie in privation.[6] But perhaps those who rely on this solution have in mind only general ideas of certain modes of acting, instead of the individual actions which are in point here. For otherwise it seems they could hardly deny that there are innumerable individual actions which, at least where a law exists, cannot fail to be bad, either sim-

---

6. Reformed dogmatists employed the notion of privation to explain sin or corruption in accordance with the Augustinian doctrine that God cannot be the source of sin or evil. But they qualified this position by insisting that sin is not mere privation but an active privation or propensity. See the *Leiden Synopsis* and other writings cited in Heppe, *Reformed Dogmatics*, pp. 323–35.

ply or in the given circumstances which the agent cannot change. And therefore in doing these actions a man sins, not because he does not add rightness to them, which *those actions* do not admit, but because he does things from which he ought to have completely abstained. If anyone nevertheless thinks that this well-known solution will be useful to him in defending the truth, he may use it so far as we are concerned, but we thought we should try to remove the difficulty without its help.[7]

If anyone does not find these arguments fully satisfying, let him reflect how dim is the sight of the human mind, and how unequal to unravelling the grounds of God's purposes. Let him not think that the clear and obvious should be called into doubt simply because he does not have the capacity to dissipate the darkness.

SECTION V

Containing the epilogue of natural theology and the transition to moral philosophy

We have considered the physical government of God, which extends to all creatures of every kind; and we have abundantly shown that rational creatures and their free actions are not exempt from it. Likewise it is clear from what we have said, that his physical government in no way conflicts with his moral government, of which only rational creatures are suitable objects and only with respect to their free actions. By his moral government God, as supreme Lord, gives laws to his rational creatures, publishing them with the sanctions of rewards and punishments and enforcing them by dispensing those rewards or punishments. It should be the purpose of all our meditation on God, to learn to conduct ourselves in accordance with these laws, lest we should not glorify as God him whom we know as God, and be found at some time without excuse.[8] It is not for this forum, but for the forum of ethics to inquire into the duties which this law requires (in-

7. This paragraph was a footnote in Carmichael's text.
8. Cf. Romans I.20.

sofar as they are known by the natural light) and to infer them from the perfections of God and from the nature and character of man and of the things which assist human life. And thus practical philosophy will begin where the theoretical philosophy of God ends.

THE END

Logic

A Short Introduction to Logic:
an elementary textbook for
students of philosophy
(particularly at the University of Glasgow)

Second edition

revised and corrected by the author.

Edinburgh

At the press of John Mosman and Co., for John Paton,
Bookseller, and for sale at his shop in Parliament Square

1722

Editorial Note

Carmichael's logic was an abridgment and an adaptation of the Port Royal logic, or *Ars Cogitandi,* or *The Art of Thinking.*[1] In his account of his teaching method,[2] he described *The Art of Thinking* as "the best Logick that I know under the name of Logick, and that is tolerably adapted for the Use of teaching in a University."[3] The principal attraction of the Port Royal logic for Carmichael was the importance it accorded to simple apprehension (or conception) and judgment: "there are basically just two modes of thinking which require the special direction of Logic, Apprehension and Judgment."[4] Other logics, notably those in the Aristotelian tradition, continued to emphasize the third part of logic, discursive reasoning.[5] Carmichael's concern, like that of the logicians of Port Royal, was to ensure that the terms used by logicians in their reasoning should represent, with some accuracy, the ideas they are supposed to signify or express.

Carmichael's endorsement of the logic of Port Royal was not unqualified. He did not consider it necessary "to follow the Author through all his Digressions."[6] He also amended the text in classroom presentation by referring students to Locke's *Essay* for a closer examination of the distinctions among clear and obscure, distinct and confused ideas.[7] He agreed

---

1. *La Logique ou l'Art de Penser* [Logic or the Art of Thinking].

2. Carmichael's account of his teaching method, Glasgow University Library 43170, appended below, pp. 379–87.

3. See below, p. 380.

4. See below, p. 292.

5. E.g., Wallis, *Institutio Logicae;* and Aldrich, *Ars Logicae.*

6. See below, p. 380.

7. In his *Annotationes ad Artem Cogitandi* [Annotations on the Art of Thinking], pp. 14–15, Carmichael refers his students to Locke's *Essay Concerning Human Understanding,* II.29 ff., for discussion of clear and obscure, distinct and confused ideas.

with Antoine Arnauld and Pierre Nicole, the logicians of Port Royal, that
not all ideas have their origins in sensation; but he considered that the origin of such ideas had been better explained by Locke. Ideas of physical or
corporeal things have their origin in sensation; ideas of thinking, judging,
reasoning, willing, have their origin in the operations of the understanding.[8] This was a consideration of the first importance for Carmichael; for
he discovered in reflections on the operations of the understanding the origin of ideas of God, of lasting happiness, and the other central ideas of his
natural theology and moral philosophy.

Carmichael's *Logic* was, by his own account, an elementary text, "directed primarily to first-year students." It should be read as an introduction to the *Philosophical Theses* which follow and represent "the higher
studies which follow this in my course of instruction."

8. See below, pp. 293 n. 2 and 338.

Preface

To the reader

There is no need to speak at length about the scope of this little work. Anyone may readily see that it is a short and simple course of instruction designed merely to prepare the minds of beginners for a deeper understanding of logic and for the more fruitful approach to other branches of knowledge which it may facilitate. With this end in view some years ago I prepared for publication a short *Introduction to Logic*.[1] This was at the time when the use of handwritten systems, which had prevailed for too long, to the great inconvenience of teachers and students, was beginning to disappear from our university. My hope in preparing that text was to ensure that the students of the university would not be deterred from the study of philosophy as soon as they began by long, tedious, and unrewarding labor. Now that the first edition has sold out, I am allowing the book to reappear in a second edition, with corrections in many places and additions in others. It is directed primarily to first-year students, who are to go on, if God so wills, to the higher studies which follow this in my course of instruction.[2]

I have had two aims: not only to lay out for beginners the usual precepts (at least, all that is useful among the precepts usually taught at this stage), but also to explain the reasons for them in a manner suited, so far as possible, to the capacity of beginners. I hope that in this way students will

1. In the account of his teaching method prepared at the request of the faculty in August 1712, Carmichael reported that a "Compend of Logick" composed by him was printing in November 1711. See below, p. 379. An earlier version of the text translated here was published in 1720.

2. Logic was the first of the philosophical subjects which, as regent, Carmichael would have taught to his students over four years. See pp. 379–81.

realize from the beginning that the study of philosophy does not consist in mere reading, nor in the understanding and memorizing of what they read, but above all in the exercise of judgment and reason, by which they may come to see the truth as it were with their own eyes, by perceiving the self-evidence of principles and seeing the necessary consequences which lead to the conclusions that follow from them. This is the reason why I have gone beyond the practice adopted in most compends of this kind by focusing not so much on the differences between words and the various forms of speech as on the various modes of thought that underlie them, which I would wish learners to pay particular attention to. That is also why I did not think it right to omit brief demonstrations of the rules about the relative modes of propositions, about the legitimate forms of syllogisms, and so on, which are normally taught (though most authors reserve these for a larger treatise). For these rules (as the distinguished John Harris rightly observed in the case of trigonometrical rules)[3] can be more easily learned with the aid of demonstrations; certainly nothing better assists the memory than calling in judgment to help her.

My purpose in writing this introduction however does not require me to say anything in detail about *the causes and remedies of obscurity and confusion in ideas, or of error in judgments; about the method to be observed in the investigation and demonstration of truth; of the different kinds of arguments that are appropriate to the various natures of the things to be known,* and so on. These topics are much the most useful part of logic as well as the most beautiful, and in the fuller course on logic one should devote much time to them. They are the additional subjects which should be taught in their own place, and tackled by students only after they have been properly prepared by prior instruction in this elementary instruction in *the forms of propositions and syllogisms.* The facts themselves prove that those who despise this elementary teaching or urge the omission of it are doing the worst possible service to the progress of students in any branch of knowledge they may subsequently study. . . .

In the final chapter I have added a section on logical practice, not because I think that it should be taught along with the rest right at the be-

---

3. Harris, *A new short Treatise of Algebra.*

ginning of the study of philosophy, but because it is useful for certain exercises which instructors should prescribe in their proper place, and which
are not to be found in the other books which are most in use today. I have
taken less trouble at the present with this part than with the rest, and have
readily adopted what particularly pleased me in the teachings of others,
changing or adding only a few things.

As for the alterations made in this new edition, most of them are intended to render more obvious and evident for beginners, at the glance of
an eye, each particular part of the doctrine, so that they may more easily
mark them and commit them to memory, when they go back over the
book.

Farewell, reader, and wish well to this little work dedicated solely to the
use of the students. *Such a work* (to use the words of a distinguished man)[4]
*should find such a favorable reception that no one will think the trouble taken
over it to be unworthy of him, even though it brings him no intellectual repute
or prestige.*

G. C.

The College of Glasgow
October 1st, 1722

---

4. Carmichael is quoting Pufendorf, *On the Duty of Man and Citizen,* p. 6.

A Short Introduction to Logic

Logic is the *science which exhibits the method of discovering truth and of expounding it to others.* Since we can be said to attain truth or deviate from it, strictly speaking, only by the act of judging, it is clear that the purpose of teaching it is the formation of true and, so far as possible, certain judgments about things which everyone should learn. Now forming judgments about things requires a prior apprehension of them; and both the truth and the certainty of the judgment depend in no small degree on the correctness of the apprehension. There are therefore just two modes of thinking which require the particular direction of logic, i.e., *apprehension* and *judgment.*

CHAPTER I

On Apprehension

1. On the nature of apprehension. On the idea, and its comprehension and extension.

Apprehension is *the act of the mind by which it merely perceives a thing* or simply thinks about it, neither affirming nor denying it, neither desiring nor avoiding it. The representation of a thing in the mind which enables us to perceive it, is called an *idea*. A fuller inquiry into the relation of an idea to the actual act of apprehension belongs to the domain not of logic but of pneumatics.[1] Meanwhile what is usually taught about ideas in logic may be appropriately understood of both.[2]

The thing which is represented to the mind through an idea is said to be its *object*.

---

1. In the longer treatment of logic provided in his dictates, *Logica, sive ars intelligendi* [Logic or the Art of Understanding] (1697), Carmichael included discussion that he here consigns to pneumatology, or the science of the mind, of how ideas are formed. See also below, pp. 326 ff. In the *Logica* he also prefaced his logic with a historical account of the origin of philosophy. In that account, he underlined the importance of direct study of the nature of things, following the lead of great philosophers of the current age, in contrast with the scholastics.

2. The two sentences preceding were a footnote in Carmichael's text. In his *Annotations on the Art of Thinking*, p. 2, he asked his students to write: "See this question more correctly addressed by Locke, in his *Essay Concerning Human Understanding*, Book II, where he teaches that ideas of things and of corporeal modes derive their origin from sensation; of spiritual things (among them the idea of thought) from reflection on our thoughts; and more general ideas (among them the idea of being) derive their origin from both sources."

Finally the word or complex of words, by which the idea, or the object as represented by it, is signified (as *triangle, good man,* etc.) is normally called a *term* (the reason for which we will give).[3] It should be distinguished as a *verbal* term, since the idea itself is sometimes called a *mental term;* as the thing represented is also sometimes called an *objective term.*

Ideas are classified above all (not to touch here on other differences between them) either by their *comprehension,* i.e., by whether they include in themselves one or several representations, or by their *extension,* i.e., by whether they represent one or several objects.

In the former respect, an idea is either *simple* or *complex.* A *simple idea* is one *which cannot be resolved into several different ideas;* such are ideas of *being, power, thought,* etc. A *complex* idea on the other hand is one *which comprehends several different ideas, into which it can be resolved;* such is the idea of *spirit,* i.e., of *a thing which has the capacity to think.*

In the latter respect, an idea is either *singular* or *universal.* A *singular idea* is one *which represents directly one object alone,* so that it cannot be truly attributed to more than one individual: such are the ideas of *Alexander, Bucephalus, this tree,* etc. I say, *directly,* because a singular idea can represent one thing as conflated from several or related in another way to more than one; however, it cannot be predicated of these individual things in a direct, but only in an oblique, case. See what is said below about the proposition [pp. 299–300].[4] By contrast, a *universal* idea is one which represents several direct objects indiscriminately, so that it can be truly applied to each one of them: such are the ideas of *man, horse, tree,* etc.

Here one must note that from singular or less universal ideas, more universal ideas are formed by means of *abstraction,* by which some part of the former comprehension is lost, and they become as a result more simple. By contrast, from universal, ideas become singular or less universal, by means of *composition,* by which they are made more complex by the addition of some idea to their comprehension.

---

3. See below, p. 300.
4. The two sentences beginning, "I say, *directly,* . . ." were a footnote in Carmichael's text.

2. On division as the resolution of the extension of a universal idea.

The *extension* of a universal idea is resolved by *division,* by which we mean here the *particular enumeration of ideas differing in their whole extension, by which the extension of a given universal idea is exactly exhausted.* Thus *animal* is divided into *man* and *brute;* brute in turn into quadrupeds, flying beasts, fish, and reptiles. The more universal idea which is divided, is here called the *whole;* and the less universal ideas, into which it is divided, are called *parts.*

The *division of a thing* very much differs from this *division of a universal idea* of which we have spoken. It is the *particular enumeration of things totally different, by which the constitution of any given composite thing is briefly described.* By this means *man* is divided into *soul* and *body,* and body in turn into its various members.

3. On definition as the resolution of the comprehension of a complex idea.

Just as the *extension* of a universal idea is resolved by *division,* so the *comprehension* of any complex idea is resolved by *definition.* By this we mean *a phrase which explains a complex idea corresponding to the given name, by means of several connected words, by which are signified both the simpler ideas which make it up and the order in which they unite to do so.*

The use of definition does not arise because when one has a complex idea before the mind, one may at the same time be unaware of its comprehension (just as one may be unaware of its extension). Rather it arises because, owing to the shorthand nature of speech, fairly complex ideas are normally denoted by simple words, and so it quite often happens that others do not understand what we mean to signify by some phrase, or we ourselves are not careful enough always to attach the same determinate idea in our minds to the same word.

Both these difficulties are remedied by *definition,* by which the meaning of a given word is both declared to others and determined with greater certainty in ourselves. We both instruct others and at the same time fix it in our own memories that the simple word covers the same complex idea which is explicated more clearly by several words in the definition. So, for example, *spirit* is defined as *thinking substance, virtue* as a *habit inclining to morally good acts.* If anyone should say that *definition,* as we have explained it here, is merely *ideal,* or rather *nominal,* I would not feel obliged for that reason to introduce a *real definition* which would be distinct from it, until I know how to explain *real essences* of things, distinct from ideal or nominal essences. And I have no doubt that it would be highly beneficial to all disciplines, if writers of every genre would imitate the *precision* of mathematicians in this respect, and never use a definition which they would not accept as a substitute for the word itself.[5]

From this it is obvious that if a definition is to have the use it is intended for, i.e., if it is to determine the idea which corresponds to a given word, one must first clearly understand which idea is expressed by the actual words of the definition. To understand this, it is important both to know the simpler ideas attached to the various words which enter into the definition and to perceive the relationship between the ideas which is expressed by the arrangement of the words. Therefore the definition must be designed to make both of these more evident than the notion one would have of the meaning of the word to which the definition is applied, if one did not have the help of the definition.

This is precisely the point of the cardinal rule of definition, which is almost the only rule we need: *the definition must be clearer than what is defined.* But provided clarity is preserved, *a definition is thought to be all the better for being shorter* and therefore easier to remember. For this reason, first, avoid all unnecessary words (such as words whose meaning is adequately included in other parts of the definition, except so far as the demands of grammar require them). Second, so that the definition may consist of as few words as possible, choose words that signify ideas which are immediately simpler than the idea to be defined, and in particular one

5. The previous two sentences were a footnote in Carmichael's text. Carmichael's insistence on merely nominal essences, as distinct from real essences, derives from Locke, *Essay,* III.III.17 ff. See also below, pp. 328 ff.

word (if it can be found) which signifies the idea which is immediately superior in the categorical series. This idea, together with the word by which it is signified, is usually called a *genus,* as *substance* is in the definition of *spirit* given above. Anything added to the definition to fix its limits, is called the *differentia,* as *thinking* is in that same definition. And with respect to these parts, the whole complex idea together with the word by which it is signified, is called a *species,* and in fact, with respect to them, a *subjicible species;* but if it has no other universal class subject to it, of which it is the genus, it is said, with respect to particulars, to be a *predicable species.*

On Judgment in General, and on Immediate Judgment in Particular

1. On the nature of judgment; and on the difference between immediate and mediate judgment.

Judgment is the act of the mind by which it gives a verdict on two ideas in comparison with each other: i.e., a verdict as to the identity or difference of the objects represented by them.

The relationship of the ideas so compared is learned either from their immediate juxtaposition (without the intervention of any third idea) or with the assistance of one or more intermediate ideas, with which both of the given ideas are compared. Therefore, one kind of judgment is *immediate,* by which a verdict is given about ideas which are directly compared; the other is *mediate* judgment, by which a verdict is given on ideas which are compared with each other through the intervention of some third idea, or even of more, properly ordered in relation to each other.

Mediate judgment has an alternative name, *discourse;* for it is one and the same thing to deduce one verdict of the mind from other verdicts and to give a verdict because of other verdicts or with regard to them. Therefore just as one must treat *discourse* under the name of *judgment* as one species of it, so what is said in this chapter about judgment in general should also be understood to be appropriate to discourse, insofar as discourse is concerned with the relation of two extreme ideas.

2. On affirmative and negative propositions, and their subjects and predicates.

The particular aim of any judgment is what it defines or what relation it determines to exist between two given ideas; hence we often utter it in words, while not indicating whether that relation between ideas is known to us immediately or mediately, much less what the intermediary is.

Now a judgment precisely considered, since it defines the relation of two given ideas, may be considered a *statement.* The statement which expresses a mediate judgment as such is not a mere proposition but an argument. However, it is not altogether appropriate to restrict the term "proposition" to statements which express immediate judgments, since the obvious and universally accepted use of the word is against it.[1] Such a statement is commonly called a *proposition,* and, to differentiate it, a *verbal proposition;* for the act of judging itself (considered, as I have said, precisely, and so as far as it is signified by a verbal proposition) has also usually been called a *proposition,* but that is a *mental proposition.* This latter use of the word, though perhaps less proper and not so common in the usual books of logic, is to be especially kept in view in what follows. For most of what is commonly taught about the proposition, which we shall explain below, properly and primarily applies to the judgment itself, or to the mental proposition, and fits the verbal proposition only secondarily, so far as it is a sign of the mental proposition. The few things that relate particularly to the verbal proposition will become clear as we go.

By virtue of their *form,* or (as some call it) their *internal quality,* propositions are divided into *affirmative* and *negative.* For in making a judgment, the mind gives a verdict on two ideas in one of two ways. It either *unites them because they belong to each other,* that is, because they are *representations of the same object,* and this proposition is said to be *affirmative* (e.g., *the human mind is immortal);* or *it distinguishes them from each other because they are discrepant from each other,* that is, *because they are not representations of the same object;* and this proposition is said to be *negative* (e.g., *the human mind is not material*).

---

1. The previous two sentences were a footnote in Carmichael's text.

Here one must note that of the two ideas, on whose association the mind gives a verdict in making a judgment, one is, as it were, fundamental (since the other idea is summoned to it to be compared with it); it is commonly called the *subject*. The other may be called accessory (in the sense that it is brought in to be compared with the other); it is usually called the *predicate*. Thus in both of the propositions given above, *the human mind* is the subject; in the affirmative proposition the predicate is *immortal;* in the negative, *material.* If the distinct notions of *subject* and *predicate* do not seem to be adequately discriminated by the explanations offered, the difference will become clear enough (at least in the propositions where it matters) from the properties of each which we are about to explain.

Here then we note that the words *subject* and *predicate* (used in nearly all treatises of logic) are usually applied not only to the actual ideas which are being compared, but also, analogically, to the words by which those ideas are signified; in such a way however, that the epithets mental and verbal may be added, in order to remove ambiguity (as we noted above for the words *term* and *proposition*).

Note further that both subject and predicate are commonly called by a single name, the *terms* of the proposition, which are either *mental* or *verbal,* depending whether they refer to the ideas themselves or to the words by which they are signified. The reason for that appellation is that in the simplest and most regular form of the verbal proposition, the subject occupies the first place, and the predicate the last place. Placed between them is a substantive verb, either alone or qualified by a negative, which is commonly called the *copula;* and which more directly signifies the act of affirming or negating. As these parts frequently change their relative positions, so it very often happens, that the *copula* is included in the same words as the predicate: e.g., *Peter reads,* that is, *Peter is reading.*

[Sections 3 and 4, which contain technical rules of argument, are omitted.]

5. On propositions which are composite, complex, etc.

Besides the simple and regular form of propositions which we have assumed so far, logicians differentiate several other forms and specify a corresponding number of different classes of propositions which they call *composite* or *complex*. However all of them are either (1) of such a kind that *each of them is not one proposition or one judgment in the mind, but several taken jointly together in one statement;* or (2) *really simple propositions* in the mind (although consisting of complex terms) by which one predicate is affirmed or denied of one subject, *but are expressed in a sort of cryptic manner* (in which the true subject and the true predicate do not reveal themselves clearly) because of the shorthand nature of ordinary speech.

To the *former* class we refer all *copulative* propositions, such as *Peter and Paul read* (i.e., *Peter reads* and *Paul reads*), and all those which have the force of *copulative* propositions: that is, propositions which join two or more propositions together in such a way that they assert the truth of each one, whether they distinctly contain the words of each proposition or the second is contained in some part of it: such are the propositions called *causal, adversative,* and *exclusive.* We leave to class discussion anything more that needs to be said about them in this first course.

To the *latter* class (that is, the class of those propositions which are simple in the mind, though they are not expressed simply and in regular form) belong particularly *conditional* propositions, such as, *if God exists, the world is ruled by providence.* Such propositions contain as it were the material of two propositions (the proposition which is supposed is called the *antecedent,* and the one which is said to follow from the supposed proposition is called the *consequent*). But they do not absolutely posit the truth of either the one or the other, but only go so far as to assert the consequence of the latter from the former. They are easily reduced to a *simple,* or (as it is usually called) *categorical,* form. For we note that a particular conditional, *if,* has precisely the value of, *in the case that;* and thus the proposition just quoted comes out as, *in the case that* (or *in every case in which*) *God exists, the world is ruled by providence.* But if in turn we transpose the terms which are here put forward obliquely, to the direct case, we shall have the following categorical proposition, by which one predicate is affirmed of one subject: *every case which posits that God exists* (i.e., *in which God exists*) *is a case which posits that the world is ruled by providence.* In the same way, any other conditional can be reduced to categorical form, some more easily than others.

[Several paragraphs of section 5 are omitted.]

6. On certain and uncertain judgment.

A judgment may be *certain,* in which case it has in itself a certain inexpressible gleam of truth, which is found only in true judgments (though not in all of them), and thus excludes all suspicion of falsity; or it may be *uncertain* or *doubtful,* in which case, since it is without the infallible character of truth, it does not escape all suspicion of falsity. We may understand from what was said at p. 299, why we use the term *judgment* here rather than *proposition* when we are considering *subjective* certainty (i.e., the certitude which is actually present to the mind) and the uncertainty opposed to it. Hence too it is quite evident that *objective* certainty is more correctly attributed to the *proposition* in the case where we can know with certainty the relationship which it defines between ideas; and similarly the uncertainty opposed to it, where it cannot.

7. Of immediate judgment in particular, and of its double kind.

Of immediate judgment as such, little remains to be said, except to stress that *all our knowledge of every kind must be resolved ultimately into immediate propositions, or propositions known by their own light.* Hence whether the relation of terms of any given proposition is known from one term or through several mediate terms, it is always necessary that the relation of any intermediate idea to the ideas which are directly compared with it on either side be immediately knowable.

The principles on which our knowledge rests may be reduced to two kinds. Some principles are abstract. What *abstraction* is, we have said above at p. 294. We may understand from this that one idea can be said to be abstracted from another whenever it is recognized by the mind as separate from the other with which it had previously constituted the same complex. But an *idea* simply is called *abstract* when it is abstracted from the particular consideration of any singular thing which is offered to our senses or reflection, such as the ideas of a *whole*, of a *part*, etc.[2] Their truth is known from the mere comparison with each other of abstract ideas, without the mind's taking notice of the thing itself as it exists in nature; an example is: *every whole is greater than its part*. Others are *intuitive,* or *experiential,* and these consist in an intimate sense, or awareness which the mind has, of a thing's being intimately present to itself; an example is the proposition, *I thinking exist.*

Propositions which are deduced solely from principles of the former kind are purely *hypothetical,* and do not absolutely posit the existence of anything. Such are the predications by which a property is attributed to something on the condition of its existence, a property which, though it does not enter into the actual concept of the thing, still has a necessary connection with that concept. The logicians call this a *property,* as in the following: *Every rational creature is subject to the moral rule.*

All *absolute* propositions presuppose principles of the latter kind, that is, propositions which absolutely attribute actual existence to some thing or which attribute a predicate that actually belongs to it. In this sense one normally attributes any predicate which belongs to a subject only contingently, such as logicians call a *common accident,* as in the proposition, *Peter is learned. Property* and *common accident,* together with *species, genus,* and *differentia* (see pp. 296–97) are the five usual *predicables* of the logicians.

2. The previous three sentences beginning, "What abstraction is . . ." were a footnote in Carmichael's text. In his *Annotations on the Art of Thinking,* p. 90, Carmichael asked his students to write the following note: "It is not only the existence of our thoughts that we know by reflection, properly so called, but also innumerable abstract truths, which by collation of abstract ideas become more certainly known than any of those external things which we perceive by the evidence of the senses."

On Mediate Judgment or Discourse

1. On mediate judgment or discourse.

Whenever the mutual relationship of any two ideas is not adequately understood by the direct comparison of them, some other intermediate idea has to be brought in (as we have pointed out above), so that one may infer the relation of these ideas to each other from the perceived relation of both of the ideas in question with this mediate idea (or with several ideas properly related to each other). The act by which we give a verdict on the relation of ideas with each other in turn, resting on judgments previously given about the relation of both with the third, is called a *mediate judgment* or *discourse,* as we said above.

It makes no difference to the consequence, whether both of the extreme ideas are directly compared with the same intermediate idea, or whether only one of the extreme ideas is directly compared with the first mediate idea, and this with the second, and so on, until we end at the other extreme idea, in accordance with rules to be established below. However, because the order of nature and of teaching requires us to begin with the simpler ideas, we assume for the time being merely that the two extreme ideas are compared with one and the same intermediate idea in the same number of propositions; for the moment we ignore the question whether the relation of both of the extreme ideas with that mediate idea is known directly or by the assistance of one or several further mediate ideas.

2. Of the affirmative and negative syllogism and of their principles and parts.

A statement by which a mediated judgment as such is expressed, together with the two other judgments on which it immediately rests, is called a *syllogism;* in other words, it is *a statement by which one proposition is explicitly inferred from two others, by which its two terms are compared with the same middle term.* This is a *verbal* syllogism; for the actual *progress of the mind through two judgments, by which the same number of ideas are separately compared with the same middle idea, to a third judgment by which the relation of the same two ideas with each other is determined,* is called a *mental syllogism.* For reasons analogous to those I noted above under the name of *proposition,* most of what will be said below about the syllogism, should be particularly and primarily understood of the mental syllogism, and secondarily of the verbal syllogism.

A syllogism may be affirmative or negative. The *affirmative* syllogism is defined as *that by which one concludes that the objects of two ideas are the same as each other, because it had previously affirmed the identity of both of them with the same object of a third idea.* It rests on the axiom that *things that are the same as some third thing are the same as each other;* for example:

> Every thinking thing is immortal;
> The human mind is a thinking thing:
> Therefore, the human mind is immortal.

A *negative* syllogism is that by which one concludes that the objects of two ideas are not the same as each other; because it had *affirmed the identity of one of them, and denied the identity of the other, with the same object of some third idea.* It rests on the axiom that *things of which one is the same as some third thing to which the other is not the same, are not the same as each other;* for example:

> No thinking thing is material;
> The human mind is a thinking thing:
> Therefore, the human mind is not material.

In both cases we are considering only a syllogism which proceeds correctly (i.e., only a valid syllogism).

The conclusion from what has been said is that in every syllogism *three ideas* are compared. They are *two* ideas whose *congruence* or *incongruence* is inferred and which are usually called the *extremes* (in the example given above of the affirmative syllogism, these are *the human mind* and *immortal*), and a *third* idea, with which both of the extreme ideas are individually compared, so that either both are seen to be congruent with it, or one is and the other is not. This third idea is commonly called the *middle;* an instance, in the same example, is *thinking thing.* These three ideas, together with the words in which they are expressed, are commonly called the *three terms* of the syllogism.

Likewise it is also agreed that *three propositions* are contained in every syllogism. By one proposition the congruence or incongruence of the two extremes is inferred, and it is called the *conclusion;* as in the example given above, *the human mind is immortal* (of which the predicate, *immortal,* is called the *greater extreme,* and the subject, *the human mind,* is called the *lesser extreme*). In addition there are *two* other propositions, by which the two extremes are individually compared with the middle, and these are called *premises.* Of these, that which compares the major extreme with the middle is called the *major proposition,* as in the aforesaid example, *every thinking thing is immortal;* that which compares the minor extreme with the middle, is called the *minor proposition,* or *assumption,* as *the human mind is a thinking thing.*

3. On the general rules of syllogisms.

From the definitions given of both syllogisms (affirmative and negative), and from the axioms on which they are constructed, it is quite clear that *in order for two extremes to be united with each other in a conclusion, it is necessarily required that both of them, in the premises, be united with the middle;* and, *in order for the extremes to be separated from each other in the conclusion, it is no less necessarily required that one of them be united with the middle in the premises, the other separated from the same middle. It follows that, if both extremes are separated, in the premises, from the middle, neither the congruence of the extremes with each other, nor their incongruence, will be able to be inferred.* Hence naturally flow the rules which are commonly but rather confusingly (since they are mixed with others) taught as *the rules on the quality of syllogistic propositions:*

First, *if one of the premises is negative, the conclusion will be negative.*
Second, *if both of the premises are affirmative, the conclusion will be affirmative.*
Third, *from two negative premises, nothing follows.*

[Further specifications of these rules of the syllogism follow (sections 3–9), which follow the rules given in *The Art of Thinking* about the extension of terms, which as Carmichael notes, are not found in "the scholastic logics."[1] However the rules on "the quantity and quality of syllogisms," which are found in the scholastic logics, and which include the "moods" and "figures" of the syllogism, may be deduced from the rules of the extension of terms. This Carmichael proceeds to do. In accordance with the plan of an elementary textbook, there is no discussion of sophisms and paralogisms. The chapter ends with the following general account of the nature of argument.]

10. On the syllogism considered with reference to its content.

Every perfect argument (such as all, in intention, seem to be) which is constructed according to the rules laid down above, if it rests on true premises, yields a true conclusion, and if it rests on certain premises, yields a certain conclusion; this is called *demonstration.* The certain intuition of the connection between the extreme ideas which is inferred in the conclusion is normally called *knowledge.* This intuition may be achieved in the very act of drawing the conclusion (an act which gets its own self-evidence and certitude directly from a distincter perception of the truth of the premises), or in a subsequent act which relies on a more general recall of an earlier demonstration.

But if even one of the premises on which the argument rests is uncer-

---

1. E.g., Franco Burgersdyck, *Institutiones Logicae.* Carmichael's colleague John Law reported to the faculty in August 1712 that "in the logicall years I began always the logicks by teaching those of Burgersdick." (Glasgow University Archives 43227).

tain, then the conclusion deduced is also doubtful and uncertain (so far as it flows from these premises). Such a mental verdict is called an *opinion*. It may be reached either in the very act of drawing the conclusion, by a particular inspection of the premises, or accepted from our confidence in a previous chain of reasoning.

Finally if any of the premises is false, it carries no weight, supposing it is false, toward establishing the truth of the conclusion. However it sometimes happens that a conclusion deduced from false premises is true, just as a conclusion drawn from uncertain premises is sometimes certain on other grounds.

But a syllogism which does not conform to the rules given above is said to be a *paralogism,* although this name is normally applied particularly to syllogisms in which the fault in form is obvious. Other paralogisms, in which the fault of form is concealed by some convoluted fallacy of ambiguous words or phrases, are usually called by the more particular name of *sophisms.*

❧ CHAPTER 4 ❧

On Method, and Logical Practice

1. On the general rules of method.

To investigate the truth or expound it to others with success, we need to do more than look at individual acts taken separately, we must also arrange them in due order among themselves. We would not wish this compend to omit any of the essential parts of logic, and so we have included here the three following general laws of method. We postpone to another place a more detailed explanation of the individual methods and the rules belonging to them.

i. *In the individual steps of our reasoning in pursuit of knowledge, we must preserve self-evidence; that is, nothing must be admitted as true which is not evidently seen to be so.*

ii. *One must not carry one's reasoning about things beyond the point where determinate ideas of them are present to the mind.*

iii. *One must always begin from the simpler and the easier; and one must stay with them for quite a while until they may become familiar, before one passes on to the more difficult and the more complex.*

2. On logical practice, and first on the treatment of the simple theme.

The special practice of logic is the careful and precise investigation of truth, and virtually the entire discipline seeks to direct this investigation and remove obstacles to it. But what is called *logical practice* usually gives precepts about certain exercises which pertain to the disclosure of truth, and it has been found to be extremely useful to bring these precepts to the attention of the students of the university. We therefore include here some of the most important and useful of them.

Logicians reduce these precepts to two classes: one concerns *genesis,* the other *analysis.* They define *genesis* as *the mode of using the tools of logic by which one forms and produces for oneself a discourse on a theme.* They define *themes* as *anything that may be put before the intellect as a subject of knowledge,* and divide them into *simple* and *complex.*

A *simple theme* is said to be a *term,* whether *complex* or *noncomplex;* or rather, *the thing itself so far as it is merely represented by an idea, and is signified by one or more words which denote that idea.*

A *complex theme* is any *proposition;* or rather *the very truth of the thing, so far as it can terminate the act of affirming or denying, and is expressed in the form of a statement or perhaps a question.*

In treating a simple theme the following rules must be observed.

i. The origin of the word itself under which the theme is proposed must be indicated, if the derivation is not too obscure. If the word admits of different meanings, they must be distinguished; and one must also mention any other preliminary points required for accurately determining its significance. This is to be done for each and every word, if the theme is put forward in a phrase of several words.

ii. One must also explain by a lucid definition the present signification of the proposed term and so the essence of the thing itself, or at least its nominal essence.

iii. One must deduce the secondary attributes, if there are any, from the essential concept by clear and evident inference.

iv. One must take into consideration any accidental attributes that may pertain to a given theme, and one must show to what variations it is liable because of them.

v. One must investigate the origin of the theme, and if dealing with a manufactured object, one must indicate how it is produced.

vi. One must also think of its end; that is, one must consider whether it will utterly perish, and if it is determined to be corruptible, by what and by means of what.

vii. One must also observe its relations and connections with other things.

viii. If the theme is composed of parts, these must be examined, and inquiry made as to how they are united in the composite theme.

ix. Finally if a proposed term is universal, one must also survey its inferiors, especially the immediate ones.

3. On the solo treatment of a complex theme, or on exegesis.

If a complex theme is put forward for treatment, it is handled either in a speech by one person, which is called *exegesis,* or by argument between two or more persons, which is called *disputation.*

There are three important and essential parts of *exegesis.* The first is called *paraskeuê,*[1] or *preparation* for treating the question. The rules are as follows:

i. The terms of the question must be distinctly explained, if they are liable to any ambiguity of meaning.

ii. Then the state of the question must be clearly and lucidly settled.

iii. The various opinions of different authors must be briefly and faithfully expounded.

The second part is called *kataskeuê,* or *confirmation* of truth, of which the rules are these:

i. The true position is to be taken and established by means of arguments.

ii. Weight, rather than number, of arguments is the principal weapon; and one must use no argument which does not have solid force and importance.

---

1. Carmichael's use of these Greek terms indicates that he was following a version of the "preliminary exercises," or *Progymnasmata,* of Aphthonius (especially chs. 5 and 6). This text was widely used in Latin translation in grammar schools in England in this period. See M. L. Clarke, *Classical Education in Britain 1500–1900* (Cambridge: Cambridge University Press, 1959), pp. 2, 184.

iii. One must meet any objections which opponents urge to elude the force of the reasons we have given.

iv. Finally, if there are any famous testimonies of great authors, they should be adduced to lend further confirmation to our position.

The third part is *anaskeuê,* or the *solution of objections;* these are the rules:

i. Opponents' arguments must be faithfully rehearsed, in such a way that they lose nothing of their force.

ii. They must be refuted firmly and clearly, and the difficulties contained in them lucidly resolved, not only by denying what is falsely alleged, but also by adding a firm ground for the denial.

iii. Contrary testimonies from great men are to be given due weight, and reconciled with the previously established truth, if this can be done; if not, they must be modestly rejected.

One may preface all these matters with a *proparaskeuê* as a proem on the importance and timeliness of the question; one may also annex to all the aforesaid parts an *episkeuê* as a peroration, which gives the gist of the whole dissertation in a few words, together with the corollaries that flow from it.

However, for the right treatment of any theme, whether simple or complex, no rules direct us so well as a well-formed judgment and an accurate knowledge of the subject under discussion. For the method must be suited to the different conditions of things, and the things must not have their necks twisted, so to speak, to fit the more rigid laws of method. No one therefore will expound any proposed theme more elegantly than one who has looked thoroughly into it and has set himself carefully to observe this one rule above all others, *to give a simple account of what he has learned by paying serious attention to the matter for himself, with an attitude of benevolence toward others and a desire to make clear the truth, for the glory of God.*

4. On the social treatment of complex themes or on disputation.

The next subject is *disputation;* its laws regard either the matter or the form of disputation. Of the former there are three:

i. The subject of the disputation must be useful and serious, something it would be worth learning the truth about.

ii. It must also be suited to the capacity, condition, and studies of the disputants.

iii. It must be such as may be a subject of disputation without absurdity or impiety.

As for the form, since three persons are necessary to the proper organization of a formal disputation, i.e., opponent, respondent, and president, some rules are common to them all; some are peculiar to each.

The rules all three must observe are these:

i. No one should seek to attract vain glory by disputations, but each should seek the truth with honest sincerity.

ii. The state of the controversy should be clearly put forward, and kept firmly in mind through the whole disputation.

iii. It is useful for the disputants to agree among themselves on certain principles on which the arguments are founded. In formal disputations, however, principles are not normally adduced before the opponent comes to use them.[2]

iv. Wait patiently for the other person to finish his speech.

v. Strive above all for brevity and clarity; and therefore avoid pointless periphrases and digressions.

vi. Both sides are to abstain from all abuse and insult.

vii. No one should use, or allow another to use, without interpretation, any word or phrase on whose current significance the disputants are perhaps not altogether agreed. No one therefore should be ashamed to request explanations of the terms used by his adversary, and no one should neglect to interpret the terms he uses himself, until words are found whose meaning no one in frankness and candor can claim to doubt. It is not good enough to make the allegation (which is the common refuge of ignorance and idleness) that the words employed are accepted in common usage and well known to philosophers, since no words can be more ambiguous than

---

2. This sentence was a footnote in Carmichael's text.

most of the technical terms of the scholastics, or less suited to raise clear and distinct ideas in the mind.[3]

The rules peculiar to the opponent are these:

i. He must carefully examine the meaning of the thesis.

ii. The first argument he puts forward should explicitly contradict the thesis. We should completely banish from the schools the silly, long-winded practice that some have of taking a third or even a fourth argument to arrive at a contradiction of the thesis; which is what they should have started from.[4]

iii. The proposition denied by the respondent should be the conclusion of the next argument.

iv. The argument should be put forward, as far as possible, with clarity and in syllogistic form (especially among beginners in formal disputations).

v. As soon as a sound response has been given which destroys the force of the argument, there should be no further dispute.

The rules to be observed by the respondent are these:

i. After an introductory salutation of congratulations or goodwill, he must faithfully rehearse the whole argument of the opponent; and he must once again repeat how far the proposition to which the response is to be attached has been taken.

ii. In rehearsing the argument, he must consider, if it was the first, whether it contradicts the thesis; or if it was not the first, whether it proves the proposition which is denied. If it turns out that the opponent has not succeeded in this, he is said to be committing *ignoratio elenchi.*

iii. If the argument does contradict the thesis, or if it proves the proposition just denied, he must examine its form; and if it is not good, he must show what is wrong with it.

iv. If it proves what it had to, and the form is good, the proposition, if false, must be denied, or if ambiguous, analyzed.

v. If none of this appears, but on the contrary it becomes clear that the argument is demonstrative, the truth must be frankly acknowledged.

3. The previous two sentences were a footnote in Carmichael's text.
4. This sentence was a footnote in Carmichael's text.

As for the president, he intervenes either merely to keep order (*eutaxia*)[5] or also to give assistance to the respondent. A president of the first kind merely has the duty to admonish the disputants to follow the aforesaid rules, and to bring them back to the proper form of disputation, if they wander from the straight path. But a president of the latter sort, in addition to the duty just mentioned, which he shares with the first kind of president, must also solve a difficulty which has been advanced when the respondent fails to do so, and defend the truth of the thesis; but in such a way that he also finds out how much the respondent can do for himself, and should lead him gradually to the true solution of the argument rather than do all the work himself, which makes the respondent uninterested in the outcome of the disputation.

5. On analysis.

The other part of logical practice is *analysis*. This is defined as, *the mode of using the tools of logic by which we resolve a discourse which has already been made and composed into the principles from which it was made and composed.* It is particularly useful in understanding other men's writings, and since we owe to them by far the largest part of our knowledge, it is rightly considered all the more useful and necessary to have an acquaintance with analysis.

Our first concern should be to reach the real meaning of the author; to this end we must use means to guide us in understanding an ambiguous or obscure sense. These are either *external* or *internal* means.

The external means for discovering the sense of a statement are these:

i. One must take into account who is speaking; for individuals usually fit their discourse to their own condition, intelligence, and interests.

ii. One must take note of what the subject of the discourse is; for words must be understood in accordance with the subject matter.

iii. One must take note of the end and intention of the discourse; for we usually try to address others in order to bring them to our point of view.

5. Cicero discusses *eutaxia* at *On Duties,* I.142.

iv. One must note the audience of the discourse; for we are bound to address others in such a way that we will be understood.

v. One must weigh the occasion of the discourse, whether it was premeditated or really an accidental and casual remark.

vi. Finally, one must take account of what went before and what comes after it and of parallel passages; for an author must be presumed to speak so as to be consistent with himself; and darker passages may be illuminated by relevant passages which are clearer.

Internal means are those which regard the discourse itself considered in itself. In this, *lexicons* give the meanings of individual words; *grammar* indicates the construction and its force; *rhetoric,* the figures of speech. In making out the real sense of a complete discourse, there are sometimes difficulties which cannot be removed by any of these aids. They are overcome most especially by careful attention to the subject under discussion and by previous knowledge, if not of the actual doctrine being given, then at least of the principles on which it rests (and which are assumed rather than laid out in the actual treatise).

After reaching a good understanding of the sense of the piece of writing whose resolution we are attempting, the following preliminaries are usually prefaced to the actual analysis:

i. An indication of the argument, or of the theme, under discussion.

ii. An indication of the author and of the occasion of writing.

iii. Something on the utility, dignity, and agreeableness of the writing itself, but in such a way that we always stay within the bounds of truth.

Analysis may be of a single proposition which has to be resolved into its subject and predicate, or of a whole discourse; whether it treats of a simple or a complex theme, we should observe the same order in taking it apart as the author followed in writing it. If the discourse consists of all or some of the parts which we assigned to the treatment of a theme above, whether simple or complex, we should note them and point them out one by one. If the author has departed from the usual rules of method, such departures should also be pointed out, and emphasized for imitation or avoidance, as they seem to deserve. In a word, the meaning of the treatise should be frankly laid bare, without trickery or deceit, and by distinguishing what is particularly pertinent from the digressions, the sequence of the thoughts and their connection with the proposed aim are to be revealed as clearly as possible.

Corollaries or conclusions deduced from the doctrine as expounded are sometimes annexed to an analysis, but one must be careful that their consequences are quite evident. It would certainly be very unfair to ascribe a conclusion to any author as his own, of which the author himself might question whether it follows from the doctrine he has taught.

১০২ PART IV ১০২

Early Writings: Philosophical Theses

Philosopical Theses were presented to students as a graduation exercise to be defended (in Latin) in the presence of distinguished guests, other professors, and students. In the regenting system, in use at the University of Glasgow until 1727, this exercise took place at the end of the fourth year of study. Carmichael chose to publish the theses he assigned his students in 1699 and 1707. It will be evident that the second set of theses may be read as a sequel to the first set presented here. In both Philosophical Theses (and occasionally elsewhere) the editors have divided sections of the original text into paragraphs.

The full text of Carmichael's
Philosophical Theses,
Which, under the Guidance of Almighty God,
Students of the renowned University of Glasgow,
Scholars and Gentlemen,
Who are Candidates for the Degree of Master,
will submit to Public Examination by Learned Men
On the 3rd. of May

Under the Presidency of Gershom Carmichael

Glasgow

Printed by Robert Sanders, Printer to the King and University,

1699

The majority of men are so careless and unreasonable that they make no distinction between the word of God and that of man when they are joined together; as a result, they fall into error by approving them together, or into impiety by indiscriminately condemning them.

(Nicolas Malebranche, *The Search after Truth,* bk. II, pt. 2, ch. 8)[1]

1. Nicolas Malebranche, *De la recherche de la vérité où l'on traite de la nature de l'esprit de l'homme et de l'usage qu'il en doit faire pour éviter l'erreur dans la science* (1674). Malebranche (1638–1715), following the purpose of the Oratorian order to which he belonged, set out to renew the study of St. Augustine, in the light of Cartesian philosophy. He was influential in Britain in the last years of the seventeenth century, as two contemporary English translations testify: *Father Malebranche's Treatise concerning the Search after Truth,* translated by Thomas Taylor (Oxford, 1694), and *Malebranche's Search after Truth. . . . done out of French from the last edition by Richard Sault,* 2 vols. (London, 1694–95). A more recent translation is now available: Nicolas Malebranche, *The Search after Truth,* translated from the French by Thomas M. Lennon and Paul J. Olscamp (Columbus: Ohio State University Press 1980); all references are to this translation. Carmichael's 1699 *Theses* show the influence of Malebranche at several points; his epigraph is at Lennon and Olscamp, pp. 158–59.

To the high and noble Lord,

[BASIL HAMILTON OF BALDON,]

the most worthy Son
of illustrious and noble Parents,
Leaders of their Country in Peace and War,

DUKE WILLIAM AND
ANNE DUCHESS OF HAMILTON,

As remarkably distinguished by the splendour of their Birth
as by Virtues worthy of that Eminence,
Generous Benefactors of the Muses,
these Philosophical Theses are dedicated and devoted
in Honour of his Patron[2]
and in witness of his devotion and everlasting respect
by

Gershom Carmichael, President,

and
all the Candidates
who have submitted their names for examination for the
degree of Master at this time: to add the names of others,
not on the list, even though they may have completed
their course of studies, is not permitted by the
Rules of our University.

---

2. See above, pp. x–xi, on the involvement of the Hamilton family in Carmichael's appointment at the University of Glasgow.

Philosophical Theses, 1699

On directing the mind to lasting happiness

I. It is universally acknowledged that reason is the highest prerogative of human nature above any other part of the visible world. Accordingly, it has been repeated *ad nauseam* in the schools of philosophy that man is a *rational animal.* Nothing more is meant here by the term *reason* than the power or faculty of thinking (*cogitandi*), i.e., of understanding, willing, and initiating actions with self-awareness (*conscientia*) and self-approval (*complacentia*). But it is clear from the very notion of reason that man should not simply rest in this essential characteristic of his worth, but on the contrary, since every power is intended to be realized in act, he should put all his effort into the single aim of making right use of his rational faculty by aspiring to happiness. One aspires to happiness by aspiring to knowledge and love of the true and the good, however manifested, and such happiness is the proper perfection of thinking things.

Although the human mind has been miserably vitiated by original sin and thus rendered incapable by itself of making right use of its faculties so that only supernatural grace can effectively redeem this fall, yet there are certain natural means which in conjunction with the rational nature of the mind can give considerable help toward uncovering a good many truths both speculative and practical. Of these means some are in our power, others not. But the vulgar so confound these two kinds that they seem to attribute much more to the former and much less to the latter than they should. The aids to the right use of reason which are beyond our power are either internal, for example, intelligence, retentiveness of memory, etc., or external, such as a liberal education, the company of good and learned men, books, experience, and the like.

Internal factors have less importance in either intellectual or moral activity than is commonly thought, whether they are taken to be based on some natural difference between souls or (as is far more probable) on the actual arrangement of the brain and of the organs subordinate to it (which the goodness of God has made more naturally able in some men than in others). This is partly because those who consider themselves superior in the endowments of nature too often do too little work, but mostly because a natural ineptitude to carry out one function of reason is usually compensated by a greater aptitude for another, and vice versa. Consequently one may say with confidence that only a very small proportion of the errors into which men fall have their origin in any natural dullness or defect of intelligence.

As for external aids to cultivating reason, help from other people may be very useful in suggesting appropriate ideas and guiding the mind by an appropriate method; and many subjects that deserve to be investigated can only be known by external and elaborate experiments. Yet one must agree that the knowledge of what each man must know to secure his own safety and carry out the duties of social life is not dependent on the authority of precepts or books (with the exception of the divine pronouncements) or on difficult and elaborate experiments. On the contrary such knowledge (insofar as it is natural) is derivable by each man from the observation of himself and of the things he sees all round him and by the accurate comparison with each other of the ideas he gathers from his environment.

II. Thus the natural assistance which is most valuable for making a right use of reason, and whose lack is the source of most errors, is within our own power. It is clear that it consists in just one thing: in weighing all our thoughts with unfailing attention, and at the same time in striving to direct our minds along the most suitable and direct road to the knowledge of truth.

III. The attention required for successfully discerning truth and thus for duly controlling our inclinations and passions (so far as they depend on the knowledge of practical truths) has to be exercised both in the formation of ideas and in their comparison with each other. There is certainly a need for attention in forming ideas. Admittedly we cannot be deceived in the bare perception, whether simple or complex, of an object viewed in itself. But in abstracting ideas, in combining them together and in storing them in the mind stamped with definite names (all of which pertains to their formation in the wider sense), we often go wrong in various ways which commonly obscure our path in the pursuit of truth. First then we must be careful that each and every idea which is to be compared in our judgments and reasoning is as clear as it can be made, i.e., that it is quite vivid to the mind; this is the best way to ensure that it is distinct, i.e., that it is not confused with any other idea. This is not because the mind which is properly aware of all its thoughts ever takes one idea for two or two for one in inspecting its own ideas. It is because in thinking as well as in speaking men often lose track of their ideas, particularly if they are quite complex and have little natural affinity with the images depicted in the brain, and substitute words or other image-signs which because they have no natural connection with the ideas to which they are attached, may easily, without the closest attention, badly confuse the ideas which they are employed to distinguish. Sometimes a word is used now for one idea, now for another, without any awareness of a difference between them; sometimes two words which are supposed to express different ideas, are used for the same idea because of tiredness. Hence it is clear that we cannot really be too careful to ensure that every word we use in silent thought or talk or writing have a fixed and definite meaning for us.

IV. This is more difficult to achieve than is commonly thought, as will be shown by considering separately the various classes of ideas which may enter our thoughts. Singular ideas are less liable to this confusion; for proper names have a closer connection with the objective or material thing signified than with any idea by which it may be represented; and their signification is grasped with sufficient precision, if the singular object to which they refer is understood, whatever the singular idea by which it is distinguished from others. But we do not need to take much notice here of singular ideas, since almost all the terms of the different branches of knowledge are universal.

Of universal ideas some are simple, others complex. And the former too are not simply one class, for some can quite easily be accurately attached to their own names, others with considerable difficulty. But however precisely all names intended to express complex ideas are supposed to be understood, yet there may still remain a serious difficulty about the names of

complex ideas, whether they are ideas of modes or of substances. In the
case of modes, the reason is the frequently large number of simple ideas,
variously arranged, which have no definite corresponding exemplar in nature. In the case of substances the reason is ignorance of the innermost
essences of the substances to which they are related and the different accounts given by different individuals of the properties which are substituted for them.

V. To deal with this confusion of ideas, and to give to words that denote
complex ideas a definite and fixed meaning for ourselves and our interloc-
utors, the most useful tool is *definition*. Definition is an utterance by
which the simpler ideas involved in expressing a complex idea by some
given name are unfolded in an individual and orderly fashion by means of
several words.[3] And since in this and no other sense definition, as it is commonly used, is rightly said to explain the *essence* of a thing, it follows that
philosophers are wrong to allege some *real* definition beyond the nominal
definition. Indeed in defining modes, it is not self-evident that any real
essence distinct from the nominal is in view at all. And we cannot penetrate the absolute essences of substances nor enumerate all, or even perhaps
the most noticeable, relative properties which proceed from them; consequently we cannot rightly be said to deliver the real definitions of them.

It is indeed true that in these ideas of substances which we fashion for
ourselves, we normally assemble the most noticeable of the properties
which fall under our observation. But apart from the fact that this method
of making a definition does not come up to the magnificent promises of
the philosophers who offer real definitions, this approach is inappropriate
except in the case of substances which are designated by reference to a singular exemplar. For if the definition (as is usually the case) is attached to a
specific name, either the idea to be explicated by definition is understood
to this extent to underlie the name, in which case it is superfluous to offer
a definition, or the meaning of the proposed name is uncertain and vague,
in which case it will not be possible to get a fixed and definite sense out of
the utterance which purports to give the real definition of the objects signified by that name. For the common method of distinguishing different

3. See Locke, *Essay*, III.III.17.

kinds of substances is by reference to some individual objects of each kind which someone has at some time seen or come to know individually in one way or another. And while this method is valuable for everyday use, it is by no means accurate enough to satisfy the rigorous requirements of philosophy, since it only goes as far as giving standard names to a few of the most obvious properties. Hence arises the need to employ definition to explicate the names of substances no less than of modes, although we will not deny that, to designate some of their more sensible qualities, it is useful to point to the things themselves or to pictures of them.

VI. We have restricted the use of *definition* to names signifying complex ideas, for it is quite clear from the very notion of it that simple ideas cannot be explicated by definitions, since they do not admit of resolution into a number of ideas. Hence the names by which such ideas are to be expressed should be explicated by indicating the subject to which they belong, in conjunction with certain other circumstances. Those who seek definitions here find a continually increasing obscurity rather than clarity. An excellent example of this (to pass over many others which occur often in philosophical texts) is furnished by the simplest and most general of all the ideas which our mind can form, namely the idea of *being* or of *existing* or of *something* (for we do not doubt that one and the same idea is expressed by these three terms). The metaphysicians make absurd efforts to define this idea, and in so doing destroy the universal significance clearly distinguished by these general words.

VII. Not only do we habitually attach ideas which we abstract or combine in our minds to certain names, we also assume that they more or less conform with the ideas which others have attached to the same names, and often also with actual objects existing in nature (which is particularly appropriate with ideas of substances). Hence we must be careful here to ensure that they do conform, as we assume they do, on both counts. For if they are deficient on the first count, we will not be able to understand others or be understood by them; if on the latter, the science which is meant to investigate the properties of things existing in nature will just be chasing chimaeras.

VIII. But it is not enough to have attached clear and distinct ideas, conforming to the nature of things, to definite names in accordance with common usage. For our minds would achieve no sense of completion from this unless they also made judgments, i.e., unless they gave opinions on ideas in comparison to each other, with regard to the identity or nonidentity of the objects represented by them. Any other relationship that some persist in seeking among the given terms of any question may be reduced to this one relationship among the proposed ideas. In investigating this relation we must pay the most careful attention, so that it will not impose falsehood upon us in the guise of truth. The opinion which we give of the identity of the objects represented by two ideas has regard either to the identity which they are assumed to have, or not to have, on the basis of a real difference of time, past, present, or future; or to the identity which they would have, or would not have, on the basis of a possible time in which they might exist; the former may be called *absolute,* the latter *hypothetical,* judgments. And hence we infer (since every idea, which can be predicated of another idea, involves the idea of a *being* or of an *existing* thing) that nothing can be truly affirmed of things impossible; and nothing can be absolutely affirmed of things purely possible. If this had been properly noticed, the usual course of metaphysics could have been shortened by half (by cutting out the part which is occupied with what are called *nonentities*).

IX. In the case of both kinds of judgment, some are *immediate,* others *mediate.* In direct judgments the relation between the two proposed ideas becomes known by comparing the one with the other without the interposition of a third idea. In mediate judgments the relation of the two extreme ideas is inferred from the relation which connects both of them with a third idea. It is an agreement if both concur with the third in clearly designating in both cases at least one object which is the same; and a disagreement, if under the same condition one concurs with the third but the other does not. But it is not required that both extreme ideas be directly compared with the same middle term; it is enough if one of the extremes is directly compared with a middle term, and this is compared with another, and so on, until one arrives at the other extreme idea, provided that each of the middle terms, as it is repeated, clearly designates on both occasions at least one object which is the same, and provided that there is not more than one negative conjunction; if there is, the conjunction of the extremes will also be negative.

Hence we may infer in passing that in every piece of reasoning, the number of principles, that is, of propositions that are assumed to be known of themselves, exceeds the number of middle terms by one. Hence the attempt to deduce all knowable truths from one or the other principle will never succeed. Furthermore the common rules of syllogisms may easily be demonstrated from our account. But as virtually no intelligent person (except those who have learned the common rules but have never penetrated to their foundations and cling to the husks of the words) would allow himself to be deceived by a viciously formulated argument, we have to admit that the majority by far of the errors into which we fall every day have their origin in false principles which we accept as true, because we are carried away by the heat of the passions or other people's authority or some other foolishness.

X. Propositions which are to be considered as principles become known in different ways depending on whether they are absolute or hypothetical. In order that the absolute existence of any thing may become known to us without proof, it must be intimately present to our mind and give a sense of itself; this is the way the mind observes its own existence and that of its thoughts. But the hypothetical connection or conflict of abstract ideas, i.e., the identity or nonidentity of objects which would be represented by them if they existed, becomes known from the mere comparison of such ideas despite the absence of the things themselves. On premises of the former kind depend all absolute propositions, which we also come to know by the use of reasoning. This includes propositions which are concerned with the existence of singular objects, and many also concerning the co-existence of properties which enter into specific ideas of substances and which are for the most part either singular or particular. But all propositions which are purely conditional, being concerned with the relation of abstract ideas, are free of that dependence. Countless universal propositions about the relations of modes in mathematics and the moral disciplines are like this; since they are free of all regard to this or that time and to the contingent existence in time of a created thing, and could not be distinctly conceived to be otherwise, they are rightly said to be in the most rigorous sense *necessary*. Hence one may incidentally infer the logicians' fourth predicable in the modes; and that the fifth is particularly appropriate in the case of substances. And in these too, especially in the more general types of them, a necessary connection or conflict of attributes may sometimes be quite clearly detected by the abstract use of reason. The first three predicables, however, are either trivially predicated or yield only explications of words.

XI. In all these judgments, whether absolute or hypothetical, whether direct or indirect, due attention requires us to avoid all rashness and precipitancy and not to accept anything as certain and indubitable in which the splendor of truth does not flash out and compel the mind intent on tracking it down to give its full assent, even in spite of its own reluctance. So far as we observe this rule, so far and no further shall we assure ourselves of immunity from error. It is no objection that many people, in clinging obstinately to errors, display complete certainty and firm mental acquiescence in their opinions as true, whether by words or by anything else that one can offer as a sign of a true and certain judgment. For all that we may legitimately infer from this is that the criterion by which truth so manifests itself to our minds as to exclude all suspicion of falsity does not lie in the external profession or forms of speech which vain and dogmatic men may use, but is to be sought in the quiet recesses of the mind itself and in the innermost depths of our thought. Here everyone who refuses to cast himself headlong into hopeless skepticism must admit that some criterion of this kind is present when we assent to certain truths (or rather to any matters of which we can say that we are certainly convinced), and this cannot coexist with false assent.

XII. To achieve the requisite attention in the formation and comparison of ideas, we must partly remove obstacles and partly use them to help us. First, there are vivid sensations and images which engage both body and mind together and are apt to divert the mind's gaze and draw its attention away from the purely intelligible. We must therefore avoid objects which strike the mind with such overly vivid sensations or images. But in our present state of union the human mind cannot avoid being strongly affected by things which affect the body, hence it should use those modes of perception in such a way that they conduce to a more distinct understanding of things. This will happen if we connect a specific sensible or imageable sign with each intellectual idea,[4] and constantly preserve the connection; this is especially true of any sign that has a natural affinity with the intellectual idea itself. This has been the remarkable privilege of geometry, both to ensure that the truths which it demonstrates by itself were easily perceived and to throw a brilliant light on the sciences which it is employed to illustrate. But if we cannot find such suitably simple natural signs, we may profitably make use of other arbitrary signs which not only get attention, particularly if they are very simple, but also may be substituted for more complex ideas and lessen the difficulty that the mind has with these and augment its capacity. The more violent emotions also put another obstacle in the way of attentive contemplation of abstract things; these too we must silence if we wish to make successful progress in this area. Here too we must make a virtue of necessity, and fight the harmful passions with more useful ones, such as the desire to know the truth, the desire to successfully perform the duties which depend on knowledge of truth, etc.

XIII. It may be further established from what has been said, that the genuine method of discovering truth turns on these two cardinal points. *First,* we must collect for ourselves ideas of the things we intend to reason about that are clear, distinct, and conforming to their originals. *Second,* in connecting a series of several truths with each other, we start from those that are simpler and easier (i.e., those which are known by themselves and those which are close to being so, or even those which, other things being equal, have simpler terms), and not only grasp their unshakeable truth but also spend some time on them before we take the step toward more composite and difficult truths (those which need a longer chain of arguments or are composed of more complex terms). However, it is not the more general truths which we should immediately regard as simpler. For just as it is far from being the case that the most general ideas are the first to take their places in our minds, so their relation is not always especially obvious to the intellect. It is true that in teaching certain abstract disciplines, espe-

---

4. For intellectual ideas, see Malebranche, *Search after Truth,* bk. III, pt. 2.

cially mathematics, it proves useful to begin with some rather general axioms which dispose the mind to give assent to more particular truths, because they are few in number and contain within themselves many other
propositions which have been rendered familiar by use. Yet these very sciences (which are taught in this manner today) could not have been discovered by that method. And there are certain other disciplines (such as pneumatology and physics) which cannot be rightly taught by the same
method. Since they investigate the actual existence of things and the properties which experience alone teaches belong to them, they require us to
proceed from the singular and less universal to the more universal.

XIV. Among all the absolute truths, none becomes known to the mind
earlier or more easily than the existence of oneself and one's thoughts; and
therefore the famous phrase of the celebrated Descartes, *I thinking exist,*[5]
does nothing to demonstrate abstract truths and should certainly not be
laid down as their absolutely first principle; yet it may without absurdity
be assigned the first place (first in the order of our knowledge, that is) in
the class of propositions which are concerned with the actual existence of
things. This at least is clear, that no physical object's existence is knowable
by us with such ease and certainty. For whether a physical thing which
sensation leads me to believe exists, actually does exist or not, yet I cannot
have doubts about the fact that there is such a sensation in me. For this
purpose it does not matter whether the *thinking thing* which is in me (or
rather which I myself am) is distinct from all matter (as we shall demonstrate below) or whether it is merely modified matter. For likewise the
truth of our assertion is sound that the existence of our mind as *a thinking
substance* becomes known to us earlier, more easily, and more certainly
than the existence of any physical thing.

XV. However the absolute essence of our mind does not become manifest to us in the same manner as its existence does. For in forming a positive idea of itself, it can scarcely itself ascend higher, since it knows about
itself by primary intuition and apprehends by inner awareness that it is
itself a *thinking thing,* i.e., a thing which perceives, affirms, denies, wills,
refuses, etc. And since these individual modes of thinking are only acci-

5. *Ego cogitans existo* (Descartes, *Meditations,* II).

dental perfections of the mind, one succeeding the other in a continual stream, it is clear that they must in no way be confused with the essence of the mind, even though we conceive of it somehow or other in relation to them. Of general and permanent thought (in which certain celebrated authors locate the essence of mind)[6] the mind itself has neither awareness nor idea; especially since that kind of thought is defined by its patrons as *an awareness of all that goes on in the mind.* For awareness is either concerned with the particular thoughts of which there is awareness or presupposes particular thoughts; certainly it cannot be taken as a *subject* of thought. Thus the mind knows itself only in relation to its modes, and they are such that the mind itself only imperfectly conceives what relation they bear to their own subject. We should therefore abandon the vain hope of tracking down the absolute essence of mind and be content that the mind should look within where the way is open and reflect on the various modes of thinking in which it engages and their order and dependence; especially since each act of thought which it performs, though it does not lead to an absolute grasp of its being (*entitas*) as it is in itself, yet discloses an essential aspect of it, namely, its ability to perform such an act.

XVI. Here *sensation* first offers itself to our consideration. Sensation is a perception in the mind excited by the occasion[7] of something physical being present and moving the organs of our body. And we are so intimately aware within ourselves that sensation resides in the same mind as the rest of our thoughts, that it seems extraordinary that there have been philosophers who taught that the sentient mind of man is different from the rational mind; nor on the other hand do the other philosophers seem to make sense who refuse to classify sensations as thoughts (notwithstanding the manifest self-awareness which they have in themselves). Nevertheless sensations do not represent any objects (properly so called), nor is there anything like them among external objects nor anything which bears a greater resemblance to them than motion or figure to thought or the body itself to mind. Hence the only account which can be given of the connection between our sensations and the properties of the bodies which

6. Descartes, Malebranche, and Arnauld and Nicole.
7. This term alludes to the Malebranchian doctrine of occasionalism.

arouse them is the will of the creator, who has so closely united substances of such different natures and established such a correspondence between the modifications of both, that the sensations aroused in the mind in the presence of physical things serve to tell it what it should pursue or avoid for the preservation of animal life. We do not however deny that the senses are useful for the investigation of truth, provided that we derive this conception not from the sensation itself but from the intellectual idea which naturally takes it up, and provided that we attend carefully to the various cases in which that idea normally designates, faithfully or otherwise, the condition of an object.

XVII. We experience perceptions similar to those described in the last thesis not only when an external object exists to arouse them but also in the absence of objects, except that these (which are commonly called *imaginations*) are noticeably less vigorous than the former and usually depend more on the determination of our will. When we dream we take them for sensations; for then we lack the sensations themselves, and there are no witnesses to correct the error of the imagination, nor do we have access to the greater clarity which would show up the obscurity of the imagination by comparison. In both these respects the cases of the dreamer and of the man caught in persistent error are neatly parallel to each other; nor is there a sharper distinction between the former and the waking man than between the latter and one who truly knows. But the primary use of the imagination is not only to retain what we have learned by sense, but also to implant other ideas more deeply in the memory and to save them from confusion; this has been shown in thesis 12.

XVIII. Besides the perceptions so far mentioned (which we usually claim to share with the animals) our mind has other perceptions of a completely different kind (which are usually called pure intellections). No one can be ignorant of these who is not too much a stranger in his own home; for only intellectual ideas make contact even lightly with thinking things. Only intellectual ideas are so general that they can stretch to include objects which present themselves to the senses in different guises; on the other hand they alone are so accurate that they distinguish between objects which are offered to the senses in the same guise (for example, a circle and an ellipse, one of whose diameters is imperceptibly longer than the other's). Finally only intellectual ideas represent objects other than themselves or can be predicated of them; for when the names given for the purpose of distinguishing our sensations are applied to external objects, they import no more than an aptitude for exciting such sensations in us, and since the notion of this aptitude is relative, it is certainly represented not by the sensation itself but only by a pure intellection.

XIX. It is abundantly clear therefore that there are pure intellections in our minds. But the question of their nature and even more of their origin, has always been considered a difficult one, and rightly so. For although we seem to be intimately aware that they are directly produced by the mind itself and do not, when viewed *materially* (as they say), contain anything in themselves which should be reckoned beyond its powers, nevertheless the further question remains as to where our minds learned that variety of forms by which they can adapt their notions to represent the almost infinite variety of external things so exactly. Experience hardly allows us to believe that the earliest exemplars of all our intellectual notions were co-created with the mind from its very origin (as one part of the learned world contends). For experience teaches us that our minds form singular notions earlier and more easily than universal notions and, even more, abstract notions (though these, if any, ought to be immediately aroused by exemplars innate to the mind). Experience also teaches that each person's mind is stocked with more notions and more perfect notions, the more they are provided by familiarity with things and by a richer supply of objects, and the more apt the structure of his organs is for perceiving them.

We can at least infer from this that the furniture of knowledge which is actually found today in the human mind suggests an origin quite other than that which these authors propose. In forming a conjecture on this question, no one seems to us to come nearer the truth than those who take the view that the exemplars of all our original notions owe their origin to the actual presence of the objects represented through them. I say *original* because there is no doubt that from the singular notion which the mind has itself formed by the occasion of a present object and which includes several obvious features of it, the mind can abstract various simpler notions which are contained in it, and in turn combine these abstract notions in a new order among themselves; but in such a way that the mind owes the material of all its natural notions (for we are not speaking of those which are suggested supernaturally) to the actual presence of objects.

Since therefore physical objects, though present, do not come to our notice except by the mediation of sensations, we safely conclude that notions of corporeal things take their origin from sensation; there are however particular reasons for hesitation about the means by which our minds are equipped to form notions of spiritual things. But if we observe ourselves, if we carefully consider the objects which are most familiar to us, by whose means the rest become more or less amenable to conceptualization, they will all be seen to urge the mind to advance from contemplation of itself to form notions of the supreme deity and of other spirits. The mind will also be seen to be aroused to reflect on itself precisely so far as it is directed to some particular thought by another object (i.e., an external object). In thinking this thought it finds itself in action, and in reflecting on it it acquires, by a supervening act, a more explicit knowledge of itself and of its powers. At any rate we will not find a trace of any other origin or process in all the notions which our minds naturally perform. And so we do not doubt that the primary furniture of all our natural knowledge may be deduced, in all likelihood, from *sensation* and *reflection*.[8]

XX. Now since we are not able with any appearance of truth to claim for ourselves or concede to external objects (even though it is attributed to them in common usage) a truly active power of producing those first exemplars of our notions, it must be fully admitted that they are produced in the mind by God at the presence of objects. Since in this and many other respects God alone is rightly said to illuminate us and to be the cause of all our knowledge, there is no reason at all why, with the celebrated Malebranche, we should have recourse to what he calls intelligible entities (unintelligible though they may be) which exist in God as the immediate objects of all our notions.[9] For if we contemplated all other things in God, God would necessarily be the most familiar object of our perception, and we would not be able to conceive any other objects whatever except by

8. See Locke, *Essay*, II.VII.10.

9. Carmichael follows Arnauld in rejecting Malebranche's view that what we actually perceive in our intellectual ideas are the archetypal ideas in the mind of God (Arnauld, *Des vraies et des fausses Idées*).

analogy with him; which flatly contradicts experience. Nor is anything to be gained by the observation of that celebrated thinker about the general idea of *being* circulating continuously in our minds; for this idea is aroused by any object whatsoever, and has no more in common with the idea of God (unless the notions of *infinity* and *independence* are also added, which are not at all ordinary notions) than with the idea of a creature.

XXI. But our minds can not only form, abstract, and combine notions or ideas (for we use these terms interchangeably)* but can also compare them with each other (as we have suggested in the eighth thesis) so as to yield an opinion whether and to what extent they are representative of the same object. On this topic there is just one point to be added at this time, namely that certain celebrated authors do not seem to us to explain its nature with sufficient accuracy by locating the judgment, partly in the perception, which they credit to the intellect, of a relation occurring between two ideas, and partly in the assent or acquiescence of the will. They do this despite the fact that to anyone who pays attention, it is quite obvious that the act of affirming or denying, in which lies truth or falsehood, differs totally both from perception and from volition. In fact it is so far from having affinity with either of these acts that the dispute between the Aristotelians and the Cartesians, as to whether judgment is an act of the intellect or of the will, is beside the point, since judgment cannot be reduced to either of them without one of the two terms being rendered equivocal.[10]

XXII. Now among all the thoughts that we have of every kind, some please us by flooding the mind with pleasure or delight, others are unpleasing, irksome, and painful. The mind naturally loves pleasing thoughts, and any things which tend to bring them to us or shut out unpleasing thoughts (to which we tend to give the general name of *goods* for ourselves); it pursues them and desires to have them present. But it hates,

---

*Carmichael's note: The term *idea* is sometimes used in philosophers for the notion itself or act of apprehending (which is the sense in which it is taken by us here and elsewhere), and sometimes for the exemplary form of the same remaining in the mind (even when it is not actually attending to it). To avoid this equivocation, we have thought it best to abstain from the term *idea* in the two previous theses where we were treating of their origins).

10. See above, pp. 31–32.

avoids, and longs to be free of unpleasing thoughts, and any thing which tends to bring them on or drive out pleasing thoughts (and such things are commonly called *evils*). The former act has usually been called *volition*, the latter *nolition;* either act in scholastic language is an *act of will.* And since the mind perpetually aspires not to this or that particular good, but to supreme happiness, i.e., the most exquisite pleasure and the most absolute freedom from pain, it cannot fail to pursue by its will every particular object which, considered in conjunction with all its circumstances, it believes will contribute in some way toward attaining that most desirable state. Hence the celebrated Locke seems on this topic to have parted unnecessarily from the common opinion of philosophers which was at one time his own, when he contends that the will is not always determined by a judgment passed on the goodness of the object but by desire for it as requisite to man's happiness.[11] For these coincide, since we always desire as pertaining to our happiness what we judge to be best, after we have taken into account not only the value of the object itself but also the toil and danger we must undergo to get it. We freely admit however that in conducting this examination, the mind is often led badly astray, as what is present to the mind has more influence with it than what is absent, and what we sense by immediate perception has more influence than what comes to us only in the form of abstract ideas, and indeed the tendency to avoid pain has greater influence than the desire to enjoy positive pleasure: these are the sources of most of the most dangerous errors in human life.

XXIII. Whenever the good or evil things which seem to make for the conservation or injury of the natural composite of mind and body are considered in the light of their presence or absence, they tend to arouse powerful determinations of the will accompanied by noticeable bodily agitation, and these are commonly called *passions*. The number of the passions is differently given by different thinkers. To us the most accurate computation seems to be that of the learned Malebranche, who allows only three primary passions: desire, happiness, and sadness.[12]

XXIV. We also experience that the will to produce certain bodily move-

---

11. Locke, *Essay,* II.XXI.35 ff.
12. *Search after Truth,* V.VII, p. 375.

ments initiates the execution of these movements, whether our minds truly produce them by some activity of their own whose mode of operation it cannot detect, or (as seems equally probable) the first cause truly produces these motions in accordance with the conditions of union which it has itself ordained, taking its occasion from our will. So far as man has it in his power for these movements to be begun, continued, and suspended according to the determination of his will, he is declared *free* in respect to them. It is also true that many of our thoughts often depend on the determination of the will in the same way, but in their case the dependence is not so constant nor equally noticeable for another reason, namely that all the internal actions of our minds involve both implicit self-awareness and self-approval, and for this reason all thought may be said to be in some sense free, i.e., it has to be voluntarily initiated by us. Since only actions which are free in this way are essentially free, and consequently (as necessarily flows from created liberty) subject to the rule of morals, it follows that these alone are the measures of both the liberty and the morality which are to be attributed to external acts. Those who have insinuated into the doctrine of *liberty* the notion of *indifference,* which has nothing to do with it (and which, strictly understood, cannot occur in an agent), have introduced great obscurity into a subject which is in itself easy enough.

XXV. There is nothing which the mind observes more frequently in itself than the remembrance of past thoughts and its ability later to reproduce similar or related thoughts in various circumstances. This experience hardly allows us to doubt that definite traces remain in the mind of individual thoughts, but their nature is most obscure. All the same if we look at the simple nature of the mind and meanwhile reflect on the variety which it continually undergoes in the way of habits and acts, perhaps we shall not be able to explain it without admitting entities in the mind which are fairly distinct from it however dependent they may be on its substance. We submit therefore to deeper examination by learned men the question whether the real accidents of the Aristotelians, as explained by Reformed writers, must necessarily be retained in the intellectual world though eliminated from the material world.[13]

13. De Vries, *De Natura Dei,* pp. 146 ff.

XXVI. From our previous explanation of the functions of the human mind, it is abundantly made out that mind is a different substance from matter, seeing that it acts by itself and in an indivisible mode. For every mode of a composite thing (such as every material object) is composite with regard to its subject, and thus divisible; so that one part of it belongs to one part of the subject and another to another. But this cannot be claimed about thought with respect to the mind. For in that case every mind would contain in itself innumerable others, each one equipped with its own portion of thought. On the contrary, since the principle of thought which is in us is intimately aware that it and its thought are a unity so that it conceives that if any part of it is removed, nothing at all survives. For the sake of brevity we pass over the other reasons which the most learned authors give to confirm the same truth, though they are quite forceful (at least in the opinion of those who derive all the differences among bodies from mechanical properties). We merely point out that the argument we have given quite overthrows that absurd figment of Master Henry More's, in which he claimed that extension is a universal attribute of being and that it belongs to spirits though in its penetrable form.[14] For extension, whether impenetrable or penetrable (if we can accept this notion), necessarily involves a multitude of parts, which we have proved does not belong at all to that which is cogitative.

XXVII. It necessarily flows from the simplicity of mind just demonstrated, that it could not be produced from a preexisting seed whether physical or spiritual, and cannot be resolved into the same, and so is by its nature ingenerable and incorruptible. Granted this, the celebrated Poiret's conjecture will not seem at all likely that every single mind (also every single particle of matter) is endowed with a certain essential fertility by which it can produce others like it. For there is not the slightest evidence in nature for attributing an influence of this kind to any created cause (i.e., an influence by which a completely new substance begins to exist).[15]

14. More, *Enchiridion Metaphysicum,* pp. 73 ff.
15. Poiret, *Cogitationes rationales,* pp. 146 n., 148 n. His theory of the fertility and productivity of things was elaborated at greater length in *The Divine Oeconomy: An*

XXVIII. But whether the cogitative principle which is found in us is said to be empty of all matter, as we have just proved, or whether it is composed of material parts, as the atheists would like, it is in either case certain, from the multiple defects which it daily experiences in itself, that it could not exist by itself. For just as the perfection of any effect depends upon either the power or the will of the producing cause, so the perfection of an independent thing can only be what is best for itself, i.e., a supreme and infinite perfection. Since our mind therefore is aware in itself of multiple ignorance, weakness, and other imperfections, it must necessarily derive its existence not from itself but from another superior cause, and one which is cogitative and immaterial. This last point admits of no doubt on the supposition that our mind is immaterial; and it must also be conceded by supporters of the opposite view. In fact, the less perfection we claim for the elements of our nature, the more excellent we are forced to infer is the architect who has constructed so excellent a fabric from such poor material. Since matter is the poorest of all things and has perfection of the lowest order, it is far removed from the highest eminence of perfection involved in independent and necessary existence, and hence presupposes a superior cause. But besides this, given matter's existence, it still cannot be put into motion, of which it does not have the principle within itself, without the influence of an external and superior cause, since by its nature it is indifferent with regard to motion or rest; and in any case thought does not belong essentially to matter whether at rest or in motion. Matter therefore requires a further influence of a superior principle, and of a principle which is essentially cogitative, in order that it may be raised to so great a perfection which is not essentially due to itself.

But the atheists say (though nothing is more absurd) that there are certain combinations of matter, which, whenever they occur, necessarily bring thought with them. Since the combination of movements required for such a singular effect is (as they themselves admit) so delicate that

---

Universal System of the works and purposes of God towards men, demonstrated, I, 7 (London, 1713). Robert Wodrow described Poiret's theology as "a neu and connected systeme of Quietisme, Molinisme, [and] Quakerisme, and the refined mysticall Divinity of the Papists, leading quite off the Protestant doctrine, and the truth as it's in Jesus" (*Analecta,* III, p. 473).

barely one or two of an infinite number of equally possible combinations is adequate for this effect, it will certainly seem strange that, despite this, the combination happens so frequently, is so constantly and regularly maintained, and rises to such noble effects. Certainly if thinking agents produce such things as this, which it would be absurd to claim were fabricated fortuitously and without design, how much less should we suppose that the very power of deliberation from which such wonderful effects flow arises from a fortuitous concourse of atoms without the design of a superior cause? Whatever therefore we suppose the mind to be in its inmost constitution, it does presuppose some intelligent cause, one which is far more perfect than itself. More than this it must be a cause which, essentially and indeed independently, involves thought and all the other perfections which are essentially found (to whatever extent) in our minds. It is quite obvious that every total cause which is superior in a direct line to any effect has to contain all its simple perfections, and that a first cause of this kind possesses them all essentially, independently, and without defect.

That there is a first cause for any effect, and that an infinite series of subordinate causes cannot be admitted, is clear from the fact that the influence by virtue of which any given effect exists has necessarily to be transmitted through all superior causes in a straight line, though no influence can be transmitted through an infinite series of causes since infinity cannot be traversed. The force of this argument will appear more clearly if we reflect that the series of which we are speaking here must be understood not as a series of successive causes, but as a series of causes which have influence at one and the same time, since every effect (i.e., a thing not sufficient to itself for existence) must depend, so long as it exists, on some cause which necessarily influences it now.

Moreover, the necessity of recognizing some first and independent cause also becomes obvious from the fact that a cause may be sought not only for every dependent thing taken individually, but also for the whole collection of them. Grant this, and you also grant what we seek, an *independent cause,* since it is exempt from the whole sum of dependent things; but if it is not granted, then the whole sum of dependent things is independent, than which nothing is more absurd.

XXIX. Our mind therefore gives evidence of a supreme cause of itself, which contains within itself, essentially and without defect and independently, all pure perfections, not only those which we dimly see in our own minds but (because of the connection between independence and supreme perfection which we noted above) all other possible perfections whatsoever, absolutely free of every imperfection; this is *the great and good God himself.* From the notion of God so established, one may infer by easy reasoning various attributes of Deity, both individually and in relation to the primary idea of him. We will mention only a few of them. It manifestly follows that *God is one,* since he contains every absolute perfection in himself and that he is *most simple,* so that he is not composed of several things, and cannot be composed with several things. It also follows that he is *immutable,* since he does not have parts or components by means of which he could change, for either of these would indicate dependence; and that he is *eternal* and *immense,* i.e., that he exists always and everywhere, without either succession or extension on his part; and that he is also *incomprehensible* to every intellect except his own. It likewise follows that we should attribute to God the common perfections of mind with a certain special eminence and prerogative; this means that he is *cogitative* not successively and variably like us, but by one utterly simple act which is identical with his essence. Still more particularly, he does not *apprehend* a limited number of things, he apprehends all things, and not by abstract and inadequate ideas but by intuitive and perfect ideas which are not drawn from outside but contained in the plenitude of his own nature. It also follows that he makes judgments but never strays from truth, never wavers, and is never ignorant of anything; hence he needs no discursive thought nor depends on drawing knowledge from outside, and never changes his mind; but at one and the same time he has all truths of all kinds before him in their archetypes, truths which are hypothetical in his power but absolute in his will. Hence it also follows that God *wills,* not rashly or inconstantly like us, not with a hesitant or ineffective willing nor determined by external things, but by his most wise, most absolute, most free, and most efficacious will, he disposes all things as is most congruous with supreme reason and most fit to illustrate his infinite glory. It also follows that God is *powerful,* i.e., his will is efficacious in disposing external things as he wishes; nor does his efficacy merely extend (as ours does) to a few things put in his power by the influence of another cause, or which could be obstructed by another cause; rather it extends to absolutely all possible effects, independently and irresistibly. And in his full awareness and approval of his own perfection, without the intervention of any external possession at all, he is supremely and necessarily happy. Finally from these foundations it is safely inferred that God is *the first and universal cause of all things that exist in nature,* whether spiritual or corporeal, not only of permanent substances but also of their successive alterations and modifications. For all other things result from his eternal and efficacious will, each with its own times and other circumstances defined by that will.

From what has been said it is clear that in many cases when the attributes of created spirits are analytically distinguished from the imperfections which adhere to them in their combined condition, so that they can be rightly attributed both to the father of spirits and to the spirits created by him, these attributes are still so proper to spirits that they distinguish spirits from bodies, though, on the other side, the properties of bodies cannot be mentally separated from the imperfections which they include, without being converted into the universal attributes of all *beings.* So there is an easy reason why the great and good God, though he contains in himself the simple perfections of all things, is yet rightly said to be *spirit,* not *body;* for spirit is distinguished from body by its (mentally or analytically) pure perfections, but body is not distinguished from spirit in this way. Hence the reason which Jean Le Clerc gives as the chief reason why God is called *spirit* rather than *body,* namely that a name is usually derived from the nobler part, is too feeble and indicative of a quite absurd error.[16]

XXX. The primary aim of all our thinking about God (as of all other things) should be to acknowledge in a spirit of veneration that the creator of the universe, its preserver and ruler, the good, the almighty, is our supreme Lord, and Lord of all things, who directs his works, of every kind, by his own right; and to offer to him as our Lord every kind of worship and obedience in the whole course of our lives. And although it has become more than obvious from what has been said that we have a great obligation to do this, yet we can find another persuasive argument by

16. Le Clerc, "Pneumatologia," in *Ontologia,* III.III, pp. 152–53.

looking more deeply into the condition of our own minds in comparison with the truths which we have deduced by easy reasoning from introspecting them. For our minds yearn with unbounded and unceasing desire for the highest happiness which we can achieve; so constant is this direction of our minds that we need no other obligation to do or not do anything than the understanding that our happiness in any degree depends on its performance or omission. This is the hinge on which all human deliberation turns. Hence it will complete our task if we show that man cannot better serve his happiness than by worshipping God and conducting himself well toward him. This is not difficult to demonstrate. For since it is certain that the one God, good, almighty, Lord of mankind and of all things, can make us happy or miserable at his discretion, it is obvious that the sum of all the prayers that we make to obtain happiness should be reduced to this, *that God may will that we be happy.* Consequently any ordering of our actions that has even the remotest connection with the benevolence of the supreme deity toward us should be pursued with every effort at every moment of our lives. It is true that we cannot define by the light of nature the extent to which our happiness can be promoted or our misery averted by any action we may take. Nevertheless it is obvious that the good God almighty, who has arranged all things in the manner most fit to illustrate his glory, and who has adorned man with the most ample abilities to know and love his creator (though he may turn them to neglect or even hatred of him), has so constituted this order of things that the more man gives evidence in his actions of love and veneration toward him, the happier, or at least less miserable, he is; and the more he shows neglect or contempt, the more miserable, or at least less happy. For nothing is more conducive than this order to manifest the supreme excellence of the deity and the dependence of the best creatures, i.e., the rational creatures, upon him. Hence follows the conclusion we set out to demonstrate, that there is no path that every man may follow in every moment of his life equally suited to promote his happiness or avert his misery, than to make himself obedient to the divine law by so ordering his actions that he expresses by them his love and veneration of God.

This may be proved not only from consideration of divine justice and power, but is also confirmed by the fact that in the acts in which the mind is acting most rationally (which are acts which involve the most perfect admiration and love of their object), it experiences the greatest delight and pleasure; in acts of the opposite kind by contrast, it unwillingly suffers pain and remorse, even as it tries to enjoy itself. The obvious conclusion of all this is that every kind of obligation falls upon every rational creature to temper all its actions to the will of God as the supreme legislator. For he has no less good cause to require the liberty of the created will to be curtailed at his discretion than he has power to visit extreme suffering on those who oppose him. It is altogether the gift of his abounding grace that he has sanctioned his laws not only with penalties but also with rewards.

There is a rather more substantial difficulty in determining the duties, so far as they are known by the natural light, which God requires men to show as symbols of love and veneration toward him. But this is less concerned with the actual substance of the precepts (which are mostly not at all obscure) as with the technical method by which they may be set out with the greatest clarity and incontrovertibly demonstrated. For there are two extreme errors into which different authors seem to us to have fallen here. Most philosophers who have professed to teach ethics, taking too loose a way, have multiplied the number of moral precepts which they supposed to be known of themselves to such an extent that they have considerably weakened the force and certainty of that most noble science. But when in our own century certain learned men, the restorers of moral philosophy, noticing the inconveniences that method had caused, took a completely opposite tack, they made too rigid an effort to reduce all the precepts of natural law to some one proposition. Such was the conclusion of the celebrated Pufendorf *that every man must cultivate and preserve sociability, so far as he can.*[17] Most inappropriately, the great man seems to subordinate all our duties (the most important part of which are to be directed toward God himself in direct worship) to the advantages of society (at least so far as they are known by the light of nature). This is why the learned Cumberland gives us a more comprehensive summary of the natural laws, i.e., that, *every man is bound to make every effort to promote the common good of the whole system of rational agents, in which his own happi-*

17. *On the Duty of Man and Citizen,* I.3.9, pp. 35–36; and see above, p. 51.

ness is included as a part.[18] The great man commends this endeavor to us under the name of *universal benevolence*. But apart from the fact that whenever the words *common good* and *benevolence* are applied to God who lacks nothing, they seem to become equivocal, it is even less appropriate to propose to us that the good God almighty (to whom all things should be subordinate) and rational creatures form a single *system of rational agents* which should be the object of benevolence.

It would be more appropriate to make a distinction here and say that the duties which are taught by the *natural law* (i.e., the duties which are known[19] by the natural light to pertain to the due expression to God of love and veneration) have regard to God himself either directly and immediately, or only indirectly and mediately. Among the former are: *the duty to hold correct opinions about God and his perfections; to seek all goods from him; to give praise and glory to him alone for all we possess; and to display these due sentiments toward the deity by suitable external signs.* The duties of the latter kind are comprehended in the single rule, that *it pertains to the declaration of due sentiment toward the deity that we should promote the perfection of all creatures to the best of our ability, but especially the happiness of rational creatures (so far as this does not conflict, to the best of our knowledge, with manifestation of the divine glory).* For veneration toward God is to be expressed by benevolence toward his creatures to the extent that they bear his image and are not opposed to him. The rule of the celebrated Pufendorf which we mentioned above comes to the same thing, and we could give various reasons as to the necessity of observing it, but we will omit them for the sake of brevity.

It cannot be denied without absurdity that the duties just mentioned, with innumerable particular duties which necessarily flow from them (the elaborating of which is the business of moral philosophy), are enjoined by the natural law, i.e., become known to us as duties by the light of nature. But these precepts of natural law are not scrupulously kept by any of us, but are violated daily by each one of us in many ways; and there is no argument that proves that it is possible to arrive at absolute happiness by

18. Cumberland, *Treatise on the Law of Nature*, p. 16.
19. Amending *innotescit* to *innotescunt*.

keeping these or any other precepts. A holier faith, moreover, declares to us other and sublimer precepts than these, and yet teaches that we should not put the hope of our happiness in keeping even them, but place it on another footing. Therefore no sane man should be content with natural religion as a sufficient guide to happiness; and no wise man will deny that natural religion is the proper helpmate of revealed religion and rightly subordinate to it.

I had intended to add to this continuous thread of discourse some particular topics from each of the parts of philosophy. But when I had got this far, I realized that I had already passed the limits both of labor and of time (having taken up this task later than I should have, and still not being able to devote myself to it without interruption because of the teaching duties which my position requires every day and with as yet no intermission). But I also recognized that wide areas of philosophy, both moral and natural, remained untouched. So I laid aside my former design, and in place of what I was originally going to add, I decided to append these short excerpts from two parts of philosophy.

Corollaries

From ethics and politics

1. Justice cannot depend wholly on agreements nor the obligation of agreements on the civil state, since the civil state itself is founded on an agreement.

2. It is wrong to deceive even an enemy not only by fraudulent agreements but also by fictitious stories, since even here a tacit agreement is understood to exist on the right use of signs.

3. Although nature has left all the external things that are necessary to the support of human life common to all, yet it was advantageous and agreeable to reason that individual ownership was subsequently introduced in most things, and that (even without the universal consent of men) ownership could be based upon the actual labor which was spent on improving the common thing and bringing it closer to human uses.

4. It is repugnant to natural equity that the goods of shipwrecked men be seized by others when the owners or their heirs are surviving and known.

5. Legitimate civil power is especially based neither on the power of the father nor on victory but on the consent of the subjects, but despotic power on a capital crime on their part.

6. Since the right of using force is inconsistent with the right of resistance, and since no one can confer on another a right which he does not have himself, no minister of a supreme power can, with any appearance of authority, be justified in conscience in using force on another person who is duly defending his right.

From physics

1. Astronomers truly assert that the earth rotates daily about its own center, yearly about the sun.

2. It is more likely that the planets revolve about the center of their system in free ether than in vortices.

3. The earth has the shape not of a sphere but of a spheroid flattened at the poles; and its widespread seas, lofty mountains, and the oblique position of its axis to the plane of the ecliptic, as well as its daily revolution about this axis, give so many advantages to the earth's inhabitants, that we should not take the view (whatever modern theorists say) that the earth in its infancy was without them.

4. We should not suppose any intrinsic difference between bodies which does not consist solely in the varied size, shape, place, motion, or rest of the parts of which they are composed. However the major phenomena of the universe cannot be explained on the basis of these alone, however consistent they and the rules of reaction between them may be, without accepting the postulate of gravity, which is the common bond not only of bodies on earth but of everything contained in the solar system (or in any other distinct system). Apart from the properties just mentioned, gravity denotes no intrinsic disposition of bodies but only the general and uniform will of God.

5. The belief which claims that the ordinary government of the material world has been entrusted by God to some subordinate *spirit of nature* who operates without his counsel seems to be devoid of any shred of reason. And if we reject a universal hylarchic spirit, there is no reason why we

should admit particular spirits assigned to tasks of this kind. Even less should we attribute perception, even of the lowest order, to brute matter.

6. We have no idea of *space* distinct from body. Yet it is not necessary that every particle of matter contained in the world be touched at all points by some other particle. Much less is it necessary that this world be infinite in extent; for the nature of space itself (whatever the prejudiced imagination may say) is contingent and finite.

THE END

The full text of Carmichael's
Philosophical Theses,

Which, with the Corollaries attached,
under the Blessing of Almighty God,
Students of the renowned University of Glasgow,
Scholars and Gentlemen,
Who are Candidates for the Degree of Master,
will submit to Public Examination by Learned Men
on the 27th. of June
at 2 o'clock in the Afternoon,
in the Church by the University

Under the Presidency of Gershom Carmichael

Great is truth and Most Powerful

Glasgow

Printed by Robert Sanders, Printer to the Queen and University,

1707

To the most Noble and Illustrious Lord

JOHN

Earl Hyndford
Viscount Nemphlear
Lord Carmichael of the Same, Etc.
Distinguished Head of the Name and Family of
Carmichael,
Of the Privy Council of Her Most Serene Majesty
Distinguished Chancellor of the University of Glasgow,
munificent Patron worthy of honours untold,
these Philosophical Theses
are given and dedicated
by Gershom Carmichael, President,
and by the Candidates

Philosophical Theses, 1707

*On natural law: how reverence for God is signified
by respect for human rights*

In the previous series of inaugural theses which were defended eight years ago under the same President,[1] it was argued that the duties by which Nature itself teaches that indirectly and mediately we are to give evidence of a due sentiment of love and veneration for the supreme being, are appropriately reduced to one general law, and may be deduced from it. This law is that *we should promote to the best of our ability the perfection of all creatures, but especially the happiness of rational creatures* (in which the perfection of the rest is contained), *so far as this does not conflict, to the best of our knowledge, with manifestation of the divine glory.*[2] So, without further preface, we may proceed to take up the thread of the argument which we broke off at that point, and deduce particular kinds of duties from this principle in accordance with the law of nature.

I. First, therefore, as there is no reason to suspect that the greatest happiness which men can obtain for men can detract in any way from either the illustration of divine glory or the happiness, consistent with it, of rational creatures other than man, we may deduce from the general law just established and at the same time substitute for it the following law (which contains in itself all the duties owed to men and which comes a little closer to demonstrating them): that *God wills and requires from men as a sign of reverence due to him, that each man do whatever duties he can to promote*

---

1. The reference is to Carmichael's *Philosophical Theses* of 1699.
2. See above, p. 349.

*the common happiness of the whole human race, and scrupulously avoid the
contrary actions.*[3]

II. The universal law about promoting the common good of rational
creatures proposed at the beginning does not cease to obligate men, even
if we suppose that there are no rational creatures other than men whom
men can either help or harm. Similarly the obligation of the law laid down
in the previous thesis would still exist for a man who lived so much apart
from everyone else that there could be no exchange either of benefit or
injury between them. In both cases, *he who benefits any one part without
harm to the other, increases the resources* (so to speak) *of the whole system;* and
the way the solitary man would respect either of the aforesaid laws would
be by simply preserving his own safety and by diligently looking out for
his own interests. But (with occasional rare exceptions) such a solitary state
is more represented by fiction than truly existing in any part of the earth.
To the contrary, individuals in general live so intermingled with others
that the opportunity cannot long be lacking to share benefits with each
other, or to offer harm. Moreover the human condition is so framed that
one man's private benefit is often another's harm, and *vice versa.* And
therefore it is clear that the law about promoting the common good of
men can only be observed by the man who in ordering the whole series of
his actions sets before his eyes and prepares consistently to follow what is
universally useful rather than what is good for himself without regard for
others.

III. We recognize that those too who are not separated from the company of others should advance the common good of men not only through
the duties which men do for each other, but also through the duties by
which each individual takes special care of his own safety, cultivates his
own mind, and endeavors to fortify himself as strongly as possible against
dependence on external things, in accordance with the rule set out in the
previous thesis. Yet the nature of men is so made that individuals need the
help of others to live decent lives; they are equipped with various gifts of
soul and body with which they may do more good to each other than any
animal can, and they are well disposed to do so. But equally they may

3. See above, pp. 24–25, Supplement I.10.

abuse all these prerogatives of their nature by harming one another, and may give in to the assaults of temptation that provoke them to do so. It is therefore obvious that if the human race is to be safe, it *must be sociable;* that is, men must readily join with their fellows and treat them well in order that, so far as they can, they may win and preserve mutual benevolence and mutual trust; these are the two hinges on which depends the speedy performance of all the mutual duties which relate to either preserving human life, or making it happier. Moreover neither the duties which relate to the immediate worship of God nor those which pertain to each man's self-cultivation are ever in conflict with the cultivation of *sociability* among men (as we have just explained it); to the contrary they very much encourage it and make it more sacred and more useful, and *vice versa.* From this we safely infer a universal obligation to *cultivate sociability* as the means instituted by God himself for preserving the common safety of the human race and procuring its advantage. From this rule, as well as from the other rule previously given that each man should *seek his own interests without harming others,* it is easy to deduce (following the law established in the first thesis) all the duties we must perform toward men. From this latter rule follow the duties which we owe to ourselves, so far as they aim at our own intrinsic perfection. And from the sociability rule follow the duties which we must perform to others, and also to ourselves so far as they relate to making us more useful members of human society.

IV. He who wills the end, normally wills also the means necessary to that end. Hence we should infer that everything which conduces to the common happiness of the human race, and especially to the cultivation of sociability among men for the sake of happiness, is prescribed by natural law; and on the other hand that everything that is in conflict with those things is forbidden by the same law. However in neither category are all these things of the same order. Some are duties whose performance in such circumstances is so absolutely essential to the *being* of society, that anyone who has not obliged himself to do them of his own accord may be rightly compelled to do them. There are other duties, however, where performance should be left to each man's sense of shame, since they pertain not so much to the *being* as to the *well-being* of society, and should not be forced out of the recalcitrant, since it would be foolish to apply a medicine which was far more painful and difficult than the disease itself. Duties of the former kind should be said to be due of perfect right; duties of the latter kind are due of imperfect right. The justice which is related to the former is not inappropriately called by Grotius *expletive justice,* and to the latter, *attributive justice.*[4]

V. This distinction should not be understood in quite the same sense in the natural state as in the civil. For in the natural state we have to decide by our own private judgment what things are owed us on the basis of perfect right and seize them by our own strength or that of our allies; in the civil state, we should claim them by action taken in the courts and with the help of the magistrate's authority. And in addition to this, the discrimination of perfect and imperfect right does not rest on quite the same foundation in both cases. For just as in the natural state each claims for himself by his own right all and only that which, antecedent to any civil decree, satisfies the above-mentioned condition of due perfect right, and leaves the rest to the humanity and sense of shame of those from whom they are expected, so in civil societies the distinction is to be taken, at least in the first instance, from the civil laws which give or deny an action. Often, for special reasons, the laws make some performances perfectly owed which nature had otherwise left in each man's judgment; on the other hand they leave to the judgment of individuals (at least so far as external courts are concerned) other performances which nature otherwise had given the right of forcibly exacting. It does not follow from this that these civil laws are in conflict with the natural laws, provided that they follow their footsteps in the heart of the matter and aim at the great goal for which civil societies are formed, which is to preserve, for each and every citizen, so far as possible, his liberty and his property. In taking up these positions, we have before our eyes (as befits philosophers) not the civil laws of any particular nation but only the natural laws.

VI. We indicated just now that some of the duties which, by the fundamental laws established above, each man owes to the human race have direct and immediate regard to the agent himself, and some to other men. With regard to the former, the law laid down in the first thesis, together

---

4. Grotius, *Rights of War and Peace,* I.I.8; and see above, p. 44.

with the comments about the purpose of the second law, tells us that every man is obliged to put his own advantage after the common happiness of the human race; but as the strength and faculties of each man are finite and not capable of everything all at once, and as each man can contribute more by his labors to protect his own safety and to advance his own interests than anyone else's, it is certain that every law commends to each man a certain particular *care for himself* as his own proper province, urging him not only to promote the happiness of the human race, at least in this way, by looking out for himself without harming others but also to make himself fitter to bring advantages to others by duly cultivating his faculties.

VII. Now the care which each man is obliged to spend on himself extends to both parts of a man, but in the first place to the mind. The mind should be furnished with correct opinions about things relevant to duty; it should learn to make correct judgments about the things that arouse human desire; it should get used to controlling its feelings by the norm of reason; and it should be early trained in some honest profession (suited to the individual's condition and mode of living). As for the body, its life and health should be preserved and its strength improved by all good means; to this end one should make a moderate and timely use of food and labor and avoid excess in either; one should also avoid immoderate passions, since they weaken the body's strength; and finally one should develop a habitual spirit of courage, in order to fight off the many dangers that threaten to ruin the body.

VIII. A man not only may but should expend care and labor in performing various duties toward God and mankind, which may exhaust his life and conclude its term earlier than if he had lived softly (for life is not to be measured by how many breaths we take but by the number of good actions we do). One is sometimes bound to expose one's life to a present danger to save others. But it is never right for any man directly to cut off his life nor to hasten his end in any way, even to avoid by death the most grievous temporal ills, nor to neglect for such a reason any decent means that lies in his power to prolong his life.

IX. Due care for the body's security not only permits but obliges one to defend it by inflicting violent harm on an unjust aggressor, even (if there is no other way) by killing him. This self-protection is circumscribed by

completely different laws, according as one lives in the natural state or under civil government, whether we are considering a just cause for doing it
or the time when we may start it or the condition of ending it. It is indeed
true that in both states the ultimate defense is permitted not only to preserve one's life but also to maintain the body's integrity and chastity,
which are of course irreparable goods. In the natural state this extends also
to external property, unless it is of such little importance that for its sake
(in the absence of other persuasive reasons) prudence does not allow us to
expose our own lives, nor humanity the lives of others, to danger. But in
the civil state it is for the civil laws to define what is permitted for the preservation of property, except that here too there is room for prudence and
humanity, especially where the laws rather give permission than a command.

Further, in natural liberty violent defense rightly begins as soon as it is
quite clear that another person is engaged in inflicting violence upon us,
and there is no hope of turning him from his hostile intention by gentler
means. It is rightly continued until not only the actual danger is repelled
and losses made good (whether the losses which originally gave rise to the
war or the loss we have sustained in the war), but also till a guarantee is
given of not doing harm in the future, a guarantee which gives assurance
that the enemy has dropped his intention to do harm or has been deprived
of opportunity and means. But in the civil state, we must not embark
upon a defense that threatens death or grave bodily injury to someone else,
until the unjust aggressor has driven us into such a position that we have
no opportunity either of running away or of invoking the help of magistrates or citizens, before the assault against which the ultimate defense is
here admitted has had its effect. It must not be continued beyond the
point at which we have an opportunity to escape after repelling the actual
danger. For vengeance for the injury, guarantee for the future, and compensation for loss (if there has been any so far) should be left in this case
to the care of the magistrate.

X. In all these cases humanity requires us to look for a safer means of
avoiding injury and not to expose ourselves or others to danger without
necessity, especially when the cause of the threatened injury is mistake or
madness rather than malice. However a man engaged in a lawful and hon-

est activity does not lose the privilege of defending himself even though he could avoid danger by giving it up. But anyone who challenges another to a duel does lose the privilege. (We extend the term "duel" here to any fight which is formally appointed and settled on certain terms, on whose outcome a dispute depends by agreement of the parties.) So does anyone who when challenged offers himself of his own accord, except perhaps in the case where the safety of innocent men or some other quite valuable right of our own or another's cannot be defended against an unjust aggressor by any other equally suitable means, though in a civil state which is truly civil this hardly seems likely to happen between private individuals. And "wrongs" properly so called (i.e., insults), which are nearly always the reason why fellow citizens engage in duels, would not provide a just cause for extreme violence even in natural liberty, since it is completely contrary to equity and humanity to repel or take vengeance for an insult in that manner. For the compensation for damage to one's reputation which is commonly said to be afforded by taking so cruel a revenge for such a "wrong" is purely and simply an illusion cherished by conceited fellows who need to be taught that true reputation (which is simply the opinion men have, and particularly upright and judicious men, of one's excellence) is to be won and preserved by behaving properly and deserving well of human society. The observation of thoroughly wicked customs, which pass among certain ferocious Desperadoes[5] as *laws of honor,* disgrace a man as a *man,* as a *citizen,* and most of all as a *Christian.*

XI. If someone has taken the initiative in causing harm to someone else but then repents and not only stops doing the harm but also satisfies all the obligations he incurred by it, and if the injured party in the bitterness of his soul does not himself cool down, at that point (but only at that point) the first party begins to enjoy the right and privilege of self-defense; and in this case some have rightly said that the just cause has passed from his enemy to himself. Here it is rightly asked whether between equals in the state of nature it is right to inflict a punishment in addition to all that we indicated in Thesis ix is owed by the wrongdoer to his victim. With Gro-

---

5. *Thrasones,* named after Thraso, the arrogant and boastful soldier of the Roman playwright Terence's play *Eunuchus,* and a stock figure of ancient comedy.

tius and Locke[6] we hold that the answer must be "yes" (at least in the case of the more horrible wrongs, maliciously perpetrated), but the injured party, who will still be seething with anger, should not proceed to punish with the same violence he had used in defense of himself or the recovery of his property.

XII. Further, the care for self-preservation which nature commends to every man not only permits license against an unjust aggressor, but also allows exceptions to otherwise universal laws in other cases. In this sense *necessity knows no law* (as they say). This is not because any necessity allows us to violate a law, but because it shows that the present case ought to be understood as excepted in the law. The present *case of necessity* causes no exception in the general precepts *of worshipping God and promoting the advantages of human society* but only in the particular precepts derived from these fundamental laws, and ought therefore to be taken as prescribing simply the particular duty which in the given circumstances brings the latter into line with the aim defined by the former.

XIII. Thus the necessity of saving a life gives permission not only to amputate a limb afflicted by an incurable condition, but also to hasten the death, in certain cases, of men who would die in any case, and even more allows us to refuse aid which would slightly prolong someone else's life, if by giving such aid we would doom ourselves to an early death. But as the outcomes of such things tend to be uncertain, and therefore we often have a reason to be uncertain as to what we owe to our own safety and what to the safety of other people, three particular kinds of reasons, it seems, should be brought into the calculation and balanced against each other, viz., the seriousness of the evils feared on both sides, the probability that they will occur, and the number of persons at risk on both sides; in the last case number may be supplemented by worth in the case of a person who is useful to many, but other things being more or less equal, each man is permitted to favor himself.

XIV. There is even less doubt that one may take by force or stealth property which ordinarily belongs to someone else, in order to save one's

---

6. Grotius, *Rights of War and Peace,* II.XX, pp. 40 ff.; and Locke, *Second Treatise,* ch. 2, secs. 7–8; see also above, p. 69.

life from threatened death. The provisos are: that the owner himself is not exposed to the same crisis; that the taker cannot get what he manifestly needs to preserve his life by any other means; and that he does not refuse to give whatever compensation may be in his power now or later for what he has taken. For separate ownership of property cannot to be supposed to have been introduced without leaving this particle of primitive community in a case of necessity.

XV. Furthermore, an emergency affecting our property sometimes gives us leave to destroy or spoil articles of relatively low value which belong to others, provided that the danger, which without fault on our part threatens a far more valuable piece of our property, cannot be removed in a more convenient way, and provided that we promptly make up the loss which the other man suffers. This principle of equity is followed and at the same time more clearly defined by the laws of most states in the case of threatened shipwreck, fire, and the like; the same is true, and rightly so, for almost all branches of the law.

XVI. Some of the duties which should be performed toward other men are *absolute;* since they arise from a common obligation, they should be performed toward all men indifferently. Other such duties are *hypothetical;* as these derive their origin from the voluntary agreements of men or from some particular adventitious state, they are only owed to those with whom we have an agreement or with whom we share some such state.[7]

XVII. Among absolute duties, this rightly takes the first place, or perhaps rather embraces all the others, that *every man should respect and treat any other man as naturally equal to himself.* Such equality not only implies that each man is *equally a man* and consequently subject to a moral obligation from which no one can exempt him, but also that he has certain rights belonging to him which no one has the right to violate. It also implies that no man may claim for himself in his own right any power over others or a greater share of the things that are available to all, merely because he is better furnished than others by nature with certain gifts of

---

7. Pufendorf, *On the Duty of Man and Citizen,* I.9, p. 68. Carmichael came to regard this distinction as unhelpful in the delineation of rights and obligations; see above, p. 77.

mind or body. On the other hand it also implies that nature *distributes* to all men in the same manner in accordance with the same laws the acquisition of dominion or government. The same point is also made by the golden and universal rule taught by our Lord: *As ye would that men should do to you, do ye also to them likewise.*[8] This also (to omit other clear consequences) refutes the empty claim of the ancient Greeks that they had been made masters by nature and the barbarians their slaves;[9] certain Christians should ask themselves whether their own minds are not possessed by a similarly outrageous opinion.

XVIII. Of the elements of a due recognition of natural equality, the most essential to the practice of social life is: *let no man harm another or cause loss to another in any way,* whether by harming, spoiling, diminishing, or removing that which is now his; or by intercepting what is due to him by perfect right; or by omitting or refusing the performance of any duty to anyone which he is bound to do on the basis of a perfect obligation. So whatever belongs to anyone by legitimate title (whether as given by nature, or assigned by the agency of a human action or law), this precept forbids it to be taken away from him, or spoiled, or harmed, or removed from his sphere of use in whole or in part.

XIX. From this it follows that *if harm is inflicted or loss caused by any means to anyone by another, the man found to be responsible for it must make it good so far as possible:* no one's right is abrogated by another man's wrongdoing. Relevant to the estimation of loss is not only the thing itself which is harmed, destroyed, or stolen, but also the fruits, whether natural or civil, which would have accrued to the owner if the thing had been saved, after deduction of the expenses which would have been necessary for collecting the fruits. Finally, all that subsequently flows from any act of harm as by natural necessity, is regarded as one loss.

XX. Compensation for loss is due not only from those who have inflicted a loss on another person themselves, but also from those who by act or omission inconsistent with perfect obligation were part of the cause of the loss. Where several men in agreement have conspired in one act caus-

8. Matthew 7.12; Luke 6.31.
9. See the criticism of Aristotle above, p. 74.

ing loss, each individual has an obligation proportional to his influence. However if any one of them is caught and is able to pay, he is obligated for the whole in the absence of the rest; once he has paid, the rest owe nothing to the injured party on the score of compensation. Also obligated is the man who has harmed another not by malice aforethought but through culpable negligence, but not the man who has been the occasion of another's loss absolutely by chance. On the natural equity of *noxal actions* and on *damage by animals,* the candidates will respond in the examination room.[10]

XXI. One should also include among absolute and general duties the duty that *everyone should promote the advantage of another, so far as he conveniently can.* Each person owes this duty both in an indefinite manner, to become a more useful member of human society by a proper cultivation of mind and body and (so far as the genius and condition of each man allows) by inventing arts and sciences useful to the human race or by developing them to a more perfect condition, and also in a definite manner by doing good to specific persons as opportunity arises. Anyone who refuses to do services of *harmless utility* to others can very rightly be accused of churlish ill will, i.e., if he refuses services which help the receiver without cost to the giver. But we should probably not stretch the phrase *harmless utility* to make it the foundation of a perfect right, unless the ground of necessity is also involved; we have admitted above that necessity lends it considerable strength, and indeed we have recognized above that in an extreme case necessity is enough without harmless utility.

XXII. But it often happens that from extraordinary benevolence we should freely do something for someone which involves expense or hard work, in order to relieve his needs or achieve some outstanding advantage for him. These are the only duties (strictly speaking) which deserve to be called *benefits.* In conferring benefits with generosity as well as prudence, taking account of the condition of the giver and of the receiver, men have an ample opportunity to win conspicuous praise and to deserve well of others. In return the beneficiary is required to show a grateful spirit, which

---

10. For noxal actions and damage by animals (*pauperies*), see above, p. 176, n. 3 and p. 177, n. 4.

should be attested by the return of equal or even greater benefits when occasion requires and his condition permits. Neglect of this duty betrays a mind which is all the more disgustingly mean in that no action for simple ingratitude is allowed in the courts nor should it be.

XXIII. One obviously does not satisfy the obligations of natural law merely by observing and performing the duties which it enjoins independent of agreements between men. Furthermore, in order to develop human society with beneficial consequences for the human race, it is necessary for men sometimes to take voluntary obligations on themselves by making promises and agreements about the mutual performance of duties which before that act were at each individual's discretion but which, once the obligation has been voluntarily contracted, have to be performed by those who have made the promises or agreements. Consequently, it is rightly included among the primary precepts of natural law, *that every man should keep his pledged faith.*

XXIV. Sometimes we speak of future actions which lie in our power in such a way that we express a merely present intention and not a will to impose any obligation upon ourselves; sometimes we speak in such a way as to indicate a will to obligate ourselves but not to confer a perfect right on someone else to require performance; and sometimes we clearly declare either by words or by other signs our will to give away a small portion of our liberty, so that not only are we obligated on the ground of fidelity but the other party acquires a perfect right to require from us the thing or service promised on the ground that it is owed to him, and to extract it out of us against our will if we do not offer it voluntarily. This will so signified, whether it arises from a mutual agreement or a unilateral promise, provided that no legitimate counterclaim may be brought against it, has no less full strength and force to produce a personal right than the actual alienation of his property by an owner has the force to found a right to property.

XXV. The first requirement of the obligation of promises and agreements is consent, both by the party which undertakes the obligation and by the party for whom it is undertaken, and it must be a consent which has been made manifest by appropriate signs by both parties. But since clear consent to a proposal cannot be either given or declared without the use of reason, it follows that the promises and agreements of those who do not have the capacity to use reason (at least to the extent of understanding the matter of the proposal, so far as it refers to them) entail no obligation directly.

XXVI. But one must not suppose that a man has clearly given his consent, who at the time was persuaded that the matter was otherwise than it actually was, and thought in good faith that the point in which he is deceived was recognized by the other party to be a condition of his consent because of the nature of the transaction, even if he did not explicitly state that. Suppose therefore that the event shows that some circumstance was lacking which it is clear that the promising or agreeing party assumed in good faith as a condition of his act (for a judgment about a thing which is not apparent is the same as a judgment about a thing that does not exist, so far as the external forum is concerned, even in natural liberty). In that case the obligation for him to perform the action is dissolved, so far as it is founded on that assumption; except that if he was negligent in investigating the matter or in expressing his meaning and the other party suffers a loss for that reason, the promisor is obliged to make it good, not directly on the strength of the promise but on the basis of a loss culpably inflicted. We caution therefore that in reciprocal agreements no event is readily understood as a condition, unless it is either expressly stated to be such; or is affirmed by the other party to the transaction truly to exist; or is such that the promise would be manifestly impossible or absurd to perform apart from the condition which it is clear that the promisor was not able to perform; or finally unless it concerns the thing itself or the material which is the subject of the agreement, its valuable qualities, or lack of them. But things not assumed as conditions do not vitiate an act otherwise properly conceived, even though they perhaps disappoint expectation, except so far as the party with whom one is dealing can be held responsible for the error, in which case the obligation would be lifted as a form of compensation.

XXVII. Another frequent question is whether a man who has made a promise or an agreement with someone under the influence of force or fear should be deemed to have given the consent which we said above was requisite to the obligation of promises and agreements. We take it as certain that we cannot validly oppose to the obligation of a promise or agreement either fear inflicted by a third party without collusion with a party to the transaction, nor fear justifiably inflicted by any party, nor the fear that the other party to the transaction will inflict an injury, if this fear is rashly conceived and without serious grounds. Therefore we think that much the safest opinion is given by those who teach that whatever can be legitimately promised for the purpose of saving life or averting serious loss must, after it has been promised, be fully performed on grounds of fidelity, even though the promise was extorted by the most unjustified force on the part of the one who required the promise be given. Admittedly this wrong renders him incapable of obtaining by that act any right which he may legitimately use (not to mention that any claim to perfect right is removed from this case by way of compensation because of the wrong inflicted). Yet the bond of veracity and fidelity is in no way dissolved by this, and that prevents the other party from making use of the counterclaim of *force and fear* (even though it was quite obvious when he was making the promise).[11]

XXVIII. Further, the object of promises and pacts has to be within our physical and moral power. We cannot therefore be obliged by any agreement to do things which, literally or morally, we cannot do. But it does not follow from this that every promise of something which is impossible or illegitimate is totally without effect, so as to give rise to no obligation. When the recipient of a promise was invincibly ignorant of the circumstances which would render performance impossible or illegitimate, if the promisor knew of them or fraudulently contrived them after contracting the obligation, there is no doubt that he is obliged to make good all the adverse consequences of his act. It seems the same thing must be said in the case of a reciprocal agreement, if the maker of the agreement ought to have known the impediments to carrying it through or afterward caused them by culpable negligence. But in simple promises, where fault on the part of the promisor alone is involved, all that is required is to make good the loss incurred by the recipient of the promise. Moreover the obligation disappears, if the impediments to legitimately performing what was promised were invincibly concealed from the promisor or supervened afterward by sheer chance, with the proviso that if anything in the agreement has to

11. See the discussion of promises made under duress above, pp. 85 ff.

this point been done by the other party in prospect of the performance now impeded, it must be returned, or if that is impossible, then its equivalent. But one must note that by *illegitimate* we do not here mean everything which is rashly promised and which would not be performed on the ground of duty if no promises had been made. For in many such cases one must apply this third principle that *many things which ought not to be done are valid when done.* So by illegitimate things which may not be done by any promise or agreement we simply mean those things which are prohibited by law without exception: such as things by which reverence for the deity is directly violated; things by which extreme disaster will fall upon anyone who does them or requires them; and things which damage a perfect right of a third party. Hence it follows that any promises or agreements we make are void if they concern the property or actions of other men, insofar as they depend not on our own will but on that of another. And the same thing must be said about property or actions of our own which have already been pledged to someone else.

XXIX. We may promise to other men and make agreements with them to take over the promises of others, and in general to transfer or acquire any alienable rights, not only through ourselves but also through a third party whom we have made the interpreter of our will. Whatever he does in good faith in accordance with the procedure of a public mandate (i.e., a mandate declared to the person one is dealing with) obligates the mandator himself.

XXX. To preserve sociability among men, as one should, it is as important that *veracity* should be scrupulously observed in assertions as *fidelity* in promises and pacts. It is true that in many cases we are not bound to reveal to others the sense of our mind, to the extent that in such cases we have the choice either to speak or be silent, or perhaps, if we are pressed, to brush off an importunate person by turning the talk in a different direction or by giving some rather general response. Nevertheless the universal law of nature which is superior to every exception is: *no one should deceive anyone by words or by any other signs which may rightly be regarded as employed for the purpose of expressing concepts to him*—i.e., by employing such signs as he judges that the other will duly interpret as intended to signify something to him which is not in fact true or which is not thought to be true by the speaker. For in making an assertion to another, whatever signs a man uses for that purpose, he is taken to be making a tacit agreement with him to use these signs in the same sense in which he thinks they will be understood by the other person with the aid of reason, i.e., in a normal way and in the sense in which such signs are usually understood in similar cases where no particular convention suggests anything different. Therefore equivocations and mental reservations do not avoid the vice of mendacity; and it is in vain to add the limitation, *if he to whom the utterance is addressed has the right to understand.* For although not all have the right to understand the sense of our mind on any and every matter, yet this right of not being deceived by false speech is common to all. Without it, the use of speech would be largely banished from human life; it would be pointless to tell anyone anything, and no less pointless to listen to it.

XXXI. An oath is rightly held to give a serious weight to both promises and agreements as well as to assertions. In an oath God is called upon to witness to fidelity in the one case, to truthfulness in the other, and in both cases to avenge any falsehood there may be. But since oaths do not so much produce a materially new obligation as add a kind of supplementary bond to an obligation which is valid in itself, the requisites of the obligation of an oath are all the same conditions which are requisite to the strength and validity of the act to which it is added. However, because of the use of the name of God whom one cannot in fact deceive and whom none can mock without punishment, the effect of oaths is not only that a more drastic penalty is to be feared by one who has broken his sworn faith than unsworn faith, but also that every frivolous interpretation is excluded from acts in which they are employed. For it is indeed rightly presumed that a transaction in which such a grave sanction is used is serious and of great importance.

I planned to treat in a similar compendium the rest of the topics of natural jurisprudence also, especially those which concern the doctrine of ownership or dominion and government, and to give a short account of them; for it seemed to me that nothing I could do would be more opportune than a synopsis of that most noble science which has been taught to these candidates with particular care, as to others before them, following the method of the famous Pufendorf.

But as the topics already dealt with have grown quite long enough for this kind of work, I once more break off the thread here. I append however the following points, so that no one may complain that specimens of the other parts of philosophy are altogether wanting.

Corollaries

From logic, ontology, and pneumatology

1. The sorites, which, besides the syllogism, is the one perfect form of argument, admits all the same figures, the same moods of individual figures, and the same rules, both general and special, *mutatis mutandis,* as occur in the simple syllogism. But in the fourth figure, besides the five moods which are usually attributed to syllogisms of that figure, the sorites admits another six, all of them yielding conclusions both negatively and positively. The candidates will explain all this in detail in response to questions.

2. The most useful and universal rule both of syllogisms and of sorites is that one of the premises must be shown to contain a conclusion, in the former case through the other premise, in the latter by taking the other premises together.

3. In order to apply this rule correctly, it is very useful to observe that not only a negative particular but also any mark of universality both distributes a propositional term which it qualifies and which would otherwise be taken particularly and cancels the distribution of a term which would otherwise be taken universally.

4. Propositions which are said to be *of eternal truth,* about the essential attributes of created things, are merely hypothetical; nor to be true do they need to be verified in terms of any being in actual existence at that time, but only in terms of the being which things would have at that time if they existed.

5. It is wrongly said that an independent thing is positively of itself.

6. The human mind experiences in itself not mere internal sensations, but ideas so named, in the strictest sense, of thought and of the various modes of thought and thus of thinking things themselves.

7. Although we form concepts of physical things earlier and more easily than we form concepts of spiritual things, the existence of our minds becomes known to us prior to and more clearly than the existence of any body.

From physics

1. It is false that there is always simply the same quantity of motion in bodies in collision taken together as there was before collision; but it is true that there is the same quantity against the same blow, apart from the quantity of contrary motion.

2. The rebound of colliding bodies is not continuation of a direct motion with a new qualification (for that implies a contradiction), but an altogether new motion produced by an elastic force.

3. Matter fills just a small part of this vast mundane space through which it is diffused.

4. For gravity (which is a property that is not essential to matter but is yet common to all its parts and against all its parts) no cause can be given, nor should be sought, beyond the efficacious will of the great Creator. Its effect and the laws by which it works in terrestrial bodies in relation to the globe of the earth have been seen by many; but it was left to the insight of the incomparable Newton and after him of the learned Gregory to reveal and demonstrate gravity with regard to the great bodies of the world in their relation to each other.[12] Thus there is no room for doubt that the planets and comets are kept in their orbits by gravity, which pervades the universe in such a way that its accelerative force in a given distance varies directly as the quantity of matter in the body which it relates to, and in a given body, reciprocally as the square of the distance from the same.

5. It is clear from the equable description of areas that the five primary planets, Mercury, Venus, Mars, Jupiter, and Saturn, are kept in their proper orbits by gravitation against the sun, and the moon by its gravitation against the earth; and the ratio of the periodic times, which is one and a half times the ratio of the distances from the center, is found in these five

---

12. Newton, *Philosophiae Naturalis;* Gregory, *Astronomiae Physicae.*

compared with each other and itself proves, by the law given in the previous corollary, that they tend toward their own center; this ratio holds with equal accuracy in the annual period, which is related to the distance of the sun and the earth, if comparison is made with the five planets though not with the moon. From all this it follows of its own accord that this force of gravity on which the annual revolution depends is to the force with which any of those planets tends toward the sun as the square of its distance from the sun; but to the force with which the moon tends toward the earth it is not as the square of the distance of the moon from the earth is to the square of the distance of the sun from it; though it has been discovered by observation and calculation that this general law of gravitation holds in the case of the moon and the other bodies that gravitate toward the earth. Therefore the force with which the annual revolution is kept in its orbit tends toward the sun not toward the earth; and thus the annual motion is to be attributed to the former not the latter. It is at any rate clear that the Pythagorean system can be maintained only by means of mere gravity disposed in an even manner through the universe.

6. The unequal accelerative gravity of terrestrial bodies at the different parallels also confirms the diurnal motion of the earth; this shows itself unequally in the long shafts of isochronic pendulums. For this inequality whose size is almost the same, as is found by experiment and brought out by calculation (on the assumption of a daily rotation of the earth), seems incapable of any other explanation than centrifugal force arising from circular movement. This is greater near the equator and more opposed by the force of gravity; it is smaller further away from the equator and at the same time less directly opposed to gravity; and therefore in the former case it takes more from it, in the latter case less. By the same principles also the shape of the earth is established as a spheroid flattened at the poles.

7. The ebb and flow of the sea is due not to the pressure of the moon but to its attraction. The parts of the sea facing it gravitate more toward it, and the parts of the sea opposed to it gravitate less toward it, than the mass of the earth itself. Both the former and the latter gravitate toward the earth itself less in the lateral parts, and thus under pressure from them they rise to a greater height. And as there is a similar, though much smaller, inequality in the sun's action in attracting waters because of its different as-

pects, tides are higher or lower depending on the conjunction or opposition of the forces of the sun and the moon. The authors cited above have given a very accurate explanation of these things as well as of other phenomena of the tides.

8. The sensation of light seems to be caused not by a mere impulse communicated from a lighted body to our eyes through innumerable intermediaries, but by an immensely fast projection through the surrounding space of the same particles which were in the lighted body. In particular the celebrated Newton has proved by many experiments that not all the rays emitted by the sun are suited to showing all colors, but that there are various kinds of rays which are each endowed with their own degree of refrangibility and reflexibility, and of themselves can only show one color, specific to itself, however distorted by refraction or reflection, and therefore the whole diversity of colors depends on the fact that the different kinds of rays are variously mixed or separated by means of refraction or reflection. In a word, we put forward for discussion all the parts of that wonderful theory (which it would take too long to rehearse here even in summary form).

9. From the observations of that great author and others (who establish that nearly all natural bodies consist of minute particles, each of which taken on its own is transparent), it definitely follows that the smallest particles of matter which are perceptible to our senses even with the help of artificial aids, not only leave spaces between them when they form larger bodies (spaces which are either quite empty or filled with some tenuous fluid), and when light strikes them, it is reflected or refracted; these particles themselves are also shot through with innumerable tiny pores which are pervious to the material of light. But this should not be taken to infinity as if there were nowhere in nature a thoroughly solid portion of matter; for though matter may extend to infinity and be divided, it cannot be infinitely divided. For this reason we must reject the recent doctrine of actually infinite vessels in plants and animals; nor is such infinity necessary to the nutrition of individual parts.

10. However it is a no less rational conjecture that all plants and animals (that have ever existed or will exist) were formed once and for all by the Author of Nature in the first individuals of each species.

Gershom Carmichael's Account
of His Teaching Method

Gershom Carmichael's Account
of His Teaching Method

(Written in August, 1712)

The Method I have taken and propose to take with ye Class now under my Charge, is as followes.

When they enter'd Semys,[1] I employ'd them, for some time, in expounding the Greek Testament & going over ye most necessary things in ye Greek Grammar.

In November, so soon as I could get them furnish'd with ye first sheet of my Compend of Logick (which was then printing) I began them to it, largely exploring every Lesson, when I gave it out, & afterwards examining them upon it, with a repeated explication. Thus I went thro' ye Compend two or three times, save that I did not prelect the Lesson at giving it out, after the first time. Here I insisted verry largely on the forms of Propositions & Syllogismes, both Categoricall & those that are not so; still shewing them how all are reducible to ye Categorick form. But I reserv'd at least ye half of ye day for ye Greek, till their publick Examination was over.

After the Examination, I turn'd their Lesson, in the Greek Testament, from the Use of an ordinary Greek Lesson, to that of a sacred Exercise; no longer asking a Grammaticall Account of Words; only causing them first read a whole Verse distinctly in Greek, & then say it over in Latin. Thus they went thro' a page or two, every Morning before Prayer (at least four

---

1. In the regenting system, still in place at the University of Glasgow when this report was drafted, "semys," or the semibaccalaureat year, was the second year of the undergraduate program. The first year was called the "bajan" year, the third year was the baccalaureat year, and the fourth year was the magistrand year. See Coutts, *History of the University of Glasgow,* p. 178.

Mornings in ye Week) & in the Semy Year finish'd ye Evangelists. I have continued ye same Method since, so that in their Course they'll go thro' ye whole New Testament.

In January I began [them] to Ars Cogitandi, as being ye best Logick, that I know extant under ye name of Logick, & that is tolerably adapted for ye Use of teaching in a University. Here likewise I prepar'd their way, for reading what was prescrib'd (as I do in all ye parts of my Course) by a previous Explication of each Lesson. In doing this, if ye year be short, & I be not verry much hurry'd, I use to read over every word of ye Lesson, & comment upon it. If otherwise, I give them a more generall View of it, & acquaint them with what I think necessary for their reading it with ye more Ease & Advantage, but especially for guarding them against Errors. And whereas, for ye help of their Memory, I use to cause them write on ye Margins of their Books here & there verry short Notes of what I think most necessary to be remarked, I endeavour, if possible, to dictate these Notes upon each Lesson, before I set them to study it. The Method describ'd in this Paragraph, being what I generally use thro' ye whole, will not need again to be repeated.

In Ars Cogitandi, I did not oblige my Self to follow ye Author thro his Digressions, tho' some of his morall ones are too good to be altogether passed by. The places of that book that favour Popery are already noticed, & shortly but judiciously obviated by an unknown hand, in Notes that are printed with ye Book. Besides which, I took further Notice of some of them, in my marginall Animadversions.[2]

What is wanting in that Book, of ye things commonly treated of in Logick, I gave them some taste of (so far as seem'd necessary) in my Theses: which (in this, as well as in ye other parts) being connected, so as to contain a Compend of ye whole Science, serve not only as Matter of Dispute, but as a Text for teaching.

I began them to ye Exercise of Disputing, I think, some time in February, having first taught them ye Rules of it, from ye Praxis subjoin'd to

2. A copy of Carmichael's annotations on the *Ars Cogitandi* is housed in the Mitchell Library [City of Glasgow] MS 90.

my printed Compend. For ye Matter of their Disputes, at first I parcell'd out to them ye Compend it self, which serv'd till ye beginning of May, when they began to dispute in ye Common Hall. From that time to ye End of ye Course, ye Theses, that are to be publickly disputed that Week, are first defended in ye Class, by those that are to impugne in publick, & impugned by those that are to defend.

The Afternoons, from ye end of March, or beginning of Aprill, were mostly spent on Pardie's Elements of Geometry;[3] in which they went thro' 3 books that Year.

The same Year I taught them one half of De Vries his Determinationes Ontologicae:[4] I design'd to have gone thro' ye whole; but could not overtake to end both Ars Cogitandi & it that Session. And I made ye less haste to go thro ye Latter, that Severall of them were not then provided with it.

In ye Baccalour Year, I went again thro Ars Cogitandi, taking in, in ye proper places, what I had in my own Compend & Theses. This took us up till the publick Examination, or verry near it. Then I went thro', in my ontologick Theses, those Heads, which they had learn'd ye Year before; making them at ye same time, read over again, & reflect upon, what they had learn'd in De Vries concerning them. And from that, I went on to teach them ye remainder of that Authors Determinationes Ontologicae. But because I could not reach ye end of them against ye first of January, & I was then obliged, for ye Sake of my private Schollars, to begin ye Pneumaticks, I referr'd what then remain'd of ye Ontology to ye Afternoons.

Thus, with ye new Year began De Vries his Determinationes Pneumatologicae, which I propos'd to have ended against ye first of March. But when at that time ye part de Deo was yet remaining, I chose to cause them write that part out of my own Pneumaticks; where it is contain'd in two Sheets of Paper; & consists of four Chapters, ye first of which states ye Notion, & by severall Arguments demonstrates the Existence, of a Deity; ye Second treats of ye incommunicable Attributes; ye third of ye com-

3. Pardie, *Elementa geometriae.*
4. De Vries, *De Natura Dei.*

municable Attributes; & ye fourth of ye Operations, or externall Acts, of God.[5] This I taught them instead of De Vries his third part.

However, All I could do, was to begin ye Ethicks with ye Month of Aprill; which I did, having before caus'd them write some of my Ethick Theses, which were to be ye Matter of our first Lessons. For my Resolution was, to take ye Plan of my Method from ye Theses, & to consider ye severall Chapters or Paragraphs of Pufendorf de Officio Hominis & Civis (which I at ye same time put in their hands) as they fell in with the things treated of there. Now, that ye Faculty may judge, whether I have, by this Innovation, done any Injustice, either to the Author or ye Subject, I presume to offer ye following Index of ye Theses, & ye Order in which I was thereby led to handle Pufendorfs Book.

The Declar'd Will of God, & Supream Law, or Rule to ye Actions of Rationall Creatures; ye Denominations they receive from thence, Thes: 1, 2, 3 Pufendorf Bk. I (which is allwaies to be understood till I mention ye 2nd) Cap: 2, secs. 1–3 & 11. What Actions & how far, morall & imputable. Th: 4–10. Puf. C.1. Law of God, Natural, Positive. Th: 11. Puf: C: 2. final section. The Natural Law truly Divine Th: 12, 13, 14. How immutable. Th: 15, 16: And because I here likewise consider'd whether it admitt of a Dispensation, & whether of an epieikeia, I took in Puf: C. 2. secs. 9, 10. Knowledge of ye Law of Nature, neither innate in Mens Minds, nor only learn'd from Custom, but gather'd from ye Nature of things. Th: 17. P: C. 3. sec. 12. Law of Nations, whether distinct from that of nature. Th: 10. Morality of Persons, where of Virtue, Vice, vulgar Distinction of ye Cardinal Virtues &c. Th: 19–25. First fundamentall Praecept of ye Law of Nature, to worship God. Th: 26. Puf: C. 4. Second fundamentall Praecept, to promote ye Wellfare of Mankind. Th: 27, and that, first, by procuring all innocent Advantages to ourselves, 2ly by living Sociably towards others. Th 28. Puf. C. 3. secs. 1–4. The Divine Authority & Sanction of these Praecepts. Th. 29. Puf: C. 3. secs. 10, 11. Fundamentall Errors of Hobbes. Th: 30: Right, perfect, imperfect. Justice, particular, universall. Injury. Th. 31, 32, 33. Puf: C. 2. secs. 12–18. Particular Dutys to ourselves, deducible from ye Law of Sociality. Th: 34. Pub. C. 3 final section & C. 5 sec. 1.

---

5. An epitome of his *Synopsis Theologiae Naturalis.* See above, p. 227.

Duty's towards the Mind. Th: 35, Puf: C. 5. sec. 2. (Here, because Pufendorf in his litle book passes this subject too lightly, I caused them write about a Sheet of Paper out of my larger Ethick, where among other things, I treat of ye Government of ye Passions; for ye Nature & Distinction of them, as well as ye Determination of ye Will, its different Acts. Liberty &tc. had before been handled in ye Pneumaticks.) Dutys towards ye Body. Th: 36. Puf. C. 5 sec. 3. Wherever different Mens Interests Clash, we must have recourse to ye Law of Sociality for understanding ye Termes of which I remark in general. It requires an Acknowledgement of ye Natural Equality of Men. Th: 37, 38. Puf. C. 7; 2ly it does not exclude nay it requires a peculiar Care of ones self. Th: 39. 3ly Every Mans Right includes a corresponding Obligation upon others, either definite or indefinite. Th: 40. Every perfect Right naturally includes, when counteracted, two accessory Rights; ye One of endeavouring to maintain it, even by hurting him that attempts to violate it; the other of getting it repair'd, when it is actually violated. Th: 41. Since Sociality consists in so maintaining & using our own Rights, as to have a due Regard to every other Mans, there appears no better way of determining what it demands, than by considering, in order, what those Rights are, that every Man has, or is capable of having. Th: 42. These I reduce to six Classes. The first Classe contains natural Rights, such as Life, Limbs, Liberty, & ye Capacity of acquiring adventitious Rights by proper Means. Th. 43., Puf: C. 6, sec. 2. The Second Classe is of those Rights, which a Person acquires by his own proper Deed: Such as ye Property of externall things in ye hands of ye originary Acquirer. Th. 44. Here I treat, of ye Grant of externall Things to Mankind in Generall. Th. 45, 46, 47. Puf. C. 12. sec. 1. Of ye Acquisition of Property by Occupation. Th: 48–52. Puf: C. 12. secs. 2, 3. What things naturally uncapable of being so acquir'd. Th: 53. Puf: C. 12. sec. 4. The Effect of Occupation, in other things, naturall & perpetuall. How it proceeds in moveables, how in Immoveables, & how far it extends. Th: 54–58. Puf: C. 12. secs. 5, 6. Occupation of things abandon'd by ye former Owner. Th: 59. Puf: C. 12 final section. Acquisition of Property by Accession. Th: 60, 61, 62. Puf: C. 12. sec. 7. The Indefinite Obligation arising from Property. Th: 63. Puf: C. 13 sec. 1. The third Classe, is of those Rights which are acquir'd by ye concurring Deeds, of ye Acquirer, & of another from whom

they are derived. Th: 64. Rights so deriv'd, either Real or personal. Th: 65.
Of ye first sort, ye chief is Property. It may be convey'd, whether the Conveyance of it naturally require Delivery. Th: 66. Property is convey'd either
entire, or diminish'd: Servitudes & Diminution of Property. Th: 67. Puf:
C. 12 sec. 8. The conveyance of personal Rights, is either of such as were
before competent to ye Conveyer and now to ye Acquirer, against a third
Person, or Such as were competent to the Conveyer against ye Acquirer
himself, but now being convey'd, or rather remitted, to him, are consolidated with his natural Liberty; or lastly, such as were before contain'd in
the Conveyers Natural Liberty, but now, when convey'd, are competent to
ye Acquirer against ye Conveyer himself. This last Sort comprehends all
promissory Deeds. The frequent occasion for them & necessity of faithfull
performance. Th: 68. Puf: C. 9 secs. 1, 2, 3. Three wayes of speaking of
future Actions, viz. so as only to express or Defigne or so as to oblige imperfectly or perfectly. Th: 69. Puf: C. 9. secs. 6, 7. Perfect Promises either
single or reciprocal. Th: 70. Puf: C. 9. sec. 5. All Deeds by which Rights
are directly convey'd inter Vivos, require ye Consent of both Partyes; &
are therefore enervated by Impotency of Reason, Mistake, Fraud, Force
&c. Th: 71–75. Puf: C. 9. secs. 8–16. Its requisite that ye Matter of all such
Conveyances be in ye power of ye Conveyer: where, of Promises of things
impossible, or unlawfull. Th: 76, 77. Puf: C. 9. secs. 17, 18, 19. Promises,
absolute & conditional. Th: 78. Puf: C. 9. sec. 20. Proxys in making or
receiving Promises, or Conveyances or Rights whatsomever. Th: 79. Puf:
C. 9. sec. 21. Of ye Obligation to truth in Assertions, as founded on an
implicit promise. Th: 80. Puf: C. 10. Of Oaths. Th: 81. Puf: C. 11. Of Contracts. I.e., Bargains about such things or Performances, as come under
Commerce, & first of their price, or value. Th: 82, 83. Puf: C. 14. Contracts, onerous or lucrative. In those Equality is necessary. Lucrative are
Loan for Use, Mandate, & Depositum. Onerous are Barter, Sale, Letting
for Hire, Loan for Consumption, & Partnership. Likewise, several Sorts
of Lotteries. Contracts are secur'd by Cautioners & Pledges. Th: 84–95.
Puf: C. 15. Obligations arising from ye 3rd Classe of Rights. Th: 96. The
fourth Classe contains those Rights which a Person acquires immediately
by ye Deed of Another, without any concuring fact of his own. Such are

ye Rights acquir'd to ye Testamentary Heir, after ye Death of ye Testator, by his declar'd Will. Th: 97. Puf: C. 12. sec. 12. To ye Heir ab Intestato, by ye presum'd Will of the Defunct. Th: 98. Puf: C. 12. secs. 10, 11. To ye owner, or any having reall Right in a thing, as against ye Possessor of it, by that Possession. Th: 99. Puf: C. 13. sec. 2, & final section. To ye Owner against him that had posses'd it, without Right, tho bona fide, in so far as he's a Gainer by it. Th: 100. Puf: C. 13. secs. 3, 4. To ye Defuncts Creditors, & Legatars against ye Heir, by his entering. Th: 101. To him at whose Expence Another, without Gift or Paction, has receiv'd Advantage, against the Receiver, by his so receiving. Th: 102. The Right to reparation of Dammage, acquir'd to him that suffers it against him that did it, by ye Trespass of ye Latter. How far it extends &c. Th: 103, 104, 105. Puf: C. 6. sec. 4 ff. And lastly ye Right any one has in the necessary Maintenance of his Right, to hurt him that attempts to violate it, which Right he acquires by ye others unjust Attempt. This Maintenance consists either in Defence of Right, or in Prosecution of it. Th: 106. Defence how far to be carried in naturall, & how far in Civill Society. Th: 107–111. Puf: C. 5. secs. 5–16. Violent Prosecution not allow'd to private persons in civil Society: how far to be carry'd in ye State of Nature. Th: 112, 113. Puf: C. 5. sec. 17. The Fifth Classe is of Rights arising from ye Favour of Necessity, occasion'd by some singular Event. Th: 114–117. Puf: C. 5. secs. 10 ff. Of ye Extinction & Loss of Rights. Naturall Rights how capable to be extinguish'd or lost. How Reall Rights. Th: 118. Personall Rights commonly said to be extinguish'd when ye other ceases to be obliged. Th: 119. How many wayes Obligations expire. Th: 120–123. Puf: C. 16. Besides ye perfect Rights of particular Persons or Services, there are some such Rights competent to ye whole Body of Mankind, & in their behalf to be exercis'd by ye particular Members of it, such as that of hindering any Body to destroy himself or another without Cause, tho witting, etc. Th: 124. Puf: C. 5 sec. 4. The sixth and last Classe is of imperfect Rights: those of Humanity, Friendship, Gratitude, etc. Th: 125–128. Puf: C. 8. Of Interpretation. Th: 129. Puf: C. 17. Of particular Societys. Th: 130. Of Conjugall Society. The Termes of it by ye Law of Nature. Th: 131–134. Puf: Book 2. C. 2. Of that between Parents & Children. Th. 135, 136, 137. Puf: Bk. 2. C. 3. Between Masters & Servants.

Th: 138, 139, 140. Puf: Bk. II. C. 4. The Necessity of larger Societys. Th: 14. Puf: Bk. 2. C. 5. The Nature & Constitution of Civil Society in Generall. Th: 142. Puf: Bk. 2, C. 6, secs. 1–6.

Thus far they wrote: Which was all prelected, except the thirteen last theses, which correspond to ye 2nd Book of Pufendorf. And ye Theses which were prelected, abating a few towards ye End, were likewise examin'd, together with ye corresponding places of Pufendorf, in ye order above describ'd. In ye marginall Notes upon Pufendorf, I took Care, among other things, to refer them to ye parallel places of Grotius.

The Afternoons this year likewise, after we had ended ye Ontology, were mostly spent on Mathematicks; in which, after having shortly glanced over ye three Books they had learn'd the Year before, I carry'd them thro' ye fourth & fifth Books of Pardy & acquainted them with ye rudiments of Algebraicall Computation.

I employ'd some of them in making exegeses on philosophicall Subjects (the rules of which Exercise they had been taught from ye Praxis Logica before mention'd) & ask'd the Censures of ye rest upon them. They likewise gave in & defended a Thesis, on ye subject of their Discourse. The same Discourses were afterwards deliver'd in ye Common Hall.

In the Magistrand Year (if God spare them & me together), ye first work must be to compleat what yet remains undone of ye Ethicks, & then, if possible, again to glance over ye Pneumatick & Ethick Theses: tho' at the same time, I must endeavour, with all convenient Speed, to get them thro', at least, ye sixth Book of Pardies Elements, without which they can make verry few Steps to purpose in ye Physicks: I must likewise give them a touche of some other parts of Geometry, as time will allow; but for their more thorow acquaintance with them, refer them to ye Professor of Mathematicks.

I would fain be ready to begin ye Physicks about ye middle of November. I'll first put Le Clerks Physicks[6] in their hands, tho a book that has nothing to recommend it, but that it furnishes occasion to talk about a great many different things. But as ye two great Hinges of Naturall Phi-

---

6. Le Clerc, *Physica, sive De rebus corporeis.*

losophy, or rather ye constituent parts of it, are Mathematicall Demonstration & Experiment, we must look farther than Le Clerk for both.

For ye Demonstrative part, there's a Necessity of puting some Text into their Hands but whether it shall be Whistons Praelections[7] or ye Notes I dictated to my last Classe, or somewhat else, I'm yet to be resolv'd. Whatever it be, ye Progress they have already made in Geometry & Severall of them in Algebra, & ye Inclination they discover that way, make me presage well of their success in this part of Learning.

As for ye Experimentall part, ye University being now so much better furnish'd than heretofore, it will surely be no presumption to hope that we may be in case to teach Natural Philosophy more effectually than ever it was taught here before. And as I endeavour'd formerly to make ye best Use I could of ye few Instruments we had, so I would now make it my business to forecast, & carefully embrace, every Opportunity of illustrating what I teach by proper Experiments & Observations, so far as time & our apparatus will serve. And for this purpose I designe to draw up a Plan beforehand.[8] I propose likewise, especially if desired by ye Society, or by particular Persons, to have ye Dyers for Experiments at known & stated Hours, as mention'd in the Proposall.

This, saving personal or accidentall failures, is ye best Method I can propose for my Classe Teaching. But whether some better way may not be taken for ye Advancement both of Philosophical & Philological Learning than this of Subordinate Classes; & particularly what is to be done, that Students of all Denominations may, without a Diminution of their Character, have access to a fit Professors help in each part of Learning, Deserves ye Facultys most Serious Consideration.

Finis.

7. Whiston, *Arithmetica universalis.*

8. Carmichael later based his physics classes on the work of the eminent Dutch physicist Willem Jacob 'sGravesande. He wrote to 'sGravesande, 14 October 1721, to express his gratitude for a work that "has been so long desired, in which one may communicate to one's students the Elements of Mathematical and Experimental Physics in a summary plan of teaching, without an admixture of useless subjects or of dogmas which today one must unlearn." Letter printed in 'sGravesande, *Oeuvres Philosophiques,* pp. xxxiii–xxxiv. See also Gori, *'sGravesande,* p. 110.

BIBLIOGRAPHY

Published Works of Gershom Carmichael

Theses Philosophicae . . . Sub Praesidio Gerschomi Carmichael P.P. Glasguae MDCXCIX [Philosophical Theses (defended) under the presidency of Gershom Carmichael, Professor of Philosophy. Glasgow, 1699].

Theses Philosophicae . . . Sub Praesidio Gerschomi Carmichael P.P. Glasguae MDCCVII [Philosophical Theses (defended) under the presidency of Gershom Carmichael, Professor of Philosophy. Glasgow, 1707].

Supplementa et Observationes ad C[larissimi] V[iri] Sam[uelis] Pufendorfii Libros Duos De Officio Hominis et Civis. Glasguae MDCCXVIII [Supplements and Observations upon the distinguished Samuel Pufendorf's two books On the Duty of Man and Citizen. Glasgow, 1718] (The first edition).

Breviuscula Introductio ad Logicam. Glasguae MDCCXX [A Short Introduction to Logic. Glasgow, 1720].

Ibid. Edinburgi MDCCXXII Edinburgh, 1722 (The second edition).

S[amuelis] Pufendorfii De Officio Hominis et Civis, Juxta Legem Naturalem, Libri Duo. Supplementis et Observationibus in Academicae Juventutis auxit et illustravit Gerschomus Carmichael, Philosophiae in Academia Glasguensi Professor. Editio Secunda priore Auctior et Emendatior. Edinburgi MDCCXXIV [Supplements and Observations upon the two Books of Samuel Pufendorf's On the Duty of Man and Citizen according to the Law of Nature composed for the use of Students in the Universities by Gershom Carmichael, Professor of Philosophy in the University of Glasgow. The second edition with additions and amendments. Edinburgh, 1724].

Synopsis Theologiae Naturalis, sive Notitiae, De Existentia, Attributis et Operationibus, Summi Numinis, ex ipsa Rerum Natura haustae. Studiosae Juventutis usibus accomodata. Edinburgi MDCCXXIX [Synopsis of Natural Theology. Or, the Knowledge of the Existence, Attributes, and Operations of the Supreme Deity, drawn from Nature itself, suitable for the use of students. Edinburgh, 1729].

Select List of Manuscripts of Lectures Delivered by Gershom Carmichael at the University of Glasgow

"Logica Sive Ars Intelligendi" [1697] GUL [Glasgow University Library] MS Gen. 56.

"Annotationes in Artem Cogitandi" [1702] Mitchell Library, Glasgow MS 90.

"Theses Ethicae" [1702–3] GUL MS Gen. 168.

Other Works Referred to in the Text and Notes

Abbadie, Jacques. *Traité de la vérité de la religion Chrétienne.* London 1684. English translation, *A Vindication of the Truth of Christian Religion, against the Objections of all modern Opposers . . . render'd into English by H. Lussan,* 2 vols. London, 1694.

Aitken, G. A. *The Life of Richard Steele,* 2 vols. London, 1882.

Aldrich, Henry. *Artis Logicae Compendium.* London, 1691.

Ames, William. *Conscience, with the Power and Cases thereof . . . Translated out of Latine into English, for more publique benefit.* London, 1639. Also in *The Works of William Ames.* London, 1643.

———— [Guiljelmus Amesius]. *De Conscientia et eius jure, vel casibus, libri quinque.* Amsterdam, 1631.

Aphthonii. *Progymnasmata.* Edited by Hugo Rabe. Leipzig, 1926.

Arnauld, Antoine. *Des vraies et des fausses Idées.* 1683.

Arnauld, A., and P. Nicole. *La Logique ou l'art de penser.* Paris, 1662. English translation, *Logic or the Art of Thinking,* ed. J. V. Buroker. Cambridge: Cambridge University Press 1996.

Barbeyrac, Jean. *Discours sur la permission des loix, où l'on fait voir, que ce qui est permis par les loix, n'est pas toujours juste et honnête.* Amsterdam, 1716.

————. *Discours sur le bénéfice des loix, où l'on fait voir, qu'un honnête homme ne peut pas toujours se prévaloir des droits et des privilèges que les loix donnent.* 2ème edition revue et corrigé. Amsterdam, 1717.

————. "Jugement d'un Anonyme sur l'original de cet Abrégé, avec des réflexions du traducteur." Translation and commentary on G. W. Leibniz letter.

In Pufendorf. *Les devoirs de l'homme et du citoyen traduits du Latin du baron de Pufendorf.* Amsterdam, 1718. 6th ed. London, 1741.

Berkhof, Louis. *Systematic Theology.* Grand Rapids, Mich.: William B. Eerdmans, 1941.

Birks, Peter, and Grant McLeod. "The Implied Contract Theory of Quasi-Contract: Civilian Opinion Current in the Century before Blackstone." *Oxford Journal of Legal Studies* 6 (1986): 46–85.

Boston, Thomas. *Human Nature in Its Fourfold State.* Edinburgh, 1720.

Bromley, James. "Correspondence of the Rev. Peter Walkden: Letters from a Lancashire Student at Glasgow University during the Rebellion of 1715." *Transactions of the Historic Society of Lancashire and Cheshire* 36 (1884): 15–32.

Burgersdyck, Franco. *Idea Philosophiae tum Moralis tum Naturalis.* Oxford, 1654.

———. *Institutionum Logicarum Libri Duo.* 1626.

Calvin, John. *Institutes of the Christian Religion.* Translated and annotated by Ford Lewis Battles. Grand Rapids, Mich.: William B. Eerdmans, 1975.

Cheyne, George. *Philosophical Principles of Natural and Revealed Religion.* 2d ed. Two volumes in one. London, 1715.

Clarke, Samuel. *A Discourse concerning the Being and Attributes of God, the Obligations of Natural Religion, and the Truth and Certainty of the Christian Revelation.* 7th ed. London, 1728.

Confession of Faith; and the Larger and Shorter Catechisms ["agreed upon by the assembly of divines at Westminster, 1648; . . ."]. Edinburgh, 1841.

Coutts, James. *A History of the University of Glasgow.* Glasgow, 1909.

Cumberland, Richard. *De Legibus Naturae.* 1672. Translated by John Maxwell, *A Treatise of the Laws of Nature, Made English from the Latin by John Maxwell.* London, 1727.

Davidson, W. L. *The Stoic Creed.* Edinburgh: T. and T. Clark, 1907.

Derham, William. *Astro-Theology: or a Demonstration of the Being and Attributes of God, from a Survey of the Heavens.* 4th ed. London, 1721.

———. *Physico-Theology, or a Demonstration of the Being and Attributes of God from his Works of Creation.* 6th ed. London, 1723.

Descartes, René. *Meditationes de Prima Philosophia.* Paris, 1641. Amsterdam: Elzevir, 1642.

———. *Meditations concerning First Philosophy.* New York: Liberal Arts Press, 1951.

De Vries, Gerard. *De Natura Dei et Humanae Mentis Determinationes Pneu-matologicae. Accedunt De Catholicis rerum Attributis Ejusdem Determina-tiones Ontologicae.* 4th ed. Edinburgh, 1703.

———. *Exercitationes Rationales de Deo, divinisque perfectionibus.* Including "De ideis rerum innatis" and a dissertation, "De extensione infinita." Utrecht, 1695.

Elton, G. R. *The Tudor Constitution.* Cambridge, 1960.

Eustache de Saint Paul. *Ethica, sive Summa Moralis Disciplinae* (1609). London, 1693.

Fatio, Olivier. *Méthode et Théólogie: Lambert Daneau et les debuts de la scolas-tique réformée.* Génève: Librairie Droz, 1976.

Gori, Giambattista. *La fondazione dell'esperienza in 'sGravesande.* Firenze: La Nuova Italia Editrice, 1972.

'sGravesande, Willem Jacob. *Oeuvres Philosophiques et Mathematiques de Mr. G[uillaume] J. 'sGravesande.* Amsterdam, 1774.

———. *Physices Elementa Mathematica, Experimentis confirmata sive Introduc-tio ad Philosophiam Newtonianam,* 2 vols. Lugduni Batavorum [Leiden]: 1720–21.

Gregory, David. *Astronomiae Physicae et Geometricae Elementa.* 1702.

Grotius, Hugo. *The Rights of War and Peace, in Three Books . . . to which are added all the large Notes of Mr. J. Barbeyrac.* London, 1738. Originally pub-lished as *De Jure Belli ac Pacis* (1625).

Harris, John. *A new short Treatise of Algebra; with the geometrical construction of equations as far as the fourth power or dimension. . . .* London, 1702.

Heereboord, Adrian. *Collegium Ethicum* (1648). London, 1658.

Heppe, Heinrich. *Reformed Dogmatics, Set out and Illustrated from the Sources.* 1861. Translated by G. T. Thomson. Grand Rapids, Mich.: Baker Book House, 1978.

Hoadly, Benjamin. *The Measures of Submission to the Civil Magistrate Con-sider'd.* London, 1717.

———. *The Works of B[enjamin] Hoadly,* 3 vols. London, 1773.

Hobbes, Thomas. *Elementa Philosophica De Cive* (1642). Amsterdam, 1647.

———. *Leviathan or the Matter, Forme and Power of a Commonwealth Ecclesi-astical and Civill.* 1651. Edited by Michael Oakeshott. Oxford: Basil Black-well, 1946.

———. *On the Citizen.* Edited and translated by Richard Tuck and Michael Silverthorne. Cambridge: Cambridge University Press, 1998.

Holmes, Geoffrey. *The Trial of Dr. Sacheverell.* London: Eyre Methuen, 1973.

Huber, Ulrich. *De Jure Civitatis Libri Tres Novam Juris Publici Universalis disciplinam continentes.* 1672. 3d ed. Franeker, 1692.

Hutcheson, Francis. *De naturali hominum socialitate oratio inauguralis.* Glasgow, 1730.

———. *Essay concerning the Nature and Conduct of the Passions and Reflections.* London, 1728.

———. *An Inquiry into the Original of our Ideas of Beauty and Virtue.* London, 1725.

———. Letters to Thomas Drenman, GUL [Glasgow University Library] MS Gen. 1018.

———. *Philosophiae Moralis Institutio Compendiaria.* Glasgow, 1742. 2d ed., 1745.

———. *A Short Introduction to Moral Philosophy in three books, containing the Elements of Ethicks and the Law of Nature.* Glasgow, 1747.

———. *Synopsis Metaphysicae.* Glasgow, 1742. 2d ed., 1744.

———. *A System of Moral Philosophy in three books. . . .* Two volumes in one. Glasgow, 1755.

Justinian, *Corpus Juris Civilis.* Vol. 2, *Codex Iustinianus.* Edited by T. Mommsen and P. Krueger. Berlin: Weidmann, 1968.

Lachman, David C. *The Marrow Controversy, 1718–1723.* Edinburgh: Rutherford House, 1988.

Le Clerc, Jean. *Ontologia, sive de Ente in genere et Pneumatologia, sive de Spiritibus.* Amsterdam, 1692.

———. *Physica, sive De rebus corporeis libri quinque.* London, 1708.

Leibniz, Gottfried Wilhelm. *Essais de Théodicée.* Amsterdam, 1715.

———. "Opinion on the Principles of Pufendorf." In *The Political Writings of Leibniz,* pp. 64–75.

———. *The Political Writings of Leibniz.* Edited and translated by Patrick Riley. Cambridge: Cambridge University Press, 1972.

Locke, John. *An Essay concerning Human Understanding.* London, 1690. Edited by Peter H. Nidditch. Oxford: Clarendon Press, 1975.

———. *Two Treatises of Government.* London, 1690. Edited with an introduction and notes by Peter Laslett. Cambridge: Cambridge University Press, 1988.

Mackenzie, Sir George. *Jus Regium: or The just and solid foundations of monarchy in general, and more especially of the monarchy of Scotland; maintain'd against Buchanan, Naphtali, Dolman, Milton, etc.* Edinburgh and London, 1684.

McLachlan, Herbert. *English Education under the Test Acts.* Manchester: Manchester University Press, 1931.

Malebranche, Nicolas. *De la recherche de la vérité où l'on traite de la nature de l'esprit de l'homme et de l'usage qu'il en doit faire pour éviter l'erreur dans la science.* 1674.

———. *Father Malebranche's Treatise concerning the Search after Truth.* Translated by Thomas Taylor. Oxford, 1694.

———. *Malebranche's Search after Truth . . . done out of French from the last edition by Richard Sault,* 2 vols. London, 1694–95.

———. *The Search after Truth.* Translated from the French by Thomas M. Lennon and Paul J. Olscamp. Columbus: Ohio State University Press, 1980.

Moore, James, and Michael Silverthorne. "Gershom Carmichael and the Natural Jurisprudence Tradition in Eighteenth-Century Scotland." In *Wealth and Virtue: The Shaping of Political Economy in the Scottish Enlightenment,* edited by Istvan Hont and Michael Ignatieff, pp. 73–87. Cambridge: Cambridge University Press, 1983.

———. "Natural Sociability and Natural Rights in the Moral Philosophy of Gershom Carmichael." In *Philosophers of the Scottish Enlightenment,* edited by Vincent Hope, pp. 1–12. Edinburgh: Edinburgh University Press, 1984.

———. "Protestant Theologies, Limited Sovereignties: Natural Law and Conditions of Union in the German Empire, the Netherlands and Great Britain." In *A Union for Empire: Political Thought and the Union of 1707,* edited by John Robertson, pp. 171–97. Cambridge: Cambridge University Press, 1995.

More, Henry. *Enchiridion Metaphysicum.* 1671.

Newton, Sir Isaac. *Philosophiae Naturalis Principia Mathematica.* 1687.

Nieuwentijt, Bernard. *The Religious Philosopher: Or the right Use of the Contemplation of the World, for the Conviction of Atheists and Infidels,* 2 vols. 2d ed. London, 1720 (vol. 1), 1721 (vol. 2).

Oldfather, W. A., ed. *Epictetus,* 2 vols. London: Loeb Classical Library, 1928.

Pardie, Ignatius Gaston. *Elementa geometriae: in quibus methodo brevi ac facili, summa necessaria ex Euclide, Archimede, Apollonio, etc.* Oxford, 1694.

Pelling, Edward. *A Discourse philosophical and practical concerning the existence of God.* Part I, London, 1704. Part II, London, 1705.

The Physiological Library Begun by Mr. [Robert] Stewart, and Some of the Students of Natural Philosophy in the University of Edinburgh. Edinburgh, 1725. (EUL [Edinburgh University Library] MS DE. 10.127).

Pitcairn, Archibald. "Dissertatio de circulatione sanguinis. . . ." In *Dissertationes Medicae, quarum multae nunc primum prodeunt*. Edinburgh, 1713.

Poiret, Pierre. *Cogitationes rationales de Deo, anima et malo*. Amsterdam, 1715. Reprinted Hildesheim: Georg Olms, 1990.

Pufendorf, Samuel B. "De interregnis." In *Dissertationes Academicae Selectae*, 261–301. Upsaliae, 1677.

———. *De Jure Naturae et Gentium*. Lund, 1672.

———. *De Officio Hominis et Civis*. Utrecht, 1728.

———. *De Officio Hominis et Civis Juxta Legem Naturalem Libri Duo. Editio novissima, aucta Lemmatibus, Indicibus, Supplementis et Appendicibus, accurante Alex. Arn. Pagenstecher*. Groningen, 1712.

———. "De republica irregulari." In *Dissertationes Academicae Selectae*, 301–57. Upsaliae, 1677.

———. "De systematibus civitatum." In *Dissertationes Academicae Selectae*, 210–61. Upsaliae, 1677.

———. *Les devoirs de l'homme et du citoyen traduits du Latin du baron de Pufendorf, par Jean Barbeyrac*. Translation and commentary by Jean Barbeyrac. 4th ed. Amsterdam, 1718. 6th ed. London, 1741.

———. *Of the Law of Nature and Nations . . . to which are now added, all the large notes of Mr. Barbeyrac, translated from his last and fourth edition*. 1734. 5th ed. London, 1749.

———. *On the Duty of Man and Citizen*. Edited by James Tully and translated by Michael Silverthorne. Cambridge: Cambridge University Press, 1991. Originally published as *De Officio Hominis et Civis* (Lund, 1673).

Raphson, Joseph. *Demonstratio de Deo, sive methodus ad cognitionem Dei naturalem brevis ac demonstrativa*. London, 1710.

Ray, Jonathan. *The Wisdom of God manifested in the Works of the Creation*. 1691. 8th ed. London, 1722.

Reid, Thomas. *Practical Ethics: Being Lectures and Papers on Natural Religion, Self-Government, Natural Jurisprudence and the Law of Nations*. Edited from the manuscripts, with an introduction and commentary by Knud Haakonssen. Princeton: Princeton University Press, 1990.

Rutgersius, Janus. *Variarum Lectionum Libri Sex*. Leyden: Elzevir, 1618.

Selden, John. *De Jure naturali et Gentium juxta Disciplinam Ebraeorum*. Argentorati [Strasbourg], 1665.

Severinus de Monzambano [Pufendorf]. *De Statu Imperii Germanici*. The Hague, 1667.

Shaftesbury, Anthony, Third Earl of. *Characteriticks of Men, Manners, Opinions, Times.* 1711.

Smith, Adam. *The Theory of Moral Sentiments.* Edited by D. D. Raphael and A. L. Macfie. Indianapolis: Liberty Fund, 1982.

Spavan, J. *Pufendorf's Law of Nature and Nations: Abridged from the Original, in which the Author's entire Treatise (de Officio Hominis et Civis) that was by himself design'd as the Epitome of his larger Work, is taken. The whole compar'd with the respective last Editions of Mr. Barbeyrac's French Translations, and illustrated with his Notes,* 2 vols. London, 1716.

Steele, Sir Richard, Benjamin Hoadly, and Michel de la Roche. *An Account of the State of the Roman-Catholick Religion Throughout the World, with a large Dedication to the Present Pope giving him a very particular Account of the State of religion amongst Protestants.* . . . 1715. 2d ed. London, 1716.

Stewart, M. A., ed. *Studies in the Philosophy of the Scottish Enlightenment.* Oxford: Oxford University Press, 1990.

Suarez, Francisco. *Tractatus de Legibus ac Deo Legislatore.* London, 1679.

Titius, Gottlieb Gerhard. *Observationes in Samuelis L. B. de Pufendorf De Officio Hominis et Civis Juxta Legem Naturalem libros duos.* Leipzig, 1703.

———. *Observationum ratiocinantium in Compendium Juris Lauterbachianum Centuriae quindecim* [Fifteen centuries of explanatory observations on Lauterbach's Compend of Law]. Leipzig, 1723.

Trueman, Carl R., and R. Scott Clark, eds. *Protestant Scholasticism: Essays in Reassessment.* Carlisle, U.K.: Paternoster Press, 1999.

The Tryal of Dr. Henry Sacheverell before the House of Peers, for high crimes and misdemeanours. . . . London, 1710.

Turretinus, Franciscus. *Institutio Theologiae Elencticae.* Geneva, 1680.

Vinnius, Arnoldus. *In quattuor libros Institutionum imperialium Commentarius academicus et forensis.* Edito postrema. Amsterdam, 1692.

Voetius, Gisbertus. *Selectarum Disputationum theologicarum.* Utrecht, 1669.

Wallis, John. *Institutio Logicae.* 1689.

Wernher, J. B. von. *Elementa Iuris Naturae et Gentium.* 2d ed. Wittenberg, 1720.

Whiston, William. *Arithmetica universalis; . . . In usum Juventutis Academicae.* Cambridge, 1707.

Witsius, Hermann. *Miscellaneorum Sacrorum Libri IV.* Utrecht, 1692.

Wodrow, Robert. *Analecta: Or Materials for a History of Remarkable Providences,* 4 vols. Edinburgh, 1842–43.

INDEX

Abbadie, Jacques, 245
abstraction: of ideas, 294, 302, 303 n.
2; method of, in natural
jurisprudence, 124.
Act of Union, xiii, 187
adventitious rights: arise from some
human action, 77; may be real or
personal, 78, 214; distinguished
from natural rights, 77–78;
sanctioned by the law of nature,
78. *See also* rights
adventitious states, 124 ff.
agreements: defined, 80–82; error
in, 82–85; forced, 85–86 n. 11,
369–71; language of, 87–88. *See
also* civil society; contracts;
marriage; promises
Aldrich, Henry, 287 n. 5
analysis, 315–17
anaskeuê or answers to objections, 312
animals, 91–92, 97–99
Anselm, 248 n. 1
Antinomians, 231 n. 8
Aphthonius, 311 n. 11
apprehension of ideas, 293 ff.
Aristotle: logic, 287; method of
avoided by Carmichael, x, xii,
229; on friendship, 76; on natural
inequality, 74, 346; on virtues and
vices, 18; real accidents, 341

Arminians or Remonstrants, 262 n. 6
Arnauld, Antoine, 335 n. 6, 338 n. 9
Art of Thinking, xi, 110, 255 n. 8,
287–88, 293 n. 2, 307, 380
atheists: absurd claim of, 243, 343–
44; and Epicureans attack all
religion and morality, 55
attributes of God: communicable, 57,
257–69, 345–46; incommunicable,
22 n. 5, 57, 248–56, 345

Barbeyrac, Jean: authority of, xiv;
comparison with Carmichael,
xiv–xv; editions of Pufendorf's
writings, 19; labor theory of
property, 94–95 n. 3, 99; on
debtors and sureties, 111 n. 10; on
laws and rights, 39–40; on
morally right actions, 33–34 n. 10;
on promises, 81 n. 9; on quasi
contracts, 113–114 n. 14; on
slavery, 144 n. 9; on the
dissolution of obligations,
119 n. 2; on the interpretation of
laws, 121–23; on the original
contract, 146 n. 3, 152 n. 7; on the
right of resistance, 166 n. 6; on
the rights of citizens, 190–91 n. 9;
on the Scottish people, 210 n. 20;
on the state of nature, 127; on

Barbeyrac, Jean (*continued*)
  virtues, 196n. 13; on war, 201n. 4,
  204n. 11, 207n. 14, 209n. 19;
  response to Leibniz, 58
beatitude or lasting happiness, x, xii,
  18, 21–24, 269, 346ff.
beneficence and friendship, 76
benevolence, 63–64, 349
Boston, Thomas, 125n. 2
Buddeus, J. F., 196
Burgersdyck, Franco, 11n. 8, 22n. 4,
  23n. 7, 24n. 8, 31n. 4, 307n. 1

Calvin, John, 25n. 9, 229n. 4
Carmichael, Alexander, x
Carmichael, Gershom (overview):
  biography, x-xi, xiv-xvi;
  philosophy, xii-xiii; teaching
  method, xi-xii, xiii-xiv, 16–20,
  21n. 2, 379–87
Carmichael, Lord John, xi, 355
Cato, 45n. 10
Cheyne, George, 241
children, obligations and rights of,
  115–16, 126, 128–31, 132, 134–37,
  143–44
Cicero: on beneficence and
  friendship, 76; on eloquence, 197;
  on justice, 42
citizens: how men become citizens,
  147–53; not all fathers of families
  properly so called, 155; rights of
  may endure following conquest,
  209–10; rights of under the civil
  law, 188–91
civil government: express the will of
  civil society, 153; God the author
  of, 155–56; origin in agreements,
  146ff. *See also* civil society
civil law, ix-x, 13–14, 45, 96ff.,
  188–90, 360. *See also* Roman
  law

civil society: may derive from three
  agreements or one, 147–53; origin
  of in agreements, xiii, 146ff., 217,
  350
Clarke, Samuel, 250n. 2
communicable attributes of God, 57,
  257–69, 345–46
community of goods, xii, 92–96. *See
  also* negative community; positive
  community
compensation for loss, 19, 73–74,
  84–85, 113, 176, 177n. 4, 366–67
composition of ideas, 294
conquest, xiii, xv; and loss of
  citizenship, 209–10; and slavery,
  139–42, 207–9; and territory,
  205–7; not a legitimate origin of
  civil government, 175–81
conscience, 32, 188–89
contracts, 106ff.; dissolution of,
  118–21; distinguished from
  simple agreements, 107–8;
  real and consensual, 108–10
Cumberland, Richard, 49,
  94–95n. 3, 348–49

Daneau, Lambert, 229n. 4, 251n. 3
debt, 70, 104, 111, 139, 143–44,
  236n. 1, 247, 341n. 13, 381–82
definition, 295–97, 328–29
delict, 73–74, 215
dependents, 115–16
Derham, William, 241
Descartes, René, 246–47
despotic government, 170, 171
De Vries, Gerard, xi, 12n. 11, 36, 54,
  227n. 2, 236n. 1, 247, 341n. 13,
  381–82
discourse or mediate judgment,
  304–8, 330–31
dispensation, 41
disputation, 312–15

dissolution of obligations, 118–23, 370–71
divine court, 30 ff.
divine law: and moral actions, 25 ff., 211–12; and obligation, 40–41, 163; defined, 24–25; when called natural law, 28
division of ideas, 295
divorce, 131–32, 145
duelling, 68–69, 362–63
duties: best understood in terms of rights, 213 ff; immediate, 46–47; mediate, 47 ff.; prescribed by divine law, 24–25; to God, 54 ff.; to others or sociability, 73 ff; to self, 59 ff.

elections, 183–84
eloquence, dangers of, 197–98
Epictetus, 24 n. 8, 42
episkeuê or peroration, 312
equality, 51, 74–75, 365–66
essences, nominal not real, 296, 328 ff.
eternity, 252–53, 345
ethics, 11, 29, 212. *See* Aristotle; moral science; scholastics
Eustache de Saint Paul, 11 n. 8, 22 n. 4, 23 n. 7, 34 n. 12
eutaxia or order, 315
evil, 26–28, 55–56, 278–79
exegesis, 311–12
expletive justice, 44, 189, 360
extension, 342

fate, 55–56
fathers, rights and obligations of, 134–37
Fatio, Olivier, 229 n. 4, 233 n. 2
force or compulsion, 36–38; and validity of agreements, 85–86, 369–71

Fraser, James, x
free actions, 25–26, 36–37, 212
friendship, 76

gambling, 110
game laws, 97–99
George II, xiii, 187
God: as the author of civil government, 155–56; communicable attributes of, 257–69; incommunicable attributes of, 248–56; providence or divine operations of, 270–81; reverence for, the first law of nature, xii, 21–25, 46–48, 52–53, 54–58, 211–12, 346–50
God, existence of: Descartes's arguments for, 246–47; proved from human thought, 242–44; proved from the preservation and structure of the physical world, 239–42; proved from universal consent, 245
governments: limited and absolute, 169–74; of the land (*imperium soli*), 150–53, 177–78; origin of civil (*imperium civile*), 147 ff.; regular and irregular, 159–61
'sGravesande, Willem Jacob, xi, 387 n. 8
Gregory, David, 374 n. 12
Grotius, Hugo: expletive justice, 44, 165, 360; his natural rights theories in Scottish universities, ix-x; on conquest, 179 n. 6, 180; on duty to God, 58; on joint ownership, 100; on language as signs, 87; on legislation, 154; on lesser evil, 33 n. 9; on marriage, 132; on ownership of animals and moveable things, 98, 99; on ownership of rivers, 97; on

Grotius, Hugo (*continued*)
   prescription or usucapion, 105; on
   prevarication, 90; on promises
   made under duress, 85, 86; on
   punishment, 175, 191; on rights
   derived from agreement, 82, 108;
   on slavery, 142, 144n. 9; on the
   origin of civil society, 153; on
   the right of resistance, 164–65,
   166n. 6, 169; on the right of self-
   defense, xii, 68–69, 70, 363–64;
   on the right of succession, 186; on
   the right to pursue harmless self-
   interest, 75; on the rights of
   humanity, 75n. 5; on the rights of
   parents, 134; on the rights of war
   and peace, 199–210; on the three
   periods in the life of a child, 136;
   on value, 106; orientation of his
   jurisprudence, 33n. 10; restorer of
   moral science, 9–10; rights and
   obligations connected, 39

Hamilton, Duke and Duchess of, x-
   xi, 323
happiness, desire for lasting, xii,
   21ff., 211–12, 325ff. *See also*
   beatitude
Harris, John, 290
Heereboord, Adrien, 11n. 8, 22n. 4,
   23n. 7, 31n. 4
Heinsius, Daniel, 74
Henry VII, 179
Heppe, Heinrich, 229n. 4, 233n. 2,
   251n. 3, 262, 270n. 1, 272n. 2,
   279n. 6
hereditary right, ix, 102–3, 185–87
Hoadly, Benjamin, 15n. 5, 164–65
Hobbes, Thomas, 10; absurdity of
   his argument that civil laws
   cannot conflict with natural law,
   190; on the law of nations, 202

Horace, 3, 65n. 5, 228n. 3
Huber, Ulrich: on civil law and
   claims of conscience, 189; on
   debt in natural law and theology,
   111n. 12; on marriage, 132; on
   punishment of deposed
   sovereigns, 167–68; on rights,
   19–20; on the right of resistance,
   164
humanity, rights of, 75–76, 179n. 6,
   215
husbands, rights and obligations of,
   128–33
Hutcheson, Francis: and Carmichael,
   xv; on natural sociability, 127n. 6;
   on natural theology, 227n. 2,
   232n. 9; on promises made under
   duress, 86n. 11; on quasi contracts,
   117n. 17

ideas, 293ff., 326ff., 339n.;
   abstraction of, 294, 302–3, 326–
   27; of pure intellect, 333, 336ff;
   simple and complex, 294; singular
   and universal, 294
imagination, 336
imperfect rights, 44, 75n.5, 82, 214
incommunicable attributes of God.
   See attributes of God: incommunicable
indifferent actions, 34n. 12, 34–35,
   41, 341
Inglis, Christian, x
intention, 26–28
interpretation of laws, 121–23
interregna, 184
intestate succession, 102–3
involuntary actions, 36–38
irregular governments, 159–61

Jesuits, 262
judging rightly, 59–61

judgment: immediate (connecting two ideas), 298ff.; mediate or discourse (connecting three or more ideas), 304ff., 330ff.

justice, 41–44; as right and corresponding obligation, 43–44; covers the whole range of moral virtue, 42–43; expletive and attributive, 44, 360; not based wholly on agreements, 350

Justinian, 14n. 12, 44, 76, 80, 96, 100, 104, 109, 112, 117, 132, 136, 140, 142, 143n. 8, 154, 202, 208n. 17. *See also* Roman law

kataskeuê or confirmation of truth, 311

knowledge: divine, a communicable attribute of God, 259–62; of God, of oneself, of others, as duties, 60–63; relevance for the morality of actions, 25–26

land, government of (*imperium soli*), 150–53, 177–78

language, as signs, 87

Law, John (Glasgow regent): 307n. 1

law of nations, 202ff.

laws of nature, xii, 9ff.; summarized, 212–13, 348–50, 357ff.; the first, worship of God, 52ff.; the second, care of self, 59ff.; the third, sociability, 73ff.

Le Clerc, Jean, xi, 227n. 1, 346, 386

Leibniz, Gottfried Wilhelm, 17n. 22, 23, 266n.

Leiden Synopsis, 229n. 4, 279n. 6

liberty, xiii, 34, 142, 156

limited government: 162ff.

loans for use: 108–10

Locke, John: his natural rights theories in Scottish universities, ix-x; on conquest, 179n. 7; on definition, 328; on ideas, 287–88; on liberty of action, 35, 340; on nominal and real essences, 296; on paternal power, 126n. 5; on slavery, xii-xiii, 142n. 6; on sources of knowledge, 293n. 2, 338; on the cultivation of the mind, 59n. 2, 67; on the division of powers in civil governments, 157n. 2; on the origin of civil society, xiii, 147, 153; on the right of property, xii, 94–95n. 3, 96, 99; on the right of resistance, 165n. 5, 166n. 6; on the right of self-defense, xii, 69, 71n. 7, 363–64; on toleration, 159n. 4

logic, 283ff.; apprehension and judgment the most important parts of, 292; defined, 292; elementary and advanced, 290; method in, 309–17; teaching of, 379–81

Lombard, Peter, 248–49n. 1

Lycurgus, 45n. 11

Mackenzie, Sir George, xiii, 171–72

MacLaurin, John, 266n. 8

Malebranche, Nicolas: 244n. 4, 272n. 2, 322, 333, 335, 338n. 9, 340n. 12.

mandate, 117n. 16

marriage, 128–33, 216

Marrow men, 231n. 8

Maximus, Magnus, 210n. 20

Maxwell, John, 94–95n. 3

method: analysis, 315–17; disputation, 312–15; exegesis, 311–12; rules of, 309ff.

mind: acts of, when free, 31ff.; aware of its imperfections, 343; faculty of reason implanted in, 36; gives

mind (*continued*)
  evidence of a supreme cause of
    itself, 344ff.; knows itself only in
    relation to its modes, 335;
    perpetually aspires to lasting
    happiness, 339–340; pure
    intellections of, 336–38; takes
    pleasure in actions conformable
    to reason, 24
monarchies: civil, instituted by the
    will of the people, 181ff.; elective,
    183; hereditary, 185–87;
    patrimonial, 180ff.
moral science, 9–11; and natural
    jurisprudence, 11, 29, 212; and
    Roman law, 13–14; and scholastic
    ethics, 11; founded on natural
    theology, 17, 230, 280–81; not to
    be derived from revealed
    theology, 12–13
More, Henry, 252–53n. 4, 342
Mosaic Law, 145

natural law: basic precepts of, 46ff.;
    defined, 28, 212; distinguished
    from the law of nations, 202;
    duties prescribed by, 212ff., 349–
    50, 357ff.; scope of, 30–32. *See
    also* laws of nature, natural rights
natural rights: and adventitious
    rights, 77ff.; and moral science,
    ix-x, xii-xiii; of extreme necessity,
    71ff.; of humanity, 75; of self-
    defense, 67ff.; perfect and
    imperfect, 44; summarized,
    213–17
natural theology: 219ff.; defined,
    233; distinguished from revealed
    theology, 12, 17; foundation of
    moral science, 17, 230, 280–88.
    See also God
negation, method of: in natural

jurisprudence, 124–25; in natural
    theology, 248–49,n. 1
negative community, 92–94
Newton, Sir Isaac, 374, 376
Nicole, Pierre, 335n. 6
Nieuwentijt, Bernard, 24
noxal actions, 176n. 3, 177n. 4, 367

oaths, 85–86, 372
obligations: correspondence of with
    rights, 43–44, 78, 213–14; derived
    ultimately from the divine law,
    28, 40–41. *See also* rights
ontology, 381, 386
original contract, xii, xv, 146–53
original sin, 48, 125, 325
Oxford University, 172

Pagenstecher, Alexander Arnold, 17
paralogisms, 308
paraskeuê or preparation for treating
    questions, 311
Pardie, Ignatius Gaston, 386
parents, rights and obligations of,
    115–16, 126, 128–31, 134–37
passions, 36, 63–66, 340
patrimonial kingdoms, 180–83
peace treaties, 85–86, 209
Pelling, Edward, 241
perfect rights, 44–45, 75n. 5, 82,
    214–15, 360
personal rights, 78–79, 214–15
physics, xi, 351–52, 374–76, 386–87
piety, 43. *See also* reverence for God
Pitcairn, Archibald, 240n. 2
pneumatology, xi, 54, 227, 373–74,
    381–82, 386
Poiret, Pierre, 259n. 3, 260, 261n. 5,
    342–43n. 15
polygamy, 130
positive community, 92–94

positive law of God, 28

postliminium or recovery of rights, 206

prevarication, 88–90

probable conscience, 32–33

promises: enforced or made under duress, 85–86, 369–70; error in, 82ff.; gratuitous, improperly so called, 81n. 9; obligation of, 81ff. *See also* agreements; contracts

property: acquired by labor, 92–96; right of, xii, xiv-xv, 91ff.; things which cannot be appropriated, 96–97

property, rules for determining: accession, 99–101; occupation, 97–99; prescription (usucapion) 104–5; succession, 102–3; transfer by consent, 103–4

propositions, 299–303, 306, 331–32

Pufendorf, Samuel: decision by Carmichael to adopt his work for instruction of students in moral science, xiff., 10–11, 16–17; early reflections on his writings by Carmichael, 348, 365, 372–73; natural rights theories in Scottish universities, ix–x; order of presentation of Carmichael's natural jurisprudence distinguished from, 211–17 passim; treatment of particular themes in Carmichael's account of his teaching method, 382–86

punishment: defined, 191–92; does not justify enslavement, 139–40; in the state of nature, 69–71; limited to compensation and guarantees for the future, 175ff.; of corporations, 193–94; of sovereigns, not justified, 167–68

quasi contracts, 112–17, 214–15

Quintilian, 196n. 14

Raphson, Joseph, 35

reason: man endowed with a faculty of, 22, 28, 32, 325ff.; right dictates of, 11

Reformed scholastics, xi, xii, xv, 229n. 4, 233n. 2, 248–49n. 1, 251n. 3, 253n. 5, 257, 262n. 6, 270n. 1, 272n. 2, 274–75,n. 4, 279n. 6. *See also* Daneau, Lambert; Heppe, Heinrich; Leiden Synopsis; Turretinus, Franciscus; Voetius, Gisbertus

regenting system at the University of Glasgow, 379n. 1

regular governments, 159–61

Reid, Thomas, 117n. 17

religion. *See* God; natural theology; revealed theology; reverence for God; theology

reputation, 61–62, 68–69, 194–96

resistance, right of, xiii, 164–74, 351

revealed theology, 12–13

reverence for God, the first law of nature, xii, 24–25, 46–48, 52–53, 54–58, 212–13, 346–50

rights, ix-x, xii-xv, 9–12; classification of, 77ff.; natural and adventitious, 77–78; of conquered people, 164–72, 209–10; of extreme necessity, 71–72, 364; of humanity, 75–76, 79n. 6, 215; of parties to an agreement, 80ff.; of property, 91ff.; of resistance, xiii, 164–74, 351; of self-defense, xii, xiv, 67–71, 199, 361–62; over the property of another, 101–2; perfect and imperfect, 44, 91ff., 102ff.; real and personal, 78, 92–94

Roman law, ix–x, 13–14, 44, 45, 84–
    85, 100, 102, 104, 107–8, 112–13,
    121, 131, 141, 143, 189, 202, 206, 209
Roman Pontificate, 187
Rutgersius, Janus, 74

Sacheverell, Henry, 169n. 8
scholastics: Aristotelian, x, xii, 229;
    writers on ethics, 11n. 8, 22n. 5,
    23n. 7. *See also* Reformed
    scholastics
Scotland, government of, xiii, 12,
    172, 210
Selden, John, 10
self-respect, the second law of
    nature: xii, 48, 53, 59ff.
sensation, 332–33, 335–36, 338
servants, 138. *See also* slavery
Shaftesbury, third earl of, 230n. 7
shipwrecks and rights of humanity,
    76, 350
signification, and relations between
    God and man, 22n. 5, 46, 361
slavery: Aristotle on, 74–75;
    denunciation of, xiii, 140;
    differences with Barbeyrac,
    144n. 9; general reflections on,
    138–45; the death of sociability,
    xv, 145
Smith, Adam, 86n. 11
sociability, the third law of nature,
    xii, 49–52, 73–76, 145, 213, 348–
    49, 357–60, 367
sorites, 373
sovereignty, expression of the will of
    a civil society, 153; limitations on,
    162ff.; powers of, 157ff.; right of
    resistance to, 165–67
Spavan, J., 171
Stanhope, Sir James, 169n. 8
state of nature, 124–27
Steele, Sir Richard, 15

Stewart, Robert, 241n. 3
Stoics, 24n. 8
Suarez, Francisco, 41
succession: in hereditary monarchies,
    185–87; to property, 102–3
superstition, 55
syllogism, rules of, 305–8
system of states, 161

theology: natural, 17, 54ff., 219ff.,
    233; revealed 12–13
Thrasones, 363n. 5
Titius, Gerhard Gottlieb: his edition
    of Pufendorf's work, xiv, 18–19;
    obligation to children, 134; on
    agreements, 80, 83–84, 107; on
    conscience, 33; on interpretation
    of laws, 121; on interregna, 184;
    on laws and rights, 39; on
    occupancy, 99n. 6; on reputation,
    194; on sociability and self-love,
    49, 71–72; on sovereignty, 153,
    155, 156; on the original contract,
    146n. 3, 151, 152n. 7; on the right
    of self-defense, 67n. 6, 69; on the
    right to punish, 192; on the rights
    of masters and servants, 139; on
    the state of nature, 125, 127; on
    war, 199; slavery, the death of
    sociability, 145, 207
transfer of property, 103–4
truthfulness in agreements, 87–90,
    214, 371–72
Turretinus, Franciscus, 229n. 4,
    248–49n. 1, 253n. 5, 262n. 6,
    270n. 1

Ulpian, 13–14, 80, 202

value, 106–7
vices and virtues, 18, 24, 42–44, 196
Voetius, Gisbertus, 229n. 4, 262n. 6
voting in assemblies, 153–54

Walkden, Rev. Peter, xi n. 2,
    89 n. 14
Wallis, John, 287
war: and conquered territory, 205–
    7; and law of nations, 202–4; and
    slavery, 139 ff.; and the rights of
    conquered people, 207–10;
    declarations of, 200–2; defined,
    199–200; duty of citizens in an
    unjust war, 190–91; restraint
    during, 204–5; right of self-

defense applies to states as well as
    to individuals, 70–71
Wernher, J. B. von, 109
Westminster Confession of Faith,
    25 n. 9, 257
Whiston, William, 387
Witsius, Herman, 12 n. 11
Wodrow, Robert, xi n. 1, 342–43 n. 15
Woodsworth, Jonathan, xi, 89

Zaleucus, 45 n. 11

This book is set in Adobe Garamond, a modern adaptation by
Robert Slimbach of the typeface originally cut around 1540 by the
French typographer and printer Claude Garamond. The Garamond
face, with its small lowercase height and restrained contrast between
thick and thin strokes, is a classic "old-style" face and has long been
one of the most influential and widely used typefaces.

Printed on paper that is acid free and meets the requirements of the
American National Standard for Permanence of Paper for Printed
Library Materials, z39.48-1992. ⊗

Book design by Louise OFarrell,
Gainesville, Florida
Typography by Impressions Book and Journal Services, Inc.,
Madison, Wisconsin
Books printed and bound by Edwards Brothers, Inc.,
Ann Arbor, Michigan
Paperback covers printed by Commercial Printing Company, Inc.,
Birmingham, Alabama